PATRICIA JEFFERY
ROGER JEFFERY   ANDREW LYON

LABOUR PAINS
LABOUR POWER

Women and Childbearing in India

Zed Books Ltd
LONDON AND NEW JERSEY

Manohar
NEW DELHI

Labour Pains and Labour Power was first published in 1989 by:

In India
Manohar, 1 Ansari Road, Daryaganj, New Delhi 110002

In the rest of the world
Zed Books Ltd., 57 Caledonian Road, London N1 9BU
and 171 First Avenue, New Jersey 07716, USA

Cover design by Andrew Corbett
Printed and bound in Great Britain by
Biddles Ltd, Guildford and King's Lynn

British Library Cataloguing in Publication Data

Jeffery, Patricia
   Labour pains and labour power: women and childbearing in
India.
   1. India, (Republic). Society. Role of women
   I. Title   II. Jeffery, Roger   III. Lyon, Andrew
   305.4′2′0954

   ISBN 0-86232-485-8
   ISBN 0-86232-486-6 pbk

Library of Congress Cataloging-in-Publication Data

Jeffery, Patricia, 1947-
   Labour pains and labour power/Patricia Jeffery, Roger Jeffery.
   Andrew Lyon.
      p.   cm.
   Bibliography : p.
   Includes index.

   ISBN 0-86232-485-8.   ISBN 0-86232-486-6 (pbk.)
   1. Rural woman–India.   2. Childbirth–India.   Sex role–India.
I. Jeffery, Roger.   II. Lyon. Andrew.   III. Title.
HO1742.J44 1989
305.4′2′0954–dc19

Contents

Labour pains and labour power

Preface

The Indian sub-continent, with one-fifth of the world's population, sees almost one-half of the world's maternal deaths each year. They occur disproportionately in the northern plains, yet very little is known about the circumstances in which women there give birth. By focussing on childbearing in two north Indian villages, we demonstrate the dramatic impact of women's subordination on female reproductive health and the survival of young children, especially girls. There is little here to remind us of the romanticised views of "natural" childbirth so often portrayed in the West. Women's fertility is high, so most women are repeatedly at risk. In an area so riven with class and ethnic divisions, women occupying differing social locations and living in diverse domestic circumstances do not all experience childbearing in the same way; and women's ability to build solidarity even on the basis of common features of their childbearing experiences is very restricted. Their sources of support from other women are scant and local perceptions of female physiology involve very negative self-images. These aspects of women's position in north India help to explain the limitations of the existing medical provisions for women. Our analysis also casts serious doubt on the current advocacy of schemes to train traditional birth attendants in north India, as part of the government maternal and child health programme aimed at achieving "Health for All by the Year 2000". Moreover, village women are all too aware of the costs to them of repeated childbearing and of the obstacles preventing them from limiting their fertility. Yet India's population policy is intensely problematic and offers very little for women in such powerless positions.

This book is based on data collected during two main field-trips to Bijnor District in western Uttar Pradesh (from February 1982 until June 1983 and during August and September 1985) and during brief visits in 1984 and 1986. We performed different but equally essential tasks connected with the research and there was a constant exchange amongst us. It is scarcely possible now to trace the genesis of the ideas presented in this book, but the prime responsibility for authorship was Patricia's.

We are grateful to the Social Science Research Council (later Economic and Social Research Council) for the research grants and Andrew Lyon's linked post-graduate studentship, and for funding from the University of Edinburgh. Our attachment to the Indian Social Institute, New Delhi, facilitated our work enormously: we are particularly grateful to the late Father Alfred de Souza and to Father Walter Fernandes. In Bijnor, Kunwar Satya Vira and his family extended generous hospitality, while Sri S.M. Arya and Dr K.K. Khanna greatly aided our work. Special thanks for helping throughout the research go to Tikka Ram, Hari Ram, Rafiq Ahmed and Khurshid Ahmed and especially to our research assistants, Swaleha Begum, Radha Rani Sharma and Savita Pandey, who threw themselves into the work with such enthusiasm. In Delhi, Jennifer and Robert Chambers, Meera Chatterjee, Carolyn Elliott, Kamlesh and John Mackrell, and June Rollinson provided us with the space to relax from the pressures of village life; their interest sparked off many useful discussions of our work.

Since completing our research we have become even more indebted to so many friends and colleagues that we could not possibly thank them all here. The staff at the I.S.I., the Centre for Women's Development Studies and Operations Research Group deserve special mention. Several people have generously commented on some or all of the manuscript: among them, Haleh Afshar, Bina Agarwal, Catherine Ballard, Bruce Derr, Tim Dyson, Lynn Jamieson, Elizabeth Jones, Uma Kothari, Helen Pankhurst, Janet Siltanen, Ursula Sharma, Peggy Duncan Shearer, Hilary Standing, Alice Thorner, Judy Tomlinson, Susan Wadley, the Women in Sociological Research Group in Edinburgh and Anna Gourlay at Zed. Catherine Robin has greatly enhanced the final product with her line-drawings from our photographs. Without our parents' support, this book would still not have seen the light of day; even so, Laura and Kirin had to learn to live with the research, the heaps of paperwork and being constantly fobbed off with "when the book is finished".

Our main thanks, of course, go to our informants who tolerated our tiresome questioning, allowed their concerns to become ours, and accepted our own concerns with humour and generosity. We hope we have represented them well.

Patricia Jeffery
Roger Jeffery
Andrew Lyon

Glossary

Note: Words given here are those used frequently in the text. Words that are used only occasionally always appear with their translation. In transliteration, we have omitted diacritical marks to indicate different values of d, t, r, glottal stops etc., and have made plurals by adding "s". We have indicated different vowels (except for proper names) as follows:

a   short as in cat
ā   long as in far
e   as in début
i   short as in pin
ī   long as in chief
o   as in bone
u   short as in full
ū   long as in moon

akelī (f) **akelā** (m): alone; in this context, (for a woman) after the death of her mother-in-law or (for a man) after the death of his father

alag: separate; in this context, for a woman, living apart from her mother-in-law; for a man, operating a production unit separately from his father and brothers

ANM: Auxiliary Nurse-Midwife; originally, nurse with 18 months training, now with 2 years training after 10th grade schooling; usually posted at sub-centres or Primary Health Centres with duties covering maternal and child health, including family planning

Ayurveda: traditional Hindu system of medical diagnosis and practice (see **vaid, Unan-i-tibb**)

bādī: food or medicines which are particularly hard to digest and create wind or flatulence, and aching joints (see **garm, thandā**)

bahū: bride, wife; more generally, an in-married woman, especially a son's wife

bīghā: unit of land that varies in size in different parts of India. In Bijnor, a **kachchā bīghā** is approximately one-fifth of an acre; three **kachchā bīghās**

equal one **pakkā bīghā.** We use **kachchā bīghās,** the most common unit in everyday speech

chhatī: purification ceremony after a birth when festive food is cooked, especially but not exclusively among Muslims (see **jasthawn**)

chūlhā: cooking stove; more generally, the people who eat meals cooked at one hearth; household

compounder: pharmacist

dāi: traditional birth attendant

dāl: pulses, seeds of leguminous plants, such as lentils and split peas

dhotī: cotton sārī worn by Hindu women; also wrap-round lower garment worn by men

Diwali: Hindu festival of lights held at new moon during the month of Kartik (October)

Eid: two Muslim festivals, one at the end of the month of Ramzan (during which Muslims should fast between sunrise and sunset) and often called "sweet" Eid because of the distribution of sweetmeats; the other on the tenth day of Zulhaj when pilgrimage to Mecca takes place and often called "goat" Eid since goats and other animals are sacrificed

garm: hot, warm, stimulating; quality of foods, climates, or people, within a theory of humours, not directly equivalent to the physical concept (see **bādī, thandā**)

garmī: heat, warmth, stimulation

ghar-jamāi: in-living son-in-law, a man who has left his natal village and lives in his wife's parents' house

ghī: clarified butter

gur: unrefined sugar

hakīm: practitioner of Unani medicine (generally Muslim)

Holi: Hindu spring festival held during month of Phagun (March), marked by breaking of normal social rules (women attack men with powdered dyes and coloured water, men dress as women etc.)

imām: Muslim religious specialist

jachā: new mother, particularly during immediate post-partum period of "one-and-a-quarter months" or "40 days"

jasthawn: Hindu ceremony after a birth at which priest removes birth pollution and names the baby (occasionally known as **jasūthan**)

khushī: celebration, jollity, happiness

khushī-kī-bāt: matter of celebration

len-den: taking-and-giving; established gift exchanges, normally between kin at life-cycle events such as births and marriages

maikā: of the mother, the mother's home; among Muslims, a woman's natal village, where her mother lives (see **pīhar**)

maulwī: Muslim religious specialist

nand: husband's sister

nasbandī: "closing the tubes", that is male or female sterilisation

neg: honorarium, gifts to which people related in specific ways to celebrants of life-crisis rituals (marriages, births etc.) are entitled

nīm: tree whose leaves have medicinal qualities; also half-trained, quack

paisā: one-hundredth part of a rupee

pandit: Hindu priest

pīhar: of the father, the father's house; among Hindus, a woman's natal village, her father's ancestral village (see **maikā**)

pūjā: Hindu prayer offering

rotī: bread, generally griddle-baked unleavened wheat bread

Rs: rupee, the Indian currency; in 1982, Rs 18 were equivalent to £1

safāi: cleaning; in relation to childbearing connotes a woman's "cleansing" during menstruation and after childbirth by the removal of defiling blood; also spontaneous and induced abortion, and dilatation and curettage

sājhe: joined or jointly; in this context, (for a woman) sharing with her mother-in-law or daughter-in-law, or (for a man) being part of production unit with his father, brothers or sons

sās: mother-in-law (see **susrī**)

sharm: (negatively) shame, embarrassment; (positively) modesty, bashfulness

sharm-kī-bāt: shameful or embarrassing matter

susrāl: father-in-law's village (for women and men)

susrī: mother-in-law, term of abuse used by women

thand: cold (noun), stillness, tranquility; quality of food, people etc. not directly equivalent to the physical concept (see **garm, bādī**)

thandī (f), **thandā** (m): cold (adjective), soothing, tranquilising

Tijo: Hindu festival during Sāwan (August), when married women return to their natal villages and sing songs while being swung on swings specially erected for the festival

Unani, Unan-i-tibb: "Greek medicine", introduced into India by Muslim traders and invaders (see **hakīm, Ayurveda**)

vaid: practitioner of **Ayurveda**, more correctly **ved** (generally Hindu) (see **hakīm**)

Note on kinship terminology: kin terms used in Bijnor by Hindus and Muslims conform to the structure discussed by S. Vatuk, in *Contributions to Indian Sociology*, vol.3, 1969, pp.94-115. Terminological distinctions between kin (and their associated roles) do not conform to those in English. We have adopted the notation M = mother, F = father, W = wife, H = husband, Z = sister, B = brother, D = daughter, S = son, e = elder and y = younger and inserted them in the text beside the less precise English term where relevant (eg MBD = mother's brother's daughter). We have used "sister-in-law" solely for HBW and "brother-in-law" for HB and introduced only the following Hindi terms: **sās** =HM and **nand** = HZ.

Cooking rotī at the chūlhā

1. Muni Gives Birth

One June evening in rural north India, we mull over the day's happenings: some men complaining about how slowly the Cane Society pays for their sugar-cane deliveries; a woman bringing a head-load of wheat to the village power-mill, pausing to lament her daughter's ill-treatment by her in-laws; a landless labourer transplanting rice seedlings and talking of the lack of employment — and cash — that the imminent monsoon will bring; anxious mothers wanting remedies for the boils plaguing their young children. Suddenly, the door is shaken by an agitated knocking. A man's voice calls out, "Come, sister, come. Muni is having her pains and the women want you to come." Patricia hurriedly joins Muni's husband's younger brother waiting to escort her through the dusk. What will the night's vigil bring? Will Muni have a difficult labour? Who will be present and how will they deal with Muni? What will the birth attendant do? Will the baby be all right and how will it be greeted?[1]

The following account is constructed from several deliveries documented during our research in two Uttar Pradesh villages.[2] A woman there generally delivers at home in her husband's village, attended by his female kin and by a dāi (traditional birth attendant). By taking the perspective of women like Muni, we air issues which are more than usually hidden from history. But childbirth is not just the women's business it appears on first glance, for young married women are workers as well as bearers of children. We therefore locate women's childbearing experiences in the context of the domestic and class politics of north India's agrarian economy. This book, then, addresses the questions which are exposed when gender studies, social demography, health policy and political economy meet.

* * * * *

Stars glint in the clear sky and a mango tree behind Muni's house is lit by flickering and darting fireflies. In a neighbouring courtyard a tractor is revved up to power a fodder-chopper. Close by, cattle are slowly munching, their bells ringing softly as they periodically shake off mosquitoes. Adults are

1

chatting on beds in the courtyard, children lying in their midst. Sleeping outside, catching the rare wafts of cool air, provides a welcome respite from the searing daytime heat. Only Muni is inside, alone in the stifling stillness of her house.

In the afternoon her labour was beginning, but she told no one until she had finished her work. She prepared the evening meal, served it to her husband and toddler daughter, and scoured the dishes at the handpump outside her house. Several days ago she had tidied her house, removing from under the bed items which might be contaminated by the birth, and setting aside some old rags for cleaning up once the baby was born. Now she had quietly informed her mother-in-law whose house abuts her own, and retired inside.

Muni's husband owns enough land to feed the three of them if the crops do well, but not enough for improving their house. Some people have recently rebuilt their homes with kiln-baked bricks and flat roofs. But most — like Muni — still live in thatched adobe houses plastered with mud and cattle-dung. Her house is a rectangle some three metres wide and six long, with the thatch so low at the eaves that an adult cannot stand upright beside the walls. The floor is a dried mixture of mud and cattle-dung which Muni regularly smears with new coatings. The doorway opening on to the courtyard is in the middle of one of the long walls, and much of the lefthand portion of the house is occupied by the store where grain and other possessions are safely locked away. To the right, a new bed leans upright against the gable wall.

Directly opposite the doorway is the aged bed on which Muni will give birth, a decrepit object, its wooden legs splaying out from the frame, many of its interwoven strings threadbare or even broken. Muni has laid some straw and twigs on the strings to make the bed more secure. Muni's mother-in-law, Burhiya, covers her with a worn quilt, the design on the cloth long-faded and its cotton wadding poking out of numerous holes.[3] Soon, other women realise what is happening and begin to arrive; some stay to watch, some wander off. A tiny kerosene lamp, a bowl of sun-baked mud with a wick of cotton wool resting against its side, is set on top of the wall beside the door, just underneath the thatch. It throws huge eerie shadows on to the wall opposite as the women move around. At every sudden movement, flies buzz noisily to life and gradually subside again. In the hearth on the floor beside the door a dried dung-cake smoulders, warming a pot of milk containing tea and unrefined sugar. The acrid smoke drifts around the room.

Muni's contractions become stronger. She feels hot and tries to throw off the quilt but is told to keep herself properly covered. Burhiya puts one-and-a-quarter rupees into a sieve and covers the coins with wheat grains. She circles the sieve over Muni's head three times and puts it under the bedhead to ensure that Muni's labour will be over soon. Burhiya then goes outside and quietly tells Muni's husband to fetch the dāi from a neighbouring village. He protests embarrassment so his mother sends his younger brother instead.

* * * * *

Presently, the young man returns, with the dāi on the pillion-seat of his bicycle. She checks with Burhiya how long Muni has been having contractions. Muni still lies under the quilt, with two neighbours squatting behind her at the head of the bed. Another contraction comes. Muni grasps the side of the bed and steadies her legs by curling her toes over the edge. The women support her shoulders and, at the dāi's instruction, one presses down firmly just below Muni's ribs. The dāi crouches on her haunches on the foot of the bed and tells Muni to bend her knees and keep her thighs from flopping down. Muni gasps, "My eyes are roaming, my spirit is leaving me!"

"What baby was ever born without pains?" responds the dāi. "Just endure your pains, taking the name of God!"

"Hāi-hāi, mother! Oh, mother, save me!" Muni cries.

"Fie! How shameless to call your mother's name at this time!" rebukes Burhiya.

The contraction fades and Muni relaxes. The dāi inserts her left hand — the hand for dirty work — into Muni's vagina, to assess how the labour is progressing. Wiping her hands on the rags provided by Muni, she reports that the mouth of the womb is not yet fully opened and labour will continue for some time. When Burhiya asks what they should do to amplify the pains, the dāi suggests unlocking the padlock on the grain-store, for that would certainly help open the mouth of the womb. Perhaps Muni should also drink some hot sweet tea to stimulate the contractions. One woman unlocks the store, while Burhiya ladles some tea into a shallow brass dish and tells Muni to drink. Another woman lights a dung-cake soaked with kerosene and puts it at the doorway in the hope of discouraging mosquitoes.

Muni's back is aching and the dāi places two bricks a little apart on the floor beside the bed. She uncovers Muni and helps her squat on the bricks for a few contractions. Muni leans back against the side of the bed and clings round the dāi's neck. During the next contraction she urinates. "The 'mother-in-law' has just peed on my clothes!" exclaims the dāi. "What's that for you to fuss about? Isn't all of a dāi's work defiling?" retorts Burhiya, and she swears, unceremoniously tossing over some rags for the dāi to dry herself.

Muni is lifted back on to her bed. As the contractions become more powerful, the shadow of her belly rises on the wall and she moans in pain, sometimes groaning that she is dying. The women present criticise the noise she is making, while her mother-in-law and the dāi reel off their comments:

"Don't make so much noise. Have you no shame? The men will hear you if you continue like this. We'll leave you here by yourself if you persist!"

"Why are your thighs wandering around? Keep them still!"

"Don't take such deep breaths. There's no need to be troubled."

"Push hard, like you're trying to shit."

"Keep your mouth closed."

"God gives babies in his own time. You must just bear the pains."

Fumbling under the quilt, the dāi again feels how far the mouth of the womb has opened. The vagina is very dry, so she asks Burhiya for some cotton wadding soaked in warm clarified butter to insert. Burhiya again expresses concern over how long the labour is taking. The dāi reckons that an injection to accelerate the contractions would be sure to result in a quick delivery: someone should fetch the compounder (pharmacist) from the nearby dispensary. Muni lies silent, while the other women discuss this proposal. No one is in favour. One points out that Muni had not needed an injection last time, so why should she have one now? Surely it would be a waste of money? Another agrees, commenting that Muni would need injections every time she gave birth if they called the compounder now. Burhiya tells another woman to undo Muni's plait, and she herself circles some balls of unrefined sugar over Muni's head three times and places them in the sieve under the bedhead. She tells the dāi there is no need to call the compounder: Muni's babies can be delivered using country methods. She pours more tea into the brass dish and tells Muni to drink, but Muni does not want anything so sweet and asks for hot water instead. Burhiya agrees, saying that hot water, too, can stimulate contractions. She begins heating some water on the hearth but, as she does so, notices another of her daughters-in-law peeping under the eaves. She rounds on her, and commands her back to her own house. "Have you no sense, coming to watch this exhibition? Don't you know you shouldn't be here, you with a six-month baby in your belly! Don't you realise you could cool down Muni's pains by taking the heat inside your belly? Do you want your own pains to start? Away with you!"

* * * * *

Patricia squats on a thick board and leans against the wall, pestered by the persistent flies and mosquitoes. Between contractions, one woman remarks that she must be feeling uncomfortable. Patricia replies, "My discomfort can't compare with Muni's!"

"But sister, why not take a rest? Lie down outside for a while. This could take a long time!" she suggests.

"No, I'm fine here."

"She wants to see everything," interjects another. "I'd thought that babies were born the same way everywhere, until she told us how different her country's customs are."

"Yes, just think how she is willing to hold a new-born baby. She isn't it at all disgusted," says another.

"That's right," comments Burhiya, "Just see how different their customs are. Look, she doesn't even have her ears pierced!"

"But surely, sister, even your daughter was born because of a piercing!"

Muni's house resounds with our raucous laughter, which subsides only when the dāi shouts that the baby's head is appearing. The waters break and soak into the rags on the bed. Within minutes, the baby is lying curled up on the cloths, coughing and spluttering. One woman brings the lamp closer so that the dāi can see to unwrap the cord, which is loosely twisted around the baby. Then the dāi lays the baby across the bed underneath Muni's raised thighs, worried that the placenta is not delivering quickly enough. She pummels Muni's stomach with her right hand and firmly tugs the cord with her left. All the women are crowding over her, craning to see. One asks if the baby is a boy or a girl. Burhiya stretches across the dāi's arms and turns the baby over. "Another girl," she tells everyone.

"Are you certain?"

"Can you see properly?"

"Yes, indeed! It's a girl."

"Aah!"

"Well, girls are all right, too, you know."

"Muni's fate is bad! That 'prostitute-widow' of a dāi has produced another girl."

"What, is it my fault it's a girl? Is it in my hands to decide what will be born? Don't fight with me, but with God. Did I make the girl myself? Fie! That is God's will."

"Why couldn't I have a son this time?" asks Muni plaintively.

Burhiya looks sternly at her. "God has given this girl. It's your job to accept her."

"What's the matter? What children does she have now?" asks the dāi.

"Two girls."

Most of the women drift away, subdued. They have seen the new baby, another girl. After a boy's birth, there would be celebrations, presents, and jollity, so this birth is a disappointment. They have supported Muni during her labour. Now there is nothing for them to do, except tell the men in the courtyard. Clearing up is defiling-work and is the dāi's job.

The dāi again pulls the cord and this time the placenta is delivered on to the rags on the bed. She runs her fingers tightly along the cord to return as much blood as possible to the baby. Then she looks around. "Can't you people calculate what will be needed beforehand? I need thread to tie the cord, and something to cut it with afterwards!" Muni indicates the spool in a pot under the eaves. Burhiya tears some thread for the dāi, who ties it tightly round the cord about five centimetres from the baby's navel. Meanwhile, Burhiya removes a piece of reed from the thatch and splits and sharpens it with a small sickle. The dāi watches and asks if there is no razor blade instead. Muni says there is one somewhere in the store, but Burhiya insists that the cord is cut with the reed, just as for all the babies in their courtyard. So the dāi cuts the cord a few centimetres from the thread. She massages Muni's abdomen and thighs briefly. Then she wraps a ball of dry mud in a rag, and tells Muni to hold it against herself so that the bed is not fouled any more with dirty blood. Next, she wipes the baby with some other rags, moulds the nose into shape, and checks with her fingers that the mouth is properly formed and the throat is open. She also opens the baby's anus with her left little finger, and dangles the baby so that a plug of meconium drops on to the floor. Then she wraps her in some ragged clothes, many sizes too big, places her beside Muni, and pulls the old quilt over both their heads to protect them from cold.

The dāi asks where they plan to bury the placenta. Sometimes she is expected to dig a hole inside the house and bury it there, sometimes it is buried in the household's midden pit on the outskirts of the village. Burhiya tells her to take the placenta to the midden. The dāi demurs and tells Burhiya to do it herself. Burhiya angrily asks if this is not dāi's work, and presents the dāi with a basket lined with powdered mud to protect it from bloodstains. The dāi places the placenta in the basket, adding the straw which had protected the bed and the reed used to cut the cord. She cleans some blood off the bed with the remaining rags and adds them to the pile. Finally, she sprinkles ash from the hearth to absorb the blood on the floor under the bed, chips off the stained mud with a trowel and puts all the debris in the basket.

"Don't you realise how hard you made my work, putting Muni on this broken bed? Why couldn't she have used that one, which is not broken at all?" she asks, indicating with a tilt of her head the new one standing upright against the wall.

"But why should we spoil a new bed by having her give birth on it?" asks Burhiya. "As it is, the blood on the strings will have to be cleaned off carefully in the morning when it's dried."

The dāi grunts her assent and goes off, carrying the basket on her head. Burhiya calls after her to be sure and bury the placenta deeply so that no one can cause bad magic by unearthing it. On returning, the dāi mends the floor, pounding some caked mud into a powder with the trowel, wetting it thoroughly and spreading the paste over the broken patch. Then she goes outside to wash, her work finished for the present.

* * * * *

The baby begins to whimper. Burhiya breaks a fresh dung-cake on to the embers to liven up the fire in the hearth, and heats up the baby's birth syrup which will help expel the meconium and protect her from cold. Burhiya tugs a small piece of cotton wadding through a hole in the quilt and rolls it into a wick. She removes the birth syrup from the fire, dips in the wick and takes the baby on to her lap. For a few minutes, the baby sucks greedily on the wick and then drifts peacefully asleep. Her grandmother puts her back under the quilt. Muni has been groaning periodically with after-pains and now complains of being hot and thirsty. But Burhiya must ensure that Muni and her baby are not endangered. "You know I should not give you anything yet. You must wait until morning. Keep your head under the quilt — you could easily catch cold. Just rest quietly till then!"

Burhiya goes out, taking the wheat, unrefined sugar and one-and-a-quarter rupees in the sieve from under the bed, but Muni and the baby will remain inside for several days.

* * * * *

Meanwhile, the dāi has washed herself and wrung out the wet patches on her clothes. Burhiya fetches two bowls of wheat from Muni's store and pours them and the contents of the sieve into the dāi's shawl. She hands her a further ten rupees. The dāi looks askance. "What, is this a house of misers? Is that all I get for a night's work? Bring more wheat. Why are you being so mean?"

"It would be different for a boy. There would be some celebrations, there would be more giving. Anyway 'mother-in-law', who are you to make demands like this?"

"But still you should give more. It is not my fault the baby is a girl. That was in Muni's fate. Do I create boys and girls? Go and fetch more wheat."

Burhiya pours more wheat into the dāi's shawl. "There, take this. This is a poor house. Muni has no more to give."

The dāi sullenly ties the wheat up in her shawl and pockets the cash. She sets off home, just as dawn is breaking.

* * * * *

Cocks begin to chorus and the cattle wake. Soon, columns of pale grey smoke waft into the still air as women light their hearths and make tea. One milks her buffalo, directing the milk into a small brass pot which she holds in one hand. From several courtyards comes the rhythmic clanking of handpumps and the crashing of metal buckets as women water their cattle. Then they noisily scour metal utensils from last night's meal beside their handpumps, chatting to their neighbours, while their children play rowdily in the courtyard. Others take the cattle-dung that has accumulated overnight to the midden, and sweep their houses and the courtyard, before cooking the first meal. The sounds of women working drift into the stuffy twilight of Muni's house: today, she alone is exempt from work.

Breast-feeding

2. Someone Else's Property

On the whole, the peasant woman of Upper India has her time fully occupied. She is obliged to let her children sprawl in the sun ... while she milks the cows, feeds the calves, ... collects firewood or makes cow-dung into cakes for fuel. She has to grind the wheat and barley ... husk the rice and millet, and do all the cooking, besides taking her share of the field work. ... It is this hard monotonous labour which, with the absence of medical aid in childbearing, converts in a few years the buxom village girl into a wrinkled hag.[1]

In this late 19th Century commentary, despite his archaic and (to present-day ears) rather offensive phraseology, Crooke acknowledges the work of women in north India and makes connections between it, childbearing and women's health which have eluded many writers since his time. The issues he raises are still relevant to scores of millions of women. Childbearing is not just the domestic affair which our portrayal of Muni's delivery might suggest. By concentrating on the intersection of women's experiences of work and childbearing, we want to avoid the "purdah of scholarship" and argue that childbearing is a key element in north Indian society as a whole.[2] This chapter and the next indicate the basis of our stance and outline the class and domestic relationships in which young married women like Muni are located in Uttar Pradesh. The rest of the book examines women's childbearing careers within this context.[3]

* * * * *

Rural north India is an inegalitarian and rapidly changing agrarian economy.[4] Thus, any portrait of life there should analyse people's access to productive resources, especially land, how different people are involved in different ways in growing food to eat and to sell, and how the state affects these processes through land reform or sponsoring new agricultural technologies. Such topics fall within the remit of political economy, but they by no means provide an exhaustive account of social life.

Recently, some authors have forcefully suggested that concentrating on the public sphere, and especially on the material aspects of production, results from and perpetuates a narrow and thoroughly distorted view of the material conditions of people's existence.[5] Activities crucial for the day-by-day and intergenerational continuity of the social system — social reproduction, the reproduction of the labour force and biological reproduction — must be incorporated in any attempt at a comprehensive analysis, as also must the ways people think about the social world they inhabit. Ignoring them means that women are likely to be omitted from the picture altogether, or else stereotyped as concerned merely with reproduction and located in a domestic sphere set apart from the public world of production. Indeed, separating a sphere of production from a sphere of reproduction would produce a deeply flawed account of rural north India, for the corollary is that one sphere is characterised by issues of class and the state (and properly analysed within the framework of political economy) while issues of gender are circumscribed by the boundaries of the domestic sphere (and safely relegated to feminists).

A holistic approach dealing with production and reproduction at the same time is more fruitful than doggedly retaining boundaries between them as if they occur in separate arenas and can be captured separately.[6] Women should be given their due as workers, but not in such a way that they seem marginal to production.[7] Women are not merely engaged in reproductive activities any more than men are just involved in production. Nor are women located solely in the domestic sphere and men irrelevant there. Class and gender issues pertain right across the board, but this can all too easily be obscured by separating the realm of production from the domestic sphere. Women and men reside in household units that differ according to their access to productive resources.[8] Further, like men, women are generally family workers not employees, though within each household their work differs from that of the men. Yet there are also class differences in women's work, just as in men's. Thus, class processes and the state's intervention in them have a salience for women. But that salience has a particular character for women simply because they are women.

People's livelihoods basically depend on the households to which they belong. These households are socially constituted residential groupings, not natural ones.[9] Their members have some interests in common and others which conflict, since men and women, young and old, have different rights in household resources.[10] Household members are recruited in two ways — in-migration and birth — in both of which young women have a distinctive part which makes the material conditions of their existences differ from those of men (and from older women too).[11] Men inherit parental property (especially land, if any) and generally stay in the village where they were born, working with people known to them from childhood. By contrast, women do not normally inherit property and usually leave their birthplace on marriage, to join households where they are wives and daughters-in-law, working in the midst of strangers.[12] These same women bear the children who are future workers. Such patterns reflect taken-for-granted views of proper household organisation. But they operate on the ground as well as in the mind and have crucial implications for the lives of young married women. Thus class factors, household politics and childbearing have a profound and distinctive impact on a young married woman. Because she is both a worker and a bearer of future workers for her husband's household, it is inappropriate to analyse domestic organisation separately from the sphere of production.

Some recent commentaries have indeed tried to broaden our vision of work and demonstrate that women are workers operating within the material and political constraints of their household's composition and its location in the class system. However, this entirely proper concern to resist stereotyping women as mothers does not mean that we can ignore women's childbearing roles.[13] Clearly, extending the concept of work to include reproducing the labour force can encompass the childrearing aspect of maternity. But pregnancy and childbirth must also be addressed head-on, not avoided for fear of biological reductionism.[14] Childbearing highlights an apparently obvious and natural difference between women and men. Yet women's and men's supposed nature and the knowledge and meanings attached to biology are socially constructed and specify socially acceptable behaviour. Women's capacity to bear children is deployed within specific contexts of gender and class relationships and is not a matter of natural drives. It is essential to the continuing restocking of each household's labour force. Its regulation entails the social organisation of pregnancy, childbirth and the post-partum period within marriage. Biological reproduction may seem natural but it must still be analysed sociologically.

We are not, however, suggesting that women's position in rural north India is rooted solely in their childbearing, for there are other key elements, notably women's lack of economic independence. Nor are we saying that women share a common experience because of their biology. In an inegalitarian economic context, women's general life experiences are diverse. So too are their childbearing careers, for each baby's birth has different implications for women and their households because of its sex and birth order and the household's structure and class position.[15] Consequently, Muni's delivery cannot be understood within the circumscribed perspective of the house where it occurred, perhaps especially not in an area of high fertility where young married women spend much of their time being workers and childbearers simultaneously.

Uttar Pradesh is India's most populous State, with its 1981 population of about 110 million probably rising to over 130 million by 1991. In its villages, scenes similar to Muni's delivery are enacted some ten thousand times a day. Yet about 50 women a day can be expected to die in childbirth or from related problems and around 800 of the babies born each day will be stillborn or will die within their first week. About one in eight live-born babies does not reach its first birthday, about a quarter die before their fifth birthday.[16] Moreover, the state impinges on such matters through its provision of health services and through its population policy, which underscores the significance of

11

childbearing not just at the village level but at the national level too. However, the recent emphasis in development programmes on child survival has resulted in the marginalisation of maternal health within even maternal and child health services.[17] In practice, the state pays most attention to limiting childbearing through contraception: ante-natal monitoring is perfunctory, obstetric services scant and post-natal care virtually non-existent. Medical surveillance may be oppressive — yet its lack can have serious implications not just for women's health but also for child survival.[18]

Approaching such issues from the perspective of young married women and locating them in a complex social system without replicating the very separation between domestic and public which we wish to subvert is not easy. But we must begin somewhere. After outlining the agrarian setting in which our research was based, we concentrate on the young married woman in her husband's village, highlighting how divisions of gender and age within domestic units are crucial in the day-to-day regulation of her life and behaviour. In the next chapter, we examine these same domestic units as the basic groupings within which workers are organised. Tying these threads together provides leverage for understanding women's work and childbearing careers which form the core of this book.

Social class in rural Bijnor

On leaving the Himalayas at Hardwar, the River Ganges travels south, and Bijnor District lies on its eastern bank for the first hundred kilometres. Bijnor came under British rule in 1801 and since 1947 has been a District of Uttar Pradesh in independent India. The Gangetic plain is fertile, if adequately watered, but no irrigation canals were constructed in most of Bijnor under the British (unlike in neighbouring Districts across the Ganges to the west).[19] Nevertheless, the British encouraged the production of cash-crops (especially sugar-cane) from the late 19th century onwards.

Most of Bijnor's two million people live in small villages, and subsistence and market-oriented agriculture provides their living.[20] Village homes generally cluster on land raised somewhat above the surrounding fields, which reduces the risk of flooding during the monsoon. The women featuring in this book share their homes with their husbands and children, eating food cooked at the same chūlhā (cooking-hearth). Close by, using the same chūlhā or in houses facing on to the same courtyard live the husband's parents, his brothers and their wives and children, plus his unmarried sisters.[21] Neighbours' houses back on to each other, with narrow unpaved alleys providing access.

Our research was based in Dharmnagri and Jhakri, two adjacent villages about five kilometres north-west of Bijnor town, and five kilometres east of the bed of the Ganges.[22] Bijnor District has one of the highest proportions of rural Muslims — about 30% — in Uttar Pradesh. Otherwise it is similar to surrounding Districts in western Uttar Pradesh, but poorer and less commercialised[23] Dharmnagri and Jhakri are broadly comparable to other villages in the District, though Jhakri is smaller than average Dharmnagri, established in the 1920s, had an entirely Hindu population of just over 700 in 1985.[24] Two-thirds were Caste Hindus, the largest group being Sahni, followed in number by Dhimars, with small numbers of Rajputs, Jats and other castes. The remaining third of Dharmnagri's population are Harijan (Scheduled Caste), some three-quarters of them Chamar and the rest Jatab. Jhakri is a long-established exclusively Muslim village, with a 1985 population of just under 400, all but 100 of whom are Sheikh.[25] Almost all the rest are about equally divided between Muslim Telis and Julahas.

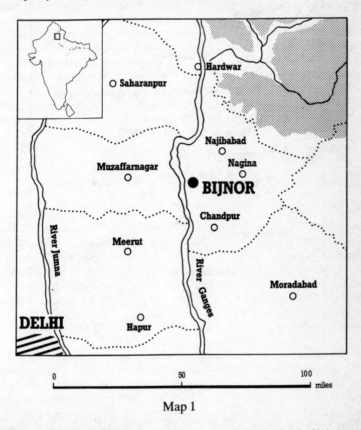

Map 1

Dharmnagri has a small temple and two government schools (primary and secondary). Jhakri has a small mosque. In Dharmnagri there are a Post Office (a small booth), a government dispensary, a couple of stalls selling items such as spices, tea, biscuits and cigarettes, and a ration shop. Further, since the early 1960s, an electrically powered grain-mill in Dharmnagri has enabled women from Dharmnagri and surrounding villages to have wheat milled into flour and rice husked rather than having to do it all at home. Nearby Begawala has a weekly market where household goods and foodstuffs are sold and a wide range of goods and services can be obtained in Bijnor town.

Jhakri and Dharmnagri are a mere 500 metres apart and Jhakri residents also use the facilities in Dharmnagri. There is, however, little other social contact between the two villages. Both villages are internally fragmented along caste and class lines, especially Dharmnagri where Caste Hindus have few dealings with Harijans.[26]

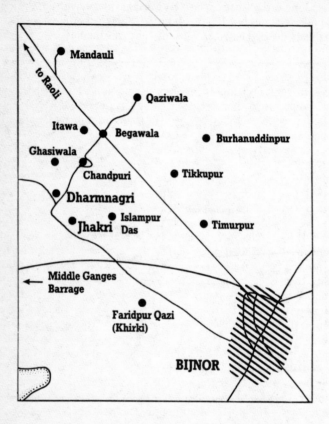

Map 2

In 1982-3, we lived in the disused operating theatre in the Dharmnagri dispensary, on the side of the village nearest Jhakri. We made further visits in 1984, 1985 and 1986. Most of the material used here comes from extensive and detailed discussions with key informants, 22 couples from Dharmnagri and 19 from Jhakri.[27] In 1982-3, the wife was either pregnant or had recently given birth and we covered a range of castes, economic positions, household structures and parities. We also completed maternity histories from all the married, widowed or divorced women in Dharmnagri and Jhakri, conducted a survey of 300 women in eleven other villages in the District, interviewed local dāis, and Patricia attended some births. We worked as a team of a woman and two men, with three local women research assistants, our division of labour entailing some "purdah of data collection", particularly on the project's core topics. Although we are particularly highlighting women here, our account of their childbearing experiences is buttressed by material from the men.

Productive resources

The land surrounding the villages is the main source of livelihood for their residents. Until the mid-1960s, agriculture in Dharmnagri and Jhakri depended on the monsoon, which usually arrives in late June and lasts, with declining strength, until mid-September. Rain was necessary for the two main summer crops, rice (harvested in October-November) and sugar-cane (harvested from November to April). Rains in January watered wheat (harvested in April) and winter vegetables. Excessive rain used to flood the Ganges and destroy crops on the villages' low-lying land. An inadequate or untimely monsoon spelt crop failure. Because the Himalayan foothills are close, the rains rarely fail entirely in Bijnor, but farmers had little protection if they were late, too heavy or too light.

Since the mid-1960s, aspects of the Green Revolution, notably the introduction of reliable water supplies, have transformed many of Bijnor's fields.[28] Around Dharmnagri and Jhakri the water-table is high. The government has provided new sources of credit, usually requiring land as surety, for instance for tubewell installation. Nationalised industries supply electricity and diesel oils to power pump-sets. The higher ground is now more fertile and less vulnerable to unsatisfactory rainfall and several crops can be cultivated on each piece of land every year. Both villages have many handpumps for domestic water supply. Land near the Ganges is now better drained and protected from flooding by a dyke built in 1965, and can be regularly cultivated rather than left as scrubland.[29] These changes have accelerated others, breaking down still further the villagers' ability to provide for their own needs. Chemical fertilisers and hybrid seeds have increased yields, but they must be bought annually and have largely replaced organic manure and seeds retained from the previous year's crop. New agricultural machinery — threshers and tractors — are commonplace. These processes operate most conspicuously in sugar-cane production, marketing and processing. In Bijnor town, a cane growers' co-operative society (established in 1940) regulates the sale of cane to the local sugar-mill, where growers receive a price guaranteed by the government. Farmers selling cane through the growers' co-operative are entitled to credit for chemical fertiliser but have to wait at least a month and sometimes six to receive their due. Cane production exceeds this mill's capacity and growers sell the surplus to middle-sized private sugar factories or to small local cane-crushers which produce gur (unrefined sugar) for sale and home consumption. In the fields around Dharmnagri and Jhakri some half dozen cane-crushers operate each year between November and April, powered by electric or diesel engines which also work tubewells. Each employs about eight men. The leaders of the gangs rent the equipment from the government and must take a chance on whether they will have made a profit by the end of the season. Dharmnagri and Jhakri were never unchanging isolated villages and the increasing involvement of markets and the state underlines that.

Access to land, however, remains the major determinant of living standards. Most landowners inherited from their fathers and land ownership is very inequitable. In the 1950s, when zamīndārī (a form of landlordism) was abolished, some sitting tenants in Dharmnagri and Jhakri gained title to the land they farmed.[30] Subsequent land-ceiling legislation (ostensibly intended to reduce the inequality of land ownership) now makes it illegal for an individual to own more than 12 acres. But escape clauses mean that little land has been redistributed and many people in Dharmnagri and Jhakri are landless, while others control large estates.[31]

Classifying people according to their access to land is beset with problems. Taking the domestic group rather than the individual as the unit for classification runs the danger of implying a unity of interest and purpose which would be inappropriate for domestic units as internally divided as those in Dharmnagri and Jhakri. Crucially, women do not own productive resources, particularly land, nor do they usually have access to income through employment. As a corollary, were we to focus on the individual as the unit in the class system, almost all women would be reduced to the ranks of the landless and unemployed. Granted, some aspects of young married women's lives are broadly comparable right across the board; yet this would not justify levelling women, for on other counts the experiences of women in Dharmnagri and Jhakri are markedly different because of their attachment (as daughters, wives and daughters-in-law) to men with differentiated access to productive resources. We prefer, then, to base our classification on domestic units, while still according full weight to the divisions within those units.[32]

However, deciding how to demarcate these units most appropriately is itself problematic. Units through which crop production is organised (production units) may coincide with those through which income is disbursed (the chūlhā, literally cooking-hearth). But production units of several brothers or a man and his sons may be comprised of several chūlhās. In illuminating the questions with which we are concerned, the chūlhā is the crucial unit: women's capacity to labour is organised primarily within the chūlhā; important aspects of distribution also operate at that level, notably food distribution and access to medical treatment, which impinge on the health of childbearing women; gift exchanges during marriages and when children are born, for instance, also largely involve chūlhās not production units; and longer-term considerations about women's childbearing careers and family-building strategies hinge on the chūlhā's present and expected access to resources and future needs for labour power. However, many technically landless men work land in production units with their fathers from whom they expect to inherit. Their access to resources is not comparable to that of men who are and will probably remain landless. Thus chūlhās need to be grounded within production units differentiated by their access to land. We have, then, allocated production units to five classes based on the amount of land owned per able-bodied adult man, the level of technology used and whether they deploy only adult family labour, hire in labourers, or must themselves seek employment.[33] Within this scheme, the chūlhā is allocated to the same class as the production unit of which it is whole or part.

Even so, some chūlhās are particularly hard to classify, as their members have craft skills, urban jobs (possibly based on education), or other sources of income, though these are few in Dharmnagri and Jhakri. Others take in extra land or release land under tenancy or sharecropping agreements.[34] In any case, allocating a chūlhā to a particular class does not provide a full account of its members' experiences. Chūlhās currently in a similar class position may be moving in different directions, for general processes of polarisation associated with population growth and land fragmentation may be offset by increased urban opportunities and rising returns from agriculture. Further, the articulation of class interests is muted because classes are cross-cut by caste and religious allegiances, while caste and religious groupings straddle class boundaries. No classification can fully resolve these problems and these class categories do not dominate village social life. However, they do broadly reflect access to resources and enable us to retain leverage over differentiation among chūlhās, and among the women and men within them.

The poorest chūlhās comprise disproportionate numbers of widows or elderly couples unsupported by their children. Thus, our sample of currently fertile couples in Dharmnagri and Jhakri is somewhat skewed away from the poorest, but it does reflect the distribution of births in the two villages.

Landlords

Landlords do not engage in agricultural labour themselves, but hire permanent and temporary wage labourers or lease out land for cultivation. In Dharmnagri and Jhakri, only one chūlhā falls into this category: the descendants of Raja Jwala Prasad, who established Dharmnagri in the 1920s. They have family houses in Delhi, another farm elsewhere in the District, links to industrial capitalists and senior members of the Indian Administrative Service and political and economic influence within the District and beyond.

Their house is a brick and plaster-faced two-storey mansion with an arched entrance-way. It is reached by a curving gravel drive through a garden flanked by a mango orchard. Separate bedrooms with attached bathrooms, dining- and sitting-rooms and kitchen quarters open on to its two large paved courtyards. The furniture is mostly Western in style. Electricity powers light and a colour television, but the plumbing system no longer works. Cooking is by calor gas, or from gas produced from cattle-dung. The tractor sheds are beside the house and the cow byre behind. Beyond them are living quarters for some of the domestic and farm servants.

This chūlhā manages the farm of about 250 acres owned by Jwala Prasad's three sons and three daughters and their descendants. They lost land to tenant farmers in the reforms of 1951, but since then little land has been surrendered. There is a farm manager, an accountant and a dozen or so men employed full-time as drivers, ploughmen, gardeners, cooks and so on. Many more are hired during harvesting. Most ploughing is done by tractor, and threshing is also mechanised. Wheat has only once been combine-harvested. The landlord paid for the first electricity connection to Dharmnagri and introduced pump-sets. As only one baby has been born into the chūlhā in the last 25 years — delivered in a private hospital in Delhi — we do not discuss the childbearing experiences of this chūlhā's women.

Rich peasants

Rich peasants work on their own land but on no one else's. Thirteen chūlhās, one in 15 in the two villages, fall into this category, owning between five acres and almost 18 acres per adult man. They must hire labour, either regularly or just at peak times such as the wheat and rice harvests. Six of our key informant couples were in this position.

In Dharmnagri, Ashok and Bhagwana are the largest of these substantial farmers.[35] They are Rajput brothers owning about 35 acres with their widowed father. They have a one-storey kiln-baked brick house with an imposing two-storey plastered facade facing on to the road. Their wives, Adesh and Bhagirthi, cook at separate chūlhās on opposite sides of the substantial courtyard. Each chūlhā has two rooms, and the men also use a men's sitting-room at the front. Apart from some cane chairs, there are just wooden board or string beds. By early 1982, Adesh had one son and five daughters (and another son had died), while Bhagirthi had one son and three daughters (and had had a stillborn son).

The land is worked jointly by Ashok and Bhagwana, but most of it is in their father's name. The father lives with his younger son Bhagwana and tensions are aggravated by Ashok's drinking and his fear that his inheritance will be reduced by transfers of land to Bhagwana during their father's lifetime. They own a tractor, a thresher and an electric pump-set. There are two ploughing sets (two bullocks for each plough), one cow and two buffaloes for milk and four calves.[36] The animals have separate quarters at the front of the house. Two permanent male farm labourers are employed, and some village council land is rented as well. The father is uneducated, as are his daughters-in-law, but Ashok, Bhagwana and their sister went to school until the eighth class and their children will probably do likewise.

They have taken loans to pay for a tubewell, and also for the chemical fertilisers and new hybrid seeds, of which they are heavy users. Ashok and Bhagwana now have lengthy dealings with markets and government offices. To be profitable, Green Revolution farming requires all the inputs at the right time in the right proportions on very intensively worked land. Protecting electric connections, acquiring diesel for tractors, negotiating sugar-cane sales to private mills or wheat and rice sales in Bijnor market, contemplating more mechanisation to avoid labour management problems and obtaining credit from the bank or cane growers' co-operative, all take time and initiative. Such worries and decisions are now part of the daily lives of rich peasants locked into commercialised agriculture.

Middle peasants
Middle peasants own between two and five acres per adult man. They farm their land mainly with family labour and hire in labourers only during peak periods. They rarely hire themselves out to work for others. This applies to more than one-third of the chūlhās in Dharmnagri and Jhakri (74), and 23 of our key informant couples.

In Jhakri, Farooq and Ghulam are fairly typical middle peasants. They are Sheikhs. Farooq and Fatima have a separate chūlhā but Ghulam and Ghazala still live with his parents, another brother married in 1982, two unmarried brothers and an unmarried sister. Ghulam's paternal grandfather and another unmarried sister also lived with them until their deaths in 1982. Altogether, they own about 14 acres of land. Their father considers tractors too expensive: oxen need only to be fed and they also provide manure. He has no thresher, but he does have an electric engine and pump-set. He rents out the engine to power a cane-crusher during the cane harvest season. They have benefited more recently than rich peasants from the improved agricultural yields. They began building brick houses only after 1980 and the animal quarters are mostly still adobe and thatch. Farooq and Fatima lived in the centre of Jhakri until 1983 in a spacious single-roomed thatched dwelling of adobe bricks plastered with a mixture of mud and cattle-dung. Now they have a one-storey brick house beside the family's other chūlhā on the village outskirts. Each married couple has its own room but the men often sleep in front of the animal quarters in the men's sitting-room. With a B.Com. obtained in 1985, Ghulam is the most educated man in Jhakri. His first job was as a clerk at the cane weighing station in Begawala for the 1986-7 season. Farooq stopped his schooling much earlier, while Fatima and Ghazala have both read the Qu'rān Sharif. In early 1982, Fatima had one son and two daughters, one of whom died later that year; another son had died in infancy. Ghazala had her first child (a son) in 1983.

Poor peasants
The land-poor comprise about one in five (42) of the village chūlhās. Their average landholding is about an acre per adult man, on which they grow mostly wheat and rice for consumption, and very little sugar-cane. Some poor peasants have a skill or alternative source of income, others rent or sharecrop land to work in addition to their own. Some Telis follow their caste occupation pressing mustard oil, and others who scrape enough capital to rent cane-crushing equipment for the season can be included here. Five of our key informant couples are poor peasants, including Shankar and Shakuntala, who are Chamars in Dharmnagri. Shakuntala had her first child (a boy) in late 1982.

Shankar, Tulsi and his eldest brother work the family land, which now amounts to only three acres. Their father had been allocated another three acres of land from surplus land from the landlord's holding by the Ganges, but the government compulsorily repurchased it in 1979 when the construction of a barrage across the Ganges began. There is a tubewell boring but they must rent a diesel engine if they need to irrigate their land.

Shankar's father has done little work for several years, and spends much of his time smoking hashish and telling outlandish stories to anyone who will listen. In 1985 he split the land among his three sons and now levies wheat and rice from them. In practice, Shankar's eldest brother manages the land, effectively renting in his brothers' land and employing them to work on it when he needs their he⬤nd if they have no other employment. Shankar and Tulsi — like several poor men in Dharmnagri — had labouring jobs on the barrage until its completion in 1985. Since then, Shankar has relied on agricultural labour. Other similarly placed young men have obtained work at cane-crushers or pedalling cycle rickshaws in Bijnor.

Shankar's eldest brother also looks after the family plough and two bullocks, which can be maintained only while the holding is farmed jointly. Even now, medical expenses or the death of animals could easily push the collective endeavour into deficit and necessitate mortgaging or sale of land. Renting the land out and seeking employment is one option, another is to rent in land and use their special Scheduled Caste entitlements to obtain loans on easy terms for equipment and livestock.[37] Currently, they do not work enough land to take full advantage of the new technology. Irrigating land is expensive and without an engine they must hire one at the very time when rich and middle peasants want to irrigate their own land.

Shankar attended the village schools until the eighth class, but Shakuntala is uneducated. They live in a single-roomed thatched adobe house, with their cow and buffalo tethered outside under lean-to shelters.

Landless

People without land depend wholly on obtaining employment from others. One in four chūlhās (48) are in this position, and six of the key informant couples.

Usman and Umrao are Teli Muslims. Usman was born in Muzaffarnagar District across the Ganges, and moved to Jhakri (Umrao's home village) after a dispute with his step-mother. Umrao's parents are dead and she has no brothers. For seven years, Usman was a permanent labourer for one of the landlord's employees in Dharmnagri. In about 1980, Usman decided his wages were insufficient and since then he has sought work on a more casual basis. Since about 1970, land fragmentation and population growth have made permanent farm employment less common, because there are fewer large holdings which are unable to meet their needs from family labour. Most of the available jobs are taken by adult men. On the other hand, more assured water supplies and new seeds provide two or three crops from one field and more seasonal work for the landless. Usman does weeding and ploughing, and harvests wheat, rice and sugar-cane, besides doing odd jobs such as making and thatching thin lattice frames for roofs. For nearly six months a year he has secure employment at one of the local cane-crushers, stoking the furnace or feeding the crusher with cut cane.

Of Umrao's nine children, only four are still alive. Both daughters are already married and Usman and Umrao live with their two small sons in one of the most ramshackle houses in Jhakri: a small one-roomed adobe hut with an aged thatched roof which leaks badly in the rain. Usman, Umrao, and their children have never attended school. Their position is very precarious: their sons, for instance, are naked while their only clothes are washed, looking (as Umrao put it) "like little frogs" squatting on their haunches. And there is little insurance against crises. When Usman cut his leg on a diesel engine in 1984, they had to sell their two buffaloes to pay for the twelve stitches and the medicines he needed.

Class and diet

A chūlhā's economic position sets the limits on its members' life-style, on their housing conditions, clothing, ability to pay for medical care, and especially on their diets. The major part of a chūlhā's income consists of grain and animal produce (home produced or as payments in kind) or cash used mainly to buy food.

In Dharmnagri and Jhakri, the basic element in the diet is grain. Wheat has long been the staple in the area, generally in the form of rotī (unleavened griddle-baked bread). Green Revolution technology has permitted more assured rice cultivation and rice is the other staple, usually plain boiled but also eaten as rotī made from rice flour. Rotī and rice are eaten with stews, mostly of pulses of various kinds (dāl) and vegetables such as potatoes, carrots and squashes. Meat and fish are only rarely eaten.[38] Grain, dāls and vegetables may be supplemented by dairy produce, milk, yoghourt, buttermilk and ghī (clarified butter), and gur is an important energy source. On rising around dawn, people in Dharmnagri and Jhakri drink sweetened tea or hot milk. Generally, their first meal is taken mid-morning after one stint of work and the other around dusk when the working day is over.

Aside from the landlord's chūlhā, however, only rich peasants such as Ashok and Bhagwana produce grain and dairy surpluses sufficient to permit their chūlhā members to "fill their stomachs" throughout the year, having ghī on their rotī and drinking milk regularly. Domestic grain-stores are filled after the rice and wheat harvests and the grain is consumed during the following year. Large surpluses are sold by the men, and the women exchange small quantities of grain to buy vegetables or fruit or (among the Muslims) meat and fish from salesmen who sometimes come to the villages. Middle peasants rarely own enough cattle to ensure a year-round supply of milk, and they cannot readily replace animals that die. Nor can they be prodigal with their grain: indeed, they ration their consumption carefully to prevent shortages before the next harvest, and they rarely eat fruit or meat.

Seasonal factors are even more important for poor peasant and landless chūlhās who buy some or all of the rice and wheat they consume. Work (and therefore income) is unevenly available during the agricultural year, while grain prices fluctuate seasonally, being low immediately after the harvests and rising as stocks decline. Opportunities for employment are very restricted during the monsoon (especially August-September) for sugar-cane is not being cut and the rice has already been transplanted. At such times, Usman's family is often penniless and hungry, though previously they would have been hungry for most of the year. Their diet is the most basic — rice or rotī with pulses or maybe just pickle; they rarely eat vegetables. Milk consumption was virtually ruled out even when they owned buffaloes, because the milk was sold to buy grain, as in other comparable chūlhās. Now, without milk animals, dairy products are even less available.

Even landowning chūlhās, however, can rarely buy in much extra food, because they have little ready cash. Payments for sugar-cane sales are often delayed and may be earmarked to repay loans taken out previously for fertiliser. In addition, fruits are seasonal, because there is no cold storage in Bijnor and fruit distribution is limited. Bijnor has a daily fruit market, but the weekly Begawala market has only occasional supplies. In any case, most fruits are relatively expensive. Fruit consumption is basically restricted to guavas and mangoes grown in orchards near the villages — but even those are beyond the means of the poorest village inhabitants.

Class and social change

Agricultural changes since the mid-1960s have had complex consequences in Dharmnagri and Jhakri.[39] The landlord and the rich peasants were the first to take advantage of the new technology. Middle peasants benefited from lower prices and easier and more widespread credit after 1970, but had missed the windfall gains obtained by the rich peasants. Even a poor peasant may now obtain water from a neighbour with a tubewell, hire a tractor for a day to plough his land or obtain credit from a co-operative. Labourers may also have more employment at harvests and other peak periods because of more intensive land use. But the new technology brings farmers problems as well as benefits, because demand for inputs has outpaced supplies. Liaqat's brother, a middle peasant, explained:

> Don't think we are rich. Only free farmers can be rich, and farmers are not free in India any more. When the diesel engines first came diesel was Rs 2 a litre; now it costs Rs 4 when you can get it. People with engines always have trouble getting diesel. They try Begawala, then Bijnor. Some men from Jhakri have had to go as far as Najibabad [45 kilometres] to get diesel to give their crops water. What is the good of this? It's the same with electricity, it has gone up in price, yet you get less of it and it comes and goes. You have to catch it when it comes or your crops go dry just the same. The sugar-mills don't pay their suppliers for six months at a time. The Cane Society forced us to take chemical fertilisers twenty years ago and now we can't get any at all, never mind on time![40]

The recent changes have thus had mixed effects. The productivity of the land has increased, but people say that farming entails more intensive work these days. Most people's living standards are improving but only slowly, for the population is growing fast. Although the uncertainties caused by the climate have been moderated, they have been replaced by the vagaries of the state and the market-place as threats to people's livelihood. There is a narrow margin between success and failure. Even rich peasants are not well-off, by the standards of the urban middle classes in India or elsewhere. All the able-bodied men, except those in the landlord's chūlhā, perform long hours of physical work during most of the year, with little scope for any kind of luxury as a reward. The expansion of credit is also double-edged. All chūlhās are indebted to some degree and seemingly small problems can make repayments difficult. A chronic illness, too many daughters to get married, or a poor harvest, can precipitate defaults on loans and enforced sales of land. So far, Dharmnagri and Jhakri have been remarkably free from this kind of pauperisation, with relatively few landed chūlhās becoming totally landless. But land is being divided among sons, average holdings are shrinking and employment opportunities outside agriculture are not increasing very rapidly.[41]

From daughter to bride

Raising a daughter is like watering a shade-giving tree in someone else's courtyard.

Women mainly relate to the structures of class and the state through men, and normally not directly in their own right.[42] Some threads of continuity still provide a key to gender divisions. The world beyond the domestic arena is basically male space: men are central in agricultural activities in the fields and in dealings with state or cane co-operative employees, marketing produce and negotiating credit. Women are largely excluded from these activities and have little opportunity for employment. Moreover, only exceptionally — for example when a woman is widowed with at least one child approaching adulthood — do women in rural Bijnor own land, agricultural tools or draught animals. Thus women are normally dependent on men, as is considered right and proper. A woman without a husband or son to depend upon is in a parlous condition. Certainly, women and men alike have a stake in the chūlhās in which they live. But, for instance, after divorce or separation the husband remains in his village, retaining the house and any land. The woman must return to her father or brothers for refuge, while they find another man on whom she can depend. Men's privileged access to productive resources and employment denies power, respect and economic independence to women and also creates patterns of vulnerability and insecurity not experienced by men.[43] A woman is subject to the man upon whom she depends. Here we explore how this affects a young married woman expected to bear children for her husband. In the next chapter, we discuss the controls over her as a worker.

Childhood, puberty and sexuality

In rural Bijnor, childhood is normally spent in the father's village, the pīhar (among Hindus) and the maikā (among Muslims).[44] Few children are employed or attend school regularly, but most help their parents from an early age. Little girls do childcare, scour dishes, take food to household members working in the fields or clear up cattle-dung, while little boys graze animals, run errands and become increasingly involved in their fathers' work.

Settling children in marriage is a parental duty, and the decision rests with them, not with their children. Parents do not wish to appear tardy or casual, for puberty transforms their child into a sexual person, possessing an immensely disruptive potential which must be carefully controlled and channelled.[45] Perceptions of sexuality are closely linked with a pair of opposites commonly used in local medical models, garmī (heat, activity, stimulation) and thand (coldness, calmness, pacification).[46] The effect (tāsīr) of climate, people's temperaments, individuals' bodies, medicines and foods can all be described in these terms. Good health requires and reflects a balance between these qualities, a balance unique to each individual and which can be upset by their diet or the climate. A naturally garm (hot, active) person (as displayed in hot temper or skin rashes) suffers during hot weather or after taking garm food, but a thandā (cold, tranquil) person is less severely affected. In terms of this framework, an ailment may indicate an internal imbalance: diagnosis discerns its cause and dietary avoidances (parhez) are prescribed to remedy the problem.

At puberty, a boy's body begins to produce semen, a highly concentrated distillation from blood.[47] Blood is garm: semen is all the more so. Accumulating semen could result in excessive garmī and (if it goes to the head) madness. This can be averted through moderately frequent sexual intercourse, which restores the body to a safe state. A sexually passionate man is garm; an impotent man is thandā.[48] Excessively frequent intercourse drains the semen and is weakening, especially for the elderly. Moreover, access to sexual partners must be regulated, for semen contains seeds from which a baby may develop. Men want children acknowledged to be theirs, to continue their name and provide security in old-age. But, indiscriminate planting — like sowing wild oats — gives the planter no rights over the resulting child. Ideally, each man has a woman to whom he has exclusive sexual access and who bears his children.

Parents of girls are influenced by parallel considerations. Puberty marks the start of fluctuations in a woman's bodily state. Garmī gradually accumulates until it precipitates the menstrual flow, which prevents the garmī concentrating in the woman's head. Thus, women are particularly anxious if menstruation is delayed or light, although an excessively heavy menstrual flow is considered weakening. Menstrual blood is also defiling: a complete and rapid cleansing (safāi) is necessary to prevent the poison accumulating dangerously in the body. A menstruating woman is considered unclean until she has had a cleansing bath after the flow ends.[49] Although sexual intercourse makes the woman more garm, and she gradually becomes more garm during pregnancy, the greater blood loss after childbirth is much more effective than menstruation in averting over-heating. Indeed, childbearing is often a recommended solution for hysteria.

A sexually mature woman should be sufficiently garm to receive sexual advances and nourish a man's seeds. The nagging worry for her parents is that, unbridled, she will allow wrongful access to her body and bear the child of a man without formal rights over her. Indeed, from puberty (and throughout adulthood too) her mobility beyond the domestic arena is closely monitored to avert such a disgrace. Her sexual maturity poses a threat to the honour (izzat) of her parents and brothers, which is best removed by her early marriage while she is still a virgin. Parents are pressured to marry their daughter quickly, for tardiness spells rumours about her character or health as well as reducing the pool of potential husbands. Basically, then, sexuality and childbearing in Dharmnagri and Jhakri are regulated within marriages that generally take place between a bride in her mid-teens and a groom a few years older.

The gift of a bride

Hindu and Muslim parents in all classes aspire to arrange their adolescent children's marriages according to a common model, although they do not always succeed.[50] The physiological changes of puberty, however, have a different significance for the parents of boys and of girls. An unmarried daughter is often described as a guest in her parents' house, to be fed, clothed, and trained at her parents' expense for the benefit of her future husband's family. She is gifted to her husband like a religious offering and her parents acquire an inferior position in relating to her in-laws.[51] Thus parents arrange their daughter's marriage with mixed feelings: sadness at losing their daughter, fear that they might fail to settle her well, anxiety about maintaining their own honour, satisfaction at having fulfilled their duty. The bride herself is physically uprooted from her parents' home and sent to her husband's house: she shifts from her father's ambit to her husband's. This is why a daughter is called parāyā-dhan (property, prosperity and good fortune belonging to someone else).

Almost all adults in Dharmnagri and Jhakri were married to a partner and at a time selected by their parents. None of the 236 ever-married women in the two villages was married across the religious boundary, nor has any respectable marriage been arranged across a sub-caste boundary.[52] Generally, parents find an appropriate partner for their child by using advice from people linked to them through marriage, a task in which older married women and their connections are often influential. Only very rarely have the bride and groom seen each other before the wedding: a girl's close male relatives inspect potential grooms and their homes while boys' close female relatives see prospective brides, who appear silent and demure in front of them.[53]

In Dharmnagri, the potential bride's parents initiate the search. The size of their sub-caste and where it lives influence how widely they range. Hindus do not arrange marriages between people descended from a common ancestor or who are already closely connected. Their matches are always in another village, mostly with partners from over 20 kilometres away. Occasionally, marriage links are reinforced when two women (sisters, paternal cousins, or a woman and her brother's daughter) are married into the same village. However, there should be no suggestion of an exchange of women between two villages. Consequently, marriage networks among Hindus tend to be widely flung.

Among Muslims, the groom's parents make the first move. In general, Muslim marriages are arranged close by within a small circle of families and villages. Muslims basically exclude only siblings, parents and parents' siblings as marriage partners. Marriage between close relatives is permitted, although only three of the 88 ever-married women in Jhakri had married first cousins: of the key informants, Nisar was married to his cousin (MBD) Najma.[54] There are seven couples in which both partners were born in Jhakri, including Liaqat and Latifan.[55] About half the remaining marriages are between partners from villages within eight kilometres of Jhakri. Only Teli and Julaha marriages are regularly arranged at distances comparable to Hindu marriages, though often between partners more closely related than Hindus would permit. Further, Muslims do not explicitly exclude exchange marriages between kin groups and villages — Jabruddin's sister, for instance, is married to Hashmi's brother.

Taking and giving

Generally, not only the bride is gifted, for she goes along with a dowry (dahej or jahez). Arranging her marriage is a trying time for her parents, because much of the preamble to the wedding entails negotiation and jockeying over the engagement gifts and dowry. The groom's family provide some clothing and jewellery for the bride, but less than the bride's parents, who also give household effects (bed, bedding, cooking pots) and clothing for the groom and his relatives.[56] Marriages are generally arranged between partners from comparable economic backgrounds and the size of dowry reflects their chūlhā's wealth. Rich and middle peasants may include a radio and cycle for the groom in their daughter's dowry as well as jewellery and several dozen sets of clothing. The poor can give just a little clothing and some household effects, and seek a groom with no greater ambitions. Hindus usually give cash in the dowry (often several thousand rupees). Among Muslims, the general level of dowry is lower and does not include cash.[57]

While the dowry is the peak of gift-giving, the marriage establishes a long-standing pattern of len-den (taking-giving) mainly from the bride's family to her husband's family.[58] A man should provide his out-married daughters and sisters (dhiyānī) with items for the rest of their days and even beyond. Initially the father gives; after his death his sons take over. Married women need male kin to continue len-den, for a sister receives but cannot give.[59] The intensity of giving is greatest when the relationship is garm (soon after the marriage) and declines as the relationship cools, but "a daughter takes all her life" and should not be sent destitute (literally, empty-handed, khālī-hāth) to her husband. Ideally, the married daughter receives a settled allowance (sīdhā), generally consisting of grain, other foodstuffs and clothing, after the wheat and rice harvests. Similar gifts called tewhārī are given at the major festivals (tewhār) especially Holi and Tijo among Hindus and Eid among Muslims, and (at least in the early years) she receives clothing and foodstuffs after her natal kin have called her for a visit.[60] Further gifts are sent when her brothers are married, when their wives give birth, when she herself has a baby, when her children are married and so on.

Such gifts are often construed as the woman's entitlement in lieu of inheritance of land but such a view is hard to sustain.[61] Rarely do the gifts contain productive property equivalent to what her brother might inherit. Occasionally milk or draught animals are gifted — but the items are generally supplies of food and clothing rather than the productive resources that provide such necessities. Not only are these gifts removed from her parents' control, but the woman herself cannot guarantee to control them. Her jewellery, for instance, may be taken by her sās (mother-in-law), for the next daughter-in-law marrying into the family, for her own daughter's marriage, or for pawning or sale if money is needed urgently. Many other items are explicitly intended for distribution among her husband's kin. Failure to send clothing for her husband would imply that she is no longer an auspicious married woman (suhāgan) but an inauspicious widow (rand).[62] Other gifts are earmarked for her sās, nand (husband's sister) and others. Further, the orchestration of len-den on behalf of her male natal kin is in the hands of older women. They store goods in readiness and protect the family's honour by giving as generously as possible, they note what was given previously, and they decide what to send and how to distribute it. Young married women, then, are crucial but basically passive conduits in these often substantial transfers of non-productive resources. Indeed, their in-laws often refer to them as auspicious wealth-bringers (dhanya).[63]

People say that women's parents have always wanted to give generously. But a widespread view is that greater access to consumer goods in the wake of increased agricultural productivity means that len-den is now more costly: daughters are regarded as more burdensome (bhāri) these days. People used to give according to their wishes and capability: the poor gave little, the rich gave more. But the giving then was khushī-se (voluntary, literally, out of happiness). These days, people say, the parents of boys display greed and want to become rich with no effort, they want a good dowry more than a good bride, they "demand from their mouth" specific items in the dowry or later len-den — and a woman's parents feel pressurised in an increasingly competitive marriage market.[64] A daughter cannot be sent empty-handed, for people will insult her by saying that she is her master's grannie (khasam-kī-nānī) and not a real wealth-bringer.

The bahū in her susrāl

> In the susrāl I cannot go anywhere and I keep purdah [concealment] from everyone. *(Bhagirthi)*
>
> In the susrāl, sharm [shame] comes. And even if you don't like keeping purdah, you still must. *(Ghazala)*

Once married, the young couple resides in the husband's village, the bride's susrāl (father-in-law's village). To her parents, she is now someone else's property. To her husband's relatives she is a bahū (bride, daughter-in-law), and the domestic authorities in her susrāl control her movements, her activities and her contact with her natal kin.[65] Her husband is surrounded by people he has known since birth: she is set down in the midst of strangers.[66] She should be docile and bear with fortitude whatever is in her destiny (nasīb, bhāg or qismat).

At least initially, she and her husband will probably share a chūlhā with her husband's parents, though her transfer to her susrāl takes place gradually.[67] After the marriage ceremony (shādī), the bride goes to her susrāl briefly along with the dowry. But the first cohabitation (gaunā) usually takes place some days, weeks or as much as a year later. In the interim, the bride remains in her natal village. On returning to her susrāl she is again accompanied by gifts of clothing and foodstuffs. Nowadays, in Dharmnagri and Jhakri, the cohabitation of most young women has taken place before they are about 17; the husband is usually two or three years older. The bride's age at cohabitation has not changed much in living memory, though the gap between marriage and cohabitation has decreased from the several years which used to be typical.[68] Even after the cohabitation, the bride comes and goes between her natal village and her susrāl, gradually increasing her time in her susrāl until she stays there most of the time.

In some respects, the chūlhā where the bahū lives in her susrāl is a single entity. Cooking and eating together generates and reflects a commonality of interests. But the chūlhā has a political dimension, for domestic units are shot through with divisions of sex and age. The bahū's shift in residence entails the transfer of rights over her from her father to her susrāl kin, especially her husband and sās. For several years, she is more controlled than able to exercise control, either over her own activities or those of others.

The husband's rule

Young men have no more say in the selection of their marriage partner than women, but once married they are established in an asymmetrical relationship. The man rules over the woman — a capacity aided by his seniority on grounds of gender and age. He is master of the house (ghar-kā-mālik), she is subject to her husband's rule (ādmī-kā-rāj).

Daily life for the bahū in her susrāl, then, involves being controlled in many aspects of her behaviour. Sharm (shame, modesty, bashfulness) is central to a bahū's proper behaviour there.[69] A young man displays sharm through obeying his parents and not inconsiderately favouring his wife or fondling his children in front of them. A young woman's sharm relates most obviously to her sexuality. Her transition to bahū necessarily entails sexual experience, but sexual intercourse is a sharm-kī-bāt (shameful matter) not to be alluded to or publicised. Further, sexual intercourse is polluting. While a man can cleanse himself by washing, a woman is permanently affected by her conversion from virgin to wife, even though she, too, always takes a cleansing bath. A bahū and her husband should give no hint of the sexual dealings between them. She should keep her head covered in his presence, and maintain a cool distance from him. Conjugal sexual activity is expected and enjoined: but a bahū's demeanour should not imply that she is sexually active. While the young couple share a chūlhā with his parents, his mother may regulate when they sleep together (at least at home at night).[70] Otherwise, however, the husband has the right of sexual access to his wife at times when he decrees: she should neither take the initiative nor refuse him. Many men in Dharmnagri and Jhakri were explicit that sexual intercourse involves the exercise of power over a woman who is degraded in the process. An essential component of a husband's rule is sexual power over his wife. Likewise, in their general dealings, the man expects obedience from his wife and slowness to offer an opinion. If he criticises her, she should hold her tongue. If he tells her to do something, she should comply even if she inwardly disagrees. She should not refer to him by name or address him as "tu", the least respectful form of address (which he may, however, use for her). If she were to be shameless (be-sharm) and assertive, his honour would be undermined.

Additionally, he has rights over his wife's childbearing capacity. He alone should plant seeds in her; his honour would be severely compromised if another man were rumoured to have attained access to her or if she is provocative and shameless in relation to other men. All the children she bears must be, beyond all reasonable doubt, produced from her husband's seeds. Thus, the bahū observes sharm by keeping long (lambā) purdah in her susrāl, covering her body, head and face properly. Hindu women wear a long-sleeved blouse and a dhotī (cotton sārī) and achieve long purdah by pulling the end of their dhotī (ghūnghat) over their faces, so that only their hands and feet are visible.[71] Muslim women wear "three-cloths" (tīn-kapre), suits consisting of trousers (pājāma or shalwār), dress (qamīz) and a shawl (chādar). They keep long purdah by covering themselves with their shawl.[72] Within the domestic compound, a bahū behaves with restraint, especially with her husband's elder male kin. She avoids eye contact, covers her face, turns away from them and stops any conversation in which she is engaged. Generally, her sasur (father-in-law) or older brothers-in-law (HeB) have little business with her and, at most, would issue an abrupt instruction to her.[73] She should not initiate conversation with them, but might ask a child or her sās to make the approach if she needs to ask them anything. Among the men, only with her younger brothers-in-law (HyB) might she develop a more open relationship. Her mobility beyond the domestic compound is also regulated: she is not allowed far from home, especially not alone, and goes nowhere without permission. She goes outside well concealed and should not linger in her errand or talk to people on the way.

A bahū is a potential threat to her husband's honour. Her observance of sharm averts this danger, as her husband appears in control of a wife whose behaviour does not reflect badly on him. Her attention to such detail demonstrates her respect and concern. Young women know what is required and generally (in the interests of a quiet life) try to behave accordingly. Indeed, many assent to the behaviour expected of them. But the standards are too stringent for complete success to be easy. The bahū who wags her tongue at her husband, who laughs and jokes in the presence of his older brothers, who ignores his comments about her cooking, or who goes about without his consent challenges his rule. Her compliance will probably be exacted through physical violence. In our conversations in Dharmnagri and Jhakri, wife-beating was regularly mentioned, by women and men alike. Men regard it as their prerogative, an appropriate way to deal with insubordination, and an important buttress of a husband's rule. Married women claim that none of them totally escapes being beaten, though some men have greater reputations for hot temper than others. Especially in the early years after marriage, a beating from the husband is not an unexpected experience for any bahū who steps even slightly out of line. Her opportunities for resistance tend to be passive self-destructive ones. She may refuse to cook, and therefore to eat. She may sit inside refusing to speak. She may wilfully cook food in ways her husband dislikes, or answer back, provoking a beating but perhaps giving herself more space in the longer run.

A man expects to rule an obedient wife. Ultimately, however, his interests are bound up with his wife and children. Men generally take the obligations of marriage seriously and the potential excesses of a husband's rule are usually moderated by his concern for his wife's welfare. An extreme example occurred a few years ago in Jhakri, when a new bride was discovered to be a deaf-mute. Apparently, the husband resisted his mother's attempts to return her in disgrace to her parents, saying that she was his wife and he would not let her be sent back and have her future destroyed.

Female hierarchy

A man's ability to check his wife's behaviour is restricted because men spend little time inside the domestic compound and cannot monitor what goes on there. The exclusion of women from the world beyond the domestic sphere is a key to understanding gender inequalities within chūlhās — but this does not imply that women are undifferentiated and equally powerless in relation to one another. Fathers command the respect of sons, older brothers of younger brothers. Through their marriages, women in their susrāl are profoundly divided from one another. The new bahū is at the low point in her marital career. More established women are further along the track she expects to follow. They are concerned for the integrity of the husband's chūlhā rather than to be supportive and welcoming: indeed, they wield authority over her.[74]

In practice, then, much of the normal policing of young married women is delegated to older women, especially the sās, older sisters-in-law (HeBW), the husband's aunts (HFBW) and his older cousins' wives (HFBSW). For years, the sās herself has been subordinate to the domestic authorities of her susrāl. But, gradually, elders die and her growing children become subject to her authority. The arrival of a bahū over whom she can exercise power, albeit localised power, is an important transition, for the bahū should respect and obey her sās and resist being provoked into answering criticism with a sharp tongue.

Close surveillance by the sās is not necessarily a source of overt unpleasantness: a sās and her bahū can live amicably together. Equally, however, many a bahū has unhappy tales to recount. Several older women talked of being frequently beaten by their sās, younger ones sometimes said their sās instigated wife-beating; significantly, "susrī" (mother-in-law) is a popular term of abuse among women. Direct and close control by the sās is supplemented with a more general scrutiny by the other women in the bahū's susrāl. Her movements are regulated, her demeanour commented on and her conversations observed. One bahū in Jhakri was gossiped about as the bride who brought only four suits in her dowry and yet speaks up so much, while Sunil's sister mockingly imitated Santosh's shamelessness at boldly striding around Dharmnagri with her shoulders erect and the end of her dhotī thrown back off her face. A bahū's female neighbours may report her misdemeanours and comment adversely if she is not beaten, saying that her husband has allowed her "to sit on his head". Women rarely rally round to intervene — unless the beating is excessive — and may comment that the beaten wife is only receiving her due. The husband's close female kin, then, are not ready allies, and a bahū's limited mobility inhibits the development of supportive relationships with other women.[75] The first years in the susrāl are likely to be rather bleak for a bahū: in their own terms, "marriage is ruination" (shādī hai barbādī).

Contact with the natal kin [76]

> In my maikā I can roam where my heart wishes. There is no hindrance nor any purdah there. *(Khurshida)*

> In the pīhar, when the mood is to go somewhere, just go. No one will say anything. But in the susrāl I cannot go anywhere easily. *(Maya)*

A daughter given in marriage belongs to her in-laws. But this does not preclude contact with her parents nor their continuing concern for her well-being.[77] In extreme circumstances, parents may provide a refuge when a bahū's life in her susrāl becomes unbearable — like Jagram's sister whose in-laws refused to provide medical treatment or convalescence, or a new bride whose husband's sexual advances had been so rough and frequent that she was terrified, or Khurshida when Khalil and his father were constantly disputing and who returned to her susrāl only after several abject visits by

Khalil's young step-brother to plead for her return. Harwan's sister was badly beaten up by her husband and sās because her dowry was insufficient: she returned to Dharmnagri while her parents fought (and won) a court case against them. Once separated from her sās her situation improved, for her husband had apparently only been obeying his mother. Promilla's sās also complained about the size of her dowry and treated her so badly that Promilla stayed in her pīhar for a year. Similarly, Nisar's cousin (FBstepD) lived comfortably in her susrāl only after her sās died: she was never given clothes in her susrāl and was returned periodically to Jhakri in rags. Her mother gave her suits and the men of Jhakri criticised her husband, but he would not contradict his mother. A woman's parents might refuse to return her to her susrāl unless they are reassured about her future treatment. As the giver of a bride, a married woman's father is inferior to her susrāl kin. But the husband's youth somewhat counterbalances this asymmetry and he may have to accept humbling criticism from his father-in-law. Yet a woman's parents dare not resist the husband's demands for her return too strenuously, lest they precipitate future difficulties for her or (perhaps even worse) her desertion.

Even in less anguished circumstances, bahūs in Dharmnagri and Jhakri were quick to contrast their life in the susrāl with their congenial existence in their parents' village. There they are loved and have warm supportive relationships with other women. Their movements and activities are not so overseen by others. They do not observe the strict deference behaviour and bodily concealment required in their susrāl: they cover their head (but not their face) out of respect for their father and can talk openly to everyone in their natal village. They find benefit (fāida), affection (māmtā), consideration (khayāl), succour (madad) and peace (ārām) there. But in the susrāl, a bahū receives no indulgence (khātir) or appreciation (qadr): she is subject to surveillance and must obtain permission for everything she does. A bahū has little room for manoeuvre, and obtains respite only when she visits her parents.

The difference is well displayed by a woman and her nand (husband's sister). When the married nand returns to her natal village the restraints of her susrāl are lifted. She is self-confident, relaxed and assertive while her brother's wife (bhābī) is concealed, controlled and self-controlled. And yet the nand transforms herself into a bahū when she returns to her own susrāl. A young married woman plays two people, one in her natal village, another in her susrāl: her passivity in her susrāl is learned behaviour, a prudent strategy for her life there.[78] Not surprisingly, the yoke of the husband and the sās does not always rest comfortably. A woman's susrāl kin understand the attractions of her natal village and the vulnerability of their authority. Her resistance, however, is curtailed by limiting her contacts with her natal kin. She cannot easily mobilise her best source of social support for she retains only fragile and fleeting links, especially with her mother and sisters. These contacts, indeed, are often mediated through men, on terms defined by her husband and his kin.

Visiting the natal village

> Once I went to my maikā without asking my husband and he beat me. Since then I have never gone without his permission. *(Sabra)*

> After marriage a woman's place is her susrāl and susrāl government operates. If it is just a question of fetching news from her parents, she stays in Dharmnagri while I fetch it. It's cheaper that way. She could never go without asking. If she did I would show her a stick! *(Udayan)*

For some years after her marriage, the bahū's brother comes to call her but her parents' claims can be fairly sure to outweigh her husband's only if she is called for festivals (such as Holi and Tijo among Hindus) or because her brother's wife gives birth, a marriage is imminent or a close relative has died.[79] Then her natal kin meet any transport costs and agree a date for her return with appropriate gifts, unless she is called because of some sadness. On other occasions, however, her husband or sās may refuse a visit altogether or grant one grudgingly for a short time because her absence from the susrāl is untimely or too soon after the previous one.

After a few years, she herself may ask to visit her parents, though generally infrequently for fear of causing annoyance. Men are apt to ask why they should agree since her brother has not called her and she will receive nothing for distribution in her susrāl. Certainly, a woman should not visit her parents without her husband's permission and agreement about how long she may stay. Few women had ever risked doing so and men insist that a wife going without permission would legitimately be beaten for her gesture of insubordination. Sometimes, however, a woman's parents manage to persuade her husband to let her stay longer than originally agreed.

A woman usually travels with a male chaperon — her brother or husband — though women married close to their natal village may walk with their children or another woman. Apart from that, having a brother to call them is considered a matter of happiness, so women do not wish to go alone. The brother, however, is calling his sister on their mother's behalf and the bond between mother and daughter is considered key. Once the mother dies, women say, the daughter's visits tail off because the brother and his wife are less likely to call her.

A visit from the natal village

Contact is also maintained through visits made to a married woman in her susrāl, though such visits do not necessarily provide her with much support. Among Muslims and Hindus alike, the wife's kin must not suggest in any way that their gift of her was actually a sale. For them to accept hospitality from her susrāl kin is inherently problematic. Her visitors might bring food with them and refuse food offered, or pay for it (even for a glass of water) to avoid any suggestion of seeking a return for their gift. A meal might be refused for fear that a special treat would cost dearly. Lengthy stays are clearly difficult under such constraints.

Further, a married woman's parents feel sharm before their daughter's parents-in-law, because of their inferior position and their virgin daughter's conversion into a sexually experienced wife. Many parents simply never visit their married daughters in their susrāl and a brother is sent instead. He, however, spends most time with the men and is unlikely to be privy to her worries. Further, he does not have the advantage of age to command respect: significantly, the word "sālā" (wife's brother) is rarely spoken, except as a term of abuse.[80]

Moreover, visits from the mother, sisters and brothers' wives are hampered by general restrictions on women's mobility. Several Muslim women married near to their natal village were occasionally visited by their mother, but this rarely happened among Hindus. Direct contact with the mother occurs mainly when a woman visits her parents. A sister's visit is very uncommon. An elder sister is like the mother and sharm keeps her away; a younger married sister needs money, time and permission from her husband — all more willingly granted for visits to her parents, for they send gifts while sisters do not; an unmarried sister is rarely permitted frequent visits anywhere. Muslim women married within walking distance of their sisters sometimes visit one another, but otherwise sisters meet only in their natal village, when festivals, weddings or births chance to bring them together, maybe after some years.

Close marriage or distant?

Distant marriage is bad. A person might die or be ill and the news not reach the woman. News can arrive from a nearby village in time. *(Fatima)*

If your wife's maikā is nearby, you or your wife can easily visit her relatives. News of celebrations, illness or death will reach you quickly and you have time to do something. Also, it is cheap to come and go. But there are disadvantages. There can be disagreements over tiny things. If you are married distantly, you live apart from disagreements. But you should ask my father about this: I was only the groom and I just did what I was told. *(Farooq)*

Marriage distance results from decisions made by parents, but young couples themselves have to live with the consequences. Generally, women are relatively positive about geographically close marriage, while men are more guarded.

In Jhakri, Muslim women who are married within walking distance of their maikā say this permits frequent contact, for reasons of time as well as money. They receive instant news of dying and living (marne-jīne) and of grief and pleasure (dukh-sukh). Their brother can easily visit them or their husband call on their parents several times a month. They themselves may hurry to finish their day's work, meet their parents for a few hours and return to their susrāl to prepare the evening meal. Such visits do not normally involve a male chaperon, though permission is rarely given as often as once a week. Negotiating longer stays can be more difficult. The contrasts should not be overdrawn, but women in Dharmnagri and other Muslim women more distant from their natal kin regret that important life-events can occur without their knowledge. Especially for poor people, travelling time and the cost of bus fares can cut women off from news. A woman's husband and brothers visit infrequently. She goes to her natal village only with a male chaperon to stay for some days or even weeks, but probably no more than three times a year, and less once she has been married several years. Indeed, a man often visits his wife's village (his susrāl) more frequently than she does.

On the other hand, a woman married somewhat distantly from her parents is more warmly welcomed when she visits. Moreover, if her parents are close by, they are needlessly grieved by her marital troubles, in which they should not meddle. Although men grant the benefits of cheap travel and rapid conveyance of important news, their comments hinge on these two objections to close marriage:

> If my wife's pīhar were too close, she would get news too often — and so would her parents. There would be too much interference. It is better for a man to be married distantly. When I visit my susrāl they think I am good to have come from so far and they treat me well. I am given the best to eat. If I were married close, what would happen? They'd toss me two-three rotī and ten minutes later (with luck) I might get some pickle and salt! *(Tulsi)*

Men say that excessively frequent contact between a woman and her natal kin permits unwanted interventions, shaming her husband and inhibiting him from beating her. Being somewhat distant means visits are less frequent. The son-in-law is treated like a prince, not someone commonplace. He is a pāhunā (guest, and by extension, son-in-law) and entertained appropriately. Moreover, his wife must settle in her susrāl: she cannot run to her parents after every little fight, because, as Naresh commented, how can she possibly go as she has no money? Dilruba came from only six kilometres away, and Dilshad complained:

> My wife goes to her maikā too often. Her father calls her and she sometimes goes alone with the small children. I should finish this marriage and make another one from much farther away — then my wife would not be able to go so often. It would be too far for her to go alone and I would not give her the fare anyway.

Amongst Muslims, dense marriage networks may protect a woman. Information can spread very quickly through third parties, since several women from one village may be married into another. Furthermore, other kin may rapidly become entangled in a dispute if the marriage is between a couple already related. Only Khalil's step-brother approved of close genealogical marriages on these very grounds.[81] In 1985 he was engaged to Khalil's cousin (MBD) from a village about six kilometres away. Out of respect for his elders with whom there is a long-standing connection, he said he would not beat his wife or swear at her. Also, he said, there is no demanding or extortion in len-den among relatives, so his wife would not suffer if she only brought a little with her. But his views and intentions are out of step with all the male key informants in Jhakri and Dharmnagri, who regard close marriage (either geographical or genealogical) as a serious threat to a husband's rule.

Aberrant marriages

Most married women in Dharmnagri and Jhakri had shifted to their husband's village on marriage, bringing a dowry with them. This was also true for most of the key informants, although for three couples the match was the second for one or both of them. Imarti was originally married to Ishwar's older brother: when he died, she remained in Dharmnagri with Ishwar. There was no formal marriage, but len-den continues from her natal village. In Jhakri, after Zakir's first wife died he married her younger sister Zubeida, while Bashir and Bilquis had both been widowed before their marriage to each other. Alternative forms of marriage are uncommon, but reactions to them potently reveal ideas about the sexual and domestic politics in which bahūs should be situated and about the proper contacts between married women, their husbands and their natal kin. Ghar-jamāi (in-living son-in-law) and within-village (gāon-ke-gāon) marriages alike pose problems for husband's rule, while the bought bride brings neither the expected dowry nor any subsequent len-den.

The in-living son-in-law

> In necessity a couple might live in the wife's pīhar. But women have sharm after they are married and stay in their susrāl. My husband would not like to stay in his susrāl. *(Adesh)*

> A man can go to his susrāl for a visit but not to live. There is sharm in doing that. People would point you out to your wife's relatives. Some people do it, when the wife's parents have no sons. That way the ghar-jamāi gets his susrāl's wealth. But otherwise a man would not like it. *(Ashok)*

For a man to depend regularly on his son-in-law is even more shameful than accepting a mere meal from his daughter's in-laws in her susrāl. Generally, a couple lives in the wife's village only if she has no siblings, particularly brothers. The ghar-jamāi works the land, cares for her parents in old-age and eventually takes possession of the land for himself and his children. In the two villages there are six instances of ghar-jamāi marriage, if Mahipal in Dharmnagri, who used to live in Maya's pīhar, is included.

Young married women's opinions about ghar-jamāi marriages were divided. Several said that they had never considered such an arrangement as they have brothers to inherit their father's land. Some thought that the woman obtains peace, love and help by being close to her parents. Others said that ghar-jamāi marriage is not honourable: on brief visits to the wife's natal village, a couple does not cohabit because of sharm, but if they lived there regularly they would. Moreover, a bad husband would still beat his wife without consideration for his parents-in-law:

> There would be no benefit for the woman, for the husband does what he likes. A man with no sharm might swear in front of her parents. Only this, the mother will show consideration to her daughter. But there is no difference for the jamāi. He does not keep his wife's parents happy and his wife belongs to him and must obey him. *(Khurshida)*

Some women considered that obtaining the wife's father's land plus his own inheritance is the major difference for the man who moves to his susrāl and becomes a ghar-jamāi. Otherwise, commented Maqsudi, he can meet his parents when he likes because his wife cannot stop him, for (as Wasila said) he is unfettered (āzād) unlike a woman. Other women, however, recognised that a man would not like being a ghar-jamāi: Tarabati commented, "A man lives with honour in his own house, but is subdued by living in someone else's." Just as a sālā (wife's brother) is not respected, so a jamāi (son-in-law) is out of place and demeaned by living in his susrāl:

> Sās-ke-ghar jamāi kuttā,
> Bahin-ke-ghar bhāi kuttā.
> At his sās' house a son-in-law is a scrounging cur,
> At his sister's house a brother is a scrounging cur.

Certainly, men's views of the ghar-jamāi are homogeneous. While granting the attractions of inheriting more land, none was prepared to concede that being a ghar-jamāi had any other benefits. The ghar-jamāi is virtually a mirror image of the normal bahū, precisely the grounds for men's objections. Being a ghar-jamāi undermines a man's ability to retain control over his wife. She has constant protection from her natal kin and can move around as she cannot in her susrāl. But her husband lacks both his normal back-up from his kin and freedom from interference from his in-laws. He may have problems retaining his position as master of the house. Men talked about ceasing to be their own man, even on brief visits to their susrāl, when they must abide by the eating and sleeping times of their in-laws and behave meekly in their father-in-law's presence. These difficulties may be exacerbated by a ghar-jamāi's in-laws. Instead of respecting their "guest" (pāhunā) they may jibe and insult him. He loses face for scrounging and may become enmeshed in tussles with his wife's hostile cousins and uncles over possession of the house and land. Maya felt she had peace in her natal village but Mahipal decided to return to Dharmnagri because of sexual insults and uncertainties over possession of Maya's father's land:

> People do not like a man who lives in his susrāl. I was sworn at all the time. They would call me 'sālā' and 'bahin-chūt'. You can never get

away from that if you live where your wife was born. It takes all your honour away. My father-in-law may give the land to his brother, so I decided not to stay and hear such things. Also, my wife's parents heard all my fights with her and matters which would cause no trouble in Dharmnagri became big in my susrāl.[82]

Landless people without sons have nothing with which to attract a ghar-jamāi. Just occasionally, however, a landless man moves to his wife's village for work. Usman moved to Jhakri after a dispute with his step-mother and another man's village was washed away by the Ganges. These are not true ghar-jamāis, as they neither scrounge from their parents-in-law nor support them. But the wife's parents and brothers are probably still at hand and compromise his capacity to exercise his rule. Such men are still vulnerable to taunts, as Pushpa commented about Punni's sister's husband living in Dharmnagri:

Men of the house and men of the entire village do not respect him. Some call out, 'Hey, Ganje [Baldie] where are you going?' Others shout, 'Kāliyā [Blackie], what's going on?' But if he lived in his own house and visited occasionally, everyone would respect him. They would say, 'Come, pāhunā, please come in', and offer him tea. They would 'stand on one leg' [make every effort] to provide good hospitality.[83]

Within-village marriage

Within-village marriage is not right. It is a sharm-kī-bāt [shameful matter] for the woman. Her parents hear everything and there will be many worries. All four parents will be pulled into fights and other relatives will be sworn at because of their connection. But there is no difference for the man as he is his own boss. *(Qudsia)*

All the benefit is from a distant marriage because you avoid fights with your in-laws. Within the village or even nearby, they hear everything and you end up on bad terms over every little thing. If the marriage is distant, you can hit your wife and swear at her but no one would find out. If it's near, you can visit often and it does not cost much to travel. But if it is within-village what would happen? Your susrāl people would be so used to seeing you that you wouldn't be special. They'd just say, 'Come, smoke the huqqa.' But if the susrāl is distant, they'd say, 'Look our pāhunā has come from far away.' They'd fetch good food and sit you down. *(Qadir)*

Only Muslims permit within-village marriages, of which there are seven in Jhakri, including Latifan and Liaqat. One attraction is that the expenses for wedding feasts and dowry are less. Latifan and her brother, for instance, were orphans married within Jhakri by their uncle (FB). Yet Muslim women and men alike are often vehement in their opposition to within-village marriage.

Women consider it shameful for a woman's parents to hear all her difficulties in her susrāl, and say that caring daughters would not like to worry their parents. Khurshida said that people's hearts become soured by fighting, Sabra that people hear only the voice of battles, Tahira that all the daughter's miseries are heard immediately. If the woman is a bit distant from her parents, she can ensure that they never hear her "little troubles". Further, managing her relationships with her elders when she is a village bahū as well as a village daughter can be a problem: those people before whom she may appear one day are the very people from whom she must keep purdah the next. In addition, she can rarely stay with her parents and obtain a respite from her susrāl. Although she can see her parents often, they make no special fuss, and her husband and sās can summon her back at a moment's notice.

Men also consider within-village marriage a problem:

> If you are married within-village like I am, you tell your in-laws that you've eaten even if you haven't. It would look greedy to take their food, as people would think you were going to make them spend money and then eat again immediately on arriving home. Apart from better hospitality if the susrāl is distant, there is also this benefit: her people would not hear about everything. Just suppose she ran back over every little thing and her brother refused to send her back. A small matter which would go unnoticed if her maikā were distant would become big within the village. *(Liaqat)*

The in-laws hear every fight and may become involved, for all that they should not meddle in their married daughter's business. Their proximity can restrain the man's capacity to rule his wife, though her relatives do not necessarily provide a refuge for her in case this offends her in-laws and threatens good relationships with them. In addition, the joys of good hospitality which a son-in-law expects are closed to the man in a within-village marriage. He becomes commonplace; the exalted son-in-law is brought down to size by familiarity:

> Usually there is good food and hospitality for a son-in-law. But just look at Farooq's young brother: he's been sitting here since nine this morning and no one has thought anything of it. He hasn't even been offered a cup of tea. He comes every day. There is nothing special for him in coming to his susrāl. *(Jabruddin)*

The bought bride

> I bought my woman from my cousin in Bijnor. No one has ever visited here from her pīhar. How could there be any coming and going or len-den? I do not know where she is from and her people do not know where she is. *(Lalit)*

Several examples, including those of Lalit and Rohtash in Dharmnagri and Taslim in Jhakri, indicate that having no parents-in-law at all is also undesirable for a man. Some men cannot secure an offer of marriage with a dowry: Rohtash, for instance, is blind and disfigured in one eye, while Taslim stutters badly. Men with some inadequacy — especially when not offset by wealth — may be able to marry only if they purchase a bride (bahū mol-lenā). Usually, they must be satisfied with a woman who is similarly disfigured, or an orphan whose relatives are more ready to take cash than give a dowry, or a divorced or widowed woman whose relatives cannot arrange a further orthodox match for her.[84] The woman in such a marriage has no more control over her destiny than other married women: her father or brother, or any other go-between decides the match, receives the payment, and transfers her. Rajballa is an orphan and was sold by her brother. Lakshmi was orphaned after being widowed in an orthodox marriage, then sold by her cousin's husband to Lalit's cousin in Bijnor who later sold her to Lalit after she failed to bear children. It was Lalit's seventh such marriage. Tahira was separated from her first husband and her second match was arranged by Taslim's sister's husband who lives in Tahira's maikā. Such marriages may cross caste boundaries and Hindus may hold rituals to set this right: Rajballa, for instance, was purified by bathing in the Ganges.

The bought bride is shorn from her roots even more than the typical bahū. She is unlikely to visit her natal village or receive visitors from it. Rohtash told us to understand that he had not made a real marriage, and that Rajballa had never been to her pīhar since arriving in Dharmnagri:

A bought thing is bought. I gave her brother Rs 800, so I bought her from him. He said he would treat us like other in-laws, but to this day no one has ever called us to her pīhar. Rajballa sometimes asks to go but I shall not go without an invitation. Without being called there is no esteem.

In Dharmnagri one woman could not go to her pīhar because her in-laws did not trust her brother. He had sold her to them for Rs 5,000 without mentioning her infant daughter from her previous marriage. Her new sās learned of the baby only when the bahū began weeping with the discomfort of her engorged breasts. The baby was brought to Dharmnagri, and the sās commented that such a brother might be prepared to sell his sister a second time if she went back on a visit.

Thus, a bought bride can expect little or no support from her natal kin. As she has nowhere to run to, her husband's rule cannot easily be undermined. She brought no dowry and sustains no len-den: she comes empty-handed and compares unfavourably with women in orthodox marriages. On the other hand, her husband had to pay for her, would probably have to pay again to replace her and consequently he may be protective of her.

A man obtains his wife's sexual services and expects her to bear his children. Ideally, she should also be a wealth-bringer, because she brings a dowry and continuing gifts. Men prefer to have good relationships with their parents-in-law, to ensure that len-den is maintained. To her parents she is someone else's property, the possession of a husband who expects to control her. Yet they can pose a threat to the husband's rule. Maintaining a balance is tricky, most feasible when marriages are arranged at some distance, a view accepted for rather different reasons by women and men.

A woman's people can say nothing if they don't like what is happening in her susrāl. They have given her away as wealth-bringer. Their only job is to give her things from time to time. *(Qadir)*

Her parents gave her away when they married her to me and that is the end of it. She is now in my hands and it is not for them to criticise. *(Pratap)*

In practice, social and geographical distance is generally maintained between a bahū in her susrāl and her natal kin, though individual instances range from within-village marriage (where the man finds his in-laws threateningly close) to bought bride marriages (where the woman's kin are non-existent or leave her empty-handed in her susrāl). A bahū should have kin, but, ideally, "one's child's parents-in-law and the latrine really must be distant" (samdhiyānā or pākhāna dūr-hī honā chāhiye).

Between pestle and mortar

3. Did We Bring You Here Just to See Your Face?

For a woman there is all the difference between her pīhar and her susrāl. In her pīhar she is someone's daughter and is not responsible for her family. In her susrāl, she has obligations and she has to work. *(Tulsi)*

You have seen how our men can't even wipe a child's snotty nose. They hand us a baby who has peed. What would they do if they had to deal with a baby's shit? *(Fatima)*

Cooking rotī and stew, collecting fodder and cutting it, removing cattle-dung and making dung-cakes, sweeping up.... Enough! I work the whole day — and even so my husband says, 'What do you do with yourself all day?' *(Zubeida)*

During the afternoon before she gave birth, Muni husked rice for the family's evening meal. After a few days' rest, she was again following her normal round of tasks. Like her, the typical bahū in rural north India is an unpaid family worker; her shift to her susrāl transfers a vital resource, her capacity to labour. The bahū, then, is not only a sexual being capable of bearing children for her husband, nor is she simply a wealth-bringer. Her marriage constitutes a form of labour migration, though it is rarely construed as such, for women's work is only partially visible: official sources grant only between 10% and 30% of women in rural Uttar Pradesh the status of worker.[1]

In accounting for women's subordination, writers influenced by the socialist tradition have generally concentrated on social and economic questions, particularly women's location in production, rather than on their roles in biological reproduction. Women seem marginal to the economy because of their low earning-power, their under-representation as employees and their lack of access to property and control over the labour process.[2] Women's invisibility in official accounting procedures is seen as indicative of their subordination.[3] Such a view, however, presupposes that work has been adequately delineated and that women's subordination is based on their ghostly presence in what is a very narrow definition of "economy". Not only does this approach sidestep controls over women's sexuality and childbearing capacity, but it ignores how women in rural north India actually spend their time.[4] An overall view of the division of labour in villages like Dharmnagri and Jhakri establishes that women contribute to "productive" activities (though not in the same way as men), as well as performing important tasks which restrictive definitions of work normally exclude from "economic activity". Indeed, women have a full and exhausting round of duties, but a feature of their subordination is that these are rarely credited as work. Women are central in social reproduction, dealing with consumption and the daily and intergenerational reproduction of the labour force. When these activities are added to women's productive work, women are more clearly seen as the workers they undoubtedly are. In Dharmnagri and Jhakri, adult women and older girls perform a wide range of tasks, which in large degree set them apart from the men of their chūlhās.[5] Local parlance divides work into three broad categories, field-work (khetī-kām), outside-work (bahār-kā-kām) and house-work (ghar-kā-kām).[6]

Most field-work, the ploughing and preparation of land for cultivation, grain planting and harvesting and sugar-cane cultivation is done by men. Some women cut sugar-cane and bring the tops back home for use as fodder, weed standing crops and participate at harvest time in cutting and threshing wheat and rice. Girls usually do field-work only if they have no brothers or just during peak harvest periods. A new bahū rarely does field-work unless there is no alternative worker, though an older married woman might.

Outside-work includes animal-work. Fetching and chopping fodder is mostly done by men, and spreading it for stalled animals can be done by women or men. Bringing buckets of water from the handpump for cattle to drink, and the milking, are mostly done by women. Dung-work, removing dung from stalled animals and making dung-cakes for fuel or tipping it into the midden pit for manure, is exclusively women's work. Women also collect firewood, rushes and dead grass for kindling, and mud from local ponds for maintaining grain-stores, walls, courtyards and chūlhās. Women are responsible for ensuring that wheat is milled and rice husked and they periodically take head-loads to the grain-mill in Dharmnagri. Women (or occasionally children) take food and water to members of their chūlhā working in the fields. Work done outside the domestic compound poses problems for women expected to maintain purdah. Much outside-work is also exhausting, because it entails lifting heavy loads (dung, fodder, fuel, buckets of water) and carrying them some distance.

House-work, mostly the preserve of women, includes numerous tasks, each taking small chunks of time and each repeated day after day: packing up bedding in the morning, preparing early morning tea, sweeping the house and courtyard clean at least twice and throwing rubbish into the midden. Preparing the meals taken mid-morning and after dusk and serving them to their husband is a lengthy business. Women may process milk into yoghourt, buttermilk and ghī. After the harvests they may winnow grain, spread it for drying and pack it in the grain-store in the house. Spices must be ground, cooking fuel — wood and dung-cakes — fetched, and drinking water pumped by hand. Dishes must be scoured in cold water at the pump, children washed and fed, clothes washed, and last thing at night, the bedding spread out again. Periodically, women mend clothes, make grain-stores, repair the chūlhā, and patch the walls and floor of their house and courtyard using diluted cattle-dung and mud. Some women also fill spare minutes spinning cotton or making rope for stringing beds. When necessary, they care for the sick and elderly. Women's activities occupy them for at least twelve hours a day, and often as much as sixteen — without counting night-time disturbances for breast-feeding and cleaning the faeces and urine of small babies and other children.

Women's work is not constant throughout the year. Seasonal variations in men's and women's responsibilities may mean that some tasks are temporarily shifted across the gender divide. During August and September, for instance, there are few jobs for landless labourers and landed men have little field-work. Men may do more animal-work than in other seasons, as well as relaxing and visiting; women can also more easily be released to visit their parents. In April, on the other hand, wheat harvesting, cane planting and harvesting, and preparing the land for rice rush the men off their feet. Some women who generally do not collect fodder do so then, others who normally do no field-work help to harvest wheat or cane. Dung-work also has a seasonal component. During the winter, women take dung to the village outskirts and make dung-cakes. Dung-cakes dry flat on the ground for about a week, are turned up on end to dry some more for another week and are finally built into stacks which stand some three metres high when completed. The stack is then dressed with cattle-dung and topped out with an inverted crock pot to keep the contents dry. This work depends on the number of cattle and can take upwards of two hours a day. But dung-cakes cannot be made in the hot weather (insects burrow into them) nor during the monsoon (since they could not dry) so for these four or five months dung-work consists of tipping the dung into the midden pit. Grain-stores are generally made gradually in either autumn or spring, when the mud mixed with straw and dung will dry even inside the house. House repair and making new chūlhās is work for the autumn, after the ravages of the monsoon. Generally, however, seasonality has less impact on women than on men, for the bulk of women's work involves a daily round of servicing their chūlhā, irrespective of season.

Class and women's work

Women are not in identical positions, however. In a stratified society, neither men's nor women's work is homogeneous. Not all women perform all the tasks that are basically women's work (cooking, cleaning, childcare). Other tasks, especially animal-work and crop harvesting and processing, are performed only by women in chūlhās in particular economic positions. An analysis that concentrates on the sexual division of labour but implies that women's work is uniform is just as partial as one focussing on economic differentiation which disregards the sexual division of labour.[7]

We can roughly sketch women's work taking class differences into account, but the picture is complicated. We have defined class in terms of land ownership, because land is the most costly, stable and productive form of property. Women's work, however, is also affected by animal ownership. All rich and middle peasants own draught animals, as do some poor peasant but no landless chūlhās. But the ownership of milk cattle (cows and buffaloes) and goats is more widespread. Rich and middle peasant women have on average five head of cattle to look after. Two-thirds of the poor peasant and landless women live in chūlhās with at least one animal, usually kept for milk which is sold either within the village or in Bijnor. The other third have no responsibility for cattle but may occasionally keep a few goats or chickens. Ownership of animals (particularly milk cattle) is unstable: cows and buffaloes are sold to raise cash in a crisis, or they die unexpectedly, and the workload depends on whether they are giving milk. But generally, in chūlhās with several animals, women's workloads are appreciably heavier than in those with few or no cattle, since milking and milk processing, watering and dung-work tend to fall to women.

In the landlord's chūlhā, women's work is largely managerial, orchestrating the servants who cook, sew, clean, wash and shop, or supervising crop processing in the courtyard.[8] In the rich peasant chūlhās of Ashok and Bhagwana, Adesh and Bhagirthi cook for the chūlhā members and the permanent employees and care for the children themselves. Their school-age children attend school, apart from the oldest girls who help around the house. The two chūlhās between them own eleven cattle. Adesh and Bhagirthi milk the cow and buffaloes and make yoghourt and ghī for family consumption. They winnow grain after the harvests, usually helped by Shankar's widowed aunt (FBW), dry it in their courtyard and on the roof and put it in stores they have made themselves. Their work rarely takes them beyond the patch of ground beside the house where they make dung-cakes: even this is relatively recent, for Shankar's aunt used to make their dung-cakes. Food is taken to men in the fields by the men servants. Their unmarried daughters take head-loads of grain for milling at the grain-mill. The men collect fodder, and the fodder-chopping is now all powered by the tractor and has become exclusively men's work.

Generally, women in middle peasant chūlhās have the heaviest workloads.[9] As Fatima and Ghazala have no hired help they cannot remain in seclusion at home. They do much of the animal-work, particularly for milk animals, alongside their sās. They rarely collect fodder, except occasionally when the men are busy, but they generally help with the fodder-chopping, guiding the fodder while a man checks the engine that powers the chopper. They themselves spread the chopped fodder and water the animals. They do the dung-work for twelve animals (six draught, three milk and three calves). They clean and store wheat and rice, carry head-loads of grain for milling in the Dharmnagri grain-mill, build grain-stores, and maintain their houses and courtyards. They cook for their chūlhās, though their sās usually takes food to the men working in the fields, unless the men have eaten before going out. Like many other women in Jhakri, they sometimes spin cotton obtained from the Gandhi Ashram in Bijnor which pays Rs 5 for every kilogram of thread they produce – which takes them about a week.[10]

Most women in poor peasant and landless chūlhās are more home-based than Fatima and Ghazala because their work does not take them out as much. They have little or no animal-work and they do little crop-processing as they do not grow enough food (if any) themselves and must rely on piecemeal cash or kind payments from their husbands' employers. In Dharmnagri, Shakuntala does house-work and some work connected with their cow and buffalo, though she does not often collect fodder or go to their fields. The only field-work she did in 1983 was nine days helping to plant sugar-cane. Shankar's older brother's wife cares for the two ploughing oxen.

In Jhakri, Umrao's work is now basically house-work. When they owned goats, she grazed them along with goats belonging to other Jhakri residents who paid for the service. She stopped doing this when they sold the goats and bought two female buffaloes. Since selling them she has had no animal-work at all. Umrao rarely obtains employment in her own right but sometimes helps Usman when he is employed on piece-rates, for instance weeding a field or harvesting cane, or when he works at a cane-crusher. She occasionally spins cotton thread, and sometimes makes dung-cakes for other women and is paid in kind. Other women in landless chūlhās may find odd jobs such as re-carding cotton used in quilts. Regular employment opportunities for women are few, however, and have probably declined in the recent past (though we cannot be certain). With changes in domestic technologies (especially grain-milling) and population increase, some tasks have declined or disappeared altogether or are now performed only by family labour. Women seeking employment can generally obtain only poorly paid casual seasonal jobs.

The work of women from rich and middle peasant chūlhās has also changed: women's work is not outside history. For example, nowadays more land is being used more intensively for rotations of wheat, rice and sugar-cane. Fewer fodder crops are grown and cultivation is also encroaching on land which used to be uncultivated. Therefore, obtaining fodder is more time-consuming and cattle cannot be sustained solely by grazing on scrubland.[11] There are probably fewer cattle per head than when our oldest informants were children, and so less milking and milk-processing. Livestock watering has been eased by the arrival of handpumps, and fodder-chopping by hand- or engine-powered fodder-choppers. On the other hand, a greater part of animal-work now consists of making dung-cakes, because wood-fuel is less readily available. Meanwhile, less cotton and pulses are grown and women's work in crop-processing is concentrated on winnowing, cleaning, drying and storing wheat and rice, whose production has increased considerably since the mid-1960s. Conversely, less wheat is milled or rice husked at home. On the whole, however, increased agricultural productivity has not been accompanied by much mechanisation, especially not of house-work. Probably the workloads of women in chūlhās which own land and cattle (especially middle peasants) have risen.[12] It is difficult, however, to tease out these changes from discussions with individual women, because women's work also changes as they themselves move through different positions in chūlhās of different kinds.

Between pestle and mortar

I myself made my bahūs separate at the same time. They were always fighting over their work. I live with my unmarried son and daughter and my bahūs give me no help at all. But I am better off separate for if I had one bahū with me she would complain that she has to meet my expenses. *(Viramvati's widowed sās)*

I used to do all kinds of work when I was joint. But my sās complained that I was slow. My husband got angry and we separated from her. *(Santosh)*

Chūlhā composition also affects the spectrum of the bahū's work, her control over it and her collaboration with other women. A bahū generally begins her marital career sharing a chūlhā, sājhe (jointly) with her sās. But being sājhe is not necessarily a long-lived arrangement.[13] Bahūs live in other domestic situations, alag (separate) from their sās or akelī (alone) without a sās at all. Of the 154 married women under 45 years old in Dharmnagri and Jhakri, about one-third live in each type of chūlhā, and only four live in a different kind of situation, sharing with their sister-in-law (HBW). In 1982, ten key informants were sājhe, 19 were alag, and 12 were akelī. Women normally start sājhe, go alag and then become akelī when their sās dies; indeed, by 1985, two more key informants had gone alag. But some bahūs arrive after their sās is dead, or start their married life alag, while others stay sājhe until their sās dies.

Collaborative relationships among women in the susrāl are inhibited by the separation of chūlhās and the view that each woman should be busy with her own work — whether she is sājhe with her sās or not — rather than spending time with other women or contributing to the work of any other chūlhā. These arrangements do not necessarily parallel those of their menfolk. Among the landed, a man and his adult sons are commonly sājhe, sharing land and draft animals and cultivating crops together. Less commonly, a man divides his land among his sons and either retains a share of the land or levies grain and cash from his sons, or he may turn his sons out to earn their own living if they are not pulling their weight. After his death, the land and livestock are usually divided equally among the sons and they may begin cultivating separately. Sometimes, however, brothers continue to work the land jointly for many years, benefiting from economies of scale with shared assets such as tube-wells or ploughs and ploughing teams. Joint operations among men are less common among the poor peasants and especially among the landless, both because they have little or no joint property to hold them together and because poor men die younger.

Overall, men tend to work collaboratively for longer than their wives do. If a woman's parents-in-law are both alive, she will never continue to be sājhe with her sās after her husband is alag from his father. On the other hand, a man may still be sājhe with his father when his wife is alag from her sās. In such instances, the jointly produced income is divided and consumed separately. The women work separately (alag-alag) and the separate chūlhās no longer share responsibilities for most expenditures, apart from those connected with the joint productive enterprise. A woman's experience of work in pregnancy and the post-partum period is profoundly influenced by her relationship with her sās (if she has one), so we shall consider domestic patterns from the bahū's point of view.

Joint with the sās

> I am the only bahū and I have never had a fight with my sās. She is very straightforward and if she ever criticises me I just listen silently. But my sās does not create fights. *(Najma)*

After the cohabitation, the bahū comes and goes between her susrāl and her parents' home. Her husband needs a sure source of cooked food, while her sās wants help with her work and may wish to educate the bahū in cooking, celebrating festivals, respect and obedience. In landed and landless chūlhās alike, the newly married son and bahū are expected to be sājhe with the husband's parents. Among our key informants, only Zubeida started her married life alag, because she was Zakir's second wife and he was already alag. If the sās has died before her bahū takes up residence, the bahū begins her married life akelī. Six of the key informants were in this position: Bilquis, Ruxana, Tahira, Adesh, Bhagirthi and Lakshmi. Sometimes the new bahū may be sājhe with her sister-in-law (HeBW) (if there is one) instead; Bhagirthi started her married life sājhe with Adesh and with their husbands' widowed aunt (HFZ).

When a sās and bahū are sājhe, they share a chūlhā to prepare food, care for jointly owned livestock and so forth. The bahū generally does all or most of the house-work. If there are animals, she probably helps to feed and water them; she may also do the dung-work with her sās. Generally, the sās and any unmarried nands (husband's sisters) do the other outside-work, collecting fodder or taking food to men in the fields if necessary. A bahū sājhe with her sās, then, is unlikely to perform the full range of tasks that comprise the women's work for her chūlhā, because her sās also participates. She does not carry the responsibility for her chūlhā's work alone. Conversely, a bahū who is sājhe must tolerate the authority of her sās. The chūlhā's work is shared, but not necessarily equitably. Often, the sās does not insist that the bahū's unmarried nands play their part and the bahū bears a heavy weight of outside- as well as house-work. Cooking for a large chūlhā can be tedious, while juggling the members' diverse tastes can be a thankless task which leaves the bahū open to complaints about the thickness of her rotī or the flavouring of her dāl. If two women remain sājhe, the structural difficulties of living together can best be overcome by a demure bahū and a sās who does not abuse her authority; they may co-operate peacefully for many years.[14]

Becoming separate

If a sās has just one bahū, the two women will probably remain sājhe unless the men separate: as Hiran put it, "How could I separate from my sās since I am her only bahū? She does the outside-work while I do the house-work." But such arrangements collapse in different ways. Most commonly, the process begins when a second son is married and a new bahū arrives; the different expenses of the brothers' families aggravate the competition between them. Men resent helping to feed their brothers' children, subsidising emergency expenses such as medical care, or meeting some of the long-term costs of marriage for a nephew or niece. These tendencies for fission can be contained by creating separate chūlhās which consume shares of the income generated while the men continue working together. Such arrangements may persist for years, but the separation of chūlhās begins a process that eventually results in the separation of land, farming equipment and draught animals too.

Generally, disputes among women are given as the reason for the division of chūlhās when the men stay sājhe.[15] A bahū is said to be caught between her husband and her sās like grain being pounded between a large pestle (masal) and a hollowed stone in the ground used as a mortar (okhlī). A bahū cannot escape marriage (and her husband's rule) but she may relieve the pressures by establishing a separate chūlhā. A bahū does not always match the passive ideals set her; she may resist her sās' instructions or answer back when criticised, or complain to her husband about his mother's treatment and ask him to press for separation. But she can only become alag if her husband is willing: there may be a lengthy period while the sās tries to keep her bahū under control, the bahū aims to escape, and both women seek the support of the bahū's husband. Eventually, he may decide that his interests lie with his wife and children, but amiable separation may be elusive.

Antagonisms between a bahū and sās are often exaggerated by the presence of another bahū. The wives of brothers may fight about the sās' favouritism among her several bahūs. Alternatively, the underlying competitiveness among women in the susrāl can easily flare up and explode in arguments about food, work, or disciplining children. Their collaboration is fragile. Each woman sees her interests threatened by other women close to her, because their destinies are linked to men who are themselves competing over scarce resources. Women say they cannot trust susrāl women, that there is no kindness or civility among them, that more than one woman around a chūlhā will certainly fight, and that women criticise one another's work. Working alag-alag prevents arguments.

Imrana: Women cannot remain sājhe. They fight. One says that she has done more work, another says she has done less. And that way fights begin.

Patricia: Don't men fight?

Imrana: Even if one does less work than the others, there is no fight. Women do not have good morals.

Patricia: What if the two women are sisters, could they not work well together like brothers do?

Imrana: There will be fighting even between sisters. Women fight more than men.

Other women emphasise features of their working environment, such as satisfying the different tastes of the father-in-law, the husband and his brothers eating from one chūlhā, or working in the midst of children:

Swaleha: Why don't you work with your sister-in-law [HyBW] Zubeida? After all, the two brothers work together on the cane-crusher.

Wasila: The men's thing is something else. They can just do their work. But we must work with children around us. Sometimes the children delay us, sometimes children fight. That can result in fights among their elders too. Two women cannot live in one place.

In Dharmnagri and Jhakri, two or more bahūs rarely remain sājhe with their sās for very long. Only eight chūlhās out of 197 include more than two married women. Sometimes the bahū who is on best terms with the sās remains sājhe while the other becomes alag or the older bahū moves out and the younger stays, perhaps until a further brother is married. The sās, indeed, may make her bahūs separate or make one bahū become alag when the next bahū arrives rather than having to live constantly with fighting.

Occasionally arguments among the men are the agreed cause of the separation of chūlhās, for example when the production unit divides at the same time as the chūlhās.

My sās never criticises me or fights with me. But my father-in-law is a very angry man. One day he told my husband and his older brother that since they do no field-work they should go alag. They will only get grain if they work. *(Kamla)*

My sās is not sharp but my father-in-law is. A few months ago he divided the land among his three sons and that is why I went alag. My father-in-law does no field-work — his sons do the work and they each give him a quintal of rice and wheat after the harvests and some money from the sale of cane. *(Shakuntala)*

The father who thinks his son is slacking may force him to find another source of income rather than benefit from the joint farm. Alternatively, the son may opt to go alag from his father because he wants independence from disputes about work or about financing his younger brother's wedding. Once the men are alag, the women also separate.

We cannot say whether the separation of chūlhās is more commonly caused by disputes among women or among men. Because consumption arrangements are especially contentious and women are particularly identified with the domestic sphere, they may be receiving an unfair share of the blame. Men's continuing co-operation may rest on being able to pretend that chūlhā separation is just a women's matter. Certainly, the people closely involved often provided incompatible accounts.

Separate from the sās

When you're sājhe you must do the work even if you don't want to. But if you are alag, you don't have to make dung-cakes if you are ill or you can make them when you want to. That is why I have been alag in making dung-cakes for the past year, although the animals are still sājhe. Before that I was just alag for cooking. *(Hashmi)*

When chūlhās are alag, women's work and the chūlhā incomes are no longer jointly organised. Separation may be achieved smoothly or with mutual hostility, and either in a once-for-all break or a protracted process. Moreover, going alag has complex implications for the content of bahūs' work. For women whose work is basically house-work, the division may be simple and quick and the bahū's workload will probably be considerably eased. In livestock-owning chūlhās, however, complete separation may take some years and entail several changes in the women's working patterns. Separate cooking may initially co-exist with shared animal-work for jointly owned draught and milk animals. Later come rotas for feeding, milking and dung-work for sājhe animals and separate animal-work for separately owned animals. Finally, the animal-work becomes entirely separate once the men are alag. Consequently, some bahūs acquire a more diverse workload after going alag, others a more restricted one. For instance, when Pushpa was sājhe with her sās and Omvati, Omvati and the sās did the animal-work, Pushpa cooked and Omvati scoured dishes. After going alag, Pushpa cooked for her smaller chūlhā, but added scouring dishes, her share of animal-work for cattle jointly owned by her husband and two of his brothers, and caring for her new baby. On the other hand, Kamla's father-in-law made Krishnu alag without any share in resources, land or livestock:

So my work is less since becoming alag — I just have cooking and dishes work but I used to do animal-work too, feeding, watering and making dung-cakes. Now I help my sās only if I feel like it.

When bahūs who are alag describe the benefits of their situation, they generally contrast them with the difficulties of being controlled by their sās and managing conflicts within the chūlhā when they were sājhe. Once alag, they are not necessarily free from their sās' interventions but they can say, "What's it to do with her, now we are separate?" A bahū can wrest some control over her daily life in her susrāl, where self-determination is otherwise hard to achieve. The sās no longer operates such strict surveillance over her bahū, while the bahū can more actively schedule her working-day and cook what her husband wants without regard for his relatives' preferences.

Set against these benefits, however, are some costs entailed in the shift in the social relations within which women organise their work. The bahū who is alag attains a position of greater self-determination in her work schedule, but she is now the only adult woman in her chūlhā and entirely responsible for the chūlhā's work. Self-determination has attractions for day-to-day business, but its costs become apparent in a crisis. Women who went alag under some cloud can be distinguished from those whose separation was not acrimonious (as when the father-in-law forced the separation and the sās and bahū remained on good terms). Eight of the key informants are alag but are on such bad terms with their sās that their own or a child's illness can pose problems, for they have no one to help them. Similarly, obtaining permission to visit their natal kin can be difficult. Asghari, for instance, is still sājhe with her sās, and often visits her parents in an adjacent village because her sās takes over her work. Asghari's sister-in-law (HyBW), however, separated from Asghari and their sās within a year of marriage: her sās describes her as a slacker (kām-chor, literally work-thief). She rarely goes to her natal village: as her sās commented, "How can she go, for who is there to do her work here?"

The bahū who separated on good terms with her sās is more favourably placed. She may negotiate help from her sās when sick and needing a rest, or if her children need medical attention. She has more day-to-day independence from her sās than the bahū who is sājhe, but not at the cost of help in an emergency.[16] But visiting the natal village remains a problem, for even a willing sās can hardly be expected to remain so if the bahū makes excessive requests for leave. The key informants often explain changes in their own visiting to their natal kin and that of their married nands to Dharmnagri and Jhakri with the simple refrain that once a woman is alag she cannot easily leave her susrāl. The husband prevents his wife visiting her parents if there is too much work. His difficulties over food and dealing with the daily round of animal-work are more than he will tolerate when he is busy himself. Irfan, for instance, said that he rarely stops Imrana going for brief visits, but he would not hesitate to do so if she asked during the harvest. As Shankar put it:

> My wife cannot visit her pīhar without permission. She asks more often than I permit for I do not let her go if there is too much work. I have never suggested to her that she goes. When she goes away, I have problems. Why should I make difficulties for myself?

The sās has authority over the bahū and may not be very supportive, yet she is probably the most reliable source of help for the bahū in her susrāl. Other women have their own work and cannot be expected to rally round. Being sājhe may be irksome, because the bahū should submit to her sās' discipline. Living alag may ease this for the bahū, as she has to face only her husband's authority. But this must be offset against losing potential help with her work (either regularly or during a crisis) and the stronger ties that consequently now bind her to her susrāl.

Being alone in the susrāl

> This is my situation in the susrāl: I am alone and have to do all the work myself. But then, even bahūs with other workers in their chūlhā must work hard, for that is how things happen here. *(Khurshida)*

> I did not go alag from my sās. If she were still alive I would still be sājhe. When she was alive there were three of us to work, myself, my sās and my nand. I mostly did house-work. Once my sās died, my nand refused to work so we got her married. Since then I have done everything, house-work, animal-work, field-work. *(Chandresh)*

Becoming the only adult female worker in a chūlhā does not necessarily entail separation from the sās. Several key informants have never been sājhe with a sās, others were sājhe until their sās died. The wives of brothers are unlikely to be joint after their sās' death, although their husbands may continue working together. Ashok and Bhagwana still farm jointly, but their wives have cooked separately since about 1970:

> My sās was dead when I married, but I was sājhe with my husband's aunt [FZ]. She died shortly after Bhagwana was married. Then Bhagirthi said she would not cook for so many people, so she went alag. *(Adesh)*

Such women describe themselves as akelī (alone), a term which underlines their lack of support in their susrāl village. Women who are akelī are solely responsible for their chūlhā, without a sās even in the wings to take over. Four key informants have a sister-in-law (HBW) in another chūlhā who might briefly be prevailed upon in an emergency. The remainder do not have even this fall-back position. For example, Jamila's sās is dead and Jabruddin has no brothers. One day Jamila was making dung-cakes while suffering from a fever which had been recurring for several months. She listed her work, which included cooking and taking food to the fields, washing clothes, dealing with the livestock, making dung-cakes:

> Sometimes the baby stays hungry as I cannot take a break to breast-feed him. With all that work, just tell me, how could medicines succeed? I do all my work alone and never rest. I sometimes feel like lying down — but who would do the work? Everyone just does their own work.

Since women's work is so tied to a daily routine, those who are akelī find it particularly difficult to visit their natal village often or for extended stays. Being akelī roots a bahū even more firmly in her susrāl. For such women, the attractions of self-determination often seem outweighed by a sense of having no support in the susrāl, although if they reach this stage at the age of 35 or so, they may already have help from a daughter or bahū of their own.

Domestic cycles and secular change

Elderly women say that bahūs today are eager to separate from their sās much more quickly than in the past, that bahūs used to remain sājhe come what may, but now want to avoid the heavy workloads of joint living, and that they no longer respect their sās. The balance of power has been reversed: now the bahū "sits on her sās' head". Asghari's sās commented:

> These days the sās is the bahū and the bahū the sās. A bahū doesn't listen to her sās. In Jhakri there are two or three bahūs who are very bad — like Fatima, and my younger son's wife — who answer back all the time. They don't do any work. They have no manners at all.

Today's bahūs are considered more cunning and less compliant than before, they want to control their dowry jewellery rather than permit it to be used for another marriage, they talk secretly at night to their husbands and persuade them to separate from their parents. Nowadays, people are averse to sharing things and men work hard for their own wife and children, not for the greater good. As one landless Hindu woman in her late 50s said:

> When I was young, I didn't say anything or answer back, even when someone hit and beat me and left me hungry. Enough, I just stayed silent. But today's bahūs, that's enough! Say one thing to them and hear two! Who wants to waste their honour and standing. It's better to remain silent. Who can beat them? You can't even tap them with a single knuckle!

We cannot be entirely certain that the incidence and rapidity of going alag have increased like the older women allege, but economic and demographic changes suggest that the proportion of bahūs now alag is probably higher than previously, and the proportion akelī may have declined. Thus, competition among brothers probably reflects endemic rather than novel struggles, which may be more common now than before. Parents are more likely to live for longer after their children are married and, with more children surviving to maturity, the sās is likely to have more bahūs to orchestrate.[17] Solitary bahūs still generally remain sājhe with their sās in Dharmnagri and Jhakri: but a sās can rarely keep two sons and their bahūs in one chūlhā for long.[18]

While we do not have to accept a "myth of a Golden Age" when bahūs did as they were told, local historians may also be right in suggesting that bahūs now go alag more rapidly. A bahū can still do so only with her husband's consent and there may be new factors that make men more prepared to separate from their parents. The Green Revolution seems to have increased the returns from cash-crops to peasant farmers, and male labourers can probably earn a better living than before. If so, young men — whether landed or landless — may want independent control over their earnings sooner after their marriage than their fathers would have done. In addition, the age at cohabitation may be slowly rising, and bahūs may arrive in their susrāl more mature and self-confident.[19] Young women are exposed to some messages of self-assertion from the radio or via examples of government female teachers and health staff. But it is difficult to specify and assess the possible mechanisms of such changes, and we can only speculate. In any case, even if today's bahūs are less subordinated than those of a generation back, their freedom of action still seems, to them and to us, extremely limited.

Just a couple of dung-cakes, a couple of rotī

All women in Dharmnagri and Jhakri are workers, but the work of women in different class positions and chūlhā types is not the same, although it has some common features. In particular, women's work is set apart from men's; the daily round of life for men and women is tough, but in different ways. But women's lengthy and varied work burden does not mean they have much influence over their own lives. Women working long hours may have little control over productive resources, over their work or the produce of their labour or how they spend their time. Nor do women with the heaviest workloads necessarily receive greater credit. Simply listing women's tasks can result in an overly materialistic account, which must be moderated by outlining local perceptions of women's work. Many of the activities performed by women are as much under-rated by local views of women's work as in official accounting procedures:

> Women in Jhakri do no work. They cook and clean and look after the children. And they sometimes milk animals if they have any.
> *(Jabruddin)*

Mahipal contrasted men's and women's experiences of their susrāl by saying that a man must work in his own village but can rest in his susrāl. By contrast, according to him, women do no work in either place and the only difference is that a woman finds purdah in her susrāl. Many men in Dharmnagri and Jhakri need to be pressed quite hard before they concede that their womenfolk really work. In discussing family labour use, Andrew was repeatedly told that women — like children — simply eat food and do nothing economically important. Trying to persuade men to put a price on women's dung-work — in savings on cooking fuel when they make dung-cakes or on chemical fertilisers when mulched rubbish and dung from the midden is used in the fields — resulted in many a lively debate. Real work is what men do, behind their ploughs, planting crops, dealing with sugar-cane, marketing surpluses. Men's work is burdensome (bhārī) and crucial to household survival, women's is trifling (halkā) and ancillary at best. Local views of women's work conceal women's huge energy expenditures, and are reflected, for instance, in differential entitlements to food.[20] A man expects the lion's share and takes his fill before his wife eats. A bahū knows that her sās could report her for taking food surreptitiously while her husband is out, and the man who suspects his wife of withholding food or purposely making it unattractive is likely to beat her. But women generally concur with men's views of women's work, and consider themselves entitled to less food than their husbands. They say a dutiful wife cares for her husband first and then her growing children. When food is short, or when the buffalo gives less milk, she should ration herself and give milk to the men first and then to the children, especially boys. Swaleha (one of our research assistants) responded to Patricia's exasperation over women's self-abnegation with the comment: "But you see, the men here have subdued their women so completely that the idea has perched in women's minds that they are indeed inferior."

But consent is incomplete. Khurshida typifies this well. When Patricia and Swaleha questioned her about her work in her susrāl, the "interview" was conducted inside her house, during her pauses for breath while she winnowed husks from the recently harvested rice. She had completed three sacks and had another ten to do. Finally, conversation turned to the sale of the husks for horse-feed. Patricia asked who would keep the money. Khurshida rested back on her haunches, winnowing basket in her hands. By now she was covered with a fine film of white dust: she grinned mischievously as she answered:

Khurshida: The money goes into my father-in-law's pocket.
Swaleha: What, even though you are working so hard?
Khurshida: Yes, that is it. He just says that I make a couple of dung-cakes, a couple of rotī and spend the rest of my day breaking the bed! He does not consider my work to be work.
Swaleha: Then one time you should exchange your work: make him work in the house while you work in the fields!
Khurshida: But I could not do his field-work.
Patricia: You should go on strike — then he'd understand your work!
Khurshida: On the contrary — then I'd get a beating!

Men prefer to define women as only consumers, but women are expected to work hard to justify their existence. Indeed, in a labour-intensive economy, men need wives, and depend on their labour in general and especially for tasks that men find demeaning. It is difficult for a man on his own to cope. So women cannot escape their work on a whim. Women's work must continue — and Khurshida is by no means alone in resenting men's definitions of women's work. As one woman commented:

Women do a lot of work but even then the men ask, 'What do you do all day?' If I lie down and my husband sees me, he asks what I am doing and says, 'Enough! Get up!' Men make women work and work until they are ground into the earth — but even then it is not considered work!

Nevertheless, numerous women explained the short gap between their marriage and cohabitation by their in-laws' demands that they be sent quickly to compensate for a shortage of female labour, possibly because their nand had just been married, or their sās was unwell. The timing of a marriage relates primarily to the sexual maturity of the partners, but the bahū's capacity to labour is also important. Certainly, once the bahū is living regularly in her susrāl, her in-laws' expectations of her as a worker are a key feature of her life there. Consequently, parents are anxious to choose their daughter's susrāl well, but they may have to juggle incompatible considerations. If they find people who are comfortably off, with neither too much work nor too many people to feed, they will probably have to provide a big dowry. And if their daughter is accused of coming empty-handed, parents fear she will be taunted, made to work excessively hard, and her sās may be dissatisfied with everything she does. Since paid employment for women is rare, bahūs' time and work are regulated exclusively within their susrāl chūlhās by the same domestic authorities who oversee their general demeanour. Until their own children's labour can be commanded, bahūs exercise little control over other people's activities. Married women readily talk about having responsibilities (zimmadārī) in their susrāl, the obligation to complete work required of them by others. Jamila commented that women survive in their susrāl only with great intelligence, for they must heed and obey their susrāl kin to the letter. Others said a bahū must do all that her husband requires. Because she knows what is expected of her, explicit instruction may be unnecessary: in some measure, she may protect herself by working assiduously. Her husband should have no cause for complaint; his meals should be provided punctually and taken to him in the fields if his work is particularly pressing. Her sās should have no reason to think she is slacking or has refused to fulfil her duties.

Women see their natal village as a haven, where not only the restraints of purdah but also the responsibilities of the susrāl are lifted. The tensions between a woman and her nand may surface when the married nand visits from her own susrāl. Jumni commented that while her sās is alive her nands come to Dharmnagri only for a holiday from their own susrāl and they do little work. Not surprisingly, young married women enthuse about their carefree times in their natal village. They say they can refuse to obey their mother once, but their sās never. As Fatima put it, a woman is not frightened of anyone in her maikā. In the natal village there is peace and a woman chooses to work alongside her mother or not. The work in the susrāl and the natal village may be almost identical, but the atmosphere in which it is carried out could hardly be more different:

There is this difference between the maikā and the susrāl: in the susrāl whatever work I am responsible for I must complete. But in the maikā there is no necessity, as my mother and sisters do the work and I can work with them if I please. I cannot abandon my work in my susrāl — my husband, my sās and other women would ask why I had not done the work which there is for me to do. No one asks me that in my maikā. *(Imrana)*

In the susrāl I fear my husband the whole time. If his food is not ready on time, then his shoe strikes my head. In my maikā I can work or not as I please, but I still get fed and no one beats me. *(Wasila)*

Visits to the natal village are carefully regulated. Susrāl kin are entitled to their bahū's work. Her absences cause problems for others, if her sās has to take over her responsibilities, or her husband faces food worries. Every day, her waking hours are largely occupied by her work: that in itself keeps her in her susrāl. Women often said they had no free time to take children for medical treatment in the nearby dispensary: how much harder would it be to stay with their natal kin for a while? Susrāl kin may resist requests for leave, for the bahū in her natal village is beyond her husband's control and her work is also lost.

Bought brides have no such refuge. Similarly, women in within-village marriages cannot easily escape their susrāl obligations. Latifan, for instance, would prefer a somewhat distant susrāl because she cannot visit her natal kin for long without being called by Liaqat. Ghazala regards herself as well-placed: she is from a neighbouring village and can remain there happily and rest from her susrāl. But Farooq and Ghulam's younger brother had just been married within Jhakri: although the cohabitation had not taken place, the new bahū was called to her susrāl one day to winnow rice and spread dung-paste on the courtyard:

> Within the village a woman cannot rest peacefully at her mother's house. Let there be just a little work and the susrāl people will call her immediately, saying, 'This work is to be done, come along!' *(Ghazala)*

Several women considered ghar-jamāi marriage particularly beneficial, for the woman's mother helps with the work and gives her peace — though Umrao is compelled to work in her maikā as she is akelī there. Otherwise, a susrāl some distance from the natal village is thought best, for a woman can stay with her parents once in a while and obtain some respite from her susrāl. Even that, however, remains an eagerly-awaited treat. Basically, a bahū stays in her own house, that is, her susrāl; and while there, she should perform her own work. As Asghari commented:

> It is not that anyone tells me to work. Having come to my susrāl, I must do everything. If I did not, then my sās would certainly say something, just like a sās would anywhere. She would ask, 'What, did we bring you here just to see your face?'

Women in middle peasant chūlhās, then, have the greatest pressures of work, while others are rather less heavily laden. Furthermore, women without another woman sharing their chūlhā have full responsibilities, while others may have some opportunities for respite to offset their subordination to their sās. These contrasts are important in women's experiences of work in pregnancy and the post-partum period. However, in detailing women's tasks, we must keep sight of another crucial point: when considering control over resources, and over work and its products, class and chūlhā differences among women retreat. Among the landed, land is vested in men, while women are dependent and controlled. Among the landless, without direct access to productive resources, people must seek remunerated labour, working for pittances if they can obtain work at all. But the conditions of employment for women are generally worse than for men: jobs are scarce and poorly paid and hardly grant any prospects of independence or equality for women. Whatever their chūlhā structure, married women are not released for full-time paid employment, nor able to use their time to establish independent means. A key feature of women's position — whatever the class position of their menfolk — remains their dependence on men.[21]

Childbearing women and the state

Distinctive forms of marriage arrangement have implications for bahūs' relationships with their natal kin, particularly visiting patterns and the lenden between their natal kin and their susrāl. Further, class location and chūlhā composition in the susrāl affect bahūs' work and their life in general. Several pervasive and crucial features are, however, shared by almost all women as they follow similar sequences during their marital careers. We are concentrating on women in their susrāl at a particularly powerless phase in their life-cycle when, moreover, childbearing has a special salience.

Not surprisingly, a girl's parents feel pressured to marry her at an early age. They should not depend on her in their old-age and they must send gifts to her susrāl kin for the rest of her days. They worry over demands they cannot meet, they fear the power her susrāl kin can exercise, yet they know they must give her away. The bahū herself has little say in the events which have such a momentous impact on her. Barring serious physical or economic impediments, she is married in her teens and will not have achieved much independence. She controls no productive property that could provide economic independence, but is transferred into her husband's custody, normally in another village. She has little control over her own sexuality and must bear children for her husband. Even if her sās does not subject her to detailed supervision, she must accommodate to her husband's power, fulfil her responsibilities, be submissive and do nothing to dishonour him. Only in her natal village is she released from the control of her husband and his kin, but contacts with her natal kin are carefully regulated by her susrāl kin. These patterns of kinship, marriage, property ownership and work have material consequences for young women. The bahū in her susrāl is more controlled than controlling, and has little space for resistance that is not self-destructive.

Concentrating on the childbearing careers of young married women compellingly highlights the relationship between women's work and biological reproduction. Childbearing women in rural north India are subject to immense pressures of work, including childrearing. They have little spare time, freedom of mobility, reward from their labour or access to cash. Apart from anything else, this constellation of factors impinges on maternal and child health. Within a general context of poverty and of gender and class inequalities in access to resources, good health — for mothers and young children alike — is additionally undermined by the shift of young women's residence to their susrāl on marriage, which further restricts their access to health care. Indeed, these features help to account for the distinctive patterns of fertility and mortality in north India, where fertility is high, as is infant and child mortality (especially of girls), and women in the childbearing ages have higher death rates than young men.[22] Unlike most other regions of the world, males outnumber females. This is especially striking among the 200 million or so people of the north-western states of Punjab, Haryana, Rajasthan and Uttar Pradesh.[23] Women's experiences in Bijnor District basically reflect this pattern. In rural Uttar Pradesh as a whole female death rates at all ages up to 40 exceed male death rates, which are themselves high. Excess female mortality, in combination with excess male births, results in a skewed sex ratio. The 1981 Census recorded 886 females for every 1,000 males in Uttar Pradesh. The Bijnor District figures showed an even greater disparity, with just 863 females for every 1,000 males.[24]

State policy and women in India

Women's general situation, as well as the demographic picture, have been the subject of legislation and Indian government action for many years.[25] Legislators, administrators and social reformers have regarded women's social position as a key factor to be remedied. But efforts to ameliorate it have almost always tackled women's location only in the domestic sphere, through marriage law reform (concentrating on the age of marriage, dowry and inheritance) and maternal and child health services.[26]

Raising the legal age of marriage has long been seen as a way of enabling brides to arrive in their susrāl more mature both socially and physically, but this has been politically contentious since before Independence.[27] In 1930, the minimum age at marriage was set at 14 for girls and 18 for boys. The minimum age for girls was raised to 15 in 1949 and to 18 in 1977. Marriage ages are generally lower in north India than the rest of the country. Although the average age of marriage for girls has been rising, many are already married and cohabiting before the legal minimum age. In Dharmnagri and Jhakri, women were often uncertain about their age, but generally reported being married by the age of 14 or 15 and cohabiting by the time they are 15 or 16.

Dowry has also been viewed as problematic for females, for parents have strong financial reasons to prefer sons. Again, attempts to reform or abolish dowry date from before 1947, but political obstructions delayed the Dowry Prohibition Act until 1961.[28] Giving, taking or demanding payments "as consideration for the marriage" are now illegal. Knowledge of the law and its provisions is still not widespread, however, though women often complain about the anxieties that dowry generates. Prosecutions under the Act are rare and the Act has few real teeth. Further, the parents of girls often fear that their daughters would be victimised by their susrāl kin if there is any protest. As Mahipal put it:

> You can complain to the government if you are being asked for too much dowry, but what would be the benefit? You'll then have to hand out bribes in all directions to get any action, and either you won't manage to get your daughter married or she'll have no peace in her susrāl.

Evidence at the national level parallels what we found in Dharmnagri and

Jhakri: dowry is not declining but there are powerful secular shifts in its nature, including increases in its scale, mounting pressures to give where voluntary giving was standard and harassment of young brides who have not brought "enough" dowry with them.[29]

Inheritance laws are different for each main religious group, but are alike in now entitling women to share their parents' property with their brothers. This entailed a sharp break with traditional Hindu law and practice and was stiffly opposed. Traditional Muslim law accords women inheritance rights (rarely met in practice) which are now formally enshrined within Indian Muslim family law. As with dowry legislation, legal rights are rarely claimed. Those few women who are aware of their entitlements hesitate to demand their rights from their brothers, who are their only refuge if their marriage collapses. In any case, women's departure to their susrāl hampers them in staking their claims to parental property. These legislative reforms in relation to marriage and property have had little impact on women in Dharmnagri and Jhakri.

A further plank in government interventions has been female education.[30] The effects of schooling are probably indirect, for the curriculum contains little explicit reference to women's rights or even principles of home economics and childcare. But educated girls tend to be married later and have fewer children, fewer of whom die.[31] They may deal more confidently with shopkeepers, doctors, nurses and perhaps with elders in their susrāl. Hardly any bahū in Dharmnagri and Jhakri has started her married life with such advantages: very few attended school regularly or for long. Most are illiterate in Hindi (though a few bahūs in Jhakri can recite the Qu'rān Sharif in Arabic). Attendance at the Hindi-medium government primary school in Dharmnagri is low, and few children from the village go to the secondary school on its outskirts. Children from Jhakri do not attend, though some boys and a few girls from Jhakri go daily to a mosque school in Begawala, where they learn Arabic and Urdu. There have been short-lived Arabic and Urdu schools in Jhakri itself. Many girls in Dharmnagri and Jhakri never attend school, or do so only irregularly, and few continue even until they are ten. The government's formal commitments to equal opportunities and free, universal education have had little impact in this part of Bijnor.[32]

The resistance to passing and implementing legislation giving women equal rights with men is mirrored in the government's own unwillingness to take women's contributions to agriculture seriously. Little provision has been made for economic and agricultural changes explicitly intended to transform women's relationships to resources and work.[33] Land reforms, the introduction of new crops and production methods, and processes of commercialisation have all proceeded on the assumption that men, and men's work, are crucial. In Uttar Pradesh, economic programmes targeted at women are rare and forms of out-work (cotton-spinning, for example) have little impact, because they are so badly paid. Yet this is not to say that such interventions have had no effect on women's activities. Rather the lack of attention to rural women has had consequences which were unplanned and largely unmonitored. We cannot specify exactly how women's work has changed, but, basically, government interventions have not enhanced women's access to employment, property and credit. Women remain economically dependent and powerless.

Health services

More direct assaults on the demographic situation in north India have been attempted through health service provision. Again, the impact has been rather slight.[34] Public health and preventive medicine have had low priority, yet environmental factors, such as water supply and drainage, nutrition and general poverty are powerful influences on villagers' health. One example is malaria (jārā-bukhār, literally cold-fever): anti-mosquito campaigns in the 1960s reduced malaria to a very low level, but it has now returned despite the annual sprayings of insecticides. Such diseases affect anyone, irrespective of age, sex and (to a large extent) class, and are important in understanding the high overall levels of mortality. Since 1965, for instance, the death rates of the children of rich peasants in Dharmnagri and Jhakri have not differed greatly from those of poor peasants or the landless.[35]

Mortality rates could probably be reduced by curative health services, but their limited quality, availability and accessibility in the rural areas impair this potential. A government hospital was opened in Bijnor town in the 1850s; and in 1905, as part of the government programme to make medical services more accessible to women, a women's hospital was opened.[36] But only in the 1960s were more concerted efforts made to take health services beyond the larger towns and into the rural areas, and now Primary Health Centres and sub-centres provide a network of facilities covering Bijnor's villages. Dharmnagri has a government dispensary and sub-centre in the same compound. The dispensary employs a doctor, a compounder (pharmacist) and two other staff, and has an operating theatre and male and female in-patient wards. The sub-centre has a male worker, whose job includes public health and family planning, and a clinic for women and children, run by an Auxiliary Nurse-Midwife (ANM). Despite its limitations, anti-malarial insecticide spraying has had more impact than any other public health measures. Generally, health workers wait for clients to seek treatment, rather than going out to the villages served by the dispensary. It is an unpopular posting, and has sometimes been without a doctor, or with one who attends clinics infrequently. Most medical care is provided by the compounder. The wards are rarely used, and the operating theatre had been out of commission for some years before we took up residence. People prefer to go to Bijnor for in-patient treatment.

From the villagers' viewpoint, government health care suffers from many weaknesses: the dispensary and clinic have insufficient supplies; treatment should be free for the poor but, in practice, drugs and dressings are rarely provided, and must either be bought from the market or staff have to be bribed to provide them. Staff at government hospitals in Bijnor may be officious (as well as expecting larger bribes), and free medical supplies there are little more reliable. In any case, villagers believe they obtain better treatment from the doctor and compounder at the Dharmnagri dispensary by being treated privately. Many consider quality care is available only in Bijnor itself: dispensary staff refuse to deal with complicated medical complaints.[37] But considerations of cost may inhibit the poorest villagers from seeking medical care speedily, or even at all. Having medical services on the doorstep, then, does not necessarily amount to being especially well-placed in relation to access to health care.

These general limitations are exacerbated for women and small children, whose levels of morbidity are the highest. Women's and children's health care has low priority both within the domestic sphere and the health services. The maternal and child health service is very limited and, moreover, female staff are often unwilling to live at rural postings.[38] During 1982-83, the ANM lived in Bijnor and came irregularly to the clinic; she rarely attended births and promoted only the family planning programmes with any enthusiasm — and village women are inhibited from using general health facilities provided by male staff, especially for gynaecological problems. Women's limited mobility and access to cash make health services less accessible for them and their children than for men. Further, work obligations make trips as far as Bijnor hard to arrange, for women depend on men to transport and chaperon them over distances too long to walk with a sick child or when sick themselves.

Alternative sources of medical care

Nīm-hakīm khatre jān,
Nīm-imām khatre imān.
A quack doctor endangers life,
A quack religious leader endangers faith.[39]

For all that government posters proclaim the dangers of "quackery", government facilities in Bijnor and surrounding villages cannot match the demand for health care. Many ailments are dealt with using domestic remedies or country medicines (ghar-kā-ilāj, desī dawā) — herbal medicines and dietary regimes — or with patent medicines bought without medical consultation. Otherwise, villagers often prefer to consult private practitioners, with a variety of qualifications or none, in Begawala or Bijnor itself.[40] People tend to be pragmatic in their choices of healers, relying initially on those who are easily and cheaply available, and moving further afield and paying more only if the first choice seems to fail. In recent years, private medical practice has expanded considerably in response to increased demand, especially in the rural areas. Few of these practitioners have a full Western-style medical qualification. Some have been trained within a local medical system as vaids (practitioners in the system of Ayurveda, "knowledge for the continuation of life", linked to Hindu texts). More common in Bijnor are hakīms (practitioners of Unan-i-Tibb, "the medicine of Greece", introduced to north India by Muslims). Though vaids tend to be Hindu and hakīms Muslim, clients are drawn from both communities.

Homoeopathy, the Hahnemann system introduced to India in the 19th century and now in a distinctly Indian form, is a third alternative to Western medicine. Other healers have no formal training but have learnt their trade as pharmacists or as apprentices to a doctor in a local town, and simply set up in practice as Registered Medical Practitioners. Spiritual healers (bhagats and maulwīs) also provide services, divining the source of a disorder or providing amulets for protection.

Most of these alternative healers prescribe and sell Western-style medicines, and injections are a very popular form of dispensing such drugs. All kinds of medication — vitamins, steroids, antibiotics — can be readily purchased over the counter in the chemists' shops in Bijnor, despite the official government drugs policy supposed to ensure that dangerous drugs are available only on prescription from qualified doctors. But the villagers do not regard these healers as quacks. They work longer hours, treat clients with greater respect, and may be cheaper than government services. Most lack operating facilities, but few of the villagers' ailments require surgical intervention, and indeed there is little reason to believe that formal qualifications are necessarily a good guide to the quality of care they provide.

Most practitioners, however, are men and offer only a limited service for women.[41] Some are reputed to sell infertility remedies or abortifacients, all medical rather than surgical treatments, usually administered after a verbal account of symptoms rather than a physical examination. If treatment entails something "for putting inside" (that is, a vaginal pessary), the practitioner does not complete the treatment himself. In 1982-83 there were only two female Western doctors in private practice in Bijnor. At their clinics, they offer maternity, obstetric and gynaecological services but at a price beyond the reach of most middle peasants, let alone the poor and landless. The other female medical personnel are the dāis, the traditional birth attendants, on whom most rural women rely during their childbearing careers.[42]

Being financially independent is inherently problematic for a woman in north India: women should be dependent on their menfolk. However, if a woman has no supporter or depends on one whose earnings cannot keep his family, she may be forced to seek employment. But the few opportunities available for rural women are mostly in low status poorly paid work, such as agricultural labour, domestic work for rich peasants, or craft-work. Some women in such a position become self-employed dāis, mostly completely outside the government health services.[43] Most village dāis in Bijnor do the work out of necessity (majbūrī-se):

> How can I think this work is good or bad since I do it out of necessity? I have to do it. I have no education, so there is no other work I could do. *(dāi)*

> I must think well of work which gives me two rotī to eat. But I work as a dāi out of necessity. Would I do this work or would my sons be labourers if we owned land? *(dāi)*

Most dāis are from poor backgrounds, usually landless Harijans or

Muslims. Some were childless, but most had grown sons who either could not or would not support them. Generally, widowhood or the husband's incapacity had precipitated them into the work so that they could "fill the stomach":

> I used to go out very little and I never liked to take food and water in other people's houses. I used to be very careful about cleanliness. But then my husband died — so, out of necessity, I became a dāi. *(dāi)*

> My husband sat at home ill, while I worked to feed him instead of him supporting me. I removed the worries from the house, so should he think badly of my work? If the stomach gets filled through being a dāi, then being a dāi is good work. *(dāi)*

The dāis themselves employ a rhetoric that the work is undesirable.[44] Most say they were unwilling recruits, some, according to their own accounts, having been dragged protesting to their first delivery when another dāi was unavailable or had died. Dāis generally claimed not to seek out clients but to go "just where I am called". It is shameful enough for a woman to need to earn her living but the work of a dāi is even more despised than the other occupations available to such women, because it is defiling-work (ganda kām).

> When I became a dāi my sons thought very badly of it. But I replied that without work, how could I eat — unless they provided my food and clothes? At that they became silent. But my oldest daughter's husband is still angry that I do this work. Since I started it he has never visited me. *(dāi)*

Most dāis, indeed, reported objections from their kin: two even claimed that their own relatives had refused to eat food they had cooked ever since they became dāis.

> **Patricia:** Some people will not eat food cooked by a dāi. Is that why your relatives don't like you to be a dāi?
> **Dāi's bahū:** That is one reason, for there is disgust at the dāi's hands.
> **Dāi:** I wash myself thoroughly after delivering a baby. I change all my clothes. So what is the trouble?
> **Dāi's bahū:** What is removed by washing the hands and bathing? Does the skin come off?
> **Dāi:** Look, you think badly of my work, but in heaven my hands will be made of silver.
> **Patricia:** [disingenuously] Isn't the blood of childbirth just the same as the rest of the body's blood?
> **Dāi's bahū:** Not at all. There is all the difference between the blood from a wound and the blood of childbirth.

Those dāis who were widowed young may practise for many years, like those who begin the work while their husband is still alive.[45] But many became dāis only relatively late in life. Partly, this simply reflects the age at which women are likely to become bereft of a male supporter. Further, the mobility of women in the childbearing ages is restricted by considerations of propriety and because their obligations in their susrāl are not easily compatible with providing an obstetric service. Moreover, pregnant women should not attend deliveries, and menstruating women endanger new-born babies. Thus, post-menopausal women are the most likely and appropriate candidates for the work.[46] Consequently, village women do not expect or obtain long-standing relationships with individual dāis. The maternity histories of the older women in Dharmnagri and Jhakri, for instance, indicate that women often call on a succession of dāis during their childbearing careers, as dāis become senile or die. Dāis, then, are very different from the typical bahū. They are often living alone or heading a household without an adult male; their weak financial position compelled them to seek work and counterbalances the respect otherwise due to their age.

We discuss the dāi's work in more detail later. Here it suffices to indicate that few dāis are literate or have had any formal midwifery training. Some Bijnor village dāis come from families in which being a dāi is part of a family tradition and young women are inducted into the lore by their elders: just under half reported learning to deliver babies by accompanying a relative (usually the mother or sās). Most of the remainder, however, had simply watched a few deliveries, like many other women, and then began being asked to do the work themselves. Periodically, the government has attempted to draw dāis into the ambit of its health services and train them in obstetric techniques.[47] For instance, the ANM at Dharmnagri organises three-week courses, including visits to the local Primary Health Centre. During this training, dāis receive a stipend and delivery kits which can be replenished periodically; but only one-third of the dāis we interviewed had taken such training, usually after several years' practice. Village dāis are not considered to have esoteric knowledge or specialised techniques; their distinctiveness rests on their willingness to accept payment for cutting umbilical cords, unpalatable defiling-work that no ordinary woman values or wishes to perform.

Dāis themselves and village women say the dāi's main work is at the delivery. Dāis have little involvement in ante- and post-natal care. Nor are they likely to administer remedies for abortions or infertility. Most reported attending births only in their own village, though a few also work in neighbouring villages. Muslim and Caste Hindu dāis often claimed not to attend Harijan deliveries because the defilement is too great, while some non-Muslim dāis denied attending Muslim births. Case loads were generally somewhere between 20 and 40 births a year, though some dāis reported as few as ten deliveries and a few more than 60. Such restricted clientele limits their experience and keeps their income — at Rs 15-30 plus some grain at each delivery — low. Indeed, financial insecurity meant that several dāis had additional sources of income, such as weaving cloth, making baskets, rush mats or hand fans, or labouring jobs on cane-crushers, hand-milling grain or cutting fodder. A few also work as sweepers, removing night-soil and performing other tasks too defiling for their caste superiors.

The few historical sources that feature dāis and women's experiences of childbearing are often written by doctors patently biassed against their competitors.[48] Thus we cannot be sure about how dāis' skills and status might have changed, especially in the wake of the major secular changes since the mid-1960s. Possibly, in the face of what are probably more restricted employment opportunities for women in the poorest classes, proportionately more women are being pauperised and more women from families without traditions of dāi practice may be resorting to an occupation that is becoming increasingly de-skilled.[49] Further, as urban medical facilities have expanded, any ante-natal, abortion and infertility work of dāis may have declined, and dāis may have become more restricted to delivery work. Yet elderly women (including dāis) generally denied any reduction or enhancement in the skills of village dāis. Some urban dāis have reputations as wise-women healers but they are few, and whatever they may have been in the past, they are not now birth attendants. The average labouring woman in rural Bijnor is attended in childbirth by a dāi such as we have described.

The poor, low-status dāi and the restricted access of women to health care services are yet more indications of the general position of the bahū outlined in this and the preceding chapter. The bahū in her susrāl is essential as a worker, wealth-bringer and childbearer. But she receives little credit for her effort, either from her susrāl kin or from the institutions of the state, and she has little scope for self-determination.

The moment of childbearing captures this most forcefully, and is the focus of the rest of the book. We explore the lives of childbearing women and people's understandings of them by interweaving women's common and diverse experiences. We follow women in Dharmnagri and Jhakri through pregnancy, childbirth, the immediate post-partum period and the longer-term consequences of repeated childbearing, in the light of class and women's work, of domestic politics and ethnicity, and of health service provision. The final chapter addresses the implications of our analysis of childbearing for government policy, particularly for maternal and child health services. To begin, we examine how two facets of the bahū — as worker and the bearer of future workers — converge when she is pregnant.

Churning milk and making ghī

4.   With a Drum Strapped to Her Belly

Everyone in the house was happy when I was pregnant. This was my first child and I had been married for less than a year. *(Shakuntala)*

I wouldn't like to visit my parents when I am pregnant. I would feel too much sharm in front of my father. *(Viramvati)*

What could I know about women's anatomy? Do I go inside a woman's body to see? I know nothing about that, I am not a doctor. *(dāi)*

Certainly pregnant women should have special foods like milk, fruit and ghī. Such foods make the baby healthy. But I could not eat such things during my last pregnancy, for we were short of money at the time. *(Urmila)*

I stopped doing outside-work after the eighth month and my sās did it for me. What, does it look nice for a woman to go out with a drum strapped to her belly? *(Najma)*[1]

Irrespective of ethnicity and class position, a bahū's in-laws have many expectations of her — central among them that she will bear her husband's children, preferably demonstrating she can do so quickly. Yet pregnancy is not something about which she should be openly proud. During childbearing, women undergo physiological processes which are regarded as shameful and also (at times) polluting and defiling. In rural Bijnor, pregnancy is not publicised through celebratory and supportive customs.[2] Moreover, local understandings of biology assign to women a role in childbearing — basically nourishing their husbands' children — which parallels their marginalisation as workers and legitimises their lack of control over the products of their work and their pregnancies alike, for instance, following divorce or widowhood. Nevertheless, a woman's own condition is believed to affect the outcome of her pregnancy. Consequently, some changes to the bahū's daily life (especially her diet and work) are considered desirable.

Pregnancy: a matter of shame

Pregnancy is not a polluting condition. Menstruation, sexual intercourse and childbirth, by contrast, all are and a woman is required to remedy the pollution by bathing.[3] But pregnancy resembles these other conditions in one respect: they are all sharm-kī-bāt (shameful matters), to which a bahū should not readily allude. When menstruating, she may say she is not bathing or her hair is dirty. In reference to sexual relations, she might talk of having bathed or joining. Women do talk about a pregnancy taking up residence (garbh rahnā) or becoming with-pregnancy (garbh-se), with-belly (pet-se) or heavy-legged (pānw bhārī honā), but there are also several popular euphemisms: people talk of expectation, of waiting for the purpose to emerge, or, more graphically, of something suspicious (dāl-me kuch kālā, literally, something black in the pulses). Older susrāl women delight in teasing the recently married women who cannot answer back, "Is there anything yet?", or, "Haven't you got any earnings [kamāi] yet?"

A pregnant bahū should display more sharm than usual, for pregnancy demonstrates her sexuality. Her sās may guess that she is pregnant only by noting when she last had a purifying bath signifying the end of menstruation, though some women regularly interrogate their bahūs to check if they are menstruating normally. But no bahū is likely to make an explicit statement when she believes she is pregnant. A pregnant woman practises more than usually rigorous bodily concealment by pulling her shawl or the end of her dhotī down over her belly; to wear tight clothing during advanced pregnancy is shameless. Indeed, some women consider that pregnant women should restrict their movements outside the domestic area in their susrāl to avoid being seen.

Contact with the natal kin

> Does it look good to show a belly like a pitcher to your parents? *(Adesh)*

> It is not good for a pregnant woman to appear before her parents, for they have given her away as a wealth-bringer. *(Ahmad)*

In Dharmnagri and Jhakri, the most striking change for pregnant women is the curtailment of contacts with their natal kin.[4] Until her first pregnancy, a bahū comes and goes between her natal village and her susrāl, probably making lengthy stays (of around a couple of months) with her parents. We might anticipate that pregnant women would visit their natal village at every opportunity, but this is rarely so, especially during a first pregnancy. Hindu women expect to visit their pīhar for the Tijo festival — but not if they are conspicuously pregnant. And when Vikram took a temporary labouring job in Viramvati's pīhar, Viramvati remained behind in Dharmnagri because she was pregnant. Displaying pregnancy to the natal kin (especially the father and brothers) is a sharm-kī-bāt and a woman is unlikely to visit them after the fifth or sixth month of pregnancy.[5] Indeed, women were appalled when we asked if pregnant women would not benefit from visiting their parents:

> Where women visit their pīhar, it must seem proper. But for us it is a sharm-kī-bāt. *(Jumni)*

> A woman should not go to her maikā once her belly looks big. *(Najma)*

Those few women who had visited their natal kin late in pregnancy generally provided a justification in terms of necessity: illness, death or a marriage among a woman's close natal kin are generally sufficient reason, even if her pregnancy is advanced. After being orphaned, Jamila was raised by her uncle (MB) and she regards his village as her maikā: when his infant son died she went to give her condolences, although she was pregnant. But such a visit is not necessarily sanctioned by a woman's susrāl kin: when Santosh's parents became ill, her sās tried to prevent her going to see them, even though Santosh is alag. Santosh insisted and her wilfulness was frequently thrown back at her as the cause of her own subsequent illness. Similarly, Adesh went to her pīhar because her mother was ill:

> When I was about a couple of months into my first pregnancy, my mother became ill so I had to go back to my pīhar. You see, my only brother wasn't married then and so there was no other woman in the house. My mother died, so I stayed until about two or three weeks before I gave birth. My husband came and stamped his feet in a tantrum saying, 'What, haven't you got two sisters who could do this work for you? Has your brother rented you back from us?'

Once in her natal village, a woman cannot return to her susrāl on her own initiative: she must be collected by her husband with her parents' consent. Occasionally, marital disputes leave women involuntarily stranded in their natal village, their sense of sharm mounting as the pregnancy proceeds. Zubeida, for example, went to her maikā early in pregnancy. After she complained about frequent beatings, her mother refused to send her back with Zakir, although he came for her several times. Eventually, Zubeida felt so ashamed at her maikā that she agreed to return to Jhakri.

Distancing women from their natal kin can present acute problems for pregnant women living in their natal village. Indeed, such women's problems are yet another objection to ghar-jamāi and within-village marriages. In ghar-jamāi marriages, such as Maya's used to be, the issue is usually resolved by sending the woman to her susrāl in late pregnancy. Exceptionally, after Umrao left her susrāl with Usman, she never returned there: but she now has no close kin in Jhakri whom she should avoid while pregnant. Women in within-village marriages are necessarily close to their natal kin and cannot be removed to a distant susrāl. Of the key informants, however, Latifan's parents are dead and her brother rarely visits her. When she goes to his house she spends time only with his wife.

Some contact is usually maintained by visits from the pregnant woman's natal village. Nearly half the key informants had been visited by a brother during their recent pregnancy. Most reported feeling *sharm* during these visits: often the brother remained outside while his sister stayed out of sight indoors. Many fathers, however, discontinue visiting during their daughters' pregnancies, though seven key informants, generally those without brothers, had been visited by their fathers. Only two were visited by their mother: Pushpa, who was ill, and Chandresh, who had neither father nor brothers.[6]

Generally, then, the first pregnancy cuts *bahūs* off even more from the social support of their sisters and mothers and ties them more firmly than before to their *susrāl*. This pattern applies to Muslims and Hindus, rich and poor; future pregnancies reinforce it. Thereafter, women can make only occasional short visits to their natal village: they belong in their own house and their natal kin become increasingly marginal in their day-to-day concerns.

Ethnoembryology and the physiology of pregnancy

> How should I know when a baby can be conceived? Doctors know such things, or people who are educated. All I know is that a baby gets made when a man and a woman join. When milk is churned, there will certainly be ghī!

All systems of knowledge (including folk biology) are socially constructed. Folk biology, however, has an exceptional resilience and power over people's behaviour and understandings, since it does not seem to local participants to be socially constructed.[7] In Dharmnagri and Jhakri, childbearing is viewed as a universal; it is part of the world as it is, not open to debate or interrogation. Alternatives are unthinkable, and normal and abnormal pregnancies alike are comprehended through taken-for-granted understandings of biological processes. Thus, it was difficult to persuade women to give accounts of their childbearing experiences. Typical retorts were, "Don't babies get born in your country?" and, "Aren't bodies the same everywhere?"

But after Patricia told them about ante-natal and obstetric care in Britain, the customary nature of their own arrangements became clearer, although some puzzlement remained. Why was an educated British woman asking illiterate village women about such defiling and shameful matters: surely she did not want to become a *dāi*? Yet, women adamant that pregnancy is a *sharm-kī-bāt* were uncertain about anatomical and physiological details.[8] Even *dāis* lack confidence: several responded, "But you are educated, you know better than I do", although some were more forthcoming about anatomical details than other women in Dharmnagri and Jhakri. The most detailed accounts, from *dāis* and other village women alike, revolve around the physiological processes that occur during pregnancy, and their ideas about what happens hang together sufficiently for most women's purposes.

The black hole
Women in Dharmnagri and Jhakri could not provide detailed descriptions of

female anatomy (banāwat or construction) and dāis commonly answered, "I know nothing" or, "How can I know? Am I a doctor? Have I had any training? I just deliver the baby, that's all." Women often described the human body as a black hole (kālī-kothrī) in which the belly or abdomen (pet) is a conglomeration of tubes (nas or nālī, the nerves, intestines and blood vessels) linked to the liver, kidneys, stomach and other organs such as the uterus (bachā-dānī, or baby-receptacle). Most women referred to one uterus which is normally closed by the cervix (munh, mouth or orifice). The vagina (bachā-kā-rāstā or baby's path) and rectum connect with the tubes inside, but women were unclear about urination and about how these tubes all interconnect.[9]

Churning milk and making ghī

People use a variety of euphemisms when talking about sexual intercourse. In addition to the coy terms mentioned above (meeting, or joining) some suggest that intercourse is like farming, referring to work or even ploughing.[10] Semen (pānī, or water) contains the seeds (bīj) that a man plants in his wife. The children (like crops) belong to whoever ploughs and owns the field. The heat of sexual intercourse opens the woman's cervix and permits the man's seeds to enter the fertile environment which her uterus provides. Few people said that the woman produces a seed or an egg to merge with the man's seed. Much more commonly, women are thought of like a field capable of conceiving at any time in the menstrual cycle.[11] If pregnancy occurs, the cervix is understood to close, thus preventing another conception. It opens again only during labour to permit the baby to pass along the vagina. Several dāis claimed to diagnose pregnancy after two missed periods, for an internal examination indicates if the cervix is closed or if the amenorrhoea has some other cause.

Women in Dharmnagri and Jhakri, however, rarely consult dāis and generally rely on their own diagnosis, in which the cessation of menstruation is a key factor. Additionally, the retention of blood (which is garm) is evidenced in symptoms of garmī, such as nausea, vomiting, and rashes. Most women note the start of their menstruation according to a lunar calendar and, if their next period does not begin, they say that one month is completed.[12] Women consider that pregnancies should last between nine and ten lunar months. Several women, for instance, specified pregnancies lasting nine months and 20 days, nine months and 12 days or ten months and three days. Others simply said that their baby was born during the tenth month. A few could not recall their menstrual dates: Rajballa's sās cuttingly told her to check with Rohtash since he must know when he planted the seeds. Some women conceive during post-partum amenorrhoea and do not realise they are pregnant for some months: a child conceived in that fashion is called locally a lamrā bachā. Hashmi, for example, does not experience vomiting and only realised she was pregnant after about five months, when she felt her health slowly deteriorating and began to dislike some odours.

At first, women talk of delayed periods (din charhnā, or the days being in arrears). Vaginal bleeding at this stage is considered a late period, as "there was no pregnancy", merely a "blob of flesh" (mās-kā-pinda). "There are only clots of blood, no eyes or nose, don't you know that?"[13] When three months are nearly completed, however, life (jān) enters the baby, its body parts begin developing and its sex is settled. From this stage, the baby's sex may be predicted in several ways, though several dāis (in particular) were very sceptical: craving for bitter foods or dust signifies a boy, sweet foods or ashes a girl; a female foetus moves earlier than a male; male babies lodge on the woman's right side, female on the left; with girls, women become languid and develop ruddy complexions, with boys, their buttocks do not enlarge much and late in pregnancy they sit with their right leg forward; the previous baby's placenta may have indicated a boy would follow (if it was round) or a girl (if it was thin and flat); or (among Hindus) the woman's palm can be read or her birth horoscope consulted. When three months are completed women talk of pregnancy and say that the baby has adhered or flourished, using jamnā (a verb which also connotes germination in plants). Thereafter, vaginal bleeding would be called a baby or the belly falling (bachā girnā, pet girnā).[14] Generally, after three months, the woman stops feeling nausea because her food is digested properly again and the worst symptoms of garmī abate somewhat. By about seven months, the baby is fully formed but spends the rest of the pregnancy growing and gaining strength.

In this process, the woman's role is essentially nurturant. Indeed, while kālī-kothrī means black hole, kothrī alone means granary or store, and sometimes uterus. The baby is nourished and prevented from drying out by the blood which would otherwise flow if the mother continued to menstruate. The mother's contribution to the baby's development, then, is towards its growth rather than its essential make-up — and that, too, using defiling blood (ganda khūn). Some women said the amniotic sac (thailī or burqa) and placenta and umbilical cord (ānwal-nāl) are produced from the mother's menstrual blood, though most were non-committal.[15] Early in pregnancy, preparations begin for nurturing the baby after birth: some blood is believed to congeal into breast milk, which remains in the breast and becomes heavy or solidified and yellow in colour ("like pus"). Pregnancy-milk (garbh-kā-dūdh) or "pregnant cow's milk" (bākhrī-dūdh) is bādī and thus capable of producing bloating, rheumatic pains, vomiting, stomach pains and diarrhoea in the breast-feeding child. Thus, ideally, a toddler should be weaned if its mother becomes pregnant.[16] Sometimes breast-feeding children dislike pregnancy-milk, but others are weaned by using applications of bitter nīm leaf juice to the mother's nipples.

Since the pregnant woman is like a field nourishing her husband's seeds, her general condition and activities can affect her own and the baby's well-being. The developing foetus takes its strength from the mother's retained menstrual blood. In itself, breast-feeding in pregnancy is not thought to affect foetal development unless the woman's diet is woefully inadequate. But people said that the woman's own strength can easily be sapped by pregnancy, even if she is not breast-feeding. Further, the accumulating menstrual blood can result in the unpleasant symptoms characteristic of garmī and even stimulate untimely uterine contractions. Moreover, the baby might fall if the woman lifts heavy loads (while doing outside-work) or if she is affected by evil spirits (which reside particularly in places away from human habitation). Such perceived threats suggest precautions which (in local terms) the pregnant woman should observe. Her diet should be supplemented with foods regarded as beneficial for coolness and strength, but not by so much that the baby becomes too fat; she should have respite from heavy work, but not total rest, since that weakens the body and may make the delivery difficult; and she should be relieved of any need to run the gauntlet of evil spirits.

Here we are not judging pregnant women's diets and rest against Western standards, but using the women's own assessments of how their situation matches local standards.[17] Women say that they rarely attain these ideals in practice and they consider this is costly for themselves and their children.[18] The demands of a labour-intensive economy and overall levels of poverty partly account for these shortfalls. Implementing the precautions which a pregnant woman should ideally take would entail additional work for other people and their sacrifice of food. The position of the bahū in her susrāl is not conducive to obtaining such allowances.

Diet during pregnancy: issues of entitlement

The pregnant woman should have ghī, milk, fruit, coconut, anything she desires. Everybody is different. Some women are damaged by garm things, others are not. A woman should just eat whatever suits her.

The different effects of foods might imply that pregnant women would systematically consume thandā (cooling) foods such as milk and most fruits.[19] Several dāis, indeed, said that avoiding excessively garm foods is particularly important in early pregnancy, when garmī could stimulate uterine contractions and result in a miscarriage. Women list garm foods that may be avoided or taken only in moderation, including gur, tea, and certain pulses (urad and masūr). The most garm foods (especially eggs and meat) are insignificant in even our Muslim and Harijan informants' diets. In excess, bādī foods which cause flatulence, such as rice (although it is thandā) and potatoes, may distend the woman's tubes, cause a miscarriage, constrict the baby or cause the woman's ankles to swell. Rice, however, is somewhat preferable to rotī made from wheat flour, which is garm. But few women rigidly adhere to a diet of thandā food or avoid bādī foods completely.[20] Parhez (avoidances) usually only apply to the post-partum diet. Indeed, we unwittingly worried one woman when we asked about parhez during pregnancy: "What?" she asked anxiously, "Should I have been keeping parhez when I was pregnant?"

> I have never kept parhez during pregnancy. Who keeps parhez before the baby's birth? But it is another matter if a pregnant woman does not feel like eating something. Then she will just stop eating it. And if she has any special craving, then she can ask for it. *(Adesh)*

Some women had cravings for earth, ashes from the chūlhā, uncooked rice, bitter foods such as pickles, or sweet things. Others stopped eating foods that became unpalatable, such as potatoes, aubergines, onions, fish, and garm masālā (hot spices), all of which are either garm or bādī or both.

Moreover, since the baby is nourished by the mother's blood, dāis and village women alike said that a pregnant woman requires foods locally defined as those which produce blood and therefore strength (tāqat), such as milk, fruit, and also ghī (which is garm but not excessively so). Some dāis, probably influenced by health education, mentioned green vegetables. Most said a pregnant woman should "fill her stomach", by having the customary two meals a day, one mid-morning and the other around dusk. Many women, however, said that excessive eating results in such a large baby that the delivery risks being hard and even dangerous.[21] Some said the day's first meal should contain no strengthening food, as the benefits go directly to the foetus. But views were not always consistent. For example, Santosh, who was initially criticised for greed and warned that her baby would be too large, delivered a small sickly baby and was then blamed for eating so much that her tubes filled with food and the baby became cramped.

Broadly, then, some special regulation of a pregnant woman's diet is in order. She should eat well, though in moderation, and include items which are both strengthening and thandā. Yet few of our key informants reported any changes at all in their diets during pregnancy.

Who eats well in a village?

> Pregnant women should get good food, but can you tell me where they do so? Who eats well in a village? Anyway, we can only afford fruit or milk occasionally. *(Ruxana)*

A chūlhā's economic position and seasonal variations in food availability and income influence what a woman can eat, whether pregnant or not. In Dharmnagri and Jhakri, only pregnant women in rich peasant chūlhās are likely to "fill their stomachs" with home-grown grain and dairy produce, just as they do normally. But even they are unlikely to receive extra foods, especially items such as fruit, which have to be bought:

> I was happy to be pregnant, because I could eat well. Last time I was pregnant we had enough grain from our own fields. Why, some years we even have a surplus to sell. We have ghī and milk in the house too, which I normally have. Other special things should be available — but I had none. *(Bhagirthi)*

Otherwise, few women in the two villages regularly drink milk, and they have no more access to dairy products when pregnant. This applies especially to women in poor peasant and landless chūlhās:

> Last time I was pregnant, we could all fill our stomachs, though we had big money worries. With our children, we need to buy four to five kilograms of grain daily, so labourers like us are very anxious people. We have a buffalo, but we sell the milk to meet our expenses. We very rarely drink milk. What can poor people do? It is hard to fill the stomach. *(Wasila)*

Most chūlhās survive near the margin, and pregnant women do not receive extra or expensive strengthening food. As one dāi put it, "For the poor, even dāl-rotī are special." Similarly, in most poor peasant and landless chūlhās, lack of sufficient cash or storage space to stockpile rice sufficient for the whole year, mean a woman's ability to take rice rather than rotī as her staple is a seasonal matter.

Economic constraints are somewhat exacerbated by problems of food distribution in rural areas and women in Dharmnagri and Jhakri contrast their life with urban living. City women, they believe, obtain special foods before as well as after delivery: "Who would not like to have special foods when they are pregnant, but who in a village can do so?" But the difficulties are not utterly insurmountable. Both villages are relatively accessible to Bijnor and there is regular traffic into town. Many of the problems of availability lie elsewhere.

What else is a woman for but to have children?

> You think I should eat more now that I'm pregnant? I tell you, the men here say that their susrī wives are just building up their strength if they ask for more food when they are pregnant! *(Santosh)*

Chūlhās able to provide pregnant women with extra cooling or strengthening food do not necessarily do so. Moreover, women accept that more effort would be made to bring their diets closer to the ideal in their natal village but, as Viramvati put it:

> Everyone likes being in their pīhar. But no matter how many shortages there are in the susrāl and whether there is benefit or not in the pīhar, a pregnant woman should remain in her susrāl.

Once her pregnancy is conspicuous, therefore, a bahū's capacity to control her diet during pregnancy is limited.[22] Her diet is essentially conditional on what her sās and husband permit. Her hopes of gaining extra strengthening and thandā food during pregnancy depend on establishing special entitlements which override economic constraints and the normal subordination of her dietary needs to those of her susrāl kin. This is not easily done. The ANM's assistant recounted her experiences in the villages served by the Dharmnagri dispensary:

Very few pregnant women get milk, though a glass at bedtime would be very beneficial. Many people do not have buffaloes. Those who do may get little milk or sell it, saying that they will get money and their work can proceed. If they keep back a pāo [quarter litre] it is not the woman who gets it. Women say that men work so they should have it. When I tell them that pregnant women need milk they just say, 'But what does she need milk for? What else is a woman for but to have children?' And that way all the woman's strength pours into the child.

A man whose wife is still sājhe is unlikely to buy special food because (after it has been shared among the chūlhā members) the pregnant woman would have little benefit. Indeed, any suggestion of special treatment for the bahū may be ridiculed by her seniors:

I am still sājhe. If my husband considers bringing something, he hesitates because there will be nothing left for me once it is divided up. If he does bring something for me, my sister-in-law [HeBW] and my sās taunt him, saying, 'He is coming with things for his own wife, has he not even a little sharm?' *(Pushpa)*

Being alag or akelī can give the pregnant bahū greater control over the grain store and her own diet, albeit in negotiation with her husband and according to their income. Women in this situation were among the few who obtained additional food during pregnancy, particularly those with few or no children. Tahira is a bought bride and is akelī in Jhakri; Taslim, her husband, is a landless labourer. Yet during her first pregnancy in Jhakri she drank milk, and Taslim sometimes took her to Bijnor to buy fruit, or bought some for her.[23] But such opportunities for the alag or akelī woman should not be overdrawn. Women with several children rarely obtain special food when pregnant. Maya is alag in a middle peasant chūlhā. She said:

My husband might bring something special, but would it look good for me to eat in front of the children? It has never happened that he has brought something for me alone.

Anyway, men rarely bring extra food unprompted — and many women hesitate to ask in case they seem too shameless. Adesh, in a rich peasant chūlhā, commented, "We had no shortages nor do I have a sās, yet I had no special food because he is not quick to bring me things." Similarly, Khalil is a middle peasant and Khurshida is akelī. But Khurshida took milk and ghī only if they were in the house, because "I am not such that I ask for something." Qadir, too, is a middle peasant and Qudsia is alag:

We had no shortages when I was pregnant. We have enough grain. The baby grows from the woman's blood and she should be given milk and fruit. Also fruit is thandā and reduces the garmī which a pregnant woman feels. But our buffalo was not giving milk then. And where could we get fruit in the village? If I had told my husband I wanted fruit, he would have brought it. But it is his responsibility to have consideration for me, so I said nothing to him.

Young married women emphasise their powerlessness over their own diet. Cooling and strengthening food may be desirable — but the pregnant bahū is expected to wait passively for milk to be offered or fruit to be brought. For her to take extra food for herself would be unseemly, especially when she is pregnant. And asking for special food "doesn't look nice", for it draws attention to her condition and asserts claims to precedence over others who eat from the same pot. If a bahū spends her own money on delicacies or eats extra food sent by her parents, others snipe. Santosh, told by the dāi that the foetus was small, lamented that she was getting nothing extra to strengthen the baby:

> My husband gives me nothing for strength as my sās says that such foods make the baby too strong and big. If I take anything she threatens not to help when I give birth. My parents sent me some ghī and gur. But if I were to take any, my husband is such that he would go round the whole courtyard telling the women. Then they would all make trouble for me, saying, 'All the world eats after giving birth, but look at Santosh eating before!'

Sometimes the sās and husband do provide extra food, or the husband buys special delicacies. Gita, for instance, is in a middle peasant chūlhā and still sājhe with her sās. They grow enough grain every year to have some over for sale. Gopal brought fruit from Bijnor which Gita ate along with milk and rice produced at home, and she ate as much as she wished while pregnant. But almost all the remaining key informants said that their susrāl kin provided no extra food. Asghari is in a rich peasant chūlhā and sājhe with her sās. They own several milk animals and sell milk in Bijnor, yet even she commented: "Pregnant women should have good food but I had no milk or fruit. Village people do not have enough sense to offer good food to eat."

Thus, few pregnant women in Dharmnagri and Jhakri eat any differently from when they are not pregnant. Pregnant bahūs have no privileged access to locally valued foods, such as milk and fruit. Generally, they simply eat what is in the house, rarely taking more than normal. Only the lucky few eat special items not regularly in their diet. Whether pregnant or not, women cannot expect pampering or special delicacies in their susrāl.

Work during pregnancy: issues of responsibility

> Village women work hard — they get no peace. If the bahū asks for a rest her sās will say, 'If you do not work how will we eat?' In villages, pregnant women get neither proper food nor rest. **(dāi)**

> Pregnant women should not lift heavy loads in case the baby falls. Also, going outside causes sharm for, no matter how much you cover your belly, it still shows. But no one in a village gets much leave from work and I am no other than a villager. *(Asghari)*

Heavy lifting work can cause a baby to fall; evil spirits may attack pregnant women wandering outside domestic space, while displaying the drum strapped to her belly is a sharm-kī-bāt. How much can pregnant women in Dharmnagri and Jhakri negotiate the changes in their activities and movements which are locally viewed as desirable? Women are especially keen to give up outside-work, such as making dung-cakes, throwing dung into the midden, fetching head-loads of fodder or carrying buckets of water. Most women, however, were disdainful when we asked if their work had reduced during pregnancy:

> Who would not like some rest?
> Who gets leave before the delivery?
> The work is your own, so who can give you a holiday from it?
> There must be a woman somewhere who gets some peace in pregnancy.

A chūlhā's economic requirements cannot easily be met if women relinquish their work, even temporarily, and pregnant women generally continue with their normal duties and move around their susrāl much as usual. They can adjust their activities, sitting down to work or working in snatches, carrying lighter head-loads of dung and dumping it in the midden instead of crouching making dung-cakes. Some, too, are relieved (if only partially) of outside-work — but others carry head-loads of fodder, or water livestock even in early labour. Our informants' working days during pregnancy are minimally 12 hours and often more, just as at other times.

What is peace compared with sharm?

Within the constraints of economic necessity, however, there is some leeway. A woman's work is lighter and optional in her natal village. The visiting daughter does not have the responsibilities of the bahū and is granted rest in her natal village which is rarely conceded in her susrāl. But to visit the natal village during pregnancy is a sharm-kī-bāt. Among Muslims and Hindus alike, sharm outweighs the benefits of peace and solicitous treatment in the natal village:

> Attention, peace, whatever there is with the mother, even so it is a sharm-kī-bāt. *(Fatima)*

> No matter what difficulty I faced in my susrāl, no matter if I were akelī, no matter how much benefit I might get in my pīhar and how much was lacking in my susrāl, I would never go to my pīhar after six complete months of pregnancy. **(Durgi)**

Rarely, then, does a pregnant woman benefit from the rest afforded in the natal village.[24] Indeed, women marooned with their parents after marital rows said their disquiet counteracted the release from their susrāl obligations. Vimla was with her parents in the third month of pregnancy, because they were paying for treatment for her toddler son. After a row, Vir left her there, returning three times before she agreed to go with him, in the eighth month.

In her pīhar she worked only when she wished: back in her susrāl, she did all her normal work until she delivered.

The bought bride normally has no contact with her natal kin, so pregnancy brings no special disadvantages for her. Equally, pregnant women in within-village and ghar-jamāi marriages are not especially privileged or able to benefit greatly from the geographical proximity of their parents. Muslim women in within-village marriages curtail their contacts with their natal kin once their pregnancy is apparent, while women in ghar-jamāi marriages generally remain in their parents' home until the eighth month at the latest, when they are sent to their susrāl — and must participate in the work there.

How can a pregnant woman get peace?

How can a pregnant woman get peace? If she is sājhe, she does her work because she feels she should work alongside her sās. And if she is alag, she has enough work of her own to prevent her getting peace! *(Urmila)*

My nand stayed for a month before I gave birth but I had scarcely any rest. I don't have so much power over anyone in my susrāl that I can cause them to work. *(Jamila)*

Although the details of women's work vary, the structural position of bahūs in Dharmnagri and Jhakri is reflected in common features of their work when pregnant. The bahū is subject to domestic authorities in her susrāl; she has responsibilities, and should not be a burden on her in-laws. Thus, ante-natal maternity leave is rarely considered appropriate, even for women whose natal kin live close by. A pregnant woman's work more closely relates to seasonal factors and to the class position and composition of her chūlhā than to the stage her pregnancy has reached.

House-work is not considered heavy enough to warrant relief, even in late pregnancy. The work of those few women in chūlhās with neither animals nor land rarely takes them outside or entails lifting loads of dung or fodder. It is subject to relatively few seasonal influences, and such women generally continued their work to the end of pregnancy, whether they were sājhe or already alag or akelī. The women key informants, however, were almost all living in chūlhās owning at least one milk animal for which they were responsible during their last pregnancy. All the rich and middle peasant women were in chūlhās with draught and milk animals (sometimes jointly owned) and with some land producing grain for domestic consumption. For these women, seasonal differences can play a significant role in their work during pregnancy.[25] In 1982, Maqsudi, for instance, had heavier work late in pregnancy than during other seasons. Mansur, a middle peasant, works land with his father. In early April, their toddler son had chickenpox and could not walk far; Maqsudi, then over six months pregnant, had to carry head-loads of fodder with him astride her hips:

These days I collect all the fodder, for the men have been too busy in the fields cutting wheat, harrowing the earth and laying new sugar-cane. Men collect fodder when it's raining or when they are not so busy — at such times I get some peace. Otherwise I must do it, even if I am feeling unwell. Also, the weather is getting hotter, so I must take drinking water to my husband in the fields several times a day.

A month later she was busily winnowing the mustard crop. She had done 10 kilograms one day and said another four days would complete the job. Although the wheat crop was mostly machine threshed, she also threshed some by hand for cattle-feed. Working in the sun was making her giddy. Since the wheat harvest finished, Mansur had been chopping fodder and watering the animals, yet her working day was still about 15 hours. That, she added wryly, excluded laying out her husband's bedding, for he was currently sleeping at their tubewell to prevent theft.

Significantly, Maqsudi is alag from her sās and unmarried nands, who are disinclined to help except with the joint animal-work. Three-quarters of the key informants were either alag or akelī during their last pregnancy and their experiences highlight the importance of chūlhā organisation. Pregnant women who are alag or akelī may be able to wrest some control over their diets, but they have no help with their work. When pregnant, such women have little option but to continue performing all their usual tasks:

> If there is someone to do a pregnant woman's work she should stop doing outside-work and making dung-cakes. That work is difficult. But I am alag. I even dived in the pond to collect mud to repair the house and carried the load back home in a large dish on my head. *(Imrana)*

> I am akelī. By the eighth-ninth month, outside-work, like collecting dung and making dung-cakes, is hard. I would have stopped it if there were someone to do it. *(Latifan)*

> How could I take leave? I was already alag. My husband and daughter would have been hungry if I had not cooked for them. Why, the very day the baby was born I brought a head-load of fodder and cut it with the chopping machine for the buffalo. *(Viramvati)*

Apart from pregnant women who became seriously ill, only a minority of the alag and akelī women had any help during pregnancy. Chandresh was akelī but her own unmarried sister and a married nand who was not yet cohabiting did all her outside-work towards the end of her first pregnancy. Dilruba's married nand arrived in Jhakri a month before the delivery, while Adesh called her own married daughter to help. And Bhagwana and Mahipal took over their wives' work collecting and chopping fodder and watering cattle for the last month, though both women still did the dung-work.

Otherwise, a pregnant woman has her greatest chance of respite from her susrāl duties if she is sājhe, which she is most likely to be early in her childbearing career.[26] Almost all our key informants were sājhe during their first pregnancy and several had a number of children while still sājhe. Two women at one chūlhā regularly share the work and can adjust their loads in accord with seasonal fluctuations and the progress of the bahū's pregnancy, if only in its latest stages. Barring those who became ill, no bahū who was alag reported being helped by her sās during pregnancy. By contrast, all the bahūs still sājhe were relieved of much (if not all) of their outside-work late in pregnancy. Hiran's sās normally does all the outside-work anyway, while Hiran does the house-work: this pattern persists throughout her pregnancies. Other bahūs normally do some outside-work, such as dung-work or taking food to men working in the fields. Generally their sās took over their outside-work, for maybe two months before they gave birth. Wasila said, "It does not look nice to go out after the seventh month", so her sās fetched fodder for their buffalo. Najma's sās, too, fetches fodder and takes food to the men in the fields when Najma is heavily pregnant. Similarly, Asghari had help during the last month of pregnancy from her sās as well as her married nand, but Asghari sometimes took food out to the men and continued making dung-cakes. Although all or some of the outside-work is taken over, the pregnant bahū retains her normal house-work to the end and discontinuing fodder collection does not necessarily absolve her from the heavy work of chopping it. Anyway, being sājhe does not entitle the bahū to shirk even during pregnancy. Several women, indeed, denied that being sājhe gives the bahū any significant benefit as "it does not look nice for a bahū to rest while her sās is hard at work".

Comparing women in one compound indicates forcefully the significance of the bahū's relationship with her sās.[27] Santosh had separated from her sās after fights about work, over her jewellery and the money being spent on Punni's marriage. During her first pregnancy, Santosh had no help from her sās or any of her sisters-in-law (HBW). She even described herself as akelī, and had to harvest wheat long after sunset the evening before her baby was born. By contrast, Omvati and Pushpa were still sājhe with their sās. Pushpa became ill during her first pregnancy and was unable to work. At the same time, Omvati was due to deliver her fifth child. Their sās did all the outside-work and even called Promilla (who was alag) to do the house-work. Even so, Omvati took some of the load: "Call it necessity or whatever you like, it isn't good to sit idle in front of your sās."

Before the delivery, a married nand is not usually called (as she may be afterwards), though if she is visiting her natal village she may be kept there until the baby is born. Within the susrāl itself, even an unmarried nand and the sās cannot be guaranteed to help unless they are sājhe with the bahū. In the post-partum period, a woman is polluted, but the pregnant woman poses no danger to other people.[28] Normative statements about the desirability of some rest during pregnancy revolve around the sharm of displaying pregnancy and possible threats to foetal well-being. In practice, these considerations are heavily outweighed by the requirement that the bahū fulfils her responsibilities without disrupting other women's work. Pregnant women in Dharmnagri and Jhakri can usually obtain only negligible respites from their work, reflecting the low levels of everyday co-operation among women.

Mishaps of pregnancy: access to health care

A bahū does not always produce a healthy baby: mishaps can occur. How they are understood and dealt with is also important in women's childbearing careers. In Dharmnagri and Jhakri, this is partly a matter of understanding the location of bahūs in their susrāl, partly a question of health service provision in rural Bijnor, and partly a feature of local views of pregnancy as a condition not normally requiring medical interventions.

In addition to home remedies, various practitioners (government and private) are available, but none is engaged in any substantial outreach or systematic surveillance of the local populace for any condition, including pregnancy. The government ante-natal service is hardly worthy of the name. Formally, the ANM should give pregnant women regular medical checks, distribute iron and folic acid tablets (to combat anaemia, which is presumed universal), monitor foetal development (for example, by weighing the mother), give a course of free injections of tetanus toxoid (to avert neonatal tetanus caused by cutting the cord with an infected instrument), identify women at risk and attend such women's deliveries or refer them to the government women's hospital in Bijnor. The ANM should maintain a network of dāis, usually those she has helped to train, to identify pregnant women and register them with her. But most dāis are not trained, and untrained and trained dāis alike seldom establish contact with pregnant women and do not systematically deliver medical care to them. Equally, village women rarely report consulting dāis during pregnancy. Most dāis claim they have no treatments or medicines to administer and that women therefore have no reason to bring their troubles to them. Thus dāis cannot provide a comprehensive safety net of medical care or referral for pregnant women.[29]

In general, the government ante-natal services do not function well, even in Dharmnagri and Jhakri which have an ANM clinic in the dispensary. Tetanus toxoid injections are a telling example. Women recognise that tetanus (a word in local use) is a major threat to new-born babies, though they are uncertain about its cause or how to prevent it. Village women are commonly said to fear that tetanus toxoid injections (which are considered garm) might cause premature labour, especially as they are given towards the end of pregnancy. Only about one-quarter of pregnant women in the two villages seek out the ANM for injections, and the ANM rarely goes into the villages herself. She never visits Jhakri, and ante-natal tetanus toxoid coverage there since 1975 is only 8%, compared with the Dharmnagri figure of 35%. Coverage in more distant villages is even lower because many women have no time to attend the dispensary.[30]

Women at risk are rarely referred for more specialist care. The ANM may send them to the women's hospital in Bijnor, but there is no appointment system, nor does the ANM accompany the woman. People in Dharmnagri and Jhakri are sceptical about the benefits of services provided at the local dispensary and often prefer to consult private practitioners in Begawala, Bijnor, or other towns, whether local traditional or Western. But trips to Bijnor and beyond depend upon time and cash, as well as the willingness of the woman's susrāl kin to arrange for a chaperon.

Yet various mishaps can occur in relation to pregnancy. A bahū might fail to become pregnant. Even if she does conceive, she may deliver prematurely or bear a sickly or stillborn baby. Further, she herself might become ill.

The barren field

If people ask for treatment to get a child, I send them to a big doctor in Bijnor. Am I God that I could cause a child to be born? *(dāi)*

Some men threaten to get another wife if their first wife does not produce children. Such women sometimes ask me for treatment. I examine them and if there is something wrong I give them doctorī [Western] medicine. There can also be some lack in the man's water. But men do not talk about their own failings. *(dāi)*

A childbearing career is an essential part of adult women's lives. Not to want children is unthinkable, to fail to conceive or to have no living children is usually calamitous. In bearing children, especially sons, the bahū continues her husband's line and provides the chūlhā's future generation of workers.[31] Failure is just cause for a man to return his wife to her parents and several women in Dharmnagri and Jhakri (who ultimately bore children) recall worrying times when their husbands were pestered to replace them.

The prevailing view is that failure to conceive is the woman's fault alone. The term bānjh refers to an unproductive and sterile field as well as the woman who fails to conceive, or (according to some informants) the woman who bears no sons. She may have inflammation (waram, sūjan) in her uterus, it may be out of place or too delicate to retain the man's seeds, the mouth of her uterus may be too narrow or swollen for the seeds to enter, or her tubes too dry to retain the man's water. She may be so thandī that her husband's seeds cannot germinate, or affected by evil spirits. Several dāis insisted that a woman could fail to conceive because her husband's water contains only dead seeds, but said villagers resist this suggestion and men generally refuse to undergo medical checks. Action, then, is directed towards the woman. Local treatments consist of herbal vaginal pessaries to open the cervix or reduce swelling, dietary parhez (avoidances) to redress the woman's alleged thand, or amulets. Recently, too, Western healers have begun offering medicines, injections or pessaries (rather than surgical methods), which may also be offered by local healers. Women who conceive quickly are considered fortunate. Even a couple of barren years after marriage results in gossip and searching for remedies, often at considerable cost to the husband and his parents, and sometimes even the woman's natal kin. Some people continue such errands over lengthy periods. Ruxana was married for two years when Riasat first took her to the hakīm in Inampur who gave her medicine and a vaginal pessary. Later they went to a dāi, who inserted a pessary. Finally, she had a series of injections from a private Western male doctor in Bijnor. Ruxana's first child was born about four-and-a-half years after she began cohabiting. Kamla had light periods only every eight or nine months and her susrāl people said she would not conceive without menstruating. Her parents began taking her to local healers, who refused to begin fertility treatment until her menstrual problems were solved. Subsequently, at various times, she was treated at Nizampur, Najibabad and Sahanpur, and had tablets from the Dharmnagri ANM and a private Western female doctor in Bijnor. Eventually Kamla gave birth more than five years after her cohabitation, but her menstrual irregularity is still unresolved. Ghazala had been married almost four years when we arrived. Another woman from her natal village who was married at the same time already had two children. People were beginning to talk. She said Ghulam was initially too "flustered" to take her for treatment: what could she do unless he took her? During our research, however, she had sundry treatments over several months. Pains in her thighs, her lower back, and her pubic region plus the two days of fever during menstruation all suggested the influence of evil spirits. Thus, she first had two amulets from a maulwī in Nehtaur, one paid for by her mother and the other by Ghulam. Subsequently she had tablets from a private Western female doctor in Bijnor, and some powder, medicine and a pessary from a dāi. Finally she was taken to the Inampur hakīm, who (without examining her) diagnosed inflammation in her tubes and cervix. He provided ingredients for pessaries to be inserted twice daily for a week, though she had trouble tracking down a dāi or the Dharmnagri ANM to do this. Ghazala became pregnant, as a result, she believed, of the hakīm's treatment.[32]

The fear of being sent back to their parents hovers over bahūs who fail to bear children. One in Jhakri, for instance, had been married more than 12 years by 1982. Her periods are generally two or more months apart and very painful; and she has constant headaches "because of the retained garmī". Since she has never given birth, her "body's garmī has not come out". She has had treatments for her menstrual problems — often paid for by her brother — but fertility treatments are too expensive. Meanwhile, her susrāl people tell her husband to marry again; he refuses, saying that God might not even give children from another woman. Another example is Udayan's mother, widowed in 1982. She prefaced telling us of her anxieties about her future with a lengthy account of how well her late husband had cared for her and had resolutely refused to repudiate her (despite his relatives' constant jibing) when she had failed to conceive even after seven years of marriage. But an extreme case during our research highlights the need for a bahū to conceive: a young childless woman in a neighbouring village died suddenly in mysterious circumstances. According to rumour, her parents-in-law had poisoned her so that her husband could remarry. In Dharmnagri and Jhakri, men and women alike were as astounded as we were.

Nevertheless, people's usual responses when they suspect that a bahū is bānjh powerfully indicate the significance of childbearing: the lengthy accounts of the key informants who underwent fertility treatments indicate wide-ranging and eclectic searches. Time seems of little object when a bahū fails to conceive, though money constrains what people can do. Similarly, the frequent involvement of male practitioners and a woman's natal kin — even though childbearing is a sharm-kī-bāt — underlines the perceived seriousness of the problem.

Most women, however, do not experience infertility directly. It was temporarily an issue for six key informants as well as other in-married and out-married women in Dharmnagri and Jhakri. Only three ever-married women aged over 30 had never borne a child; another had borne one child (who later died) but had never given birth again.[33] All our key informants, of course, eventually became pregnant, even if only after an anxious wait. On average, married women in Dharmnagri and Jhakri conceived within about two years of the cohabitation and nine out of ten conceived within five years. Many just laughed when we asked if they had needed treatment to become pregnant.

Only women whose babies fall observe restrictions

Some people say pregnant women smell sweet, like a melon, and that is why they attract evil spirits. *(Imrana)*

A baby can fall if the mother is jolted or if she lifts heavy weights. Also, she can be affected by evil spirits if she goes to places like graveyards where there is dirty air. That can make the baby die in the belly or contractions begin which cannot be stopped by medicines. *(dāi)*

As with infertility, the woman is considered responsible for the successful outcome of a conception. While harbouring the baby, her own condition and behaviour influence its development, for good or ill. Prudent women take precautions.

Anxiety centres on deliveries "before the appointed moment" (samay-se pehle) rather than on overly-long pregnancies. The baby needs to remain in its mother's belly for the correct time to be strong enough to survive. Our records almost certainly undercount what would be considered early miscarriages in Western terms, but are locally regarded as "the days being in arrears" rather than a pregnancy. Even the miscarriages between the fourth and eighth months (just 2% of over 1,200 pregnancies reported) are probably an understatement.[34]

Premature labour is believed to occur for several reasons. Excessive garmī implies over-stimulated tubes in the belly and is especially dangerous in early pregnancy, before the foetus is established. A male foetus is considered more garm than a female one and more likely to miscarry precipitately if the woman herself is garm.[35] Women who are normally garm (for instance, whose menstrual periods are heavy) are prone to have babies fall. Such women and those with a history of miscarriages are the only ones likely to avoid garm foods systematically until the baby is properly rooted. Jumni, for instance, had two six-month miscarriages in succession. Subsequently, when a period was a fortnight overdue, she visited a doctor who told her the previous miscarriages had been caused by garm food. He prescribed parhez of garm foods plus very thandā tablets to be taken daily. She consulted him just once, as he lives in her pīhar; thereafter her father-in-law fetched supplies of tablets every fortnight until she gave birth. At any time, fever and garm medicines (such as anti-malaria drugs, aspirins, or tetanus toxoid injections) might make a woman so garm that her cervix dilates and uterine contractions begin.[36] Hashmi, for example, reported a six-month miscarriage due (she considered) to a bout of malaria. A pregnant woman should not attend another's delivery for fear of absorbing the garmī of the contractions. Sexual intercourse, too, causes cervical dilatation.[37] Given Santosh's history of delayed periods and failure to conceive, Sunil was prevented from having intercourse with her from her sixth month of pregnancy — and said his brothers would beat him (at his mother's instigation) if Santosh's baby fell.

Frequent pregnancies, too, can weaken the uterus so that it cannot retain the baby; being jolted while travelling by bus or cart can twist the woman's tubes and cause the baby to fall. Strenuous work, such as fodder chopping, is undesirable, but (of course) rarely avoidable. Early in pregnancy, falling heavily (as once happened to Mansur's sister) or being beaten (as Lakshmi was) can make the "blob of flesh" break up and cause bleeding. Hashmi and Imrana's sister-in-law (HeBW) reported three late miscarriages, one at eight months caused by evil spirits, another at seven months after she had lifted a heavy weight, and the third at five months while carrying a head-load of dung.

Women in Dharmnagri and Jhakri rarely call on dāis and usually resort only to domestic remedies to arrest the abdominal pains and vaginal bleeding that signal an incipient miscarriage: taking thandā foods and avoiding garm ones, refraining from sexual intercourse, resting from heavy work, or lying on a bed with the foot raised by a pair of bricks. Most dāis said they have no medicines, although the dāis who serve Jhakri offer country medicines containing thandā ingredients: dried water-lily seed and dried water chestnut pounded together with a local medicine called kamar-kas and drunk with cold milk. They advise easily-digested or light (halkā) food (such as khichrī made with rice and mūng-kī-dāl).

If the "blob" is badly broken, they (like other dāis) would send the woman to Bijnor for cleansing (safāi, in this case dilatation and curettage). Generally, however, when a miscarriage cannot be arrested, the woman simply consumes garm foods to ensure a complete cleansing. A woman whose baby has fallen should take precautions when pregnant again. She may avoid garm foods during a subsequent pregnancy. In addition, people will probably conclude that she had been possessed by evil spirits (asar, bhūt, hawā or satāo) or attacked by the evil eye (nazar) of someone envious of her pregnancy. A few dāis treat evil eye or tell the woman to obtain amulets to wear when she is next pregnant. The woman will also probably avoid graveyards, cremation grounds, and wooded areas, the favourite haunts of evil spirits, although many women say that no women have any business in such places and that spirits can strike even at home. Some dāis, however, rejected such explanations, saying that women simply require medical treatment or that their conditions are due to God's will.

Problems can also occur at full-term (pūre din). A small full-term baby may be explained by the mother's weakness or illness which prevented the baby from flourishing. But if the mother's health was good, a weak baby, a stillbirth, or a deformed baby may be explained as the work of evil spirits and the woman will probably wear an amulet during her next pregnancy. Working, eating, drinking, or leaving the house during even a partial solar eclipse can result in a missing arm, deformed fingers or a cleft palate, while eating stale food can also harm foetal development. Most dāis considered that sexual intercourse late in pregnancy can damage the baby's head (as well as causing cervical dilatation). Most women were unwilling to talk about sexual intercourse — we were often roundly sworn at when we enquired — but those who did said that men are more concerned about their own pleasure than the danger to their unborn child.

There are no routine ante-natal consultations initiated by dāis, doctors or ANMs to monitor foetal development. Self-care is the commonest way of checking on progress and gauging foetal growth and presentation. Just occasionally, if the pregnant woman or her sās are anxious about the baby's size, women reported consulting a dāi. Some dāis said they used massage to turn the baby, even in advanced pregnancy. Most of our key informants, however, had no contact with the dāi or with other medical personnel during pregnancy: they averted or dealt with minor problems using domestic remedies.

Illness in pregnancy is an affectation of the rich

> I had great garmī for three-four months. But there is no medicine for that. I just ate thandā food. When the spirit enters the child, the symptoms of garmī decline. *(Gita)*

> I did not vomit but I felt garm and weak. I did not want to do any work. But I had no treatment, either country or doctorī [Western] because I thought that everything would get better when the baby was born. *(Hashmi)*

Another aspect of pregnancy is the health of the pregnant woman herself. Pregnant women in rural Bijnor generally have heavy workloads for which their diets are scarcely adequate. Further, over half the key informants reported unpleasant symptoms or health problems while pregnant. Since pregnancy is not considered a medical condition this is probably an understatement. Symptoms regarded as "little-little troubles" are unlikely to entitle a woman to either rest or medical care. As one woman put it, "illness in pregnancy is an affectation of the rich."

Some women experience symptoms of garmī, including nausea and vomiting (ultī), itchiness (khujlī) in the genital area, white water (safed pānī, a vaginal discharge), burning urine (peshāb-me jalan) and burning chest (sīne-me jalan).[38] Some women continue eating garm items throughout pregnancy without discomfort but those suffering from garmī may seek relief by consuming fruits, milk, or yoghourt (all thandā) and excluding garm items from their diet. But as these beneficial items are often hard to obtain, self-treatment is not always straightforward. Imrana had burning chest and burning urine: she took wild Indian mulberry (considered thandā) and avoided garm foods such as greens and urad and masūr pulses. Others take less wheat-flour bread and eat more rice, which is thandā. Vomiting and nausea are expected to disappear once the spirit has entered the baby, towards the end of the third month. Swollen legs and ankles, back pain, pains in the belly, bleeding, general weakness and night-blindness (rāt-aundhā) were also reported, but these conditions are considered to right themselves only after the woman has given birth and must simply be endured.[39] Endemic diseases (such as malaria, pulmonary tuberculosis, scrofula and dysentery) can also affect a woman, whether pregnant or not. But they do not necessarily entitle her to rest, any more than the other symptoms reported.

This is especially so if the woman is alag or akelī. Promilla, for instance, had night-blindness after the seventh month. Her sās gave no help, so Promilla tried to complete her work before dusk. Her husband, however, did any remaining work after dark. Sabra fared less well: she is on very bad terms with Suleiman's step-mother, his sisters are both married and her sister-in-law (HeBW) had died. Five months before giving birth, Sabra began to suffer chest pains, cough and fever which continued after the baby was born:

> Women should stop lifting heavy loads or making dung-cakes, but I had no leave at all. The girl was born at night and I had worked right into the evening. If I had had someone to help me I would have stopped working, for I wanted to lie down and rest.[40]

Among women who are alag or akelī, only the few who became so ill that they could not leave their bed had all their work taken over, usually by the sās, a nand or the sisters-in-law (HBW). Respite from house-work, in particular, is obtained only if a woman becomes very seriously ill. Fatima had suffered pains in her lower back from the fifth month but continued doing dung-work until about ten days before the birth:

> From the time I began having pains I very much wanted to stop that work, but I continued with it until I could not get off my bed. I am alag and had to continue the work out of necessity.

Only when she was completely incapacitated did her sās and sister-in-law (HyBW), Ghazala, step in to do her house-work and dung-work for her. Tahira is akelī, but when she had malaria and became delirious her house-work was taken over temporarily by her sister-in-law (HyBW) and Taslim. Khurshida is also akelī and said that was why she had to do all her work: if she had had any helper, she would not have continued with her outside-work, particularly the dung-work. Six days before she gave birth, however, she had a fit and was unconscious for two days; her work was then done by Khalil's unmarried cousin (his FBD).[41] Jamila became so ill during her pregnancy in 1984 that by seven months, her body and legs swelled and she could not walk. As she is akelī, she called her own cousin (FZD), who did her work and even carried her to the latrine.[42]

Women suffering from "little-little troubles", and even Promilla, Fatima and Jamila had no medical treatment for their conditions. Basically, pregnant women in Dharmnagri and Jhakri are unlikely to attend the Dharmnagri dispensary or hospitals and private clinics offering Western medicine in Bijnor. They seldom consult vaids or hakīms who offer treatments for pregnant women. Equally, they rarely see a dāi before the delivery, for instance about morning sickness or other recognised hazards of pregnancy. Pregnant women's health problems are mainly dealt with by domestic remedies (such as dietary changes or rest) based on a common stock of knowledge rather than the preserve of experts. Only if these treatments seem to be failing badly is specialist medical advice likely to be sought. Crucially, however, the decision to do so does not rest with pregnant women themselves and, additionally, several features of pregnancy tend to inhibit even more than usual their access to medical care.

The pregnant bahū who claims special entitlement to medical care would set herself above others in her susrāl. Equally, taking action on her own account would leave her open to blame if anything went wrong. Her susrāl kin must first concede that her condition constitutes a medical problem, one, moreover, which it is wise and necessary to treat during pregnancy. Sometimes treatment is considered more harmful to the pregnant woman and her baby than the malady. Many Western medicines are considered garm and could cause the baby to fall, a fear that commonly results in resistance and delay in seeking medical intervention. Promilla's sās, for instance, said that "there is no treatment in pregnancy" for night-blindness. Similarly, Chandresh had fever and a lot of garmī in her chest and belly, but Chet Ram's aunt (FBW) advised against treatment, saying she would recover once the baby was born. Medical consultation may also be delayed or prevented because the pregnant woman feels sharm. Zubeida had stomach pains and a white discharge, but she saw this as insignificant and not worth jeopardising her modesty by consulting a doctor.

Further, as usual, seeking medical care is often inhibited by financial considerations. Many chūlhās cannot afford even a glucose drip or a course of antibiotics, or can do so only by borrowing money or forgoing food. Suleiman had to borrow Rs 1,500 to pay for medicines for the cough which developed when Sabra was pregnant. Even for relatively wealthy chūlhās, expense is an important restraint on obtaining medical care. Maqsudi, for instance, in a middle peasant chūlhā, suffered from griping stomach pains with diarrhoea and blood in the faeces (marore-pechish) for the last three months of her fifth pregnancy. She laughed when asked about treatment: she had some when she was most ill, but "How long should we continue treatment? I was ill for three months!" As Wasila (whose husband is a landless labourer) said, "We do not rush for treatment like our betters do. We get treatment only when the spirit is about to leave us." Nevertheless, several male key informants sanctioned medical treatment when their wives became seriously ill. Sometimes male healers were consulted, often (though not exclusively) for illnesses which were not considered directly connected with their pregnancy, such as fevers and coughs. Tahira, in a landless chūlhā, was given tablets brought from Bijnor to treat malaria; and Khurshida, in a middle peasant chūlhā, had injections costing Rs 150 from the dispensary compounder, who administered them at her home while she was unconscious.

But people often argue that it is pointless to spend money on a condition that will right itself after the birth and for which treatments may anyway be undesirable. In contrast to infertility, then, problems relating to foetal development and maternal health during pregnancy are typified by a slowness to concede that medical intervention might be necessary. Generally, pregnancy and foetal development are considered most appropriately dealt with by domestic remedies and careful avoiding action, with the support of amulets to protect against evil influences. In combination with the lack of outreach and very narrow brief of the government ante-natal services, such perceptions mean that there is no procedure to guarantee the timely diagnosis of medical problems related to pregnancy. Medical surveillance of pregnancy has many limitations and may be oppressive: but its virtually total absence makes any protection that it can afford effectively unavailable to most childbearing women in rural Bijnor.[43]

Disputed claims to illness

Sometimes a pregnant bahū's condition becomes serious yet her susrāl kin refrain from seeking medical care. Normally, a married woman's parents have only limited and contested rights to intervene on her behalf in her susrāl. None the less, during our research, a few tussles erupted between women's susrāl kin, especially the sās, and their natal kin over the custody and care of the pregnant woman. That parents intervene when their daughter is pregnant reflects the seriousness with which they view conditions that sometimes develop and remain untreated. News continues to pass between a woman's susrāl and her natal village. If she becomes seriously ill, her parents will probably be alerted by her brothers or her husband. Parents generally consider that their daughters will receive adequate food and appropriate medical care and convalescence only when they are in their natal village. A pregnant bahū's parents might even insist that she is given medical treatment at their own cost. But such assertive interventions breach the norm that they should remain marginal to their daughter's pregnancy, and they may be resisted by their daughter's in-laws.

During her first pregnancy, Pushpa was sājhe with her sās and Omvati, but on bad terms with them. Pushpa and Punni would have liked to become alag, but Omvati would not let this happen. As she said:

Punni and Pushpa would like to be alag from me and our sās, but Pushpa's first pregnancy is nearly full-term. If they went alag that would be their choice, but the whole village would criticise, saying that we have not even helped her through one pregnancy. That is why we have prevented them from going alag. Maybe they will do so after the baby is born.

By the seventh month, Pushpa was very weak. She had griping abdominal pains and began to lose blood in the faeces. She was eventually allowed to rest, though her sās accused her of slacking and making excuses. Her sās sanctioned some treatment, but that was abandoned when she did not recover. Punni had no cash of his own to pay for further medical care, so he reported the situation to Pushpa's parents. Pushpa's mother visited Dharmnagri, saw the seriousness of the situation and had Pushpa admitted to hospital in Bijnor. Apart from Punni, no one from her susrāl visited her in hospital. Punni's mother refused to pay for medicines, saying that whoever had decided to take Pushpa to hospital should pay for her treatment. Punni insisted on establishing a separate chūlhā shortly after Pushpa gave birth, precisely because he could not care for Pushpa properly while still sājhe.

Even if the pregnant woman is alag, the sās can exercise her sway. In 1985, during her sixth pregnancy, Maqsudi experienced severe swelling in her legs and body and could hardly move; Mansur was also ill at the time. Maqsudi's mother took her to her maikā so that she could rest, but shortly afterwards Maqsudi was retrieved by her sās, who commented:

Maqsudi's mother says that Maqsudi should deliver in her maikā not in Jhakri. She says that if Maqsudi dies, they will bury her there — and if she lives, they will send her back where she belongs. I know that if she dies here, her mother would rip open my plait [abuse me] and blame me for failing to get proper treatment. But Maqsudi has this trouble every time she is pregnant and we always get her treated. And if we allowed her to deliver in her maikā, her mother would soon complain about the money they have to spend. She would accuse us of refusing to keep Maqsudi with us only because Mansur is having treatment himself. That way women begin to gossip. That is why I brought Maqsudi back here.

Poverty, inadequate diets and women's heavy work burdens are compounded by several factors that militate against a pregnant woman's access to medical care if problems arise. Medical provision for pregnancy is sparse. Moreover, local definitions of pregnancy as a condition not normally needing medical care, coupled with constraints of time and money mean that treatment is not necessarily sought even if the problem is serious. Despite cultural ideals for diet and rest during pregnancy, articulated in terms of maternal and foetal well-being, despite the sharm of having a drum or pitcher strapped on the belly, in practice pregnancy is normalised. Unless a pregnant woman becomes seriously incapacitated, she is locked into the domestic politics of her susrāl, with even less support than usual from her natal kin. She is expected to continue her daily life as normally as possible, right up to the onset of labour.

Making dung-cakes

5. Women's Affliction

If I feel too much sharm to visit my maikā when I am pregnant, don't you think it would be even worse to give birth there? *(Imrana)*

My sās decides which dāi to call. What say do I have in this? *(Omvati)*

I didn't call the dāi during my pregnancy so I don't think she would have known about me until she was called for the delivery. *(Najma)*

No dāi knows anything about treatments. Enough! The baby's born so cut the cord! Dāis aren't able to do anything else. *(Maya's sās)*

Labouring women's experiences generally approximate to the archetypal account we gave of Muni's delivery.[1] Women in rural Bijnor, whether Hindu or Muslim, give birth in similar physical and social settings. The social composition of their chūlhā has little influence on who attends the birth. Even the chūlhā's economic position usually has no bearing, for home births entail little expenditure. Typically, a woman's labour is conducted like those of other women nearby and like others in her own childbearing career. For the most part, variations relate to lengths of labour, degrees of discomfort, and the differential deployment of remedies, rather than to women's differing social locations.

But it would be wrong to conclude that the relative uniformity of women's childbirth experiences amounts to naturalness. Of all the activities discussed in this book, giving birth might seem the most detached from the social world outside the labouring woman's home. Being in labour should not be broadcast and, if possible, a woman completes her day's duties before retreating inside to give birth. Certainly, she then experiences an interlude in her routines: her work is in abeyance, she does not take normal meals and her small children are cared for by another woman or an older child. Her home, lit by a flickering oil lamp or candle, with women coming in and out, is mundane compared with medicalised hospital settings in the West. Indeed, women in Dharmnagri and Jhakri regard their methods of conducting labour as natural and obvious.

As everywhere else, however, childbirth in Bijnor is shot through with socially accepted practices.[2] People's evaluations of the physiological processes involved and the procedures adopted speak volumes about how women are regarded. Childbirth carries heavily loaded meanings. It is even more a sharm-kī-bāt than pregnancy and this influences the acceptable location and attendants for a delivery. Local perceptions of midwifery and of the dāi are bound up with childbirth pollution. Moreover, labour does not always proceed at its own pace but is managed in accord with local views of physiology. The normal delivery cannot be understood except in relation to the social world beyond the labouring woman's home — and a crisis makes this even more obvious.[3] Despite appearances, then, birthing practices in rural Bijnor are interwoven with domestic and agrarian class politics that influence both the evaluation of women and the obstetric care available to them. Unravelling these elements is essential in specifying the conditions of childbirth in rural Bijnor.

Babies should be born where the "work" took place

Babies should be born in the mother's susrāl: only that is honourable. *(Maya)*

What? Are babies born in the mother's maikā! *(Khurshida)*

Babies are always born in the susrāl. What? Would it look good to give birth in the pīhar, in front of the father and brothers? *(Nirmala)*

Pregnant women do not negotiate where they deliver or even consider it debatable. Giving birth in the susrāl home is absolutely taken for granted, by Muslims and Hindus, by rich and poor, and is what the overwhelming majority of women in rural Bijnor do.[4] Some had never heard of any alternative. A woman ought to deliver where she lives, a baby should be born where the work (that is, sexual intercourse) took place. Going to the natal village to deliver is anathema — even if, as women acknowledged, more ease and better care are available there. But comfort is outweighed by sharm. We were sometimes sworn at for even asking about such a topic: "What, susrī, will you ask what happens at night next?"

Women in within-village and ghar-jamāi marriages face particular problems in maintaining this separation from their natal kin. Muslim women in within-village marriages cannot deliver away from their maikā, but they avoid their natal kin. The rule is for the baby to be born "in the house of those people to whom it belongs", in the paternal grandparents' place. For a woman to give birth with her father and brothers nearby would be a sharm-kī-bāt. Mostly, our questions about what happens in ghar-jamāi cases were hypothetical, as women's hesitant and diverse responses reflect. Most thought such women would deliver in their natal village (even though it would be a sharm-kī-bāt), because they lived there. Others said they would probably return to their susrāl if they felt acute sharm with their parents:

Yes, a child could be born in the woman's pīhar. If there is necessity, anything can happen. *(Tarabati)*

If a woman spends every day near her parents, all the sharm would have been abolished anyway. Still, it does not look good to give birth in the maikā. *(Fatima)*

A woman who feels sharm would go back to her susrāl to give birth. Many women do not feel sharm, even though it is a sharm-kī-bāt. *(Bhagirthi)*

In practice, however, women in ghar-jamāi marriages were generally taken to their susrāl late in pregnancy. If not, they gave elaborate explanations, often of being abandoned temporarily in their natal village. Before Maya's fifth delivery, for instance, Mahipal argued with her uncle and stormed off, leaving her in her pīhar. Her father repeatedly asked Mahipal to collect her, but he refused. Only after the birth did Maya go to her susrāl with her sās.

In 1982-3, only two key informants gave birth other than in their susrāl. Rajballa had a hospital delivery because of obstructed labour (see below). Umrao is completely cut off from her susrāl, and gave birth in Jhakri (her maikā): indeed, all Umrao's nine deliveries took place there. These nine plus Maya's one delivery in her pīhar are the only ones out of all the key informants' deliveries (nearly 200) which took place in the mother's natal village. We heard of only a handful of other women who had given birth in their parents' house. One in Jhakri was married to a man whose first wife had died in childbirth; in Dharmnagri, another's previous child had been stillborn. For both, the sharm was counterbalanced by fear of further misfortune.[5]

But even giving birth in the susrāl is not straightforward. Most houses have only one room which can provide the necessary privacy for the delivering woman.[6] Before the onset of labour, pregnant women clear up their possessions, stacking utensils neatly away, dragging steel trunks into a corner by the grain-store, putting other items into the store itself. The floor is swept and the newest quilts and other bedding are cleared away. Giving birth is a defiling event and possessions might be contaminated by childbirth pollution. During labour, a woman wears old clothes and lies on an old bed, so that nothing of value is damaged. She becomes intensely polluting. Moreover, despite covering herself with an old quilt, she undergoes the sharm of being touched and exposed.

Virtually all women in rural Bijnor deliver like this in their susrāl: to give birth anywhere else would be shocking. That people in Dharmnagri and Jhakri regard this as natural and unquestionable should not conceal the essentially social character of their birthing practices.

Attending a Birth

Why would I go to my mother when I have a sās and nand here in my susrāl? *(Urmila)*

99

> My mother came to visit. But she went away when she heard that I was
> having pains, saying that she should not be there at such a time. *(Sabra)*

During labour, most women are with at least a couple of other women who
stay throughout, and others who take turns to support or simply to watch. The
labouring woman's likely attendants are affected by considerations of sharm
and childbirth pollution, accentuating yet further the social construction of
birthing practices.[7]

Normal distancing between a woman and her male susrāl kin is
exaggerated when she is in labour. Childbirth is unsuitable for male
involvement. Her father-in-law and brothers-in-law (HB) would not enter
her house. It is even possible that they will not learn she is in labour, since
they generally spend little time in the domestic area. Occasionally, the
husband needs to fetch something, but he does this quickly, averting his gaze
and remaining aloof. Similarly, it would be unthinkable to call her father and
brothers to her side.

Female natal kin, especially the mother and sister, are also excluded from
the delivery by considerations of sharm. Generally, mothers and daughters
alike regard this as only proper. A woman's mother or sister is not called from
another village, and probably will not realise that her daughter or sister is in
labour. Unmarried girls — such as the labouring woman's nands and
daughters — are excluded, as they should not learn about such sharm-kī-bāt
before marriage. Generally they hover, curious, in the vicinity. Basically, the
delivery is attended by married women from the labouring woman's own
susrāl chūlhā and compound, and from neighbouring ones. Being sājhe
rather than alag or akelī normally differentiates bahūs in their daily work, but
such distinctions are usually overridden during their deliveries. Unless the sās
is dead, she is central (whether sājhe or alag). Otherwise, the sās' position is
probably taken by the labouring woman's sister-in-law (HBW) or her
husband's aunt (HFBW). Occasionally, the woman's married nand is visiting
from her own susrāl, or an older woman may be attended by her bahū or
married daughter.[7] Several women said that barren women are excluded,
although there is no consensus on this. More distantly related women come
and go, the largest crowd being present for the birth itself but quickly drifting
away afterwards.

Unusual residence patterns create awkward problems and exceptional
solutions. A woman in a ghar-jamāi marriage might deliver in her parents'
house, but some women said that her mother and sisters would remain
outside. Others considered the sharm would have evaporated long since and
the mother and married sisters could attend the delivery. One woman's susrāl
had been washed away by the Ganges; perforce, she returned to Dharmnagri,
where her mother attends when she gives birth. In practice, though, most
women in ghar-jamāi marriages give birth in their susrāl. Muslim women
were unanimous that women in within-village marriages should deliver with
their female susrāl kin in attendance, not their mother or sisters. The handful
of cases when a labouring woman's mother was present were all difficult

deliveries of women in within-village marriages (see below).

Occasionally, women from the same natal village are married into the same village. They usually attend each other's deliveries, but as daughters-in-law of their susrāl, not as village "sisters". Exceptionally, women without close female susrāl kin may call their sister. For instance, Chandresh was akelī and Chet Ram is an only son. Shortly before Chandresh gave birth, Chet Ram's youngest sister was married and Chandresh's sister attended the wedding. Her sister, her recently married nand and neighbouring women attended the birth. Umrao is even more unusual: she has lived in Jhakri (her maikā) for years, and she calls her married sister a few weeks before she is due to deliver, for her mother is dead and she has no brothers whose wives could attend her.

Rarely is the labouring woman alone: only if there are no closely related women, if she is socially isolated, or if she goes into such precipitate labour that her sās and neighbours do not realise what is happening. But even women who are alag or akelī are unlikely to be by themselves when they give birth:

Swaleha: Where was the baby born?

Zubeida: In my susrāl — and no one was with me, apart from the dāi.

Patricia: You didn't go to your maikā?

Zubeida: Who goes to their maikā, that I could go too? If I suggested going to get some ease, my husband would beat me. Who is there to help me in Jhakri? But I would feel sharm in my maikā.

Zubeida is on bad terms with her sās and her sister-in-law (HyBW), Wasila. She is one of the tiny number of exceptions who prove the rule that birth is something of a spectacle. Indeed, Zubeida's previous deliveries had both been difficult and were attended by a crowd of neighbours.

Besides being a sharm-kī-bāt, childbirth results in pollution which affects the woman herself and potentially the people around her. Several tasks associated with the delivery are considered defiling-work (ganda kām), and the labouring woman's female susrāl kin are unwilling to perform them. Thus, a dāi is usually present to do these tasks. Often there is only one accessible dāi; if there is a choice, the decision rests with the senior attendant rather than the labouring woman.

In Dharmnagri a Chamar woman attends a few births, but she resists being defined as a dāi.[8] She is Shankar's widowed aunt (FBW), yet she did not attend Tarabati's last delivery and agreed to deliver Shakuntala's baby under duress only because the other dāis who serve Dharmnagri could not be found in time. One of these is a very elderly deaf Chamar in Itawa who is occasionally called by Chamars in Dharmnagri.[9] But most women in Dharmnagri rely on a Muslim Julaha widow from Chandpuri. Without any training, she replaced a Chamar dāi from the same village who had served Chandpuri and Dharmnagri until she died. The Chandpuri Muslim dāi estimates that she attends about 20 births a year, and this enables her to supplement her income from herding other people's goats. Until a few years ago, a dāi lived in Jhakri but we were told that her brother took her away when she went mad. Since then, Jhakri women have called on two married Muslim Qasai dāis from Qaziwala.[10] They received some initiation by the sās of one of them, and have both also received government training. They serve a cluster of villages, including Jhakri, and each delivers between 70 and 100 babies a year. They say this is less than previously as they are being undercut by untrained dāis. Twice during our research a Qaziwala dāi had attended a birth in Jhakri and was immediately sought out by women from another compound to attend a second one: Latifan delivered shortly after Wasila, and Jamila after a Julaha woman. In villages with a resident dāi, women need not rely on men's greater mobility beyond the village and can fetch the dāi themselves, even at night. Otherwise, a man — often not the labouring woman's husband because he feels sharm — is sent to fetch the dāi on a bicycle.[11]

Labour management

Radha: Tell me about Pushpa's delivery. Did she make a lot of noise?
Omvati: She certainly did — but we told her to be quiet because all the men of the house were sitting outside. Punni told me that if Pushpa made too much noise and we hit her he would say nothing. But I didn't hit her, I just told her off.
Santosh: When the baby was born it fell on to the floor!
Radha: How did that happen?
Santosh: Our sās doesn't like Pushpa, so she gave her a really old bed to give birth on, and the baby fell through the holes in the stringing!

In rural Bijnor, sharm and pollution are just two elements of local understandings of birth that affect its social and physical setting. Women's labours are also monitored and (when deemed necessary) managed. Childbirth does not proceed naturally or without human intervention.

Monitoring progress

By the end of pregnancy, the accumulated menstrual blood has caused a build up of such garmī that uterine contractions are triggered and the mouth of the uterus opens. Contractions are essential and must be frequent and strong enough to expel the baby. Labour is called taklīf (affliction, distress, trouble) and dard, the term for contractions, applies to pain in general. Initially, the pains are probably light and easily endured (halkā). As labour proceeds, the pains are described as tez, connoting their sharpness, strength, swiftness and piercing quality shortly before a baby is born. The length of labour is roughly estimated in relation to daily routines of mealtimes, daybreak or sunset, and women describe very varied experiences. A few had sporadic light pains for several days during which they continued working, though often stopped eating, before severe pains lasting between about two and seven hours.

Others had light pains beginning in late afternoon which gradually intensified until the baby was born before the following dawn. A few babies were born precipitately after only a couple of hours, while yet other women reported intense pains for two days or more.

When severe pains begin, the labouring woman lies covered by an old quilt on the bed designated for the delivery. Her head is raised with a pillow, her knees bent and her heels pressed against the sides of the bed. During pains, an attending woman squats behind her on the bedhead and supports her shoulders, while another may squat on the foot of the bed keeping her bent legs upright. The women gauge whether the pains are amplifying or not, whether they are frequent and intense enough, or whether they are easing off. How does this labour compare with the woman's previous ones? Is she experiencing much greater discomfort than usual?

Only once the pains are such that the labour seems well established does the labouring woman's senior attendant summon the dāi who, on arrival, takes her station squatting on the foot of the bed. The other attendants might already have felt the labouring woman's belly to assess the baby's presentation, ascertain that it is still moving, and check the strength of the pains. This the dāi does too. But she has no instruments, nor does she shave the labouring woman's pubic hair, perform an enema or wash either herself or the labouring woman, for (women say) cleansing (safāi) takes place only after a birth.[12] Yet the dāi's arrival does presage some new developments. Touching the labouring woman's genitals and inserting a hand inside her body is both a sharm-kī-bāt and defiling-work. Other women would be appalled to do this: their nearest approach is their frequent usage of "chūt" and "bhosrī" (vulva) in verbal abuse. The dāi keeps the labouring woman concealed under the quilt and uses her left hand, the inauspicious hand appropriate for such tasks.[13] The internal examination allows her to assess cervical dilatation, check that the baby's head is engaging properly and that the vagina is not so dry that the baby's transit will be difficult. The dāi's information is added to the general discussion about how the labour is progressing.

Country methods of accelerating labour

Some women crouch on bricks as that makes them stronger and the baby can be born faster. Other women stay on their bed and I hold their legs and push their heels against their buttocks. That way the woman gets strength and the mouth of the uterus opens quickly. *(dāi)*

If the woman has weak pains, I suggest that she takes hot milk or tea. Opening locks and loosening her plait can also speed the delivery. *(dāi)*

Dāis say that birth is imminent when the cervix is dilated and the woman is having severe pains. But they expect labour to be lengthy if there are severe pains without cervical dilatation, or dilatation but an easing off of pains. In such cases, a wide range of domestic or country remedies can be called on to accelerate labour, or in local terms "to amplify the pains" (dard barhānā).

One dāi said some Hindu families call a pandit (Hindu priest) to say prayers, and some Muslims send money to the mosque or ask a Hāfyz Qu'rān (person who has memorised the Qu'rān Sharif) to pray over gur which the labouring woman then eats. None of our key informants had this done, but several had amulets retied during labour. Others reported having grain and a small amount of money (generally one-and-a-quarter rupees) in a metal sieve circled around their head, and placed under the bedhead.[14] The cash and grain absorb the inauspiciousness which may be slowing the labour, and this is later transferred to the dāi. Balls of gur may also be circled round the labouring woman's head and placed under the bedhead. Putting a small sickle under the bedhead is also regarded as beneficial.[15] Parts of the labouring woman's environment may be opened to encourage her cervix to release the baby. Her plait may be undone, for loose hair is a potent symbol of sexual garmī and associated with the opening of the cervix during intercourse.[16] Lids may be lifted off earthen braziers (barosī), and the grain-store and trunks unpadlocked, especially if the woman put something inside them while pregnant.

Altering the labouring woman's position is another tactic. Some dāis said the woman herself decides what is most comfortable. Others are more inclined to intervene, to suggest the woman adopts either a prone or upright position. Some dāis consider that lying down with the knees held up by the dāi and the heels pressed against the buttocks is sufficient to speed dilatation, especially if an attending woman increases the force by pressing down on the woman's belly during pains. Other dāis said the woman should be raised so that the baby's head presses more firmly against the cervix. Thus, the legs at the head of the bed may be lifted on to a pair of bricks or the woman may walk around for a while inside her house.[17] Several dāis believed the most effective way to speed the delivery is to have the woman "underneath" (nīche), that is, squatting beside the bed, supported by the dāi and with her feet placed slightly apart on a pair of bricks: the woman (they say) gets greater strength to push and the baby shifts forward away from the lower gut where it is believed to be in danger of becoming stuck. During their last deliveries, two-thirds of the key informants were lying down under a quilt when they gave birth. Most had been in that position throughout labour, though a few had squatted on bricks briefly before lying down again. Several claimed that babies are not born underneath, for not only is the woman exposed but squatting encourages her to defaecate. Nevertheless, one-third of the key informants were squatting on bricks for the birth and felt the delivery had been speeded.[18]

If pains become less rapid and intense, women say they have become thandā. To avert this, the labouring woman is warmly wrapped up. No heavily pregnant woman ought to be present in case she makes the pains thandā by drawing the garmī into herself. If such precautions fail to prevent the labour from slowing, steps are taken to make the pains garm again. Occasionally, the dāi is asked to insert a vaginal pessary: the dāi who serves Dharmnagri advises soaking cotton wool in ghī or in juice extracted from the leaves of a plant called kukar-chandi to stimulate pains, help the cervix dilate and also make the birth easier by moistening the vagina. But a labouring woman is more commonly given garm foods. In wealthy households, the attending women prepare warm milk with local almonds, hot milky tea, or (uncommonly) hot milk with ghī, eggs broken into hot milk, large dried grapes, or gruel made from a garm ingredient, such as barley or urad-kī-dāl (a kind of pulse). Generally, however, sugar-water (gur-kā-pānī, hot water sweetened with gur) or hot water with ajwain (medicinal seeds) are used to reactivate pains.[19] A few women had protracted light pains and consumed only tea with gur for several days before the birth. Some refused sweet infusions in favour of hot water because the sweetness nauseated them; a few, indeed, reported vomiting in labour, a sign of excessive garmī.

During one-third of the key informants' last deliveries, no domestic remedies were deployed either because their labour was deemed to be progressing satisfactorily, because their baby was born before any remedy was given or because there were no suitable ingredients available. Another one-third reported garm decoctions of one kind or another. One-fifth had nothing to eat but just squatted to help the delivery, and the remainder used a combination of techniques.

> I don't know any pain which compares with the pain of giving birth. *(Wasila)*

> If the woman is having severe pains I do not give anything to make them less. Only by having pains quickly does the baby come soon. *(dāi)*

> The pain of having a baby is such that if I think about it I don't want any more children. *(Ruxana)*

There are no remedies for reducing the pain that women experience. Indeed, intense pains are thought necessary to ensure a speedy delivery. Women suffering great affliction are criticised for shamelessness if they make a noise audible to people outside.[20] They may be told to push as if they were defaecating soon after the strong pains begin. Women in labour should "endure the pains" (dard khāo) rather than "taking too much additional air". They should "swallow back their breath" and are asked, "How can a baby be born without pains?" They should just "accept the pains, calling on God's name".

Childbirth pollution

> Of course we must call a dāi, for none of us can cut the cord. *(Omvati's sās)*

> The cord is cut only after the placenta is delivered. Otherwise they could go back inside the woman's tubes and the poison could spread and kill her. *(dāi)*

During labour the dāi plays a supportive role and may also perform internal examinations and mop up any faeces, vomit and the waters, tasks too defiling for the labouring woman's susrāl kin. After the birth, the dāi's defiling-work begins in earnest. During pregnancy, the mother has nurtured the foetus with menstrual blood. At the very moment of transition to motherhood, she loses some of this blood, which has accumulated over the months and is even more polluting than normal menstrual blood. Childbirth pollution is the most severe pollution of all, far greater than menstruation, sexual intercourse, defaecation or death. Consequently, touching the amniotic sac, placenta and umbilical cord — known collectively as pindī or lump — and delivering the baby, cutting the cord and cleaning up the blood are considered the most disgusting of tasks. Without a daî, the new mother's attendants would face a quandary.[21]

As the baby is born (paidā honā) or takes birth (janam lenā), the dāi holds its head and eases it on to the bed or the floor. If necessary, she unwraps the cord from around it. Then she concentrates on the jachā (new mother). She presses the jachā's belly and tells her to bear down. If the placenta is slow to deliver, she may massage her belly. Half the dāis said they simultaneously insert their other hand into the vagina and tug the cord robustly, but the rest said this causes sepsis. Only after the placenta has delivered does the dāi cut the cord, so that the poison in the placenta cannot spread through the jachā's body. In twin births, we were told, the first baby's cord is not cut until both babies and placentas have delivered, even if this entails some hours' wait.

Once the danger to the jachā is removed, the dāi rubs her fingers along the cord to squeeze blood towards the baby. She ties the cord about five centimetres from the navel using sewing thread. The few dāis with government training have been given a delivery kit which includes scissors for cutting the cord but several (including the two who serve Jhakri) said their clients often prefer some other instrument. In Jhakri, after the key informants' last deliveries, one-third of the cords were cut with scissors, another third using a razor blade and the rest with a sharpened piece of reed from their thatched roof. In Dharmnagri, probably because their dāi has not been trained, scissors are not used, and blades and reeds are used equally. In three deliveries, a penknife was used. Dāis say that sickles and penknives were more widely used but blades and reeds became popular when people began to fear neonatal tetanus. Whatever the instrument, any effort to sterilise it is uncommon.[22]

Hindu practice differs from that of Muslims if a woman delivers without a dāi present, for example, when the labour was precipitate or the dāi could not be found in time. Hindus invariably wait for the dāi to arrive and cut the cord. Lakshmi, for instance, has no sās or sister-in-law (HBW).[23] When her labour started, she continued working and told no one, and was totally alone when the baby was born. She was found by a neighbour who massaged her until the placenta delivered and then helped her on to the bed. But neither woman cut the cord: the neighbour sent Lalit to fetch the dāi, who arrived over an hour later. Most of the Muslim key informants were attended by a dāi who cut the cord. But Muslims do not necessarily leave the cord uncut if the baby is born before the dāi arrives. In Jhakri a landless Faqir woman will cut cords and is paid if she does so. Three other women — Ahmad's mother, Nisar's aunt (FBW), and Riasat's aunt (FBW) — will cut cords, but only if no dāi is present.[24] They are not paid and are not considered dāis. Bilquis, Hashmi and Najma all reported that the dāi had arrived after the cord was cut. On the other hand, when Qudsia's last baby was born, much of the cleaning up was done by Nisar's aunt but Qudsia said that the dāi had the right to cut the cord and be paid. Although a penknife had been washed in hot water and cleaned in the fire, the dāi cut the cord with scissors. Even more extraordinarily, Usman considers his earnings as a labourer insufficient to warrant even calling a dāi: together with Umrao's sister, he manages Umrao's deliveries. After her last one, he held a lighted match, while Umrao's sister held the cord which he cut with a penknife.[25]

Generally, the dāi also handles the placenta and cleans the floor. She chips away the stained portions of the dried mud and puts the pieces into an old basket, along with the placenta and any rags she used to mop up. She then repairs the broken floor with fresh mud and diluted cattle-dung. In Jhakri, all placentas are buried in the chūlhā's midden pit on the village outskirts, for a placenta is "not something to be buried inside". It must be buried carefully so that it cannot be unearthed and magic practised on it, possibly by a barren woman who wishes to conceive and harms the baby in the process. Its burial may be supervised by the jachā's sās or even performed by her for safety's sake. Among Hindus practice is more varied. Caste Hindus generally ask the dāi to bury placentas inside the house to preclude the danger of magic.[26] A small pit is dug in the floor, the placenta buried and a fire lit on top to ward off evil. Some said that a boy's placenta is buried by the mother's bedhead while a girl's is buried by the foot (as befits their relative status). Others said that boys' placentas are buried inside, but those of girls are buried outside, since magic is unlikely to be practised on them. Some said that only the first-born's placenta is buried inside. Several dāis said that Caste Hindus are now more likely than previously to bury the placenta in the midden, but this was not commonplace in Dharmnagri. After the Caste Hindu key informants' last deliveries, only two placentas were buried in the midden, both of girls who had older siblings. The remainder were buried inside, irrespective of the baby's sex and the jachā's parity. On the other hand, half the Harijans used their midden and half made a pit inside the house. Whatever the dāi's ethnicity, she follows her clients' practice when dealing with placentas.

Childbearing is necessary for a bahū, but also profoundly polluting, and women regard their bodily functions with distaste. Dāis perform defiling-work for which there is a demand: someone must deal with childbirth pollution by cutting the cord and removing the placenta. But, while all women who give birth are subject to defilement, only a few are obliged to earn their keep by doing defiling-work for other people.

Midwives or menials?

> Since the Chamar dāi died, my sās has called the Julaha dāi from
> Chandpuri for all her bahūs. The choice of the dāi is according to her
> wishes. *(Pushpa)*

> The dāi did not know that I was due to deliver. She had not visited while
> I was pregnant. *(Asghari)*

> Generally, women do not call me before the labour has started. *(dāi)*

Monitoring of labours and interventions during unduly slow ones indicate
that childbirth in Dharmnagri and Jhakri is a socially managed process. But
the labouring woman plays little part in the discussions about her labour's
progress and any interventions. She might refuse a chosen treatment,
whether hot sugar-water or squatting on bricks, but management of the
labour is not in her own hands. Usually, the labouring woman's sās (or other
senior attendant) calls the dāi only once she considers labour to be well
established. Before that she may have examined the labouring woman's belly
or tried to hasten the delivery through various domestic remedies. These
interventions are not esoteric knowledge known solely to the dāi or even the
sās: they constitute a familiar repertoire. Most labouring women know about
them and have seen others being similarly treated; any of the attending
women may suggest them and can cite cases where they seemed beneficial.[27]
After the dāi's arrival, the senior attendant remains central in the conduct
of the delivery, in decisions about whether it should be accelerated, about the
labouring woman's position, and so on. Certainly, the dāi voices her opinion
and her information about cervical dilatation may be important. But her
suggestions are not always heeded and she does her work under the watchful
(and sometimes critical) eye of the other women. Even after the birth, the
senior attendant reserves the bulk of decision-making for herself — and
expects the dāi to carry out tasks under her direction. She provides the thread
for tying the cord, but the dāi ties it; she decides what the cord should be cut
with — occasionally even rejecting the dāi's suggestion — but leaves the dāi to
do the job; and she instructs the dāi about burying the placenta.
Consequently, it is inappropriate to regard the dāi as an expert midwife in the
contemporary Western sense. Even in the absence of medically trained
personnel, the dāi does not have overriding control over the management of
deliveries. Nor is she a sisterly and supportive equal. Rather, she is a low
status menial necessary for removing defilement, and her lowly status is
reflected in several ways.[28]
Most Hindu dāis are Harijans (formerly Untouchable), who often also
perform other forms of defiling-work and whose presence is generally
anathema to Caste Hindus (and many Muslims as well). Moreover, Muslim
and Hindu women rarely mix socially, and many Caste Hindus regard
Muslims as little better than Harijans, because of their dietary practices.
Harijan and Muslim dāis, then, start with grave social disadvantages in
relation to most of their clients. The pre-existing social distance between
Caste Hindus and a Harijan or Muslim woman is exaggerated if she also does

the work of a dāi, although matters may be less stark for a Harijan dāi serving Harijans, or a Muslim dāi amongst Muslims. Nevertheless, by virtue of performing their work, most dāis become polluted, some even in the eyes of their own relatives. This is echoed in their clients' behaviour. Many people admit a dāi to their home only for the delivery and some subsequent cleansing work. Our key informants often commented spontaneously that the dāi would have been unaware that they were pregnant. Dāis themselves say their work begins only when the woman is in labour:

> I go at the time of delivery, not before. If the baby is being born correctly then I deliver it and cut the cord. My work is after the baby is born, not before. *(dāi)*

Once the jachā has a purifying bath, physical contact between her and the dāi probably ceases (unless they are related). The dāi is tainted by handling childbirth pollution and she is generally unwelcome at other times. The Qaziwala dāis, for instance, visit Jhakri freely but their attempts to find out if women are pregnant are often resented.[29]

After the birth, the dāi's payments further underline her inferiority in her clients' eyes.[30] She may be expected to accept the cash used to divert misfortune from the labouring woman and risk being affected by the bad luck herself. She is paid in instalments during the days following the birth for cutting the cord (nāl-kātāi), burying the placenta (pindī-dabāi), and bathing the jachā (jachā-nehlāi), all payments specifically for the removal of pollution. She receives nothing if the baby is stillborn. In such an event, Hindus do not have the baby's cord cut and the baby and placenta are buried together in the fields by a member of the family. Muslims expect the cord of a stillborn baby to be cut, but they themselves bury the placenta in the midden and the baby in the graveyard. Similarly, the dāi is not paid for advice or if she withdraws from a case before the birth. Few dāis receive customary payments from their clients, for example of grain after harvests or at the marriages of people they delivered.[31] The total payments of between Rs 15 and Rs 30 plus some kilograms of grain and gur and possibly some old clothing are often insufficient to support them without other sources of income. Thus the dāi's bargaining position is weak. Dāis often reported acrimonious negotiations over their pay. Indeed, after each delivery Patricia attended in Dharmnagri and Jhakri, the dāi was abused and sworn at for claiming "unreasonable" fees and had to accept less than she had originally requested. Several dāis reported being promised payments which were never fulfilled because they could not enforce their claims.

Safety and risks

Since childbirth is subject to social definitions that make working as a dāi undesirable, it is not surprising that women who become dāis do not claim competence to deal with complicated cases. Generally, home deliveries are managed by women who cannot monitor progress in detail. Although dāis have probably attended more deliveries than other women, they have no obstetric equipment (apart from those who use scissors to cut the cord), though they do examine the woman, internally and externally. Dāis fully understand the importance of recognising complications. Abnormal presentations protract labour, endangering both mother and child, so dāis try to assess if the baby is straight and correctly positioned (sīdhā, that is, with the head engaging on the cervix), inverted (ultā, that is, a footling breech) or askew and obstructed (ārā, terhā, that is, transverse).[32] Several dāis claimed to be able to turn a baby, even during labour. Others said that this was impossible during late pregnancy (let alone labour) but that they might try to deliver a footling breech presentation, though not a transverse one. Dāis also recognise the dangers if contractions wane and the baby stops moving or (in their terms) the woman's belly becomes thandā. But they have no foetal trumpets or other means of detecting foetal distress, except feeling the woman's belly. Equally, dāis themselves said they cannot remedy such problems as haemorrhage or failure of cervical dilatation, arrest premature labours, induce labour in an over-long pregnancy, or cope with unusual conditions such as prolapsed cords and placenta praevia.

> A dāi does nothing at all. She just cuts the cord and washes the jachā. *(Hashmi)*

> If the baby in the belly is fine and the woman is not troubled, then I deliver the baby and cut the cord. Enough! *(dāi)*

Altogether, dāis have very modest perceptions of their capabilities, as do their clients. Dāis said they like to deal only with normal presentations, their clients said that dāis are just cord-cutters (nāl-kātne-wālī). If a dāi diagnoses a problem, she is likely to withdraw from the case. Dāis generally claimed they had never had serious mishaps for that very reason:

> I have never had a woman die. I examine the woman first and judge if she and the baby are all right. If there is any danger, I say the work is beyond my competence and I cannot deal with the case. *(dāi)*

> In difficult cases, I refuse to put my hand on the woman. I send them to Bijnor. If I accepted such cases and there was trouble afterwards, the woman's people would come after me and might fight or beat me. *(dāi)*

> If the woman's belly is thandā or the cord appears before the baby, I do not put my finger on the woman. I refuse to deal with the case. That is why I have had no problem cases. *(dāi)*

If a dāi predicts a stillbirth, she may hope to avoid blame for any mishap by advising that the labouring woman is taken to hospital:

> One time I was called the placenta was delivered but the baby was still not born. I said they should take the woman to hospital but her husband said they had no money. They begged me to do the work, although I said that mother and baby might both die. I did the work but I was paid nothing as the baby was stillborn. *(dāi)*

Of course, this is not to criticise individual dāis for being unsupportive. Their recruitment to the work generally stems from financial distress and they appreciate that neither their reputation nor livelihood will be enhanced if they are held responsible for maternal or foetal deaths. For the normal delivery — the vast majority of cases — the village dāis suffice. But the way problem deliveries are handled forcefully exposes the limitations in the obstetric care available to labouring women in rural Bijnor, either from dāis or other sources.

There used to be no treatment for a woman having trouble during delivery. She might be in labour for eight or ten days without being given anything. Often the woman's lips and hands would go blue with clutching the bed so tightly. There are country medicines, but there is no hakīm in this village. Everyone just lived by God's grace. *(dāi)*

If the baby is askew I first try to straighten it. But if I can't, nowadays I send the woman to Bijnor. In the days when there were no hospitals, it was up to God's command whether the woman and baby lived or died. *(dāi)*

But now, there are other possibilities. Since about 1960, Western medicine has become increasingly accessible, even to villagers, through the government health services and independent (often untrained) private practitioners. Nowadays, the dāi may call in a medical practitioner or recommend that the labouring woman goes to hospital. But this does not necessarily improve the conditions of childbirth.

Labour acceleration using Western methods

There are country methods for amplifying the pains, but they only work slowly-slowly. Women these days want to escape the affliction quickly, so I myself may suggest that they have an injection from the doctor. *(dāi)*

Until recently, we just used country methods to amplify the pains and babies were born by God's command. But now there are these new injections. *(dāi)*

In the past, if labour seemed protracted, domestic remedies (such as garm food) would initially be tried, but if these failed, dāis occasionally sent for labour-accelerating remedies from local male practitioners, hakīms or vaids. An important change has recently taken place, which affected about 15% of the women interviewed in our 1982 survey. If the pains diminish or the labouring woman is in extreme pain for a long while, a medical practitioner may be called to administer an intramuscular injection of synthetic oxytocin.[33] Most of the dāis also call a practitioner to give an injection if the placenta does not deliver quickly after the baby is born. The practitioners are almost always men, from a variety of backgrounds. In Dharmnagri and Jhakri, these were the trained government dispensary compounder working privately and charging Rs 15-25 per injection, some private Registered Medical Practitioners from Begawala, and an untrained Dharmnagri Chamar who was establishing a reputation for medical work among the Harijans. Only two of the dāis we interviewed claimed to give injections themselves, one having been instructed by her medical practitioner husband. Occasionally, the ANM gives an injection to a labouring woman.

Several dāis said that women are no longer prepared to tolerate excessively painful or protracted labour and ask for labour acceleration by oxytocin rather than await the gradual effects of domestic remedies. Women regard these injections as very beneficial, since they give strength as well as accelerate the labour. The local term for the injections (dard barhānā) means to amplify the pains. Certainly, the effects are often rapid and dramatic. Over one-third of the Dharmnagri key informants had injections during their 1982-3 deliveries, administered by the compounder or the Chamar practitioner. Some had more than one injection, sometimes from more than one practitioner without the other's knowledge. None of the Jhakri key informants had injections, though they have become popular there since 1983, administered by the compounder or a private Muslim practitioner from Begawala. The woman herself may ask for an injection even early on in labour, though this is not always agreed to. Equally, some women felt that the dāi who serves Dharmnagri often advises an injection when it is unnecessary, and sometimes the baby is born naturally within minutes of her saying the delivery would be protracted without an injection. Women in their first labour were sometimes refused injections by their attending women, on the grounds that it would prevent them delivering without an injection in future.

The popularity of these injections could hardly be more ironic. Male practitioners display no inhibition about administering them, relying simply on the dāi's assessment of cervical dilatation and the baby's presentation. The injection of a standard dose of oxytocin (rather than a steady monitored intravenous drip) results in acute discomfort from the almost instantly amplified pains. Moreover, there are risks of rupturing the uterus, damaging the cervix or causing severe foetal distress and after-pains. Such is Western medicine's main contribution to obstetric care in rural Bijnor — the use of powerful drugs obtained over the counter without either prescription or evidence of medical competence by practitioners who administer them to labouring women whom they do not examine. This development is hardly likely to enhance either the ease or well-being of women undergoing home deliveries.

Let God send no one to hospital
During an interview with a dāi in a neighbouring village, the following dialogue encapsulated the views of village woman about giving birth in hospital:

> **One woman:** Why are you asking all these questions? Don't babies get born in your country?

Swaleha: In her country babies are born in hospital and the treatment is free. There are no dāis. That's why she's asking.
Woman: That's right. Here no matter how much trouble a woman has, she stays at home. Those people who can't pay a lot of money, their woman or child will die, or they won't be looked after properly. That's all there is to it. Only those with money can go to hospital.
Another woman: Let God send no one to hospital.
Patricia: But there used to be few treatments. Now there are hospitals. Hasn't that made any difference to you?
First woman: There is no real difference. Village people have not benefited from these hospitals, even the government ones. We can't afford to pay — there might as well be no hospitals.

Local hospitals and clinics would be incapable of meeting a greater demand for hospital deliveries.[34] But in rural Bijnor, a hospital delivery is rarely actively sought — rather it is avoided. Ideally, a baby should be born in its father's home, where the appropriate celebrations and gift-exchanges can be conducted after the birth.[35] But that is only one reason among many why hospital deliveries are undesirable. For most people, guaranteeing careful treatment is prohibitively expensive, even in government hospitals and clinics where the bed and medical advice are nominally free:

Even in the old days, people with money went to doctors if there was trouble. But poor people could not then and cannot now. If the dāi cannot deal with the case, when there is no money what can anyone do? Whether she lives or dies, the woman remains at home, for the doctor would ask more money than they could give.

Medicines have to be bought from local pharmacies; hospital staff extort cash gifts. The cost can easily exceed Rs 1,000, three or four months salary for a labourer and a sum which even rich peasants are unlikely to have in ready cash. Private clinics may charge more but at least state their prices in advance. After ten days in labour, Hashmi and Imrana's nand had a private clinic delivery by Caesarian section: the cost of that, eleven bottles of intravenous glucose and the stay in the clinic was about Rs 2,500, some ten months income for a labourer.

In hospital, doctors send everyone you know away. I was terrified when I went for a check-up, seeing all those instruments, so I did not want to be admitted. *(Bhagirthi)*

Even for such people as Bhagirthi, for whom the expense is less problematic, hospitals are frightening places, full of strange people and even stranger equipment. Other women are scared to accompany a labouring woman to hospital, where they would anyway be excluded from the labour room. Once alone, women fear what might happen. Pain and rude treatment aside, the examinations and treatments entailed in hospital deliveries may destroy a woman's sharm.[36] Women's responses to Patricia's accounts of ante-natal and obstetric care in Britain ranged from astonishment to

113

vehement disapproval. One woman from Jhakri told us about a Hindu woman from Dharmnagri whose forceps delivery was conducted by a former male compounder in the dispensary. Apparently, when the Jhakri men heard of this, they told their wives: "You must tolerate the affliction, even if you die, but you must not break seclusion [purdah mat tornā]."

Not surprisingly, then, women go to hospital only in extremis. Local dāis claim to refer difficult cases to hospital, but the accounts of women in Dharmnagri and Jhakri indicate that many women undergo home deliveries even when their condition is serious. For instance, Mansur's sister, who is married within Jhakri, described her first delivery, when the baby was transverse. Her sās called the dāi then living in Jhakri, who refused to deliver the baby. A dāi from Qaziwala was called, who considered the case beyond her competence. Finally they called a government dāi from Bijnor. Mansur's mother even joined the throng, though not with everyone's approval:

You must have heard how Mansur's sister had great trouble. Her mother even came in to look. Some people have no sense of sharm. *(Wasila)*

The labour lasted three days. The first two dāis stayed, disclaiming responsibility, with the Qaziwala dāi apparently simply chanting "Allah's command is imminent!", to the labouring woman's annoyance. Even in these circumstances Mansur's sister was not taken to hospital nor even to the dispensary. Eventually, the Bijnor dāi delivered the baby safely.

Those few women who had delivered in hospital were generally admitted only in advanced labour after their attendants had decreed their case an extreme emergency; they generally felt lucky to have escaped with their lives. Of the nearly 200 babies born to the key informants by 1985, only three had been born in hospital. During her third labour, Maqsudi was admitted to hospital unconscious. After four bottles of intravenous glucose, she recovered but stayed in hospital several weeks; her brother paid for the treatment. During her first labour (in her first marriage), Tahira was in labour for a week before being taken to hospital; the baby was born two days later. Medical staff recommended a Caesarian section but her father-in-law forbad an operation: she had several injections, one of which may have sedated her, for she recalls nothing about the delivery. She stayed in hospital over three weeks, and her in-laws paid out over Rs 2,000. Rajballa also had a hospital delivery. Hers was the first labour that Patricia attended. Its exceptional character and our own interventions in it make us hesitant about detailing it here. But it dramatically encapsulates the problems that confront labouring women in rural Bijnor when a crisis occurs — and made us appreciate why they resist going to hospital to deliver.

Rajballa gives birth in hospital

By April 1982, Rajballa was heavily pregnant, her ankles were swelling painfully and she could not work properly. She came to see the ANM with her sās and Rohtash. The ANM gave her short shrift, saying her symptoms were entirely due to the bādī effects of excessive rice consumption. Patricia suspected from Rajballa's appearance that the presentation was transverse but her concern was dismissed by Rajballa's sās. The ANM did an external examination, pronounced everything normal and said Rajballa would soon deliver; Patricia deferred to the medical expert.

Some days later, sporadic pains began, sometimes strong, sometimes stopping altogether. At about nine one evening, Rohtash's younger brother fetched the compounder at the dispensary and Patricia accompanied them to Rajballa's house. Rajballa had been given warm milk to drink, but had vomited it over her clothing and the Chandpuri dāi. The dāi announced that the baby's head was large, though dilatation had proceeded well, so without further ado the compounder injected Rajballa with oxytocin. Within minutes, she was in severe discomfort, with rapid and strong pains. She called out for her mother, for God and for her husband, and screamed that her spirit was escaping from her. The women in the room criticised her for not "enduring the pains", telling her to keep her mouth closed, to push down as if she was trying to defaecate, and not to waste her effort by gasping and making so much noise. If she persisted, she was told, they would leave her alone. Rohtash came in and again she cried in pain. In exasperation he slapped her cheek and told her to be quiet. Their small daughter shrieked hysterically, so he put his arms round Rajballa and helped her on to a pair of bricks beside the bed. He clutched her tightly, making kissing sounds to encourage her, before rejoining his brothers outside.

By midnight, the pains had completely stopped. The dāi again examined Rajballa and (as she wiped her hands on Rajballa's petticoat) pronounced that the cervix was opened, but the baby's head was large and the vagina narrow. She reminded the attending women to open all the padlocks in the house. But still nothing happened, so Rajballa's sās and the dāi agreed to call the compounder again. While he prepared another injection, the dāi told him the baby's head was too large. At Patricia's suggestion he examined Rajballa. Somewhat shaken, he said that the baby's head was at the side, and not engaging on the cervix. Patricia asked if he had not examined Rajballa earlier. "No," he said, "That is woman's work. I just did what the dāi asked. I did not know the head was at the side." Patricia asked if he could deliver the baby, possibly using forceps. He said he had no training for such work and asked if Patricia had any knowledge. The case seemed hopeless.

Patricia suggested taking Rajballa to hospital in Bijnor. The compounder hesitated, saying they would be afraid and especially anxious about the expense. Rohtash came inside to discuss the proposition; he was ready to go, though the women of the family were very reluctant. Rajballa was eventually bundled on to mattresses on the floor of our jeep, and Rohtash, their small daughter, the compounder and sweeper from the dispensary all joined her. But a woman would be needed to care for Rajballa while she was in hospital. Her sās had vanished. Her sisters-in-law (HBW) refused to come — they were too frightened, or could not abandon their responsibilities at home. Patricia prevailed upon Rohtash's sister and her husband to join a poor widowed neighbour who had agreed to help. We reached the government women's hospital in Bijnor shortly before 2 am. Our reception immediately made clear why the women had resisted coming. Several nurses were chatting in the entrance but hardly glanced up when Patricia went inside and explained the situation. The nurses complained about the time and brusquely told Patricia to leave. She repeated that Rajballa was in danger and was told to go elsewhere. Patricia explained once more. One nurse muttered, "These Punjabis even want treatments at night!" In the dull light, Patricia's garb and accent had apparently obscured her origins; but for the urgency, she might have been tempted to adopt the label. Instead, she revealed that she was British and was instantly ushered courteously inside. One nurse asked how we came to be living in an Indian village and was stopped only by Patricia's judicious mention of the District Medical Officer's permission for us to stay in the dispensary. Only then was the doctor summoned and Rajballa taken into the delivery room. Patricia went inside too, but Rajballa's intimidated relatives retreated to the jeep.

Rajballa was hauled on to the delivery table. A nurse put on surgical gloves and performed an internal examination. When the doctor arrived, Patricia was told to leave. A few minutes later, the doctor confirmed that the baby was transverse. As Rajballa was weak and her uterus still in spasm, a Caesarian section would not be possible immediately and Rajballa was given an injection of muscle relaxant. The doctor doubted if there was suitable blood for transfusion in the hospital store and was unwilling to operate without it. She advised us to take Rajballa to Meerut, four hours' drive away, partly along dirt roads.[37] We said Rajballa was in no state for such a journey, so her blood was matched and Rohtash and his sister's husband bought some blood of the correct group. Meanwhile, the doctor had Rajballa connected to a glucose drip.

By 9 am the bystanders had been swelled by our research assistants and the ANM. Inside the labour room the ANM began chiding Rajballa's in-laws for not heeding her advice. "If you had stopped her eating so much rice and brought her for treatment, this would never have happened." Then, as Rajballa began moaning, she turned to her sharply and said, "Be quiet. Keep your mouth closed. Use your breath below. Be quiet. They'll hit you here if you make a noise." "Yes," agreed a nurse, "Is she a goat or a buffalo that she cannot suffer even light pains?" Rajballa weakly asked for water. The nurse refused, saying that one should drink nothing before having an operation. Patricia explained that it was just to dab on Rajballa's lips, and the nurse allowed Swaleha to moisten some gauze and let Rajballa suck on it. The ANM commented, "If she had kept her mouth closed, her lips would not have become dry." And the nurse added, "This woman already has one child, but even so she makes all this noise."

A little later, outside, discussion resumed. Rohtash's sister defended herself from the ANM's criticism by telling Patricia that Rajballa herself was to blame. "Rajballa made her own health bad. When we told her not to eat so much rice, she thought badly of us. She told Rohtash that we were trying to prevent her from eating and that was why we said her swollen ankles were caused by eating so much rice. She is having so much trouble because she did not listen." The ANM herself had a public rebuke from the doctor for giving an injection. She replied, "But I did not give the injection, it was the compounder." "Then you should remain beside your cases," retorted the doctor as she stalked off. "But it was night-time," pleaded the ANM, unheard by the doctor. Aside to Patricia, the ANM justified herself: "You know that I examined Rajballa last week and told them to come to hospital. I told them the baby was transverse and the swelling was dangerous. But these people don't listen. They continued feeding her rice even after I'd told them not to" — a version of events very different from Patricia's notes from the previous week. And so the recriminations continued.

By mid-morning, there were signs of foetal distress and the doctor operated. A healthy son was born. On leaving the operating theatre, the doctor announced to Rohtash, "Your son has been born" (using the least respectful form of address). In gratitude, Rohtash dropped on his knees before her and touched her feet respectfully. Meanwhile, Rajballa was taken (still unconscious) to the post-natal ward, with a glucose drip in place. There were no nurses with her when Patricia and Swaleha arrived there and noticed that the drip was no longer working: blood was seeping back into the catheter. The nurse whom they we summoned detached the tubes from the bottle and blew down the air inlet. Then she tried to reinsert the drip in Rajballa's right arm but could find no veins prominent enough, and eventually found one in the left.

We continued to visit over the following days, usually bringing some of Rohtash's family with us. Soon, Rajballa was sufficiently recovered to take solids again. Her stitches were removed a week after the delivery and a few days later she returned home.

Rajballa's case highlights a number of aspects of the conditions of childbirth in rural Bijnor. Neither the ANM nor the dāi diagnosed the transverse lie of the baby, let alone dealt with it. The injection of synthetic oxytocin by the compounder was clearly especially dangerous in the circumstances. But our criticisms of the domiciliary care she received by no means amount to advocacy of medicalised hospital childbirth, particularly not within the present modes of health service provision. Rajballa's experiences in hospital are salutary illustrations of the problems facing intrepid villagers who take their womenfolk to hospital. Rajballa herself was chided while in labour, and Rohtash — a quietly dignified man in his own home — was reduced to a cringing servility, painful to watch. He and his relatives suffered rudeness and indignities from the hospital staff, who, for instance, in full view of a ward full of onlookers loudly criticised their failure to bring clean clothes and sanitary towels for Rajballa, and dismissively refused to permit the "dirty village habit" of having the baby suck his first drinks from a cotton-wool wick rather than a spoon.[38] Throughout Rajballa's stay in hospital there were problems persuading Rohtash's female relatives to stay to feed and wash Rajballa and the baby. Yet Rohtash and his relatives insisted that the treatment Rajballa received was superior to any they could have imagined if we had not pulled rank and used our twice daily trips to Bijnor to check that her medication was being properly administered. Even the ANM commented that nothing would have been done properly if Rajballa had arrived on a buffalo-cart, but that our jeep had impressed the hospital staff.

Moreover, hospitalisation cost Rohtash large sums of money. A registration fee of Rs 2 was followed by Rs 10 for the blood test, Rs 200 for blood, Rs 36 for each bottle of glucose, Rs 50 for the pre-operative injection and further sums for the other medicines. The ANM commented that bribes would also be needed: the doctor would expect gifts for delivering the baby, the nurses would require persuasion to administer the drugs correctly and on time, and hardly had Rajballa been deposited in the ward but a sweeper asked for money for the cleaning staff, without which the area around Rajballa's bed would have been left uncleaned. This all cost over Rs 1,000. Rohtash's sister's husband — never slow to seize an opportunity — lent the money in exchange for some of Rohtash's land as surety.

While we were chastened by the social costs and financial worries this crisis generated, Rohtash himself was relieved. He had feared being left to rear their daughter without an adult woman's help or (possibly worse) with a second wife who might act in a step-motherly fashion. Further, Rajballa was a bought bride and he could only hope to replace her at similar cost. The outcome could have been worse. He had been able to raise a loan without selling any land (as others might have been compelled to do), and could hope to redeem his mortgaged land in due course.

Mishaps in delivery

Taking a labouring woman to hospital is seen as a last resort to be deferred or preferably avoided, even if the labour seems likely to end in the death of the mother or baby. When we discussed women's access to health care with women in Dharmnagri and Jhakri examples of women who had died were often drawn to our attention. The numbers are small and incomplete. As one man said when we asked about deaths in his family, "The dead are gone." Those we know about are just a selection of cases and refer only to women whose deaths were publicly known to be in the course of childbirth, miscarriage or abortion.[39]

We were told of Kamla's relative, whose entire body became swollen when she was some six months pregnant. Her natal kin took her to a doctor, who said she would survive only if the baby was aborted. He administered garm medicines and injections to induce labour, but she died three days later. Another example was a susrāl relative of Haroon and Irfan's sister, whose baby died in utero at full-term and she herself then died: her susrāl kin could not pay for treatment because this was during the monsoon. We also heard of several recent cases in Dharmnagri and Jhakri themselves. One Hindu woman had five new-born babies die. Towards the end of her sixth pregnancy she had convulsions but recovered after a couple of injections administered by the compounder. Later that day she gave birth but had another fit and died; the baby died three days later. Another bahū in Dharmnagri had three stillborn girls in succession and her parents suggested that she deliver next time in her pīhar: she did so, but both she and the baby died. During 1982, a Harijan woman haemorrhaged during delivery and died a day later, and the same year the bodies of a Hindu man's daughter and her baby were fetched from hospital in Bijnor and brought to Dharmnagri for funeral rites.[40] In Jhakri, Zakir's first wife died in childbirth; Zubeida, his second wife, is her younger sister. Dilruba's oldest nand also died in childbirth, and the husband then married Dilruba's second nand, who had a difficult fourth labour and was eventually delivered by Caesarian section in Bijnor. And Sabra's sister-in-law (HeBW) died in about 1980 during a premature labour precipitated after her husband beat her. Of course, deaths during pregnancy and during or shortly after delivery are but the tip of an iceberg. We had many more accounts (from key informants and others) in which women's lives were probably in jeopardy. Women described labours with heavy bleeding, eclamptic fits, very protracted full-term labours, breech and transverse presentations.

Maternal death, though, is far less common than death of the baby. Our informants do not clearly differentiate a stillbirth (marā-huā bachā) from a baby who "in becoming, died" or "died having taken a couple of breaths". We include all such cases in one category. The 236 ever-married women in Dharmnagri and Jhakri in 1985 had carried a total of 1,210 babies to full-term. Twenty-four were stillborn and 12 more had died instantly. In other words, around one in every 33 full-term deliveries (about 3%), one or two deliveries each year in the two villages, end in a stillbirth or the instant death of the infant. Our numbers are small and some infant births and deaths may have been omitted, so this rate is probably an underestimate.[41]

Stillbirths remain common occurrences. The three Jhakri bahūs married within the village in 1982 all later had stillbirths. Ghazala's sister-in-law (HyBW) had a breech delivery. A second woman's labour began in her seventh month of pregnancy: her sās called the compounder who gave three injections to arrest the labour, but the baby was delivered stillborn a few hours later. In both cases the women's mothers were present at the labour, which was generally (though grudgingly) considered appropriate given the danger to their daughters' lives. The third woman — Liaqat's niece (BD) — had a very difficult delivery in 1983: despite two injections of oxytocin, her pains were protracted and sporadic and after a third injection a stillborn boy was born. In 1984 Latifan also had a stillbirth after a hard labour: she had five injections from the Muslim practitioner from Begawala, then the compounder gave another two, without being informed of the others. Bhagirthi's fifth baby was also stillborn: the baby was healthy but the cord was round its neck. Bhagirthi blames the dāi's incompetence, and called another dāi next time.

In each of these cases there are problems of obstetric management, most glaringly in the misuse of oxytocin injections. Other factors, however, contribute to these high stillbirth rates. As is commonly the case, boys are slightly more likely than girls to be stillborn or to die immediately. First deliveries (especially to small physically immature women) and high-parity deliveries also tend to be more vulnerable than second, third or fourth babies, so women in Dharmnagri and Jhakri are likely to have stillbirths simply because they marry young and have long childbearing careers. But a more important contribution to high stillbirth rates is women's poor nutrition. Most adult women are small, under-nourished and anaemic and bear children whose birth-weights are so low that they are likely to be sickly or stillborn. Women in relatively affluent chūlhās in Dharmnagri and Jhakri seem little better placed in this respect than their poorer sisters. This partly reflects their common positions as bahūs.

Greater availability of ante-natal care, trained birth attendants or hospital deliveries probably could not fully compensate for the effects of gender inequalities in access to food and medical care. But prolapsed cords, breech presentations or slow cervical dilatation cannot be attributed to dietary inadequacies. How such crises are dealt with exposes the institutional limitations in the obstetric care available in rural Bijnor. Fortunately, such dramas are not daily occurrences in Dharmnagri and Jhakri. Most women carry their pregnancies to full-term, most babies present normally, the dāis can usually deal with the delivery satisfactorily and most labours result in a live baby and mother. In the days immediately afterwards, in the jachā's susrāl home, the destinies of the jachā and her baby are still closely bound together. There the jachā's susrāl kin care for them and organise the celebrations that mark the new arrival.

Birth syrup for the new-born

6. A Matter of Celebration

The jachā and baby are inside. As sunset approaches, women spread matting and sacking in the courtyard. Now they have time to celebrate the birth. From neighbouring houses come girls with babies astride their hips, their mothers, and a few bahūs. The courtyard buzzes with anticipation as some 50 women and girls crowd on to the matting. When the Balmiki woman strides in with a large drum hung round her shoulders, they part to give her a central place in the crush.[1] She settles herself cross-legged on the ground, the drum across her knees, and beats out a rhythm. Women beside her suggest a song and they raise their voices. The rest join in, singing lustily:

Nand, mere budhe bel-ke-kān,
Nand, merā punkah letī jāi-o jī.
Nand hum ne dūr se mangwāi!
Nand, take away my old bullock's ears,
Nand, take away my hand fan.
We have called the nand from afar!

Nand, mere budhe bel-kī-sīng,
Nand, merā dandā letī jāi-o jī.
Nand hum ne dūr se mangwāi!
Nand, take away my old bullock's horn,
Nand, take away my stick.
We have called our nand from afar!

And so on, taking the jachā's part, with the verses becoming increasingly laden with double meanings, culminating in instructions to the nand to take away the old bullock's testicles and the jachā's "potatoes" (ālū, meaning her husband's testicles) and the old bullock's anus and the jachā's "pestle" (okhlī, meaning her husband's penis). More songs in similar vein follow. Soon ankle bells are brought out and unmarried girls dance to the songs in turn. After a couple of hours, the jachā's nand distributes sweets to the children and gives the Balmiki woman a handful of flour and some gur for her services. So it will be every evening, until the naming ceremony, but only among the Hindus —

and only after a boy is born.[2]

In the days immediately after a birth, numerous activities mark the significance of childbearing in rural Bijnor.[3] On the one hand, many features of the treatment of the jachā and baby reflect anxieties about their condition. Irrespective of ethnicity, caste, economic position and chūlhā composition, or the jachā's parity and the baby's sex, the jachā and baby are viewed in standard and apparently indisputable physiological terms. Childbirth results in pollution, which adheres especially to the jachā. Childbirth pollution represents power but, unless it is controlled, it is an evil power and the jachā cannot capitalise on it to enhance her self-respect. It can damage the jachā herself and she 'wants her condition rapidly remedied. Further, both she and the baby are capable of harming and defiling other people.[4] Equally, both are vulnerable, particularly to evil spirits and a sudden and dangerous loss of garmī.[5] Accordingly, this double-edged concern with the vulnerability of the jachā and baby and their capacity to endanger others is reflected in several procedures in the immediate post-partum period, primarily the regulation of their contacts with other people, bathing and a strict dietary regime. The extreme limit of about five weeks for these precautions is expressed by several terms, especially sawā mahīnā (one-and-a-quarter months) and chāllis din (40 days), but this period is not usually met in practice. We discuss the implications of this for the jachā's daily duties in the next chapter.

At the same time, a birth is a matter of celebration, which greets the new arrival. Central to the celebration are gift-exchanges which are a specific example of more general patterns involving out-married daughters, who (from the viewpoint of their susrāl kin) should be wealth-bringers.[6] The key figures are the jachā herself and her married nands. Beyond that, however, we cannot outline what happens concisely. The celebrations have distinctive characters among Muslims and Hindus, while class position differentiates people's capacity for liberality in gift-exchanges and hospitality. Further, the jachā's parity and the baby's sex have a considerable influence over the celebrations. Birth rituals are not standard practice: some procedures are common to all births, but many others are optional or permit differential expenditures and ostentation. Ritual silences or the abridged performance of birth rituals should not be glossed over. Actors' choices reflect the long-term significance of each baby's birth for the jachā's chūlhā. A first-born son is greeted by noise, bustle, gift-giving and feasting, which enhances the jachā's sense of worth. The jachā whose baby is a girl — especially one with other daughters — cannot but share the general disappointment.[7] Compared with the woman who bears a son, she is a failure, though even pride in bearing a boy is tempered by the awareness of vulnerability and danger.

Vulnerability and danger

> I have not been allowed outside since the birth six days ago. I have had to drink all these sweet things. I have become full drinking sugar-water and I'm feeling absolutely suffocated inside. *(Urmila)*

Blood is garm and the blood loss at birth makes the jachā weak and vulnerable as her proper balance has been suddenly upset. Thand could easily lodge in her tubes, displaying itself in parsūt, described by informants as a shivering fever with diarrhoea peculiar to jachās. Moreover, after leaving its mother's protective warmth, the new-born baby could succumb to thand. Giving birth also weakens the jachā by opening her tubes and making them delicate: thus, she is vulnerable to attack by evil spirits or the evil eye. Likewise, the baby is soft and vulnerable. Further, the jachā herself remains impure (ā-sūdh among Hindus and nā-pāk among Muslims) or simply dirty and defiled (gandī) by defiling blood. The defilement is called sūtak or, more prosaically, gandagī or mailā (dirt, foulness, filth); some of it also adheres to the baby. Although losing blood makes the jachā weak and vulnerable to thand, she is keenly aware of the urgency of a profuse flow to remove the defilement and cause a complete cleansing (safāi). She also appreciates the need for controls over her behaviour, for her own and the baby's protection.

Concealment and limited social contacts

Najma's niece [ZD]: You know my aunt [MBW] in Qaziwala? Her baby does not drink mother's milk — just like the first daughter who died.[8]
Swaleha: What is the baby being given, then?
Najma's niece: She gets cow, buffalo or goat's milk. She will not take mother's milk into her mouth — there is some evil influence.
Patricia: Does she refuse mother's milk even on a spoon?
Najma's niece: Yes, even though she takes cow's milk on a spoon.
Mansur's sister: Then there is certainly some evil influence on your aunt.

Though several dāis were sceptical, many undesirable symptoms in the new-born — persistent restlessness, crying, stiffness or failure to suckle — are widely attributed to evil spirits or the evil eye, which affect the baby directly or through the mother's milk.[9] The jachā, too, is vulnerable to evil influences. Evil eye can be treated, but many people do not know how, and evil spirits are particularly obstinate and lethal. Hence, prevention is crucial.

I've been very restricted since the birth. If I went anywhere, women would say, 'The baby is still small but Santosh has started going out.' (Santosh)

The jachā's and the baby's safety is ensured by keeping them inside the house for several days, and within the domestic compound for possibly several weeks. The chance of evil influences entering the jachā's house is reduced by the careful regulation of visitors. Basically, all visitors are discouraged, especially menstruating women whose shadows are dangerous for the new-born and people reputed to have the evil eye. Some Hindu households place an earthen brazier containing a small fire (hār) outside the door and tie a sprig of nīm leaves above the lintel. Anyone entering pauses to let the fire drive evil influences away. Muslims do not do this, but they are no more welcoming to guests. At most, people should make very circumspect comments about the jachā and baby, to avoid activating the evil eye's envy. Evil spirits are frightened by an iron sickle on the floor at the bedhead or a lamp burning through the night. Black thread tied round the baby's waist or wrists, black glass bangles, and lamp-black on the forehead or around the rims of the eyes afford further protection for the baby from the evil eye. Some people also fear magic practised on the stump of the baby's cord (nāf) once it has dropped off and they wrap it in cloth before hanging it around the baby's neck for safe-keeping. Many dāis and other women also said sexual intercourse endangers the jachā's opened body and softened tubes.

Conversely, the jachā has restricted contact with others because she endangers them. People avoid touching her, while someone who has been prescribed an amulet in the preceding five weeks fears even to enter the jachā's house because the amulet's efficacy would be destroyed.[10] Fear of defilement makes the jachā temporarily like an untouchable, even among Harijans.[11] Ingesting food cooked by a jachā is dangerous, more so for a man than his children, and a jachā should be absolved from cooking. A man's health, too, would be affected by direct contact with defilement during sexual intercourse with a jachā, though people could not specify what symptoms would ensue.[12] Women generally said that their sās or nand slept inside with them to prevent the husband sleeping with them, though rarely for the several weeks generally specified:

> For at least two-three months a jachā should not join with her husband. But it depends on each man. Why, some men do not even leave their wives when they are menstruating. (*Omvati*)

Cleansing and protection from thand

Touching the jachā and baby is an aspect of defiling-work. Straight after the birth, the dāi gives the jachā some old cloth or a lump of dried mud to clean herself. The jachā is then enveloped in a quilt to protect her from drafts, even in the hottest season. Women feel disgust at touching a new-born baby and shook their heads incomprehendingly at Patricia's preparedness to do so. The infant's preliminary cleaning is the dāi's responsibility. After cutting its cord, she wipes it over with a rag, smoothes its forehead and eyes with her hands and squeezes its nose into shape. She checks that its mouth is properly formed and opens its throat by cleaning out the mouth with her fingers. Then she opens its anus with her little finger to clear out some meconium, wraps the baby firmly in old clothes and puts it under the quilt beside the jachā.[13] More cleansing is inappropriate then, for neither jachā nor baby should be endangered by further exposure to thand.

Bathing the jachā and baby is, however, necessary as it removes defilement, and this defiling-work is generally performed by the dāi. The timing of the first baths depends on when the baby is born. Only in the hottest weather and if the birth was in the morning, are they bathed soon afterwards.[14] If the delivery was in the late afternoon or at night, or during cold weather, the first bath waits until the next day. After bathing, both jachā and baby are warmly wrapped again in the quilt on the bed where the jachā delivered. Since mustard oil is garm, women said an oil massage would be beneficial, but few jachās had one and few dāis reported massaging even the baby before bathing it. Generally, dāis complain, clients are too miserly to pay the extra for such services. Whatever the season, however, the jachā and baby are bathed in warm water, often with mustard oil added. The water is poured over the jachā, she is rubbed vigorously, and hot compresses are applied to her shoulder and knee joints, where thand is especially liable to penetrate. In Dharmnagri, the jachā crouches on a plank over a pit in the floor of her house for her daily bath from the dāi. Some Muslims are similarly bathed for a couple of days, but then usually bathe in the family bathing cubicle. Nowadays in Jhakri, few jachās are bathed daily as there is no resident dāi. Their dāis return to bath them only once, if at all, and jachās are either not bathed for several days or are helped by their sās. Latifan was one of those who complained of the poor service:

> I bath myself. The dāi does not do massage because we cannot pay what she asks. In villages, women are considered worthless.

For its first bath, the baby is suspended over a large metal dish, usually by the dāi, who rubs it while the jachā's sās or another closely related woman pours the warm water. Later baths are given by the jachā's sās or the jachā herself, because the baby is no longer so defiling.

Dealing with the soiled cloths and excreta of the jachā and the baby is also defiling-work, though not as polluting as delivering the placenta and cord-cutting.[15] In Dharmnagri, jachās generally do not take full responsibility for this immediately. Since there are no domestic latrines and people usually go out to the scrubland or fields, a pit is dug in the jachā's house. Her excreta and soiled cloths are later buried in the midden. Someone also clears up the baby's excreta and washes its soiled cloths. The dāi did this for a few days for all five Hindu women without a sās, and for four women who were alag or sājhe. Dāis generally said they prefer to avoid this work, but have little choice if they wish to be paid for cord-cutting, even though several said their clients do not pay extra for the service. Generally, women whose defiling-work was not done by the dāi had it done by their sās. Being sājhe or alag does not clearly affect the choice of worker; the sās did the work for half of the women who were alag. Only two Hindu women (both Harijans) did the defiling-work themselves. Both are alag, and neither had the normal dāi for Dharmnagri at their delivery. By contrast, the Muslim jachā herself does this work from the beginning. Some said there was no need to pay someone as the baby did not defaecate for several days or they themselves were not dirty enough to warrant paying a dāi. Jhakri domestic compounds have dry latrines and Muslim jachās use them (at least after the first day) and leave their soiled cloths there to be collected by the sweeper. They also clear up their baby's excreta and wash its soiled cloths.

Hindus and Muslims alike consider that the baby's first hair is irretrievably contaminated by its contact with the mother's blood. The hair should be shaved off, though generally not within the first week. Some Hindu households perform the shaving (mundan) on the fifth day after the moonless night in the month of Asār: they call a barber and the jachā's nand takes the baby in her lap while he shaves the head.[16] The nand receives just a token sum, while the barber is paid cash, wheat and possibly gur as well. The baby's hair is buried inside (particularly for a first-born or a boy) or simply dropped beside the domestic grain-store and allowed to disappear gradually during house cleaning. Others (even members of the same caste) perform the shaving at the bath in the Ganges after the Diwālī festival.[17] The baby is taken to the Ganges where its head is shaved by a barber. The family sing songs and place the hair on two deep-fried rotī which they float into the water. Yet others have no fixed day for the shaving. Muslims also call in the barber for the baby's head shaving (aqīqa). They have no special time for doing this, though generally wait until the baby is at least five weeks old. The aqīqa is considered a religious requirement for Muslims and among the wealthy may be accompanied by the sacrifice of two goats for a boy or one for a girl.

Women observe dietary avoidances only after the birth

The jachā eats garm things: that cleans the filth out quickly. *(dāi)*

We put gur, ajwain seeds, dried ginger and ghī in harīra for the jachā. But it is a matter of money: wealthy people can give dried fruit and nuts to rebuild the jachā's strength. *(Urmila's sās)*

The baby was born at noon. In the afternoon I had sugar-water. The next day I just had tea. On the third day, I began eating again, mūng-masūr-kī-dāl [types of pulses] and rotī. I do not eat yoghourt, or laukī [squash] or urad-kī-dāl [type of pulse] for a month after giving birth because they can cause damage. My dishes were separate for a fortnight: I myself do not like eating from someone else's dish. *(Imrana)*

It is dangerous for a jachā to eat food or take cold water too soon, for the water accumulates in her tubes and she gets pains. *(Maqsudi)*

Women talk about observing dietary avoidances (parhez) only after delivery. The jachā is weak and vulnerable to thand. Her tubes are opened and softened and still contain menstrual blood that accumulated during pregnancy. Thandā foods endanger her and retard her cleansing by reducing and slowing the blood flow. Bulky items or bādī food would stretch her tubes, enlarge her belly and even cause diarrhoea.[18] By contrast, strengthening (that is, blood replenishing) and garm foods are particularly beneficial.

Generally the jachā receives nothing immediately after giving birth. Some women had tea (which is garm) or warm water some hours after delivery while others had nothing until after their first bath, maybe the next day. Among Muslims, older female susrāl kin first share some of what the jachā will receive. Among Hindus, the jachā must generally wait until her sās or father-in-law performs a pūjā (prayer offering) called sīk nikālnā over what she will receive. Ideally, the jachā is subsequently given special foods: dried fruits (grapes, dates), nuts (cashew, local almonds, coconut), melon seeds, dried ginger, ajwain seeds, sugar or gur, honey and ghī.[19] Finely chopped fruits and nuts are fried in ghī and sugar, gur or honey according to different recipes known variously as gond, harīra, or chāron maghaz. A few of these items are thandā though strengthening (coconut, for instance), but most are garm (especially the gur, ajwain and dried ginger) so in combination produce garmī and strength. Such a sweetmeat would be the jachā's basic diet for some days, were it not for the expense. As Kamla said, "This is a village. If I get good food after giving birth, that is a great thing. In towns it is different. Women very much want good food but shortage of money prevents us from getting it."

In Dharmnagri and Jhakri, the jachā has these special foods usually only after her first delivery, although some women in poor peasant and landless chūlhās never receive them and a few in rich peasant chūlhās received at least some after several deliveries. Desirable though they may be, the fruit and nuts in harīra may be omitted to save money. Indeed, few women had anything other than sugar-water (warm water with gur, dried ginger and ajwain seeds), which some jokingly said we could call harīra if we so wished.[20]

> Here the jachā starves for a few days. When I was about eight my mother had a baby. We children were eating chicken and rice, so we shared some with her — and we got into terrible trouble with my aunt [FyBW]. *(Santosh)*

> Of course I was hungry before I was allowed to eat! But if a jachā eats too soon her belly becomes heavy. *(Wasila)*

Normally the jachā takes only this caudle and possibly hot water or tea without milk for several days. Bulky solids are likely to enlarge her belly, while a liquid diet also reduces the need to defaecate. After some days she takes solid items again. For all the Muslim key informants this was on the third or fourth day, but amongst the Hindus there was more variation; most reported between four and seven days, but for three (all akelī) it was the second or third day. Many women took their first solid food on the day of the festive meal following the birth (see below). Because this meal was delayed by the death of her brother-in-law's daughter (HBD), Viramvati had to wait nine days before taking solid foods again. Some women initially have just one solid meal a day and continue taking sugar-water before resuming the normal two meals a day. At first, the jachā eats easily digested or light food containing garm items but lacking spices and peppers. It is cooked separately by her sās or another woman, at least while the jachā is not cooking for others. The jachā eats rotī or deep-fried wheat bread, certain sorts of pulses (masūr or mūng, especially husked) and some vegetables. Women particularly avoid thandā items: varieties of squashes, such as laukī, and rice, unless it is piping hot and preferably in a khichrī (pulses and rice cooked together) in which the pulses predominate; yoghourt and buttermilk, both separately or together; and milk unless heated. Also avoided are such bādī items as urad-kī-dāl (a type of pulse) and potatoes, although both are also garm. Women talk about five weeks of dietary avoidances. In practice, however, this applied to only about half the Hindu key informants and about one-third of the Muslims. Muslim women more commonly observe avoidances for one to two weeks, and about a quarter of the Hindu women only until the jasthawn a week to ten days after the birth (see below). Some had kept lengthy periods of avoidance after earlier deliveries, but not after their most recent one.

Many women consider themselves so endangering (especially to their husband) that they said, "My heart would not let me eat from the same dishes as other people." For about two weeks, Muslim jachās use separate crocks which are later broken and discarded. Hindus use separate brass dishes, for a week longer on average, and purify them with hot ash from the chūlhā once the jachā is considered clean again. The length of time a jachā's dishes are kept separate varies considerably, six women (three Muslim and three Hindu) doing so for less than a week, and nine (two Muslim and seven Hindu) for a month or more. Separate dishes are sometimes used during the whole period the jachā observes food avoidances, but sometimes less. Moreover, although separate arrangements for the jachā's food create extra work, there are no clear relationships between these arrangements and the composition of the jachā's chūlhā or its class position.

Such variations are perhaps all the more surprising, given the apparently compelling reasons for caution, for the jachā's sake and to protect those around her. Certainly, women who observed lengthy avoidances justified doing so in terms of their own health:

> I had dāl and rotī after the fourth day and then observed avoidances for one-and-a-half months. You see, I am the only person who looks after my children and I should do nothing which would endanger my health.
> *(Khurshida)*

On the other hand, Adesh observed dietary avoidances for just a fortnight. When asked why not for the full five weeks, she commented: "In the midst of agricultural work, who could observe avoidances for so long?"

The baby's well-being

> The baby has birth syrup for three-four days to clean out its belly. *(Imarti)*

> If the jachā has good food, her milk becomes blossoming milk and after drinking it the baby itself blossoms.

> My baby has a fever and cries every night from eleven o'clock until the dawn call to prayer. I've consulted doctors in Mandauli and Bijnor. The ANM's assistant in Dharmnagri advised an amulet for me in case there is some evil influence in my milk. *(Fatima)*

Mother's milk is neither garm nor thandā. Its effect depends on the mother. If she has a fever, that influence will reach the child. If she eats very garm things, that could cause illnesses like thrush [munh ānā]. If she takes very thandā things, the thand could lodge in its belly or give it shivering in its ribs [paslīyā].

The baby's well-being is bound up with the jachā, especially with her diet once lactation is initiated, and also with her health and other activities. Accordingly, protecting the baby from evil influences or excessive thand entails controlling the jachā.

Mother's milk (mā-kā-dūdh) is normally first given on the third day, or, if the baby is very weak or cries incessantly, perhaps on the second day, though never earlier.[21] Occasionally, cow's milk is given first rather than mother's milk. Most women provided no other rationale than that "this is a custom from the past", which they follow because their elders instructed them. Some older women, however, consider mother's milk is initially excessively garm and potentially damaging for a new-born baby. One dāi explained:

We have no special name for the jachā's first milk, though we could call it khīs, our name for a buffalo or cow's first milk. New-born babies are very soft inside and this first milk could cause belly-ache. It is very garm and could give the baby severe diarrhoea, as happens to adults who drink too much khīs from a buffalo. After a while, the jachā's milk becomes less garm — like goat's milk — and is safe for the baby to drink. *(dāi)*

New-born calves are given sugar-water rather than being exposed to the undue garmī of khīs. Bovine khīs is cooked with gur and distributed among neighbours to celebrate the calving.[22] No one consumes the jachā's first milk, but the new-born baby is treated rather like the calf: its grandmother (FM), mother or possibly aunt (FZ) feed it birth syrup (janam ghuttī) until breast-feeding begins.[23] The ingredients of birth syrup are garm but less so than the mother's first milk. They simultaneously protect the baby from thand and clean its throat and tubes by stimulating intestinal contractions which expel the "black-black stuff" (meconium), which is considered more defiling than normal faeces. Patent birth syrup can be bought, but villagers make their own using ingredients easily available locally: basically, ajwain seeds, flat-bean pods (sem-kā-pattā[24]), gur and turmeric cooked in water. A few women mentioned dried ginger, leaf of betel tree, salt, a nīm leaf or white sweet (batasha). Birth syrup is cooked in a small crock on the chūlhā. Once cooled, some is decanted into a crock saucer or brass dish and the baby sucks on a cotton-wool wick submerged into it.

Breast-feeding begins only after the "washing of the milk" (dūdh-dhulāi).[25] The jachā's nand wets a sprig of dūb grass with water and strokes the jachā's breast with it. The nand expresses some milk into a dish containing ashes, and throws the milk-soaked ash into the midden. Squeezing the jachā's nipple is said to open the holes in the milk sacs and ensure a good flow of milk — though a few women regarded this as "just a custom", neither harmful nor beneficial. The nand receives a cash honorarium (generally between Rs 5 and Rs 15) from the jachā: in return, she gives a token sum (maybe Rs 2) to the new baby. Only then does the new-born drink mother's milk.

Thereafter, the jachā's care is for the baby's sake as much as her own. A weak woman cannot produce enough milk to sustain a baby properly and some women reported taking solid items soon after delivery because their milk was insufficient. Strengthening foods are beneficial, though not always available, and garm foods can help stimulate a plentiful supply of milk. But quantity is not the only consideration. The effect of mother's milk is influenced by the jachā's diet. She should eat garm items to protect the baby from thand and complete the expulsion of meconium begun by the birth syrup. Thandā and bādī items in her diet would harm the baby's soft tubes and make it prone to constipation:

> The jachā's tubes are very soft. Eating thandā things will give her belly-ache and even shivering fever and diarrhoea. Water would accumulate in her tubes. Her belly would enlarge. And the new baby drinks the jachā's milk. If the jachā is ill, the baby becomes sick too. That is why she should not take thandā things. *(dāi)*

In caring for herself, then, the jachā ensures that her milk is not damaged by her own ill-health. Thandā food or a cold bath could make her ill and her milk dangerously thandā. The excessive garmī of a fever could harm the baby. Sexual intercourse too soon after delivery can make the jachā dangerously garm and the opening of her tubes can result in her being attacked by evil spirits which make her milk blue, her breasts painfully engorged and the baby fretful. During pregnancy, to visit a house where a death has taken place might later result in evil influence in the milk. And a jachā afflicted by evil eye produces harmful milk: indeed, women conceal themselves while breast-feeding for fear that the evil eye will strike. The jachā's maternal responsibilities are underlined by breast-feeding, for her behaviour, diet, health, and mobility all affect the quality of her milk and, thereby, her baby's welfare.

Celebrating the birth

Although the details vary somewhat, most of these procedures to protect and cleanse the jachā and baby cost nothing or require simple items already in the house. Neither is their practice marked by major class or ethnic differences. Basically they reflect a common concern about the vulnerability and dangerousness of the jachā and baby in the days after the birth.

The restraints on the jachā all highlight the urgency of re-establishing her usual condition. An important marker of this is the jachā's specially cleansing bath that takes place some days after the delivery. The earlier baths aid her transition to cleanliness, as well as counteracting the dangers of thand, but one bath is particularly significant for her return to normal life. If the dāi baths the jachā daily, she continues only until the day before the jachā's special purifying bath, at which one of the jachā's female susrāl kin usually pours the warm water. The bath is associated with the chhatī (especially among Muslims) and the jasthawn (exclusively among Hindus).[26] These generally take place between five and ten days after the delivery and signify the end of the jachā's extreme defilement, though not of the defilement altogether.

Among Muslims, this bath is called the chhatī (literally, the sixth). Afterwards, the jachā wears clean clothes. Her sās or nand spread diluted cattle-dung over the jachā's floor and the courtyard outside to purify them. A celebratory meal of dāl and rice, sometimes (among the more wealthy) topped with ghī and finely ground sugar, is prepared, often by the barber. The chhatī is not considered a religious requirement for Muslims — informants spoke of it as "just a custom" or a matter of celebration — and they do not employ a maulwī or imām either to remove the defilement or to give the baby a name.

Hindus, however, are dependent on religious specialists. With them, the jachā's specially cleansing bath is generally associated with the jasthawn (also called the jasūthan by some informants). The jachā is bathed, puts on clean clothes and new glass bangles, and probably also applies an auspicious mark on her forehead and makes a new parting in her hair, using vermilion.[27] Diluted dung is spread over the entire floor of the house and the area outside by the jachā's sās or nand to help remove the defilement. Among Caste Hindus, the pandit (temple priest) makes a sacred pattern on the floor of the jachā's house and performs a pūjā to remove the defilement. He also decides upon the baby's name by consulting the birth almanac and he purifies the jachā and baby by giving them some Ganges water to drink. Then there is a festive meal of dāl and rice, again sometimes topped with ghī and sugar, cooked by the pandit, who also joins in. Among Harijans (the Chamars and Jatabs), the jasthawn is not performed by a pandit as he neither visits their houses nor eats food cooked there; they go to the temple, where he consults the birth almanac, and they perform the pūjā and cook for themselves. Some Hindu informants said they do not have a separate chhatī and that the jachā's bath is simply part of the jasthawn. Others have a separate chhatī, though sometimes only for the first baby, when a cooked yoghourt dish with rice is placed on a tray along with a dhotī; the jachā's sister-in-law (HeBW) performs a pūjā and receives the dhotī. Adesh and Bhagirthi said that, as Rajputs, they do not hold pūjās while the moon is waning and they perform the chhatī on the sixth day after the new moon, which may place it after the jasthawn. Otherwise, the chhatī generally takes place (if at all) before the jasthawn or as an integral part of it.

After the chhatī or jasthawn, the jachā can leave the house, move around the courtyard and be involved again in the life of her chūlhā. Many jachās begin going out beyond the courtyard soon after the bath, though others refrain from doing so for several weeks. But the chhatī and jasthawn baths do not erase the jachā's impurity completely; her defilement continues as long as she is bleeding and is only finally eradicated five weeks after the delivery. She may continue to avoid thandā foods, to eat from separate dishes, and refrain from cooking for other people. Indeed, these restrictions on her activities are not lifted simultaneously. There is no sharp division between being totally impure and totally pure or being utterly vulnerable and being able to take the full range of foods. Rather, the jachā gradually introduces a greater range of foods to her diet, but should take greatest care immediately after the birth; and she eases back into the social world outside her house, first just talking to people, later eating with them or cooking food for her chūlhā.

But the chhatī and jasthawn are not merely concerned with the removal of defilement. A birth is a matter of celebration (khushī-kī-bāt) and the chhatī and jasthawn are also components of the khushī (that is, celebration, merriment, happiness) that welcomes the new baby and endorses motherhood and childbearing. Among the key informants, Pushpa was alone in citing khushī — rather than just sharm — as a reason for giving birth in the susrāl:[28]

> No one goes to the jachā's pīhar to celebrate. If the khushī takes place in her susrāl, a lākh [one hundred thousand] people could be invited! But that would not be auspicious in the jachā's pīhar. No one from her pīhar can eat the jasthawn food — but all the susrāl people may attend. Just think, after a woman's first baby, there is the chhatī in which the jachā's sister-in-law [HeBW] has work. If it is a boy, the jachā's nand and her brother-in-law [HyB] both have work. What, should they all go to the jachā's pīhar? That is why it is suitable to deliver in the susrāl.

Khushī provides the opportunity for ostentatious display which demonstrates generosity and economic well-being. Costly khushī that takes place soon after the birth (rather than after some delay) reflects best on the honour of the jachā's susrāl kin. The feasting following the chhatī and jasthawn involve entertaining relatives and neighbours in the jachā's susrāl. The barber and pandit who cook for the Muslims and Caste Hindus also expect generous fees for their work. Moreover, khushī entails extensive activation of links outside the jachā's susrāl: general patterns of len-den (taking-giving) in relation to out-married daughters are set in train after a woman gives birth. On the one hand, the jachā's parents seek to reinforce her position as wealth-bringer in her susrāl by sending gifts for her and her susrāl kin. On the other, the jachā's parents-in-law make presentations to their own out-married daughters (the jachā's nands) and their sons-in-law. Early in her childbearing career, the jachā herself is likely to be passive in the resource transfers that occur because she has given birth. Her elders, however, are central in marshalling the goods that are presented. Indeed, the jachā and baby often seem almost incidental, for they are not the central actors in the public procedures that khushī entails.

These basic patterns of hospitality and len-den are subject to considerable variations in practice. The orchestration of khushī is affected by the jachā's marriage type and her chūlhā's composition. Ideally, the jachā's mother arranges what will be sent from the jachā's natal village. If the jachā is a bought bride or her mother is dead, this facet of len-den is compromised and the jachā's chūlhā must meet the expenses. Again, ideally, the jachā's sās is responsible for organising the feasting and distribution of goods, but only while she is still sājhe with the jachā. The jachā who is alag or akelī should finance the hospitality and len-den from her own chūlhā's resources and from whatever her parents might have sent. Differences in class position are also reflected in khushī. Generosity and display are desirable after a woman gives birth, but not all can rise to the occasion to the extent that rich peasants can. The ceremonial meal that follows a chhatī or jasthawn, for instance, might involve numerous guests or be a simple meal for the jachā's chūlhā members. Gifts can include silver jewellery and expensive cloth or just token sums of cash and mere cotton.

These constitute the central parameters within which khushī operates. But additionally, individual women's accounts indicate that each delivery has a different significance for her chūlhā and evokes different degrees of khushī. Since Hindus have a more elaborate repertoire of celebrations than do Muslims they can more forcefully express degrees of khushī by adding or omitting different components. Tardiness of celebration contrasts with rapidity, small-scale feasting with large-scale, attenuated practices (or even their omission) with elaborate and costly procedures, minimal len-den with generous display. Two crucial considerations influence the khushī following a birth: the jachā's parity and the baby's sex. Clearly, both always operate in combination, but we have separated them here. First, we contrast the khushī greeting a jachā's first child with that following her later deliveries and then we specify the differential responses to boys' and girls' births.

There is celebration only for a first child

It is not a question of being a boy or a girl: the news of the birth only goes to the jachā's maikā after the first birth. *(Sabra)*

When the first child is born, the jachā's people send things to her susrāl. *(Urmila)*

Chandresh gave me and my next sister a sārī and blouse, and the two youngest sisters got a dhotī and blouse each. But as there are four sisters on the back of one brother, only I took jewellery: Chandresh gave me silver anklets from her dowry. *(Chandresh's oldest nand)*

The bahū's first delivery demonstrates her ability to bear future workers and results in great excitement and khushī. Even a first-born girl offers hope of sons to come. The dāi, for instance, is paid more for first deliveries — probably Rs 25-30 as against about Rs 20 — and rich and middle peasants may include a new dhotī and cloth for a blouse for a Hindu dāi or cloth lengths for trousers, dress and shawl for a Muslim one. Further, links between the jachā's chūlhā and her own parents, others in her susrāl, and her married nands are brought to life. If the new baby is unmoved by the rumpus, the jachā cannot fail to be impressed: the celebrations endorse her successful womanhood, enhance her position in her susrāl and reaffirm for everyone the importance of childbearing. She has good cause for pride.

Celebration in the jachā's susrāl

The most elaborate khushī marks a jachā's first delivery (or possibly a son's birth following several girls). Most first-time jachās are still sājhe and their sās orchestrates the celebrations. Although khushī-se (out of happiness) has connotations of voluntariness, the generosity of the jachā's sās is closely scrutinised and miserliness escapes no one. For reputation's sake, the sās appreciates that a special effort is necessary, even if cash must be borrowed. Thus, Muslims like to do the chhatī and Hindus the jasthawn splendidly, at least for a first baby. The scale of the meal to which relatives and neighbours in the jachā's susrāl (possibly including her married nands and their husbands) are entertained reflects the khushī. Generous payment of the cook (the barber or pandit) is also expected. People like to organise these meals quickly, for early celebration — around five to seven days after the birth — usually implies greatest khushī.[29] Only Tahira held no khushī for her first child in Jhakri, because her baby was born during the monsoon, the slack period for wage labour, and Taslim had no money. All the other key informants' first births were publicly marked, people with little cash giving festive food only to some relatives, and more wealthy chūlhās feasting a wide range of relatives, sometimes even the whole village.

Len-den and the jachā's parents

> News of only the first baby is sent to the jachā's parents, because they send things only on that occasion. After that nothing comes. What, should we continue to send news for no matter how many children?
> *(Wasila)*

As at other stages in the jachā's childbearing career, her natal kin keep their distance. They neither host any celebrations, nor are they guests at the feasting in the jachā's susrāl. But when the jachā's in-laws decide to celebrate, her natal kin should send gifts for distribution.

Usually, news of the birth is formally taken to the jachā's natal village by her husband or his brother only after her first delivery. The Muslims' shorter marriage distances permit men's brief absences with little notice and they generally convey the news more quickly than Hindus. Asghari's parents heard the day she delivered, but Sunil and Punni went to inform their wives' parents only after some days. Whoever takes the news asks when the jachā's parents can accept the "lump of gur", which will be taken by the jachā's husband's older "brother" (her HeB or HFBS) among Hindus and by the barber among Muslims. Once the jachā's parents receive the lump of gur, they must send gifts for the jachā, her husband, the baby, and her other susrāl relatives, items known collectively as sīdhā by Hindus and chhūchhak by Muslims.[30] Muslims send suit-lengths and Hindus send dhotīs or sārīs plus cloth for blouses for the jachā's female susrāl kin — her sās, nands, and sisters-in-law (HBW). Suit-lengths are sent for men and children, including the new baby. There may be silver jewellery for the jachā, and a silver amulet for a boy or silver anklets or bracelets for a girl. Other women and children may receive small sums of money. Food items for the jachā's special diet and for celebratory meals may also be sent, including flour, pulses, ghī, rice, finely ground white sugar, gur, and coconuts.

But the jachā's parents' financial position influences what is sent. Several hundred rupees would be necessary to provide sārīs and suit-lengths of cotton with artificial fibres, jewellery, cash gifts and food items. This is no mean outlay. When Asghari's first child was born, her father sent 40 kilograms of wheat, ten kilograms each of rice and pulses, ingredients for gond for Asghari, gur, suit-lengths for Asghari and Ahmad, Ahmad's parents, his sister and sister's husband, clothing and silver anklets for the baby — and he had a handpump installed in the courtyard Asghari shares with her sās. Others cannot be so generous. They provide cheaper items like cotton dhotīs and suit-lengths or small sums of money, and they may omit foodstuffs and restrict the recipients of the more expensive items. Santosh's parents sent cotton dhotīs only for herself, her sās, her one nand and her two sisters-in-law (HBW) — Pushpa and Omvati – still sājhe with her sās. Santosh's three other sisters-in-law simply received Rs 10 apiece and their husbands each got Rs 2 rather than suit-lengths. Indeed, three Harijan women said their parents had requested delays in sending the lump of gur:

> We have not yet sent the lump of gur. My father asked us to wait until the cold weather. After the rice harvest he will have cash for the gifts which he must send. *(Shakuntala)*

Chandresh's widowed mother wanted to wait until Chandresh's younger sister was married. And Viramvati's father had still not sent gifts after her first delivery in 1978 when her second child was born in early 1982: he was arranging weddings for his two remaining unmarried children and said he would not have ready cash until after the next wheat harvest.

No news of the birth was sent to the jachā's parents after only four of the key informants' first deliveries. Jhakri is far from Tahira's maikā and without money for khushī, they neither informed her parents nor received gifts from them. The other two bought brides, Rajballa and Lakshmi, have no one to tell and their susrāl kin received no gifts. And Promilla's experience highlights women's centrality in len-den, for her widowed father was not informed and only later sent a dhotī for Promilla and a suit for the baby — much less than if his wife were still alive. When Promilla's nand gave baby clothes, Promilla bought a dhotī for her nand, something (she commented) her mother would have provided.

Usually, however, the jachā's natal kin want to give generously.[31] They rejoice over her fulfilment of her wifely duty, as well as feeling the pressure to be generous: "My daughter's sās wants a cycle and watch in the chhūchhak. We have just two bīghās [less than half an acre] of land. What, should we sell it to buy such things?"[32] Mere cotton goods are no longer so acceptable. Expectations have risen, though rarely so much yet in Bijnor that gold jewellery or expensive household items are commonly demanded or given. But parents know that recipients cast critical eyes over the gifts, assessing the quality of cloth and quantity of foodstuffs, making comparisons with other such occasions. Omvati, for instance, complained after Pushpa's first delivery, saying eleven dhotīs were needed, but Pushpa had none: her parents had neither given any when she visited nor sent any, even though she is an only daughter.[33] Since Omvati was still sājhe with Pushpa, she and her sās had to buy dhotīs specially. Omvati acidly commented that she has two sisters, yet her parents provide enough dhotīs when she gives birth.

Pity, then, the jachā who receives nothing because she is isolated from her natal kin, or whose parents cannot match her in-laws' expectations. The jachā should be the conduit of largesse sent for her susrāl kin "out of happiness".

The nand's honorarium

As an out-married woman of the jachā's susrāl, the jachā's married nand has a special position in the days immediately after a birth. Guests at the chhatī or jasthawn feasts present cash (Rs 1 or 5 are popular sums) or cloth for suits for the baby. The nand probably gives more than them, possibly several suit-lengths. She also receives more, as she is entitled to neg (honorarium), which is ideally most elaborate and costly when her brother's first child is born.[34]

Usually, the first neg includes silver jewellery, a necklace (such as a "collar bone" of solid silver or a necklace of linked segments), bracelets or anklets. The neg also contains at least one sārī and blouse-length or several suit-lengths (preferably cotton with artificial fibres). The nand's husband and children generally receive suit-lengths (possibly more than one apiece) and she might receive several kilograms of grain or gur. Since women expect neg for each first child born to their brothers, an only sister with several brothers does well compared with women with only one brother or with several sisters. If there are several nands, the eldest is often the only one to receive jewellery, or she is given the largest piece. About a quarter of the key informants had only unmarried nands at their first delivery. In that case, Muslim women give just cloth and then give the jewellery after their first delivery following the nand's marriage. Hindu jachās give a dhotī or sārī and jewellery, but the nand cannot use them until she is married. Women without a nand give cloth or token cash (but not jewellery) to their husband's cousin (HFBD).

Most jachās are still sājhe at their first delivery, so the sās has access to the jachā's dowry jewellery, some of which she might transfer to the nand (her own daughter). Nands are said to prefer items originating from the jachā's parents, rather than from their own.[35] Clothing for the nand may be that sent by the jachā's parents to mark the birth, or something already set aside by the jachā for occasions when she is expected to give, for example, a sārī received at her brother's marriage, a dhotī from her dowry, or suit-lengths given when she visited her parents.

Only rarely does the married nand receive nothing after the jachā's first child is born. Occasionally, disputes between the jachā's and the nand's chūlhās are evidenced by lack of len-den, as in Lakshmi's case.[36] Promilla and Santosh could not give their nand any jewellery because their sās had kept all their dowry jewellery when they became alag. And in landless households, straitened circumstances prevented some jachās from giving neg: Zubeida did not even call her nand as she had nothing to give, while Wasila called her own sister and gave her just cloth, whereas nands expect grain, jewellery and money too. Generally, however, married women hope for generous gifts when their brothers' wives have their first babies, and most jachās, their sās and their mothers plan accordingly.

How long should khushī continue?

It was not a first child so news didn't need to be sent to my maikā. *(Dilruba)*

After later children we do not send the lump of gur nor do things come from the jachā's pīhar. When I go to my pīhar, my mother will give clothing for me and the baby. *(Kamla)*

There is no objection to celebrating each child's birth, but later deliveries are generally marked less elaborately than the first. Hindus usually hold a jasthawn but only rich peasants invite many guests. The rest mostly invite only the husband's closest relatives. Muslims might perform a chhatī each time; but it is "just a khushī", not a religious requirement. Excluding the first-time jachās in Jhakri, over half the Muslim key informants held no chhatī after their last delivery. They simply bathed and shared food with their immediate chūlhā. The rest had small-scale chhatīs with few guests, maybe immediate relatives and a representative from each chūlhā in Jhakri. Generally, too, financial constraints are acceptable reasons for spending little on marking a later child's birth.

In addition, the jachā's parents usually learn of her later deliveries rather fortuitously. They probably knew of her pregnancy and would be informed if she were ill, but no one is formally sent to tell them she has safely given birth. Generally, a Muslim jachā's parents do learn of the delivery within a few days, maybe mentioned during coming and going between Jhakri and the jachā's natal village, or by the Qaziwala dāis as they go about their work in nearby villages. News of Latifan's eighth delivery was probably the most rapidly communicated: she is in a within-village marriage, gave birth the day a bride from Liaqat's compound was married to a groom from her natal compound, and missed the wedding feast for reasons known to all. If the jachā's natal village is more distant, her parents may learn only through a chance meeting in Bijnor, or when the jachā visits them for a wedding or festival (when the baby is at least five weeks old) or when the jachā's father or brother visit her (sometimes as much as three months afterwards).

Women themselves see little reason to send news, as their parents rarely send many gifts after later births. Some parents send nothing, others just a solitary suit or dhotī for the jachā and clothing for her husband and children. Some women received clothing for themselves and the baby only during their first visit to their natal village after the delivery — no more than anticipated any other time. Jewellery, foodstuffs and clothes for the husband's other relatives are rarely sent. Yet the jachā's sās and nands (and possibly others in her susrāl) will expect presents of clothing. Thus, gifts distributed to the jachā's susrāl kin are largely provided by the jachā's chūlhā itself. Since women of higher parities are increasingly unlikely to be sājhe; the jācha must use items from her own store or buy specially. Generally, len-den is small-scale after later births and what the nand receives is downgraded, with the jewellery omitted and more expensive cloth replaced by cotton.

In other words, first children generate liberality, according to the jachā's parents' and in-laws' capabilities. Any khushī for second and third children is probably less costly. Later still, feasting and len-den may be forgone altogether. Indeed, it is considered improvident to provide a feast after each birth:

> After my daughter's birth we did no khushī. Why, I did not even do the chhatī after several of the boys. With so many children, how long should we continue doing khushī? If there are just one-two, then khushī will be done. *(Latifan)*

Shouting loudly, "It's a boy"

> Village people don't like girls. Much more is done when a boy is born. The taking-outside and jasthawn are done with great expense, drums will be played and hearth tongs clattered against the griddle. If I have a boy, I must give all my susrāl women a dhotī, all the men a coconut each, and my brother-in-law (HyB) a suit as well. But if I have a girl, I might just give a suit to my brother-in-law (HyB) and neg to my nand. *(Santosh)*

> I vomited when I drank sugar-water, for Hashmi's sās is burning with evil eye because I have had a son. She will not even pick him up. But the giving of boys or girls is Allah's work, so what is the benefit of burning with jealousy about other people's descendants? *(Fatima)*

> When a baby is born people shout very loudly, 'It's a boy', or they say in a dead voice, 'It's a girl.' *(Khurshida)*

Women play a central role in the immediate responses to a baby that affirm the importance of sons through more elaborate and costly celebrations.[37] Hindus have a large repertoire for demonstrating the different significance of boys and girls, so the following account largely applies to them. Muslims, however, just as readily assert that a boy's birth brings the greatest khushī. Dāis repeatedly commented that Hindus and Muslims alike greet girls' births silently, boys' with enthusiasm and joy:

> In their hearts no one wants a girl. If it were under anyone's control, no

girls would ever be born! *(dāi)*

If there are already several girls, people consider the birth of another a matter of sadness [dukh-kī-bāt], though if a girl comes after several boys they do not mind so much. *(dāi)*

Sometimes dāis are insulted for delivering a girl, sometimes the jachā's in-laws fly into a temper:[38]

Women often say that a dead widow co-wife [marī rand saukan] has been born. Sometimes women swear, but I ask if they were not girls once and chide them for what they say. *(dāi)*

If people complain when I deliver a girl, I say I did not make her and the girl was just in their fate. *(dāi)*

Moreover, while individual dāis reported different levels of income, they always receive less when a girl is born:

The women say that a prostituting widow [chudai rand] has been born, so what should they give me? Recently several girls have been born and now people say that I just bring girls into the world. That way my income has declined. *(dāi)*

Sometimes people take a loan from me for a year when a girl is born, and then never repay it. But what can I say? I do not make boys or girls. It's God's wish. Some people get boys while others get girls. *(dāi)*

A dāi getting Rs 25 plus about five kilograms of grain for delivering a boy would probably be given Rs 15-20 plus the grain for a girl. Four key informants gave Rs 10 or less after their last daughters were born. One dāi was seething after delivering a girl in Jhakri, for she had received only one rupee and 500 grams of grain and, thereafter, the jachā's sās intended to do all the defiling-work rather than call the dāi daily and pay more. Another dāi commented on people's responses thus:

Many people are sad when a girl is born, but never when a boy is born. Sometimes the jachā gets no proper food. There are no special customs when a girl is born. Parents think they first have to raise her and then collect money for her dowry. A girl is someone else's property and they will have to give to her all her life. That is why people do not do khushī when a girl is born. That is why people do not give me anything special when a girl is born. Yes, indeed, some even swear at me.

Celebration, len-den and neg

Bhārū larke-kā-dādā kharchā khenche,
Ghar-me luchchī dādī kharchī!
Kidhar gaye, sānwaliyā pyārā?
The bastard baby's grandfather [FF] is extorting,
Inside, his lewd grandmother [FM] is squandering!

Where has my beloved lord [husband] gone?

[A birth song in which successive verses name the jachā's other susrāl kin][39]

A first-born son brings the greatest khushī of all, certainly greater than a first-born daughter. And while some khushī is probably done for boys born later, there is little or no celebration for a girl born later.

Among Muslims, the chhatī for the first boy, whether or not a first-born, is· performed elaborately. Asghari, for instance, attended the chhatī for her brother's first son: his delight was demonstrated by organising the baby's head-shaving at the same time and sacrificing two goats. Asghari (the jachā's nand) received suits for Ahmad, his parents, her daughter and three for herself (from the jachā's parents, the jachā, and her own parents). After later boys, any khushī is probably smaller-scale. The jachā's parents probably send nothing for distribution among the jachā's susrāl kin or for a festive meal, and the costs must be met by the jachā's chūlhā, which is increasingly likely to be alag or akelī as the years go by. When Dilruba's third son was born, the chhatī guests were the residents of her compound and a representative from each production unit in Jhakri. By contrast, the chhatī is rarely performed for baby girls with older siblings. Hashmi's fourth daughter's birth was marked only when Hashmi's sister-in-law (HeBW) cooked flour in gur for her when the baby was already over a month old. Only Najma and Khurshida had chhatīs for their daughters: they just invited the women of their compound as "they were not first-born children".

In Dharmnagri, too, celebrations are most elaborate for a boy, even for a second or later one. Many jasthawn guests may be invited — or just a handful. Arranging the jasthawn quickly signifies happiness, but weeks or even months may elapse before a girl is named. Alternatively, the jasthawn can be replaced by the cheaper mandal, when the pūjā is as at the jasthawn, but the pandit does no cooking (so is paid less) and no one is invited for festive food. The contrast is particularly striking among rich peasants for whom financial constraints are least crucial: during our research Bhagwana had a boy while his brother Ashok had a girl. Bhagwana invited all the residents of their section of Dharmnagri (about 200 people) to the jasthawn. But after Ashok's daughter's birth, there was no chhatī and neither jasthawn nor mandal had been held even a month later. Neighbours commented that there had been weeping in Adesh's house after the birth; she now had five daughters and one son, and "in searching for a boy they had got yet another girl". Adesh herself commented, "We did no khushī for this girl. For a boy, my husband would invite everyone and there would be a big jasthawn. But, instead, he has been saying stinging things to us all."

Poorer Hindus also mark a girl's birth less elaborately than a boy's, with a small jasthawn or just a mandal and less costly gifts for the jachā's susrāl relatives. Udayan's response epitomises this. He and Urmila were pleased enough to have a girl after two boys. Yet, when the pandit performing the jasthawn instructed him to place Rs 10.25 on the sacred pattern, Udayan's retort was instantaneous: "What? Has a boy been born to me?" The pandit laughed, conceded the point, and accepted Rs 5.25. Udayan's close relatives were evenly matched by researchers as the only guests at the meal which followed.

When a woman's first-born is a boy, her parents are expected to send the most generous gifts they can afford. Indeed, news of all first sons — whether first-born or not — will probably be conveyed to the jachā's parents and they may send gifts, even if they did so for an earlier girl. The first son, at least, must be properly welcomed. The jachā's parents rarely send elaborate gifts for the jachā's wider susrāl connection after the birth of subsequent sons (generally just clothing for the jachā's immediate chūlhā and for the new baby). But they are unlikely to send anything at all if a second or later baby is a girl.

On the other hand, the jachā's parity is most crucial in the nand's neg, which is costliest after the jachā's first baby, girl or boy. Thereafter, the nand can expect (at most) just clothing but not jewellery. Only rarely was this not so, in all instances among Hindus. Durgi's first child was a girl, but her nands both refused jewellery until she had a son. Her second child was a boy: one nand received a sārī and silver necklace of eight "buds" or segments and the other a sārī and silver bracelets. Likewise, Jumni insisted on waiting until her brother's wife had a son. Adesh — in a rich peasant chūlhā — was extraordinary in giving her nand jewellery twice, after the first child (a girl) and after the boy who followed.

Extra celebrations for a boy

In Dharmnagri, further procedures take place only after a boy's birth, particularly birth songs (janam gīt) and the taking-outside (bahārī). These entail additional len-den and also bring into sharp focus the contrast between the jachā (as bahū) and her nand (as out-married daughter), for the latter plays a central role in the celebrations. For instance, birth songs, as people emphasise, are sung only after a boy's birth, for his birth is considered auspicious. Each evening before the jasthawn, women gather to dance and sing bawdy songs, whose innuendos they are often embarrassed to explain afterwards. The jachā remains inside whereas the nand actively participates.

The taking-outside is on the Sunday or Thursday evening following the birth. Among Caste Hindus, the jachā's female susrāl kin visit the three satī shrines on Dharmnagri's outskirts.[40] A Brahmin's wife makes a sathiyā (good luck sign) on the trees at the shrines, using cattle-dung, dabs of flour and turmeric, and bits of straw. Meanwhile, the women sing and fool around. For example, Jumni's nand — released from her susrāl — acted an old woman requesting in quavering tones a blind bride for her son. Then, to squeals of delight, she jigged around holding a segment of sugar-cane at her groin and made prancing runs at the other women.[41] After circling Dharmnagri, the women return to the jachā's home. Thereafter, the proceedings take place in similar fashion among Caste Hindus and Harijans alike. The oldest nand (or sometimes the dāi or a Brahmin's wife) makes a sathiyā beside the jachā's doorway, spreads diluted dung on the ground outside the door and puts a small stool or plank on it. Then the dāi and the jachā's nand and sās take the jachā's brother-in-law (HyB, or failing that, her HeBS) inside. The jachā and baby are heavily shrouded in a shawl. The brother-in-law leads them on to the stool, where the jachā faces the house and throws uncooked rice back over her shoulder seven times. She then goes inside. Her brother-in-law receives neg, the money from the top of the sathiyā, a coconut, a suit-length, possibly even a radio, for taking the jachā outside. The nand receives neg for the sathiyā, even if she does not make them herself. Dhotīs and blouses are also provided for the jachā's other nands, her sās and her sisters-in-law (HBW) and suit-lengths with token sums of cash wrapped inside for the men. Children get coins, and boiled chick peas are distributed to the onlookers. Later, birth songs are sung.[42]

In Jhakri, male circumcision, performed by the barber, is the only extra procedure when a boy is born. This is only occasionally accompanied by expensive gifts and generous feasting. Fatima's second son's circumcision cost just Rs 15 for the barber's fee and Rs 5 for the sweets distributed among the compound's children.[43]

The pressure to give

> Neg dene-ke-māre,
> Nikal-gayā pānī.
> Jachā-ke-sone-kī barī pareshānī!
> As a result of giving neg,
> Water has come out [tears are flowing].
> The jachā's sleep is greatly disturbed!

This chorus of this birth song poignantly reflects a common lament and its verses proceed to list the tasks of the jachā's female susrāl kin and how each has "demanded her own neg". The pressure to be generous weighs heavily when a boy is born. Demands may be made for a radio or cycle for the jachā's brother-in-law (HyB), expensive jewellery for the nand, or more money for the medical practitioner who gave a labour accelerating injection. Only rich peasants like Bhagwana can contemplate repeatedly holding a large-scale jasthawn as he did when his third son was born. For people on the margins, such expectations pose serious problems, generally resolved by reserving the major outlays for the first boy (especially a first child, but also if he has older sisters). The expense of a costly chhatī or jasthawn and bahārī can outweigh the joy. Umrao (in a landless chūlhā) did not hold a chhatī for her last son (her ninth pregnancy): "We did no khushī last time. We have enough difficulty filling our stomachs without extra expense." Similarly, after Imarti's third son's birth (her seventh pregnancy) there were only attenuated procedures. The Dharmnagri pandit consulted the birth almanac and provided a name. To his annoyance, the jasthawn was later performed by his aunt (FZ), who (by her own confession) is illiterate and merely mumbles what she can remember of the recitation. She was paid Rs 3 and only chūlhā members ate the food she cooked, for all that they are middle peasants.

Underscoring the importance of sons

Bearing a son, particularly a first-born son, results in a resounding confirmation of the jachā's success. As a corollary, the jachā whose baby is a girl hears powerful messages of her failings. This is also enshrined in numerous sayings, such as, "When a woman has a son, she grows one fist in height but when she has a daughter, she shrinks one fist in height", or, more crudely:

> Pūt nā sapūt,
> Chūlhe-ke-ūpar mūt,
> Rahā ūt kā ūt.
> No son, let alone an obedient one,
> There is only piss on the hearth,
> He remains sonless, just a blockhead.[44]

Again, among Hindus, for instance, when a son follows a daughter a lump of gur is broken over the little girl's buttocks to signify that even though her own birth was not a source of happiness, at least she brought a brother in her wake.[45] Such sayings and practices, along with the differentiated responses outlined above, surely make the point overwhelmingly clear. Occasionally, however, a jachā is punished or threatened because she delivered a girl, highlighting the displeasure which is usually more discreetly submerged. These cases become talking-points in the villages: Bhagwana threatened to repudiate Bhagirthi if she had another girl; Davinder refused to call his sisters or even enter his house for several days. And Lalit's younger brother even padlocked the grain-store, saying Lakshmi could hardly expect food since he was paying for the baby girl's jasthawn. For several days, Lakshmi had ajwain seeds and dried ginger washed down with hot water, not the ghī he would have granted if she had produced a son. Furthermore, the jasthawn actually ended in uproar when the pandit realised that he was not going to be paid, and he departed leaving the baby nameless and the defilement unremoved.

A death soon after birth

Sometimes, anxiety about the baby's vulnerability is not misplaced and the baby has already died or is sickly before any khushī can take place. In Dharmnagri and Jhakri, about 3% of live-born babies die within the first week, and another 3% before the end of the first month. If we add in stillbirths and babies who die at birth, one in eleven babies born at full-term (three or four a year in the two villages) were dead within one month. Boys' chances of survival in this period are slightly lower than girls'. The highest death rates were among first-born babies, but the chances of babies dying at this age differed little among the different classes or between the two villages.[46]

None of these babies died in hospital and we have only their mothers' explanations for their death. Of the 58 deaths under one month for which we were told a cause, the most frequent diagnosis (nearly one-third) was tetanus (a word used in Hindi, but its symptoms are easily confused with septicaemia).[47] Thirteen were of children born before 1975, when tetanus toxoid injections became available locally. Since then, only four deaths have been attributed to tetanus, despite the fact that only one-quarter of all births were protected by tetanus toxoid injections before delivery. Indeed, two-thirds of the Muslims who had any tetanus toxoid injections summoned a medical practitioner (the compounder or an untrained practitioner) to give both jachā and baby tetanus toxoid injections only after the delivery. Unlike the free ante-natal tetanus injections, these cost Rs 15-25 and actually offer the baby no protection from tetanus if its cord was cut by an infected instrument. Possibly these injections enable women to pass on protection to subsequent babies, though not to the baby they think they are protecting. The next largest category of cause of death was the effect of evil influences (seven deaths), followed by fever, diarrhoea, pneumonia and a variety of other causes. Some babies were reported to have died suddenly for no apparent reason.

Occcasionally, sick babies are taken to Dharmnagri, Begawala or even Bijnor for treatment, either to a doctor or (if evil influences are diagnosed) to a religious healer. Generally, however, home remedies are favoured as they do not necessitate taking the already vulnerable infant beyond the domestic area. A range of items may be applied to the cut end of the umbilical stump (sūndī), but often only if it is already septic. People use mustard oil containing turmeric, "red medicine" (lāl dawā or mercurichrome), surgical spirit, Dettol or an antiseptic cream. Ash used to be commonly employed (and was possibly a source of tetanus) but few individuals now mention it. One dāi said her clients sometimes used musk, which is very garm but expensive and often adulterated, so its use has declined.

A baby's death in this early period ends any khushī and len-den. It also puts a stop to the dāi's work and to her payments. Among Muslims and Hindus alike, the dead baby is bathed by a close relative and then buried. If its death occured before the chhatī or jasthawn, the defilement is finally removed by the jachā's close female susrāl kin, simply by bathing the jachā and plastering the floor of her house with diluted dung.

Most babies, however, do survive. In welcoming them people select from a repertoire of procedures which have very distinct class and ethnic characteristics. But within those parameters, they do so in ways which publicise the different significance of each birth for the jachā's chūlhā. Motherhood is graphically endorsed by the khushī which greets the first-born child. Particularly when this child is a boy, the birth will be marked by noisy celebration, feasting, and the extensive activation of links through len-den, to the extent that funds permit. Later children — especially girls — meet with much less excitement. From the moment of giving birth, then, jachās are distinguished by the khushī and public recognition which different births are granted. Indeed, many births — particularly those of girls and high parity babies — are scarcely treated as matters of celebration at all.

Even for the jachā whose delivery is loudly welcomed, the immediate post-partum period is one of anxiety about the baby's well-being and ambivalence about herself, whatever her class position and ethnicity. Right across the board, bearing any child, whether son or daughter, whether first-born or later, alters the jachā's bodily state so that she is vulnerable to thand and evil influences as well as being profoundly polluted and dangerous to people around her. Much as motherhood is valued and expected, all celebration is moderated by this understanding that it inevitably involves the jachā in negative self-images and necessitates virtually standard procedures to remedy her situation. These are not merely significant as evaluations of women's nature, for the jachā's vulnerability, her more than usually restricted mobility and her capacity to contaminate others jeopardise the execution of her everyday responsibilities.

Washing a child at the handpump

7. A Chance to Sit on the Bed

Women in Jhakri only stop working the very moment when they give birth, not before. *(Wasila)*

Dharmnagri is a village, so who gives a woman any rest before she gives birth? Why, I consider myself lucky to get some rest after giving birth! *(Maya)*

A jachā gets rest for just a few days. If she has a sās or a nand then she may get some rest for five weeks, but where will she find real peace in the midst of her husband and older children? *(Durgi)*

Sharm comes in front of the mother. That is why she is not called after her daughter has a baby. It is a susrāl matter, and it is correct that it is dealt with by susrāl people. *(Sabra)*

Only after the baby is born does a woman have a chance to sit on the bed. *(Kamla)*

Being a jachā is one of the rare occasions when a bahū is entitled to relief from her normal work. Her role as new mother ought to put her role as worker in abeyance and she should be temporarily replaced by another worker. Women say that the jachā should be helped by her sās, her nand (or even both) or some other woman from her susrāl connection. Ideally, the jachā obtains help with at least some of her work for five weeks.[1] But while the jachā's condition warrants some special arrangements, the details in practice vary widely and the perceived needs of the jachā are far from universally met. Help must be negotiated, and, as a bahū in her susrāl, the jachā is ill-placed to enforce these ideals herself. She cannot command anyone's services, and has no guarantee that others in her susrāl will do so on her behalf. Indeed, the weight of other considerations may be incompatible with providing lengthy help for her. Jachās in Dharmnagri and Jhakri are surrounded by other women, all of whom are workers themselves. Thus, the availability of help for more than a few days after delivery, from within the jachā's susrāl or from elsewhere (especially the married nands) is often problematic. Young women in Dharmnagri and Jhakri consider that the domiciliary post-natal care available to them cannot ensure recuperation from pregnancy and childbirth. It is part of a more general syndrome that operates in relation to childbearing women, to the detriment (women say) of their own and their children's well-being.[2]

Maternity: a matter of shame -

Husband: Say, fair one [wife], should I call your sās?
Wife: No, my king [husband], this is nothing to do with my sās!
Husband: Say, fair one, should I call your mother?
Wife: My king, now my heart's desire is spoken!

This birth song represents a dialogue between a jachā and her husband, expressing the jachā's wish to exclude her sās and call her mother. Succeeding verses contrast the jachā's husband's brother's wife with her own brother's wife, her husband's sister with her own sister, her husband's aunts with her own aunts and so on. But this inverts rather than reflects the situation of the typical jachā, whether Hindu or Muslim. Alongside the jachā's weakness, vulnerability and capacity to contaminate others is another aspect of maternity: sharm. The jachā's condition is a sharm-kī-bāt; her physiological processes are embarrassing, distasteful and striking evidence of her sexuality. Thus her access to her natal kin is restricted. We have already noted that they do not attend celebrations in her susrāl and may even not learn that she has given birth for some weeks. If a bahū's natal kin know about her pregnancy, her brothers and (especially) her father may avoid visiting her around the time the delivery is expected. If they call shortly afterwards, they stay only briefly, for their presence is inappropriate:

My father chanced to visit me the day I had given birth. Because of that he immediately went away. *(Omvati)*

My brother visited Jhakri the day I gave birth, so he got the news immediately. But he did not stay and he only came back after a fortnight. *(Hashmi)*

My brother had not visited Dharmnagri while I was pregnant, and then he came the very day I gave birth. He rushed away, he was so embarrassed. He is my baby's māmū [MB] but people began to taunt him saying, 'What, has the baby's chachā [FyB] come to eat sweets?' *(Urmila)*

By chance my brother came to Dharmnagri on the jasthawn day. When he realised that I had a son he went away and ate in a hotel in Bijnor. A baby's māmū [MB] cannot eat the jasthawn food. *(Bhagirthi)*

The jachā is most unlikely to be visited in her susrāl by her mother or sisters soon after delivery, unless she or the baby are seriously ill and this stricture is waived. Her female natal kin are not considered suitable replacements to do the work from which she is temporarily relieved.[3] This is so even for Muslim jachās in within-village marriages and women in ghar-jamāi marriages. Further, a visit to the natal village is not permissible for the jachā. Solicitous care, better food, respite from susrāl responsibilities or access to medical help might all be available there. But the sharm of being a jachā is compounded by her defilement and her own and the baby's vulnerability, which make travelling inappropriate. At the earliest, the jachā might visit her parents when the baby is some five weeks old: she has a final cleansing bath, takes the baby to her natal village, stays some weeks and returns to her susrāl with gifts.[4] Such visits are not entitlements, however, and many of our key informants did not make them. In any case, the timing of such visits does not provide for recovery from the delivery itself.[5] Viramvati said, "My parents first learnt of the baby when I visited them when she was two-three months old." Perhaps more surprising is Maqsudi's account. Her maikā is within sight of Jhakri but her baby was born during the hectic rice-transplanting season: "No one took news of the baby to my parents and they did not visit me. I went to them when the baby was two months old."

Thus, the jachā whose parents are still living, whether distantly or close-by, is effectively no better placed than bought brides or women whose parents are dead. Typically, a jachā has no access to the women with whom she can relax or the place where she is most at ease. She is tied to her susrāl and must regain her strength and her normal condition there, subject to the restraints and responsibilities of a bahū.

Someone to do the work

There could be benefits for a woman if she stays in her pīhar to give birth. But I am fine in my susrāl as my nand helps with my work. I am more fortunate than many women, who get no help in their susrāl. *(Bhagirthi)*

The jachā is unclean for five weeks. For all that time no one should eat food which she has cooked. But if there is no one to cook for the family, she may start cooking for them out of necessity after a fortnight. If she is completely akelī her husband would cook his own meals.

In the susrāl, a jachā may have a few days rest, but only if there is someone to do the work. *(Jumni)*

Preparing food is work common to bahūs in their susrāl. But, while a jachā may cook for herself, she should not cook for others.[6] Childbirth pollution endangers their well-being, though informants were vague about what symptoms might ensue. But if the jachā does not cook, who will ensure that her chūlhā members do not go hungry? Further, outside-work is compromised. Who will do the dung-work, the animal-work, or take food to men in the fields? One Muslim woman's case dramatically indicates the urgency of finding an alternative worker. Only minutes after giving birth, the jachā anxiously summoned her cousin, who is also married in Jhakri, saying (to the amusement of the other women present):

> It's time to milk the buffalo. Here, take my shawl and cover your face well with it. And don't say anything — the buffalo only gives milk to me, but she might give milk for you now if you dress like me!

Women living amid so many others might be expected to obtain abundant help and support after delivery. In practice, as at other times, the demands of a labour-intensive economy and the low levels of co-operation among women affect the rest that jachās obtain. Women in Dharmnagri and Jhakri strongly articulate the jachā's entitlement to rest, but finding someone to do the work can prove difficult. Women's experiences of the post-partum period are so diverse, however, that they cannot be captured succinctly. Different women report an array of experiences and there is diversity even in individual women's childbearing careers: Asghari was helped by her sās and married nand for several weeks, both before and after her first delivery; but Viramvati's nand was in advanced pregnancy herself and could not visit Dharmnagri; Durgi's sās helped her for a fortnight; while Khurshida was helped by Khalil's cousin (his MBD) for nearly two months.

The support a jachā obtains with her different types of work, from whom and for how long is influenced by several parameters which intermingle in different and sometimes unpredictable ways after each birth. Most salient are the composition of the jachā's chūlhā and her normal patterns of co-operation in her susrāl; the availability of her married nands to help; changes over time; class factors (principally in relation to women's work); and ethnicity. Women with the heaviest workloads, particularly those in middle peasant chūlhās, tend to obtain the least respite from their responsibilities, especially if they are Muslim.

Domestic setting in the jachā's susrāl

The jachā's support network is primarily demarcated by her residence in her susrāl and the division of labour between men and women. Basically, some other woman or women accomplish the bulk of the jachā's work: cooking, dish-scouring, household cleaning and childcare. Short cuts can be taken in some other tasks, as when dung is thrown into the midden instead of being made into dung-cakes.

The jachā can expect help only from women of her own chūlhā or of closely related ones, especially her sās. But the mere existence of the sās is no guarantee that she will take over the jachā's work, for she may have other responsibilities which put helping the jachā low on her agenda. Prior decisions about chūlhā organisation, particularly about remaining sājhe or becoming alag, are important in this. Almost one-quarter of the key informants were still sājhe at their last delivery and they all had their work taken over by their sās. By contrast, half the key informants were alag and only half of them were helped by their sās. The remaining quarter of the key informants were akelī.

Other married women, living in houses sharing the same courtyard or beyond, have "their own work" and would rarely be asked to help. Even the jachā's sisters-in-law (HBW) are unlikely to offer their services, unless (as is rare in Dharmnagri and Jhakri) they are sājhe with the jachā. Unusually, Jumni did feel obliged to help Kamla (her HyBW), although they are separate from one another and from their sās. Consequently, Jumni refused to go to her pīhar with her brother for the Tijo festival. Essentially, however, the sās is the jachā's most likely helper, but even then after only about two-thirds of the last deliveries of key informants with a sās still living.

Calling the married nand

The jachā's nand is a central figure in the celebrations after a birth and is also regarded as a potential helper with at least some of the jachā's work. Only Najma and Khurshida have no nand, though Fatima and Ghazala's nand is too young to help yet. The maternity history of Najma's sās was one of the most woeful in Jhakri. On overhearing it, Najma commented: "Three boys and seven girls! But just two boys remain. Not one girl stayed alive. If just one was alive, what would be the matter with that? Why, I could sometimes call my nand!"

All the remaining key informants have at least one nand, sometimes, of course, shared with their sisters-in-law (HBW). About one-quarter of the nands are still unmarried, sharing a chūlhā with the jachā or in a separate chūlhā with the jachā's sās. An unmarried nand aged ten or so will probably help the jachā, just as she might on a day-to-day basis. But three-quarters of the key informants' nands are married and so probably living in another village. Help from that source is less certain, as several considerations affect whether the married nand will be called after the jachā gives birth.

The jachā's own chūlhā composition is important in negotiations over calling the nand. If the jachā's sās is still alive, she, not the jachā herself, is key in the decision. It is appropriate for a mother to call her married daughters but improper for the jachā to suggest that her nand is called, especially while she is still sājhe. The initiative rests with the sās to ask one of the men to leave their work and fetch the nand from her susrāl. The jachā's sās can benefit from her daughter's helping hand while also engaging in len-den. Half the jachās still sājhe with their sās also had help from their nand. On the other hand, once akelī, the jachā herself can ask her husband to call a helper, and over half the akelī key informants obtained help from a nand. The situation of the jachā who is alag is much harder to characterise. Being alag is generally symptomatic of some distance between the jachā and her sās. The sās herself is a less reliable source of help, and, moreover, is less likely to call the nand. The jachā may face difficulties negotiating who is called to help her:

> But it is the job of the sās to remind her son to call his sisters. That is the point. If my husband does not think to call his sisters, then in anger I remain silent. *(Imrana)*

Only one-third of the jachās who were alag were helped by their nand.

153

And overall, fewer than half the key informants with one or more nands old enough to help — either unmarried teenagers or married — had any help from that source after their last delivery.

A married nand's failure to help the jachā can be largely attributed to decisions of the jachā's susrāl kin (and sometimes the jachā herself) not to summon her. When a nand is called after her brother's wife has given birth, her expectations of relief from her own susrāl responsibilities may be more than usually dissonant with those of the jachā, who (unusually) is entitled to rest herself. Certainly, some women overcome the structural tensions and develop supportive relationships, but this depends heavily on mutual good will.[7] Among middle peasants in particular, several women — key informants and their sās alike — commented caustically that the nand merely comes with such a troupe of her own small children that she creates more work than she does.

> It is not essential for the nand to come. My sās is alive and does my work for me so there is no need to call my nands. *(Qudsia)*

> My nands do no work when they come to their pīhar. Their mother does it all. That is why she has not called my nands except after my first baby. She says they do no work so what is the benefit? My sās does everything, even the work for the nands' children! So I just give them neg some other time when they come to Dharmnagri. *(Maya)*

If the nand comes, she is entitled to neg, even if she does no work.[8] Several women argued that the desire for neg and for rest are key in the nand's visit. Often, the sās herself does not want to call her daughter, reckoning that she can cope better alone. Several key informants, indeed, said they themselves had not been called after their brother's wife's delivery as their mother was doing the work. Among the poorest (especially the landless), the inability to provide neg, rather than unwillingness to call a nand who does nothing, is sometimes a reason given for not calling the nand:

> My daughter was born after I had gone alag. But we called neither of my nands then. You see, we had spent a lot on medicines for my husband's T.B. and for my baby son who died. So we were very short of money and had nothing to give to my nand. Just my sās helped me for 40 days. *(Vimla)*

> How could we call my nands, since we have nothing to give as neg. If we ever had money left after feeding everyone, then we could give. We have never called my nands. Anyway, my sās is here to do my work. *(Wasila)*

Occasionally, the baby's sex influenced the decision to call a nand. Nands are more likely to be called and given neg during the greater khushī marking a boy's birth. Once in the natal village, the nand may do some of the jachā's work. Conversely, in a few cases, the nand was not called explicitly because the baby was a girl.[9] Bhagirthi had a son and her nand stayed for several weeks; soon afterwards, Adesh had a daughter, and said she could hardly call their nand again so quickly, especially as her baby was a girl. And Durgi lost out twice when she had daughters:

> **Durgi:** One nand was married before I was, and the younger one was married about a year after my marriage. When I had my first baby, my younger nand was in Dharmnagri for a visit, so we kept her here and did not bother to call my other nand.
> **Radha:** Why not?
> **Durgi:** My sās said there was no point. What would my nand have to do? The baby was a girl, so there was no taking-outside and my nand had no sathiyā [good luck sign] to make. Anyway, the younger nand was already here.
> **Radha:** By the last delivery you were alag, so what happened then?
> **Durgi:** I worked right up to the delivery and my sās did my work for ten-fifteen days. You see, I had another girl and my husband was angry. He took his food from his mother's chūlhā and did not come into our house for three days, so how could I ask him to call his sister? When he did come inside, I asked him to call his sister, but my sās told us to check first that we had a dhotī set aside. We did not and my husband had no money, so we did not call her. But if it had been a boy, my nand would certainly have come.

Thus, assessments of the help the nand is likely to provide, financial constraints and considerations of len-den and khushī, can outweigh the voiced appropriateness of calling the married nand.

The nand is a also a bahū

> The nand can only come if her susrāl people are prepared to send her. *(Jamila)*

> Both my married nands came after I had my first child, a boy. But they stayed only five-six days as they are both akelī in their susrāl and their husbands are worried about their work when they are away. *(Vimla)*

Even if the nand is called, however, she is no free agent. Like the jachā, she is a bahū and subject to limitations on her activities. The most common restraint is the nand's own pregnancy or recent delivery, since visiting her natal village then would be a sharm-kī-bāt; her natal kin would not even bother calling her if they knew her condition. Otherwise, the nand's responsibilities in her susrāl loom large and influence her in-laws' decisions about permitting visits to her natal village to help her brother's wife. Sometimes, lack of a suitable replacement for her or the extra work created by births, marriages or deaths among her immediate susrāl kin mean that she returns only briefly to her natal village, if at all. One nand's brother comes to call her, but her sās says they cannot spare her at present. Another nand goes to her natal village, but her mother capitulates to the husband's insistence that she stays only four or five days. One nand cannot come because only she can milk a temperamental buffalo, another because her new sister-in-law (HyBW) cannot yet be left in charge, while an older nand's bahū is a jachā. The accounts given are legion, and primarily hinge on the precise circumstances in which the nand is living, on her responsibilities and the composition of her chūlhā:

> After this child, my sās did my work, even though we are alag, until my oldest nand arrived five-six days after the birth. But my second nand's husband refused to send her: he said it was too soon after she had been here for treatment for jaundice. He is like that. He never wants to send her and never lets her stay long. My oldest nand's husband is not like that: he never complains and he lets her stay as long as she asks. And he usually agrees if her mother asks for her to stay longer. *(Kamla)*

> I went to my maikā when my brother's first child was born and stayed for six weeks. But the next time, my twelve-year-old nand had just died. I told my brother that I could not go with him at such a time. *(Ghazala)*

The childbearing career of the jachā's sās gives another perspective on this. The sās' daughters and bahūs may be balanced in numbers, but sometimes there are several married brothers with only one married sister or several married sisters but only one married brother. The solitary sister with several brothers repeatedly faces the birth of their children. Certainly, she can expect more neg than other women, but this must be weighed against often having to negotiate permission from her susrāl kin to visit her natal village. Moreover, she may sometimes be pregnant or a jachā herself when one or other of her brothers' wives delivers. The only sister of Rohtash and his five brothers returned to live in Dharmnagri with her husband when her mother was widowed. Her case is instructive. All her brothers are now married, and (in comparison with all the other Hindu key informants' nands) she could hardly be more accessible.[10] Yet her brothers' wives resent her unwillingness to help when they give birth, especially as she expects costly gifts when boys are born. Pushpa considers her nand's "help" of little use as she just "works for two days, does nothing for two days", while Omvati sees no benefit because the nand "will not remain beside me throughout the twenty-four hours". Unlike nands called from another village, she is constantly distracted by her own chūlhā's responsibilities. From the nand's angle, the disruption could be considerable: by the end of 1986, her brothers had had 22 children, five born during our research.

Conversely, the jachā married to an only son or to a man with younger unmarried brothers will probably fare well, especially if there are several sisters. His calls on his sisters will be less persistent and one sister (at least) will surely be granted permission. In addition, the nands are unlikely to be all simultaneously pregnant or jachās and debarred from visiting their natal village. Several women whose husbands have no married brothers were helped by more than one nand after their first delivery, when expectations of neg are important. They are also more likely than other women to obtain help from a nand on later occasions. Dilshad is an only son with four sisters, one married in Jhakri and two married into the same compound in Qaziwala.

Until these two latter had children, one or other would be in Jhakri while the one in Qaziwala did the work of both of them. Dilruba (whose sās is blind) had at least one nand doing her work before and after each of her five deliveries, usually for several weeks.

Most jachās have less chance of being helped by a nand. Indeed, six of the 18 key informants who were helped by their nand after their last deliveries received that help rather fortuitously. Calling the nand entails becoming a supplicant, but if the nand is already in her natal village, a more effective bargain can be driven with her husband over when she will return to her susrāl, sometimes to the benefit of the jachā. Sabra has never called her nand as she has nothing for len-den, but her nand happened to be in Jhakri after Sabra's last delivery and helped for just one day; Sabra's sautelī-sās (step-mother-in-law) is the nand's step-mother and maltreats her if she does not work hard for her. Other nands were in their natal village for a wedding or festival:

> My nand chanced to be in Jhakri for a wedding when I gave birth. That's why she did all my house-work and outside-work for ten-twelve days. After she returned to her susrāl, I did all my own work again. *(Latifan)*

> My daughter arrived two months ago for the first time after having her baby. During that time her husband has been to call her twice but I refused to send her as she should be here for Tijo. Anyway, Jumni was about to give birth. *(Jumni's sās)*

Alternatives to the sās and nand

Only Khurshida has neither a sās nor a nand, so the rest of the key informants might seem able to rely upon either their sās or nand or even both. But only around half of them were helped by their sās and fewer than half by their nand, some jachās having help from both. Occasionally, the jachā's sisters-in-law (HBW) may rally round, but usually only if there is no sās, nand or alternative, and then probably for no longer than a day or two.

Generally, the men of the chūlhā are minimally affected by the jachā's inability to perform her work. They might adjust their activities or do extra work to alleviate the women's work if the jachā is alag or akelī and the men's work is slack. Occasionally, men collect and chop fodder without help from the women. Sometimes, they eat before going to the fields or take food with them. A jachā would not be expected to do field-work. But hardly any men helped their wives with "women's work", never with dung-work and rarely with house-work. The three bought brides among the key informants were all somewhat unusual in this. Tahira was akelī and her nand was not called. Tahira's sister-in-law (HyBW) did the house-work and dung-work for four days and Taslim collected and chopped the fodder. Lalit and Rohtash both did house-work for their wives. Lakshmi had no sās, but was still sājhe with Lalit's brother's adolescent daughter, who helped only grudgingly. The feud with Lakshmi's nand's susrāl kin meant the nand was not called and Lalit did some of the cooking. Rajballa, by contrast, is alag and her nand lives in

Dharmnagri. When Rajballa returned to Dharmnagri after nearly two weeks in hospital, neither her sās nor her nand offered any assistance (though both had taken turns attending her in hospital). Rohtash was so anxious about her recovery from the Caesarian section that he cared for their daughter and did the cooking for over a month while Rajballa cared for the baby boy.

But such instances are extremely rare, for the jachā's work is women's work. Sometimes, the jachā's best recourse is one of her own unmarried daughters. Sabra's daughter (aged eight) did the cooking, making tiny rotī for her father and younger sisters, after Sabra's nand had helped for one day. Similarly, Imarti's twelve-year-old daughter did the work until Imarti's nand arrived and again after the nand returned to her susrāl to care for her own heavily pregnant bahū.[11] Several bahūs in Jhakri reported having helped their sās after childbirth.[12] Occasionally, the husband's aunt (FBW), his unmarried "sister" (generally his FBD) or his unmarried niece (BD) does the jachā's work. Sometimes, jachās range more widely and call someone from outside their susrāl:

> When I had my older daughter, I was still sājhe and my married nand stayed for a month. But when my second daughter was born my married nand couldn't come as she was a jachā herself. So my husband's aunt [HFZ] helped me. She came a month before the birth and stayed another month afterwards. She can stay as her bahū is still sājhe and does her work while she is away. *(Viramvati)*

A nand might send her own daughter and occasionally the husband's married niece or cousin (his BD or FBD) may be called. Bashir has refused Suleiman (his son from his first marriage) access to his land, and Bilquis calls her married daughter (from her own first marriage) for several weeks. She has never sought help from Sabra (her step-daughter-in-law), whom she herself has never helped after childbirth. Adesh also called her married daughter after her last delivery. And Maqsudi even calls her sās' mother (HMM) to do house-work and some outside-work, since her sās and nands only perform the animal-work that remains sājhe.[13] From the jachā's point of view, all these women (including the married daughter and the sās' mother) are susrāl kin and resorted to in preference to her natal kin, particularly her own mother or sisters.

> It is not good for a mother to come after her daughter gives birth. A woman feels sharm before her mother. There is a difference between a daughter and a daughter-in-law. *(Asghari)*

> There is sharm in front of people from the pīhar. Also, they are not entitled to come or to take neg. If there is no nand then there is necessity. Only then a woman might call people from her pīhar. *(Chandresh)*

> My father would not let my unmarried sister come here as that would give him a bad name. Anyway, my sās and nand would say I have called my sister to avoid giving to them. *(Santosh)*

A woman feels sharm in front of her parents, so she would not call her mother. For the susrāl people it is something different, as it is a matter concerning their house. *(Khurshida)*

A woman's natal kin may be called upon, but only in exceptional circumstances which need elaborate justification. Their involvement is shameful, "worse even than involving them in a marital row", Imrana commented. It also leaves the jachā open to accusations that she is trying to evade len-den. Several women said a sister's help would be more congenial, but unthinkable unless they could find no one else to help. Umrao, for instance, lives in her maikā and has no contact with her susrāl kin, and calls her married sister some weeks before giving birth. Sometimes, too, a chance visitor remains to help:

My nands were both married before I was. Only the younger one came after my first delivery and she stayed just seven-eight days. My nands came after the other deliveries, but we did not call them so that they could work. I got no benefit from their coming. Sometimes my sās did my work, sometimes I did it myself. After the last baby, my aunt [FZ] helped. She happened to be visiting when I gave birth and she stayed for over a week. So I did not even call my nands this time. *(Imrana)*

It is certainly rare for the jachā to receive no adult help. If the sās or nand cannot help, another woman (generally from the jachā's susrāl connection) usually steps in. Indeed, several jachās had more than one helper, either simultaneously or consecutively. Women who are sājhe are almost certain to be helped not only by their sās but also by a nand or alternative. But only half the jachās who were alag were helped by their sās, and just under half of these were additionally helped by a another woman. Thus, nearly three-quarters of the jachās who were alag had just one helper, their sās or someone else. The jachā who is akelī is most unlikely to have two helpers: about half were helped just by their nand, the rest by an alternative to the nand. Chandresh is the only exception: her first baby was a boy, Chet Ram is an only son and Chandresh was helped not only by three of her four nands briefly in succession but also by her sister.

The passage of time

Hashmi: Let me explain what happened after the births of these four children who are still alive. Both my nands were married before me and when I had my first daughter, both came from their susrāl. The older one stayed for just a week because of her work in her susrāl. But the younger one was still sājhe and she stayed for a month to do my work. After my son's birth, we held a chhatī, so both my nands came. The older stayed just six days. The younger one stayed only a week, for she was then alag in her susrāl. After the next boy, I called my oldest nand's daughter, who arrived a week before the baby was born and stayed for

two weeks afterwards. This last time, no one came. My sās did my house-work for three days.
Swaleha: Didn't you call your nands that time?
Hashmi: No. Who calls the nand every time?

Another angle on jachās' experiences can be obtained by tracing women's childbearing careers, for the domestic circumstances of the jachā and her married nands change, and later births generate less khushī.

Being sājhe is the surest guarantee of being helped by the sās after childbirth. Most bahūs begin their married life sājhe, and the sās is expected to keep her bahū under her wing until at least the first child is born. Thus, the jachā is usually best-placed after her first delivery. Occasionally, a sās dies or they become alag before the bahū has a baby, but women generally have one or two children while still sājhe. A few key informants remained sājhe even after four or five children — Latifan had seven children while still sājhe — and all continued to be helped by their sās. Further, more of the jachā's nands will be unmarried or not yet cohabiting at her first delivery, and some of them will be sharing the chūlhā's work anyway. Moreover, a married nand is more likely to come early in the jachā's childbearing career, because the sās is so central in calling her. Almost all the key informants had help from their sās and at least one nand after their first delivery. The few exceptions were those without a nand, with nands too young to help, or whose married nand was not called because there was no cash for neg or because of a family feud.

Gradually, configurations change. The jachā who is alag is less certain of being helped by her sās. Over the years, the sās may become frail or die. Unmarried nands are converted into married, and their availability to help the jachā is compromised by their susrāl responsibilities. The nand cannot come repeatedly:

After my first child, both my nands were here, as well as my sās, for the older nand was married within Jhakri and the younger one's cohabitation had not taken place. My older nand died a few months after that. After the second baby, my younger nand came from her susrāl and did my work for ten-twelve days. But for later births, my sās just did my work for three-four days and then I did it myself. But before my last child, she had died. I've had my eight children very rapidly, and who could call her nand back every time? The nand's husband cannot send his wife every day, for she has her own work in her own house. *(Latifan)*

Urmila's account indicates the changes that may occur in a matter of only eight years, though she has always obtained some help from a nand:

Urmila: I have four nands. None was married when my first son was born, so they were all here. There was no question of calling them. The first nand was married when my son was about a year old, three years after my marriage. Soon after that I became alag. After my second son was born, my older nand was called from her susrāl. She did my work for about six weeks; she could stay that long as she was still sājhe. My second nand was married two years after the first one, after my second son was born. When I had my daughter, my second nand helped with my work. She had been here visiting for about a month. The very day her husband came to collect her, my pains began. With great difficulty, my sās persuaded him to leave her here to help. He let her stay just two more weeks. She has no children, but her sās is dead and her husband is alag from his brother, so he worries about getting food cooked when she is not there.

Patricia: Didn't you call your older nand when you had your daughter?

Urmila: No, she was pregnant. She had a girl about four months later.

Only in the early years after marriage (if at all) are married nands sājhe with their sās or sisters-in-law (HBW). Later, the nands are likely to be alag or akelī and their own successive pregnancies and growing responsibilities, including caring for their children, make it increasingly difficult for them to leave their susrāl for long. No matter what a nand's responsibilities or how many brothers she has, however, she will probably make every effort to come to her natal village after the first deliveries of all her brothers' wives, for then the khushī (and the neg) is greatest. After later births, the jachā's sās may refrain from calling the nand. This general progression is likely to be reversed temporarily only if a woman has a son after a series of girls.

Basically, then, changing demographic configurations and considerations of khushī mean that a jachā's chance of being helped by her sās and nands declines over time. Although the jachā almost always has some adult help, individual cases reflect a complex of elements that make it difficult to predict her source of support.

Women in villages can't observe restrictions for long

My nand came a month before I gave birth. She did my house-work and outside-work after the birth, but her husband collected her five-six days afterwards and then I did it all myself. *(Jamila)*

I did not cook for a fortnight, because my unmarried nand and my sās did the work together, while my husband collected fodder. I began house-work again after a fortnight and began collecting fodder again two months after the birth. *(Nirmala)*

I don't usually collect fodder much anyway, unless the men have no time. Imrana made dung-cakes for me one day and threw the dung in the midden the next day. After that I myself began to make dung-cakes again. *(Hashmi)*

Out of necessity, poor women begin their work five-six days after giving birth. Women in villages can't observe restrictions for long. *(dāi)*

The chūlhā organisation of the jachā and her nands is clearly crucial in the structuring of jachās' support networks and how they change. But even that cannot capture the variations in the quality and length of help provided. A sās or a nand might help the jachā for several weeks or for only a few days, with all her work or only some of it. Unravelling these complexities entails also considering issues of class and ethnicity.

The jachā's helpers from within her susrāl and those specially called from elsewhere cannot be distinguished with respect to the period they provide help or the work they do. One sās helps for several weeks, while another lends a hand only for a few days. One married nand concentrates on the jachā's work and once with the jachā is easily kept there, but another hardly helps at all and is soon summoned back to her susrāl. More detailed consideration of the helper's obligations, however, helps us to understand variations in the amount of help obtained by the jachā. Broadly speaking, helpers giving the most extensive help are women with the fewest responsibilities: some domestic and work situations enable women to be available for longer than others.

Within the jachā's susrāl, the sās who is still sājhe will probably help for several weeks, at least with some of the work. Likewise, the married nand or alternative helper who is sājhe can usually negotiate a longer stay with the jachā than one who is alag or akelī, especially if she has no children herself yet. This was so for Adesh's daughter, Punni's brother's daughter who helped Pushpa, and Dilruba's nands in Qaziwala, for instance. Similarly, an unmarried adolescent girl might be released by her mother to help the jachā, whether within the jachā's susrāl or from elsewhere. Khurshida, for example, was still sājhe with her sās when her first daughter was born, and her sās did all her work. The sās had died before Khurshida's son was born, and Khurshida has no nand. Thus she called her unmarried "nand" (Khalil's FBD) from the next house, who did all her work for some three weeks. After the next delivery, Khurshida called another unmarried "nand" (this time, Khalil's MBD) from a nearby village: she stayed nearly two months, did all Khurshida's house-work and outside-work, and received 20 kilograms of wheat, five kilograms of gur, three suit-lengths and Rs 5 for the dūdh-dhulāi. In another instance, Bhagirthi's nand brought two of her children and could do Bhagirthi's work for several weeks, as her own nand's unmarried daughter did her work (including caring for her three other children), a domino effect that delighted our informants. Older women can more easily help if they have a grown daughter or are sājhe with their bahū, as were Umrao's sister, Viramvati's husband's aunt (HFZ), Imrana's aunt (FZ), and Maqsudi's sās' mother (HMM). By contrast, the nand or other helper who has young children and is alag or akelī faces her husband's complaints about food worries if she is away too long and no one can easily take over her work.

Class and jachās' work

Further, jachās and their potential helpers are differentiated by their workloads. Particularly salient is the distinction between house-work that all women do and the varying amounts of outside-work that women in land- or livestock-owning households also regularly do. The length of help a jachā obtains depends on her own workload and on the leeway which her potential helpers have with their own.

Generally, women in poor peasant and landless chūlhās have lighter workloads than middle peasant women, because they have little or no outside-work. Several such jachās, including Vimla, Viramvati, Umrao and Wasila, had some weeks' help with their house-work and what little animal-work they had.

On the other hand, women who are already heavily loaded cannot easily take on the jachā's entire work for long, especially if that entails a lot of outside-work.[14] The outside-work of middle peasant women is more burdensome than that of most rich peasants or the poor peasant and landless women, involving taking food to the fields, watering and feeding several animals, collecting fodder and making dung-cakes, without assistance from servants. A helper from a middle peasant chūlhā can come from elsewhere for an extended visit only if her work can be satisfactorily taken over while she is away: otherwise she may help for only a few days before going back to her susrāl. Very few middle peasant women were helped for more than two weeks with their cooking, and for a few more days with their outside-work. Several Muslim middle peasant women, for instance, explained that a rapid chhatī was held because they had to do their house-work quickly after delivery, rather than because of great khushī; others could find no one able to do their outside-work and were making dung-cakes within a week of giving birth. Thus, the jachā may obtain help for only a short time, or for only some of her duties.

Some rich peasant women have little work which takes them beyond the domestic arena, others have work profiles more akin to those of middle peasant women. Rich peasant women, however, are generally able to find and reward helpers whose work can be done by someone else. They all had several weeks relief from their outside-work, and all but Asghari had someone to do their cooking for six weeks or more.

Women's work varies seasonally (especially for rich and middle peasants), but this was rarely mentioned to explain why a jachā was able or unable to obtain help after a particular delivery. Nor does our analysis suggest that the season of a baby's birth affects the help its mother obtains. Rather, the routine patterns of co-operation into which the jachā and her potential helpers are locked are more significant. Considerations of chūlhā composition and the availability of the jachā's helpers intersect with class differences in the work her helpers might perform for her and in the work they themselves would need to give up.

The Hindu and the Muslim jachā
Another ingredient is necessary to fill out this picture. Women in Dharmnagri and Jhakri voice identical views about the approved sources of help for a jachā and agree that help is appropriate. Yet some of the most striking differences in the quality of help received in practice indicate that ethnicity is another important component, especially with respect to the length of help,

the numbers of helpers, and the role of the sās. Basically, Muslim jachās obtain less help than do comparable Hindu jachās.

Only about one-quarter of the key informants refrained from cooking for as long as a month. Hindu women do not cook for others for at least a fortnight (but generally no more than three weeks).[15] Among the key informants, Lakshmi was the sole exception in having just a few days' help with her cooking, but she is extraordinarily isolated, being a bought bride, akelī in her susrāl, and cut off from her nand. By contrast, two-thirds of the Muslim jachās had less than ten days off cooking, and over half had less than a week off. The range of Muslim experiences is much wider than amongst the Hindus: Zubeida, Sabra and Hashmi had less than three days relief from cooking for others, whereas Umrao, Khurshida and Dilruba each had over a month off. These divergences are well illustrated by Wasila and Zubeida, married to landless brothers. Zubeida is Zakir's second wife and he was already alag when he married her. She does all her work right up to delivery and has no help afterwards from her sās or Wasila. Zakir has never called either of his sisters, saying that he cannot afford neg. After her last delivery Zubeida was the only key informant to have no adult help: her eleven-year-old step-daughter did the house-work for one day and the outside-work for a fortnight. After earlier deliveries she did not have even that. Zakir refuses to call Zubeida's sisters as he would have to give them cloth. By contrast, although Wasila has never had help from her nands (for financial reasons), her sās did her cooking for about three weeks and her outside-work for almost two months, as well as helping with outside-work for about two months before the delivery.

The ethnic contrast is especially clear-cut among jachās in middle peasant chūlhās, particularly if the jachā's outside-work is taken into account. Some Hindu women (such as Maya and Durgi) had two weeks off both cooking and outside-work. Others did no outside-work for much longer: Nirmala had two weeks off cooking but two months off fodder collection, and even Lakshmi did not collect fodder or take food to the fields for two months after the delivery. Among the Muslim jachās, virtually all were doing outside-work less than ten days after delivery: Hashmi, Jamila, Maqsudi and Fatima were all doing dung-work within a week of giving birth. Najma (sājhe with her sās) and Khurshida (helped by an unmarried "nand") each had more than one month's help, the only Muslim middle peasant women to have more than a fortnight's help with their outside-work.

Among Hindus, the contrasts between the khushī following the births of boys and those of girls are more marked than among Muslims. We expected that Hindu jachās giving birth to boys would obtain correspondingly more help than those giving birth to girls, and that the differences would be more marked than for Muslim jachās. But the baby's sex seems to make little difference to the length of time a Hindu jachā receives help, whereas Muslim jachās who gave birth to boys generally had more help than those who gave birth to girls. Even so, four Muslim jachās who gave birth to boys (Zubeida, Tahira, Jamila and Fatima) had fewer than five days help with their cooking.

This was less than any of the Hindu jachās, even those who had girls, except for Lakshmi.

Further, about half of the Hindu jachās had two helpers. By contrast, among the Muslims, only Asghari had two helpers (her sās and nand), and that only because it was her first delivery and her sās had succeeded in keeping her nand in Jhakri for several weeks before and after the delivery, after she had come to attend a wedding. Even so, Asghari was cooking again six days after the delivery, although her nand did her outside-work for 30 days. In addition, all but two Hindu jachās had help from their sās, or their nand, working alone or together, or the sās or nand with another helper. The Muslim jachās' solitary helpers were almost evenly divided between the sās, a nand or an alternative helper. Among Muslims, the sās who is alag is much less likely to help than she would among Hindus.

The upshot is that Muslim jachās generally obtain about half as much help with their house-work as Hindu jachās living less than five minutes' walk away. The differences are most marked for those with several children who give birth to a girl, and whose work is associated with land- or livestock-ownership. On average, the Muslim key informants had higher parities (though about the same numbers of surviving children) than the key informants in Dharmnagri, and this might have some effect. There were also more nands potentially available to jachās in Dharmnagri than in Jhakri. But these slight differences cannot account for the very marked contrasts in the help obtained by typical jachās in Dharmnagri and Jhakri, which remain when like is compared with like in the two villages.[16]

In some respects, this is surprising. We had expected more comprehensive women's support networks among Muslims and had anticipated that Muslim jachās would be better placed than Hindu ones. Over half the Muslim key informants with married nands had at least one within easy walking distance. Yet Maqsudi and Dilruba each have a married nand within Jhakri who provide no help after their deliveries, while Ruxana had lengthier help from her "nand" (HFBD) called from another village, than she did from Riasat's married sister in Jhakri itself. In Dharmnagri, with the single exception of Rohtash's sister, the key informants' nands are much more distant but more likely to help and for longer. In part — but only in part — this contrast reflects the greater difficulty women married close to their natal home have in obtaining permission for lengthy stays there.[17]

Defilement, celebration or help for the jachā?

Muslim nands, however, are also less likely to be summoned, which suggests that Muslims tend to regard the provision of a helper as less imperative than do Hindus. Indeed, ethnic differences in the length of time that jachās can obtain help from anyone can be more clearly understood by focusing on childbirth pollution. Protecting the jachā's close susrāl kin can be largely achieved by restricting direct physical contact. But in one particular — cooking for other people — her work should be done by someone else.[18] Although women in Jhakri and Dharmnagri alike talk of five weeks as the time during which the jachā is defiling, Muslim jachās generally begin to cook much sooner after delivery than do Hindus.[19]

This is consistent with several other features. Several Muslim women lamented that the Qaziwala dāis who now serve them provide an inadequate service compared with the dāi who previously lived in Jhakri. She would become a living-in servant, even cooking food for the jachā's chūlhā, which would be unthinkable for Caste Hindus. Further, if the dāi is late arriving in Jhakri the umbilical cord may be cut by someone else. The Qaziwala dāis rarely wash soiled clothing or deal with excreta: that is done by the jachā herself, who may also be cooking for others. All in all, childbirth pollution is treated much less seriously by Muslims than by Hindus, who generally go to greater lengths to ensure that the jachā does not cook soon after delivery. Among Hindus, even if the nand is not called, someone will probably do the jachā's cooking for at least two weeks. Paradoxically, then, the Hindus' greater sense of defilement is associated with a longer respite from daily chores: conversely, most Muslim jachās have little time to recover from the delivery.

Again, several aspects of the help obtained by jachās come into sharper focus if we reconsider khushī and len-den. Among Hindus and Muslims alike, the greatest khushī is after a first birth and the jachā is most likely to have help from her nand. Subsequently, len-den declines; so does the likelihood of being helped by a nand who has been expressly called for that purpose; and inability to provide neg is sometimes cited as justification for not calling the nand. This is particularly striking among Muslims, who have a much less elaborate repertoire of birth celebrations, even after a first birth. Without the lure of neg, the nand will probably not come and she is less likely to be called.

The help given to the jachā reflects a complex interplay of social, economic and demographic considerations. In so far as it is possible to generalise, jachās who are alag and in chūlhās that own livestock and land (in other words, women who are solely responsible for the heaviest workloads) generally obtain the least help for the shortest time. Women who are akelī, however, seem to fare better than those who are alag, perhaps because they have a freer choice of possible helper and are unconstrained by their sās' interference. Jachas who are sājhe have the most assured and lengthy help from their sās, especially those in the most and the least wealthy chūlhās. Additionally, protecting other people from childbirth pollution, providing neg for the jachā's nand, and the decline in khushī, may also have a crucial impact on the quality and length of help the jachā obtains. Indeed, the attenuation of help from nands sheds doubt on how central (rather than incidental) helping the jachā is. The jachā, then, is by no means guaranteed lengthy help after giving birth. Certainly, some women ease themselves gradually back into their normal daily chores, but this transition comes only a matter of days after delivery for many others, especially Muslims.

Counting the cost of motherhood

Bringing up the children rests on me, not my husband. And now my own health is not recovering. The more children, the more my health sinks. *(Dilruba)*

In rural Bijnor, most women's marital careers are repeatedly punctuated by times when they are a jachā. Most women's work is time-consuming and heavy, and most women consider their diets impoverished in relation to their energy outlays for work, lactation and recouping their health. While they do not regard protracted inactivity as advisable, women, especially those in Jhakri, constantly reiterate the cost of childbearing, in terms of the jachā's recovery and women's capacity to feed and care for their children. Our experiences of women visibly ageing, becoming gaunt and losing their earlier vivacity, endorse this view, albeit impressionistically.

You see how we must deal with babies' pee and shit. Babies cause a lot of worries. Last night my new baby was sleeping on my bed but my two-year-old refused to sleep with anyone else, so he was on my bed too. My sleep is always broken, never complete. My head aches. Having too many children has brought weakness into my body. With every child I lose a bit more of my spirit. Bearing a child every two years does not let us remain young for long. We are not as old as we look: women here become old quickly. *(Latifan)*

Health problems and health care after delivery

About half the key informants reported suffering from severe after-pains (gole-kā-dard, literally "pains of the swelling") for several days after their last delivery. They were divided about the cause of the pains. Some (mostly Hindus) said that the jachā's tubes had been emptied and even twisted during the baby's delivery and that the pain was basically one of wind (gas or hawā) because of the space created in the woman's belly. After-pains wane, they consider, once a jachā begins eating solid food and her tubes are no longer empty. Another cure is for the jachā to walk across a threshold. Among Muslims, the favoured interpretation is that after-pains are due to incomplete cleansing (safāi). Western pain-killers are generally shunned as they are drying (which inhibits the flow of defiling blood) even though they are garm. As Imrana put it, "Peace would be obtained from the pain but there would be no cleansing." A hot object against the woman's abdomen (senkāi, literally toasting) provides garmī, though some regard that as drying as well. Generally, Muslim women, too, just endure after-pains: only a few took patent medicines such as Dasmool and Baralgan, which are believed to cause sweating, a wet garmī which opens the body and generates cleansing. Hot oil massages are also considered beneficial but rarely obtained.

More seriously, about a third of the key informants were affected by fevers, malaria, chest pains and coughing (in some cases pulmonary tuberculosis) or chronic pains in the pelvic region. A few also reported severe

167

headaches in the weeks after delivery, due, they considered, to broken sleep. While establishing breast-feeding was rarely a problem, some women reported inflamed or enlarged breasts (thanelā) and others had septic breasts. In 1985 Dilruba resorted to feeding her new baby from one breast only and said he was not getting enough nourishment. After her 1980 delivery Fatima had problems breast-feeding, as one breast had become septic, and she was operated on. The baby girl was weaned before time, subsequently never thrived and eventually died about a week before Fatima's son was born in 1982. Again Fatima had problems, for one breast produced watery milk while the other produced coagulated milk "like yoghourt" and suckling was painful. She fed from one breast and had a fever and headache. Farooq bought milk expressing equipment (which cost Rs 5). Santosh, too, fed only from one breast: the milk from her right breast lulled the baby asleep, while after suckling on the left breast the baby remained alert. A Harijan woman told Sunil that Santosh should express milk from both breasts into separate dishes and put an ant into each. The one placed in milk from her right breast died and so Santosh fed only from the left breast in case her baby died.

Generally, these various complaints are dealt with at home or simply considered to get better by themselves. Treatment for after-pains, pains in the pelvic region, or coughs is usually considered inappropriate. Other ailments (such as fevers) are believed amenable to patent remedies, often already in the house, or to dietary observances. Otherwise, someone (often a man) is sent to the Dharmnagri dispensary or to a Begawala practitioner to fetch medicines for the jachā, prescribed on the basis of their description of her symptoms. Less commonly, the compounder or medical practitioner makes a home visit. Dāis are rarely consulted and only a few women said they had even been massaged by the dāi. The ANM provides no routine post-natal care, either domiciliary or at the dispensary. Occasionally, the jachā's condition is such that she is taken to Bijnor for more sophisticated treatment than the Dharmnagri dispensary provides. Just as when there is no helper for the jachā, the chhatī or the jasthawn may be performed quickly so that the jachā can leave the house.

Women were puzzled by our questions about jachās' crying and few had heard of jachās becoming insane or delirious (pāgal, bāolī).[20] Only Shakuntala reported being possessed by the spirit of her grandmother (FM) in a dream: she became unconscious, but recovered after her father-in-law had tied a thread on to her wrist. Without nutritional, physiological and psychological data, we cannot judge whether women's reports of chronic weakness and lethargy (kamzorī) amount to post-natal depression: such symptoms could arise from their nutritional condition (anaemia is probably virtually universal), or be hormonal in origin. Further, it is hard to evaluate the situation of jachās in the few weeks after delivery. The jachā views herself as defiling and vulnerable and she is isolated from her female natal kin (whose care is considered superior by our informants themselves). Her immediate susrāl kin surround her, but she has no guarantee of substantial psychological or practical support from them. Indeed, she does not abandon her "work" for "mothering" and face the identity crisis often considered important in post-natal depression in the West.[21] But combining mothering with her other duties may create problems of a different order.

Anxieties about pregnancy and childbirth

My brother's wife has four children and she is worried about having more. Each time, she had great pain and she fears that one time she will die. My own mother died in childbirth when I was about two-years-old. The baby was not straight and only its hand appeared. And that way, in affliction, my mother died.

My first delivery was very troubled. My husband called the ANM and her assistant and the ANM gave an injection. Only then was the baby born. The second time I was in affliction for four days. The ANM and her assistant were here, as well as the dāis from Qaziwala and Itawa. The ANM said there were twins and even after she had given four-five injections, nothing happened. I was in great pain and many women gathered to watch. Someone said that the baby's head was coming into view, and I told them, 'Clutch the baby's hair and pull it out. Let it be born no matter how!' Eventually, my husband went to Bijnor and got medicines from a doctor and then the baby was born. Everyone was crying, for my sister [her husband's first wife] had died in this affliction. Everyone was very frightened. Last time I was in labour I was terrified, for I had hardly escaped with my life the other times. *(Zubeida)*

Our key informants are, of course, survivors. The symptoms they have personally experienced as jachās have not included serious haemorrhage or untreated puerperal fevers, although several had experienced unpleasant and even life-threatening symptoms and considered they had just escaped with their life during previous pregnancies or deliveries. Moreover, all have relatives or acquaintances who had become seriously ill during pregnancy, or had died during childbirth. Most women do survive: but there are also those for whom labour is the end of the road, unless they return as churail, the ghosts of women who die in pregnancy or childbirth. In Dharmnagri and Jhakri, a woman can be expected to die in pregnancy or delivery every year or so. Only women pregnant for the first time or hoping for a son after several girls voiced enthusiasm about being pregnant: those of higher parities more often expressed dread and fears for their own safety. After delivery, they are relieved to have survived.

Imrana typifies the anxieties and helplessness which women often express. In 1985, she recounted her pregnancy (her fourth) after we had departed in 1983. Towards the end, her belly had become very large and she found it hard to work. She called her nand's daughter to help, but the child just played with others. Imrana continued carrying head-loads of fodder, even though it made her giddy. While she was tethering the calves one day, she lost her footing on the slippery monsoon mud and fell heavily. Her pains began:

I feared I would not survive. I went home. The boy was born before the dāi arrived. Three hours later the girl was born. We had not known earlier that there were two babies. Just a year later I am pregnant again and I have malaria. And I have burning-urine and swollen ankles, just like the last time. I expect this child to die at birth, for I have no one to help me. If my sās helps, my sisters-in-law (HBW) taunt me, saying, 'What, are you eating rotī made by our sās?' That is why I am still doing all my own work, even the dung-work. Why, my husband has a bad fever too, so I must help with the animal-work.

The girl twin died at 20 days, but Imrana's fifth pregnancy resulted in a healthy boy. When we visited Jhakri in 1986, Imrana was frantic. The boy born in 1984 was suffering from thrush, vomiting and diarrhoea. He was emaciated and smaller than his brother born 15 months later. In the midst of her work, she was touring local medical practitioners and divines trying to remedy his failure to thrive.

Such examples highlight the immediacy of the risk of pregnancy and childbirth to women in Dharmnagri and Jhakri. In the short-term — the course of any one pregnancy and delivery — women are well aware of the hazards to their own well-being and even survival. These fears are supported by evidence from north India as a whole. In Uttar Pradesh, women in the reproductive ages die from various causes: fevers, accidents, tuberculosis (which may affect men too), and beatings, neglect and even the outright murder or abetted suicide termed "dowry death". Adult male mortality rates are themselves high, but the mortality rates among females in rural Uttar Pradesh in the prime reproductive ages (15-34) are over one and a half times those of males in the same age bands.[22] While a single cause of death cannot always be ascertained, much of this excess female mortality is probably directly related to childbearing. Estimates of maternal mortality are poor, but in rural Uttar Pradesh at least five deliveries in every 1,000 end in the death of the mother. Women are right to fear childbirth. They cannot know that their spirit will escape death.

Childrearing and other work

I did not want to be pregnant again. It is not easy to bring up children. *(Fatima)*

I do not want more than two children. Making them is easy, rearing them is difficult. *(Santosh)*

Women in Dharmnagri and Jhakri also take a longer-term perspective, for they know that they must combine childcare with their pre-existing workloads. Each jachā must breast-feed her new baby, care for any older children, possibly undergo another pregnancy soon after the most recent one, and also complete her responsibilities around the house and outside.

In listing their work, women rarely mentioned childcare until we specifically asked about it.[23] On further questioning, women explained that breast-feeding and bathing the new baby or dealing with other children is generally slotted into the interstices of their other work or even done in tandem with it — a woman suckling a baby lying across her thighs while she squats to cook at her chūlhā, or spin cotton thread, or make dung-cakes, is a common sight. Except at night, when the baby lies beside its mother and she breast-feeds and deals with its excreta, childcare is rarely performed exclusively or for long periods, because women's other duties tend to dominate. As Jamila said: "We don't rear our children. Children rear themselves. Don't you see how we put our babies on the bed and leave them while we work?"

Women consider childrearing difficult and say they cannot do it properly. Pālnā means to rear or raise in the sense of providing for bodily needs (as in raising chickens, for instance), but also connotes cherishing and educating. But women say they cannot devote themselves to childrearing without denying attention to other work necessary for the long-term survival of their chūlhās as a whole: making or collecting fuel, caring for draught animals or those that provide milk, cooking meals, repairing the house or grain-store. Childrearing may be in direct competition with these tasks, particularly if the jachā is alag or akelī and cannot share either childcare or other work with anyone else. Udayan's aunt (MZ) in Dharmnagri told us one day:

> My bahū has been going to the fields all week, along with the children and even the baby. What can poor people do? We have to work; these days the sugar-cane needs weeding. There is so little shade out there, and they all go out early in the morning on the cart. Then the baby is left in a patch of shade to be watched by its biggest sister while its mother works.

Otherwise, a new baby spends much of its time on the mother's bed while she continues her work. When she leaves the courtyard, maybe to remove cattle-dung or take food to the men, she relies on her already busy sisters-in-law (HBW) or her sās to keep an eye on her baby, or asks a young girl to watch the infant and tell her when it needs feeding. Once when Patricia was visiting a jachā she took the baby on her lap. When he began fretting she rocked him, only to be rebuked by the jachā's neighbour: "We don't do that. What if he gets used to being rocked? How can a woman do her work if her child won't stay quiet unless he's rocked?" A baby who can sit astride someone's hips spends much of its waking time with other children, especially girls aged about five to nine who cannot yet do heavy lifting work. When the baby is hungry, it is brought to the mother wherever she is working. Once mobile, the baby crawls or toddles with older children. Otherwise, women say, their work could not be completed. None the less, the mother is responsible for feeding and bathing it, sorting its clothes, dressing it in extra layers at dusk, and is wholly responsible for it throughout the night. In the course of a discussion about her work and that of her labourer (mazdūr) husband, Wasila retorted to a question about whether she too ever did any mazdūrī: "I bring up the children. Is there any greater mazdūrī than that?"

Hashmi's experiences strikingly illustrate the interplay between her own recovery from the delivery, the demands of childcare and the pressure of other work. After giving birth to a girl in late 1982, she was back at work within three days of the delivery. She had had a quick chhatī because her three-year-old son was sick and refused attention from anyone but her. Having bathed, she said, she just had to do the rest of her work as well. One day three months later, the baby girl was crying. Hashmi explained that she was not producing enough breast milk. We asked if she was not giving additional milk (ūpar-kā-dūdh, usually cow or buffalo milk):

> The buffalo is not giving milk just now. I am thinking we should buy a cow, but really I have enough to do. I do the work on alternate days for the animals we own jointly with Imrana: three oxen, two buffaloes, one male calf and four buffalo calves. An extra animal would increase my work.

So no cow was bought and no extra milk provided for the baby. Indeed, she died aged 18 months, reportedly from diarrhoea and dehydration.[24]

The toll of childbearing

> Women become old bearing children. They can't keep their strength. Their spirit drains away.

> I was not happy to be pregnant. The first baby was still very small and I did not want to be pregnant again so soon. *(Hiran)*

> Women these days have a baby nearly every year, so how can they keep their strength? *(Rajballa's sās)*

For most women in Dharmnagri and Jhakri, each pregnancy, delivery and post-partum period is not an isolated episode but one part of a sequence. Moreover, women are vocal about the strain of combining their work (including childcare) with such childbearing careers. They consider that the physical demands of repeated childbearing damage a woman's health and that prolonged breast-feeding plays a considerable part in this.

Some solids have generally been introduced into an infant's diet by its first birthday, though breast milk remains the major part of the diet.[25] One evening, Patricia was being quizzed about childfeeding in Britain by Latifan's brother and Liaqat, both from Jhakri. Liaqat commented that their womenfolk breast-feed for two to three years: "Our children take just rotī and rice because their mouth burns with the peppers in other food and they run away to mother's milk again." To this Latifan's brother responded, "Is that the way for women to keep their strength [tāqat]?" If children refuse to be weaned, their mothers may continue to suckle into the next pregnancy, even though pregnancy-milk is considered potentially harmful to the toddler. Almost half the key informants (irrespective of class or ethnicity) were breast-feeding during their last pregnancy. Generally, they had weaned their previous child by the fifth month of pregnancy, though a handful of Hindu women suckled up to the last month and even into labour. Most of the remainder had not been in a position to breast-feed while pregnant, because it was their first pregnancy or because their previous child had been stillborn or had died. While early and abrupt weaning has disadvantages for the toddler, the local view is that to continue breast-feeding during pregnancy also takes its toll on women's health:

> When a woman breast-feeds while she is pregnant the new baby may not grow strong. But it is more likely that the woman will become weakened from two directions: the baby in her belly and the child sucking at her breasts. *(dāi)*

Even without breast-feeding, women say that being pregnant can sap strength from the body. Women undergoing their first pregnancies are not considered in great need of extra strengthening foods. Such foods are considered most beneficial in later pregnancies to prevent weakness, though they are rarely obtained. Most women survive, but they recognise the costs to themselves in comments like "jitne bache, itnī kamzorī" (just as many children, just so much weakness).

Breast-feeding and pregnancy tend to shade into one another, and few of the women approaching or past menopause have had much time free from pregnancy or lactation during their fertile years. Wajid and Zakir's mother in Jhakri and Shankar and Tulsi's in Dharmnagri can serve as examples. Wajid's mother was married at ten and began cohabiting at seventeen. She is now in her early sixties. She conceived two years after cohabiting and had eight pregnancies to full-term. Four of her children died, one at a month, the others at around two years. Shankar's mother was also married at ten and began cohabiting at seventeen. She is now approaching seventy. She conceived three years after cohabiting and had seven pregnancies. One baby was born two months before time and died a few days after birth. Two other children died, both at just over a year. Both women may have omitted miscarriages, abortions or early child deaths. Even ignoring that, though, they both must often have been simultaneously pregnant and breast-feeding. Their childbearing careers are fairly typical of women in their age group.[26] The younger women usually detail maternity histories which have occupied most of their lives since their cohabitation. Like the older women, they generally undergo pregnancy and lactation repeatedly, with little space between weaning one child and bearing another.

Furthermore, it is hard for a woman to escape her responsibilities in her susrāl, even if she or her children are sick. The work must be done; how else can the rest of the family survive? Time taken for medical treatment (especially a trip to Bijnor escorted by a man) is costly in terms of adult workers' inputs. Chest complaints and colds, fevers and diarrhoea, septic cuts, boils and conjunctivitis, mean that babies and toddlers are frequently fretting and take their mother's attention away from her other work. But seeking medical treatment is often delayed until the condition is serious.

Paying attention to women's and children's health is often squeezed to the margins. Moreover, women cannot easily take unilateral decisions about medical expenditures. Decisions may have to wait until their husband returns home in the evening. Occasionally (as discussions of some child deaths indicated) that was simply not soon enough. In any case, even rich peasants do not always have ready cash, and poor women face even greater problems:

> Either spend on food for all, or medicines for one. Bringing up children is difficult. *(Zubeida)*

> My son had blood in his shit. That continued for five months and then he died. In getting treatment for him, we have become destitutes. *(Tahira)*

But it is not simply a matter of time and money. We heard of several occasions when women's parents took them back to their natal village for medical treatment and convalescence (not only after childbirth) on the grounds that neither would be adequately granted in the susrāl. Parents, it seems, are much less likely to grudge time and money on their married daughters.

After childbirth, many women receive less help than they consider reasonable and their due, let alone than they might consider ideal. Issues of len-den and khushī and the desire of others to avoid defilement often seem to have higher priority than helping the jachā. In view of the problems of finding helpers whose own responsibilities can be set aside or passed to someone else, it is perhaps surprising that some women obtain as much help as they do. The women who get least help — disproportionately Muslim middle peasant women — are also those who have experienced higher levels of child mortality than might be expected.[27] In Jhakri as a whole, child mortality rates among middle peasants are as high or higher than those of poorer Muslims, and much higher than those of comparable Hindus. We cannot make direct links between the amount of help a woman can call on around the time of a child's birth and its chances of survival; but it is at least plausible that the two are related. Low levels of assistance after childbirth may be indicative of general problems of mobilising support. The stress Muslim middle peasant women are normally under could affect their ability to breast-feed satisfactorily, devote time to their children's needs and attend early enough to obtaining medical care if their children become sick. But such an interpretation cannot provide a complete answer, for Muslims are also more suspicious of government health services than are Hindus. They seek health care later in illness episodes and have little contact with public health staff.[28] Both villages, however, lack the public health provision to improve their environment, and the inadequate supply of affordable curative health care prejudices the maintenance of good health among the population at large. The high infant and child mortality rates in both villages are just a partial reflection of a very sorry state of affairs.

These considerations are exacerbated for young married women in their susrāl by their restricted access to food and cash, restraints on their mobility and their time-consuming work, all circumstances not of their own making. In addition, young women are in a very different situation from their husbands in relation to childbearing and childrearing. They experience costs of repeated childbearing which do not directly affect men. Death in pregnancy or delivery is a common fear, their own loss of spirit and the anxieties of childrearing are frequent refrains. Yet children are necessary for the future security of women themselves and of their susrāl chūlhā; and success in rearing robust children is achieved only against heavy odds. In such a context, young women approach family building with deep-seated ambivalence:

Hashmi: My older girl and both boys have fever. I am also worried about the baby. I don't sleep properly at night because they wake me. I have a headache all the time. One shouldn't have children.

Swaleha: But if you don't have children everyone starts getting you treatment and your sās says that you are no good because you can't bear children!

Hashmi: That's also true. If there are no children, that is also a worry. But there should be just two-three so that you can feed them, look after them and remain healthy yourself. With few children they can all stay strong. I don't need any more children. These are more than enough! If there are many children there are difficulties, because children also create worries.

Reaping the Spring harvest

8. The Spring and Autumn Harvests

Andrew: How many more children do you want?

Farooq: Do you have some in your pocket to give away?

Andrew: No, I just want to know what you want. You had three children when I went away.

Farooq: If you know so much, tell me how many I've got now!

Andrew: How could I know? You could have had no more or one or two and they could be boys or girls.

Farooq: Or some might have died also.

Andrew: Yes, that's right.

Farooq: Ah, now you are beginning to understand how God's will might work.

Men have been almost silent in the last four chapters because they are ignorant of or aloof from many aspects of childbearing. But a wife's overall fertility concerns her husband deeply. Chūlhās are aggregates of individuals united by some common interests, but divided by gender and age. Thus, decisions about fertility are made (or not) in the context of domestic and sexual politics in which bahūs are embedded, and not by childbearing women alone.[1] In addition, chūlhā interests have both class and ethnic components which are reflected in distinctive approaches to family planning and demographic outcomes. Decisions to adopt contraception are rarely taken at one time or with a fixed set of participants and we cannot confidently outline the dynamics of decision-making.[2] Yet family planning constantly recurred in our conversations in Dharmnagri and Jhakri, usually initiated by our informants themselves. We have a powerful sense of how individuals can alter their stance or spouses may express different views. People's situations change as boys and girls are born or die, and accounts of what happened or expectations of what might happen are very fluid. Thus, many factors combine to propel couples towards or away from contraceptive use.

Furthermore, in ways unparalleled in other spheres, the Indian state attempts to intervene in family-building decisions by providing different contraceptive methods and stressing the desirability of a small family.[3] "We two, our two" is a common refrain in radio messages or on clinic walls. But even those villagers who do not want many children often find the available contraceptive methods unsatisfactory and object to the incessant pressure from government personnel to toe the line. Our attention, then, cannot be limited to individual pregnancies and deliveries, or just to women, but must focus on how women's childbearing careers are constructed in the light of their own situations and the role of the state.[4]

Childbearing careers

North India has a distinctive demographic profile.[5] For many years, fertility has been high, particularly in the rural areas, and may even have risen since the 1950s. Almost all women marry when relatively young, and potentially have lengthy childbearing careers. Furthermore, most women have a limited say in the number of children they bear, while (equally) they share with their husbands the benefits of sons, especially old-age insurance, for which there are no real alternatives. High fertility is also related to high rates of child mortality, distinguished in north India by higher death rates among girls.[6] Bijnor District is centrally located within the area where this pattern obtains.

Patterns of fertility

> You ask why there are so many children in India? I'll tell you why. India is a garm country and her people are garm. You have to marry girls off young or they'll run away or be carried off by some boy. Girls shouldn't be married until they are 25, that would bring the birth rate down. But only educated people, like me, understand that. *(Nisar's uncle, FB)*

Fertility rates in Dharmnagri and Jhakri are high. On average, 40 children were born each year between 1976 and 1985, giving a crude birth rate for the two villages together of about 42 births per 1,000 population throughout those ten years.[7] This is close to the figure for rural Uttar Pradesh in the same period. Post-menopausal women (aged 45 and over) reported an average of between seven and eight pregnancies lasting to term, whether resulting in live-births or stillbirths. Fertility rates are higher for Muslim and Harijan women (just over eight such pregnancies) than for Caste Hindu women (just over six); and for women from the wealthier classes — rich and middle peasants combined — with eight full-term deliveries, than for poorer women, with seven. Women aged between 25 and 34 have had fewer births but the same patterns of higher numbers among Muslims, Harijans, and the wealthier classes can also be seen amongst them, though the differences are smaller, ranging from 4.5 for Muslim women to 3.7 for Caste Hindus. These figures may understate the case: women may not report some births, especially when the child died soon afterwards.[8]

Some differences in patterns of social organisation may contribute to ethnic differences in fertility.[9] For example, Muslim women who live near their parents rarely go to stay overnight (when they become sexually unavailable) but just visit for the day and return home by evening. Furthermore, Hindu women seem to experience more sharm at the possibility of having a child after they have a son married. The wish to avoid being a pregnant grandmother seems to inhibit sexual activity among Hindu couples in their late 30s and early 40s to a greater extent than it does among Muslim couples. Five of the 27 older women in Jhakri, but only four of the 54 older women in Dharmnagri, may have had a child when they had a bahū of their own.[10] It is more difficult to explain why Harijans have had more children. Better nutrition (lowering the age of menarche) and higher life expectancies may help to explain the higher fertility of rich and middle peasants.

Better nutrition and longer life expectancies may also have contributed to a rise in fertility over the relatively recent past. Women born in the 1930s seem to have had more children by the age of 35 than those born in the 1920s or those born in the 1940s, though the differences are small and our data on children's birth dates deteriorate as we go further back in time. Older women, however, certainly believe that women now have more pregnancies more rapidly than before. Changing social practices may have had unintended effects on fertility patterns. The age of marriage has increased, but the rise in the age at which women start to cohabit has been very small.[11] These rises might reduce fertility. But if the age at menarche has fallen, more brides are likely to be menstruating when they first cohabit; indeed, the length of time from cohabitation to first pregnancy has decreased. Similarly, older women consider that bahūs go alag more quickly nowadays. This could increase fertility because, while sājhe, the husband's sexual access to his wife may be regulated by his mother: once alag, a woman is sexually more available to her husband. Furthermore, her work obligations may make her more restricted to her susrāl earlier in her marital career than the bahū who is sājhe, and thus less able to stay overnight with her parents. This tendency may have been exaggerated if increasing expectations in len-den at times of daughters' visits inhibit parents from calling them back, and if the intensification of work (as a result of Green Revolution changes) has also extended the periods when women are sexually available to their husbands.

We do not, however, have evidence of changes through time in such potential contributors to fertility variations as the length of time children are breast-fed, the impact of post-partum taboos on sexual intercourse, changes in the rates of widowhood or the possible impact of better nutrition on fecundity and foetal wastage. Locally, people say that the Green Revolution, with a wider use of artificial fertiliser, has made people more garm (meaning, here, sexually active as well as aggressive) and increased the rapidity with which women become pregnant. But even if fertility has not been rising, population growth has certainly taken place, largely because of the other side of the equation: a decline in mortality.[12]

Patterns of child mortality

Children in Dharmnagri and Jhakri are being raised in an environment which poses several threats to their health, from infectious diseases, inadequate nutrition and poor access to medical care when they are ill. Most children die without medical diagnosis, which is often difficult even for trained medical staff. A malnourished toddler whose intestinal infection hampers fluid-retention can rapidly succumb to dehydration during a fever: ascertaining a single cause of death is problematic. Mothers identified specific causes for only small numbers of children: accidents, tetanus, pneumonia, smallpox and typhoid.[13] We were given no reason for nearly one in ten of all deaths. Unspecific fever was cited in one in five cases and another one in six children apparently died suddenly, from unknown causes or the influence of evil spirits.

In the two villages, 9% of all babies delivered at full-term do not survive to the end of the first month. But most child mortality takes place in the following few years, mainly among toddlers.[14] This was forcefully impressed on us during the 1985 research, when Patricia left her daughters in Edinburgh. Repeatedly, she was asked about her two daughters, "Are they still alive?" not, "How are they?" Returning the question revealed an extensive catalogue of disasters (longer in Jhakri than Dharmnagri) since our departure some two years earlier. Of the 78 children born alive to the key informants after January 1980, almost one-quarter were dead by September 1985.[15]

Grim though these figures are, the maternity histories indicate that matters were much worse before about 1960. Until then, most people had great difficulty ensuring the survival of their children. Of babies born prior to 1960, fewer than 65% reached their fifth birthday.[16] The survival of young children was lowest amongst the Muslims and the Harijans (55%), whereas nearly 75% of Caste Hindu children survived. The survival rate was also much better for the children of rich and middle peasant households (67%) than for poor peasant and landless children (58%). The maternity histories of some older women hardly bear reporting. In Jhakri, one woman had ten children, two of whom are still alive, and another who had five children has only one living. Only one post-menopausal woman (Bilquis' sister) had all her (nine) children living. No women in Dharmnagri had quite such disastrous maternity histories. All the women who had ten or more children had at least four still alive, and eight post-menopausal women reported no child deaths.

Of the children born in the 1960s, 74% lived to the age of five, as did 82% of those born in the 1970s. Harijan children born in the 1970s were almost as likely to survive until the age of five (85%) as were Caste Hindu children (89%), but Muslim chances of survival (74%) were still much lower. Class differences have almost disappeared, with almost equal chances of survival for rich and middle peasant children as for those from poor peasant or landless chūlhās.[17] Of our key informants in Jhakri, only two (Asghari and Ghazala) have had no children die; and they have only had one child each. Another three have had a late miscarriage or a stillbirth, but nine of the 19

Jhakri key informants had had two or more children die by 1985. The extreme example is Bilquis, in a rich peasant chūlhā, six of whose children had died. In Dharmnagri, by contrast, over half the key informants had no live-born child die, but one (Bhagirthi) had a stillbirth. Four women had had two children die. In Dharmnagri the extreme case was Jumni, with two six-month miscarriages and two child deaths.

Even without a rise in fertility, declining child mortality would result in larger completed families. Although post-menopausal women had given birth to more than seven children on average, fewer than five were still alive. Older women in Jhakri have had more children than those in Dharmnagri, but (because of the lower survival rates) have fewer children still alive: under 4.5 on average, compared with an average of five each in Dharmnagri. But women born between 1940 and 1950 have larger numbers of children still alive: more than five in both villages. For younger women, the ethnic differences are insignificant. In both villages, the relatively poor have fewer living children than the relatively wealthy. Rich and middle peasant women have had more children, more of whom have survived.

Overall, then, the possible rise in fertility and the certain decline in child mortality suggests a relatively recent switch in family-building. Prior to the 1960s, couples were probably most anxious about ensuring the survival of their children; since then, although fear of child deaths has not evaporated, the possibility of having "too many" children has begun to face people in Dharmnagri and Jhakri. Family-building is still very risky, but people's judgements about desirable family size and composition are increasingly influenced by the changing balance between the benefits of having children (especially sons) and the costs of bringing them up (especially daughters).

The value of children

The chūlhā is the basic unit of consumption and prime source of welfare. It is often also the unit of production. Even small children can be economically useful in this enterprise, tending goats, running messages, helping in the fields or performing childcare.[18] Generalising from such evidence from India and elsewhere, some authors have argued that villagers are being economically rational in having numerous children. Few people in Dharmnagri and Jhakri, however, concede great value to child labour: even children who do not attend school are viewed primarily as consumers, making only small contributions to the chūlhā's well-being. Since education beyond the age of ten is still rare, most children are already making some contribution by that age. But adults generally take a longer-term view. By middle age, landed men are unlikely to be operating their land jointly with their brothers, and landless men have probably been alag for many years. Thus, when a couple's ability to work declines, they need children of their own to grow or earn their daily bread. Without that, they face a dismal old age.[19]

People without sons would have to work till they drop

Boys have always been preferred, like they are now. It's because the pleasure stays in the house, the light of the house keeps burning, and the name continues. Even when sons separate, the name continues. It's the same for the landless and those with land. Even if one son is no good, in your old age one at least will be some use to you, will feed you, love you and fear God. *(Umrao)*

The need for children, however, is more accurately construed as a need for sons.[20] A son's labour power is considered more valuable than a daughter's, and more important for the chūlhā's maintenance, whether it is unpaid family labour or paid employment. Gradually, sons learn men's work and by adolescence are probably performing an adult man's load alongside their fathers. Moreover, a son's work should continue to benefit his parents, even when they are too old to work. From this perspective, a son's work during childhood pales into insignificance. Sons are the best — indeed almost the only — way of dealing with the hazards of old age in a society without pensions, life insurance or substantial personal savings. Women's and men's security alike is bound up in their sons. Daughters are a very poor substitute, for they generally move away on marriage. Parents should always give to their daughter. Depending on a daughter in old age offends against all local views of propriety and honour, and is resorted to only in the absence of sons.[21] Bringing in a ghar-jamāi is a plausible strategy only for people with land to lure the daughter's husband. It is an exceptional and difficult solution, to be avoided if possible:

Boys look after their parents when they are old but people without sons would have to work till they drop. They will always be in difficulty. Besides, boys keep their father's name going and as soon as they are old enough they will do field-work. Girls don't do field-work, and if they were to, it is never for their parents. They don't earn money for their fathers. When a girl goes away to her own house who will look after her parents if there is no son? You can bring in a ghar-jamāi but this is not the same as your own line. Instead of saying it was your own son, people would comment it was your son-in-law who was doing the work. *(Liaqat)*

Sons, then, should provide "comfort and shade" (chain-chhān) for their parents' old age, though they cannot be absolutely guaranteed to be dutiful.[22] Landowning parents may attempt to control sons by refusing to allot land to them until after the parents die. Parents also have all the might of moral pressures on their side to bring sons into line. But poor peasants and the landless have least hold over their sons, for there is little or no resource in which they share an interest. Not everyone with sons expects to benefit, although boys do provide psychological rewards even if they make little financial contribution to the chūlhā. Vikram, a landless man, said that sons eat from their father's hand until they marry, and then go alag: he just expected that the light of his house would keep shining. Others also said the glory of their name would be perpetuated by their sons: a daughter cannot provide a man with a sense of continuity, of being able to outlast his own death.[23]

> It's wrong to say that boys and girls are the same. Boys stay at home but girls go away. Boys fill your house but girls empty it. Without sons you lie on your bed and worry in your old age, but people with sons have their work done for them. And your name will live on. People say that's your son walking down the path when they see him. *(Irfan)*

As many children as I have, that many will benefit me.

Despite the undoubted economic and psychological benefits of sons, only three key informants (all men) thought an almost unlimited number was desirable. In Jhakri, Dilshad — a rich peasant — said he wanted as many children as God would give. He had four sons and one daughter (another girl had died of chickenpox), and saw no limit to the number of sons who would benefit him. He himself is an only son and he and his father have difficulty working their land; indeed, his oldest sister's husband lives in Jhakri and works some of the land, and his two other married sisters are often there too, helping Dilruba and doing field-work. He looked to a time when his own sons could work all the land. Likewise, in Dharmnagri, Bhagwana (also a rich peasant) favoured a large family; he had three sons and three daughters. That, he told Andrew, was enough. But a friend burst into the discussion, saying Bhagwana had told him he wanted many sons, in order to avoid the nuisance of employing labourers. Later, on his own, Bhagwana grudgingly assented that the government was correct in saying that two children are enough; but then, seeing Andrew's quizzical expression, promptly said he did not really agree:

> As many children as I have, that many will benefit me. They can all work for me. True, the girls will go away. But the boys will bring brides in, and I have equal numbers of both. I am not worried about having too many. I will inherit 90 bīghās [about 18 acres] from my father, so I will be all right in my old age.

For Dilshad and Bhagwana, who expect to work their land using the same technology, having several sons reduces their dependence on wage labourers and enhances their income.[24] Each son can still expect a reasonable inheritance. Ashok, another rich peasant, was more equivocal, reflecting his own family position. He was uncertain how many children were "too many" for he had only one son, but said people should not have many children.[25]

Among the rest, only Nisar (a middle peasant) positively endorsed the argument that a large family makes economic sense for farmers like him and for labourers:

> **Nisar:** It's the same for farmers as for labourers. If a labourer has three sons they would earn ten or fifteen rupees a day but if he only has one

son he would only earn one-third. Isn't there a benefit in that?

Andrew: But won't they have to be fed and clothed also?

Nisar: Yes, but they'll bring in more than they use up.

None of the others argued in this way. Labourers, in particular, felt the future looked bleak, because farmers like Dilshad and Bhagwana increasingly use family labour and reduce the employment opportunities for people like themselves.

The costs of children

Most people consider children bring benefits but also impose costs. In the short run, they are costly to feed and clothe.

I do not want any more children. Why, the two I have give me a lot of worries. It takes a lot of money to raise children. *(Nirmala)*

If you have lots of kids you can't look after them properly. You're never under control, some would be fighting, some would be sick, they'd be pissing and shitting all over the yard. That's useless. The smaller the family the easier, the bigger the family the more difficult. *(Naresh)*

This couple's comments are typical. While women certainly pay more attention to the physical costs to themselves, they and their menfolk alike express concern for the other attendant costs of parenthood. Young children must be fed and clothed. If they are sent to school they should be clean, well-clad and properly equipped. When they fall sick, medical care may be necessary. Even for middle peasants, to have many children cannot be an unmitigated good, since the expenses of rearing them loom large.

One son will be as big as his father

That's right, two or three children are best. You can look after them well and they'll get good food, good clothes, and a good marriage. One son will be as big as his father. If there are three or four they'll all be smaller, whether they have a lot of land or a little. *(Naresh's father)*

Immediate anxieties co-exist with a longer perspective. Having many children can be detrimental to the parents' and their children's long-term prospects. None of the landless or poor and middle peasants (barring Nisar) said unlimited fertility was desirable: rather they are exercised by their responsibility to enable their children to find secure livelihoods. If there are many, how can they all be well settled? For most of those with land, its fragmentation comes to the fore. Poor peasants foresee even more inadequate holdings for each of their sons, and fear being reduced to landlessness.[26] Even middle peasants are conscious of the division that takes place at each generation:

Irfan: Two children are enough. That would be intelligent because your expenses will be less. My father had only one brother to share his inheritance, but we are three brothers and we have many children between us.

Mansur: But the land is more productive now, so that doesn't much matter.

Irfan: My father had three sons. But my uncle [FB] had only Farooq's father. Now tell me, who is the richest?

Latifan — also in a middle peasant chūlhā — had had six boys and two girls, all living. When she described her pregnancies, Jamila's nand (who was visiting Jhakri) remarked, "You must be about the only woman without a child who has died".[27] Latifan retorted that this simply meant she had to rear them all, and she was praying that no more would be born. Liaqat himself described their situation:

Liaqat: Only two sons are necessary to help their father, and for their wives to help in the home. Look, I've got 20 bīghās [four acres] of land. That's going to be split amongst my six sons. Two sons and a father are sufficient for 20 bīghās or even two men can work it themselves if one falls ill or the father is too old.

Andrew: Is there any benefit or only trouble from so many children?

Liaqat: I'm telling you, trouble. The children have been born. Of course they are my children, so I will look after them and love them. But they are going to be very expensive. The land will have to be divided and I've got to get all of them married. And clothe and feed them in the meantime. And send them to school.

All in all, children are an expense and worry for parents, but not such that anyone says they want no children. There should be children, but in moderation. However, sons alone compensate in their parents' old age.

A girl is not necessary

Boys and girls are good. But the girl's people stay down, they can never get their feet out of the mud, while the boy's people are racing for the sky with their mouths open shouting all the way. Bringing up a boy is like eating food that is hot but it cools down quickly — you spend money on bringing him up but then he stays and pays you back. Bringing up a girl is like eating food that slowly-slowly makes your mouth hotter and hotter until it burns the skin off the roof of your mouth. *(Ishwar Das)*

The differences between sons and daughters are marked from the very moment of birth. They are also highlighted in describing women's childbearing careers.[28] After overhearing Khurshida's maternity history, her neighbour commented "her wheat and pulses have come forth": here, the wheat stands for girls and the pulses for boys. In similar vein, an elderly dāi commented that she had "reaped the spring and autumn harvests equally", meaning she had given birth to identical numbers of girls and boys. But such differentiations are not limited to linguistic distinctions or differences in len-den and khushī.

Given the structuring of work, marriage and residence, there are no economic grounds for wanting a daughter. Women with several daughters bemoan their fate; those with sons fear the jealous evil eye of those without. Support in old age ought not to come from a daughter, for she should go to "her own house" when she is married. For parents in all economic positions, providing dowries and continuing through the years to give to many daughters benefits other people. It is better, they say, to have few daughters, so that each can be well settled in a good marriage. Granted, a girl's mother may appreciate her in childhood for the help she gives. Some people said that a daughter is wanted only for her work, and that a son's marriage may be timed with an eye to replacing the loss of his sister's labour when she is married. And that is the crucial point. No matter how useful a daughter is before she marries, her contributions are short-term, devalued because they are female labour and inadequate compensation for the expenses her parents subsequently face on her behalf. In the long run, her parents-in-law (not her parents) stand to gain from her work.[29]

Nevertheless, some people — generally those with several sons already — indicate religious and social reasons for wanting a daughter. Ishwar Das and Bhagwana liked the composition of their families — three boys and three girls — because each son had a sister to consider his own. Jumni and Jagram have four sons and no daughters. Both said that they would stop having children if they had a daughter:

> **Jagram:** You need to have at least one girl because of Raksha Bandan.[30] A boy with no sisters will be upset because he has no one to tie his rakhī [wrist-string]. A cousin-sister could tie it on, but that wouldn't be the same. A real sister is a real sister.
> **Jagram's grandfather (FF):** It's not right about wanting a daughter. You shouldn't say you want a girl. It's up to God to decide.
> **Jagram:** But I said what I would like myself, so it's not wrong.
> **Jagram's grandfather:** Yes, it is wrong. A girl is not necessary like you said. You have four sons — won't they all get married? When they are married won't four daughters come to your house?

Jagram was supported by his mother, who argued that a real sister is necessary for len-den at weddings and when children are born; a distant "sister" may not come when she is called. Certainly, a substitute sister may be called if there is no real sister. The jachā, after all, can call a substitute nand if she has no real one. But a woman has more need of a real brother than he has of her. She relies on him to call her from her susrāl and he continues the link through len-den even after their parents are dead, a link which a sister is highly unlikely to provide.[31]

Several men mentioned the religious importance of giving away a daughter in marriage, but only Udayan construed this as a reason for actually wanting daughters.[32] After having two sons, he and Urmila went to Hardwar to make a vow and pray for a daughter. He explained:

> I'll tell you straight: boys and girls are not the same. You do need both, because otherwise people will say you've only got sons or you've only got daughters. Girls are good because you can give a daughter away. But boys are better because they receive a bride, they bring people in and continue the family. Girls go away and do this work for someone else.

Generally, however, organising a daughter's marriage was not a welcome religious duty but a source of worry. Shortly after the death of Nisar's uncle's (FB) fourth daughter, Swaleha commented to him that bringing up daughters is an act of merit for Muslims and a route to Paradise. He responded:

> But it's very hard to bring up girls these days and get them married. Because of girls, families get dishonoured. A man I know had a good daughter and got her married. But later her husband left her with her parents saying the dowry was not big enough and he wanted a divorce. Just think of the dishonour to her parents!

Briefly, few people without daughters were anxious about failing to fulfil religious requirements. Rather, they felt relieved of an onerous chore, one moreover which many said was becoming harder. A widow in Dharmnagri had married her one daughter with some difficulty. She commented:

> My own mother was widowed with two daughters to marry, but she did not face my problems. When I was married, people didn't think badly about daughters. But now the dowry has got so big, and the boy's people's belly is not filled even so. That's the only reason why people now think that one or two girls are enough. If there are just a few girls they can give them each something, and they won't be miserable in their susrāl. Otherwise they may be taunted and made to do more work, and neighbours will say they brought nothing when they came.

Yet girls are often said to be more dutiful and repay parental affection with obedience and love, while it is believed that boys (necessary though they are) are more likely to cause trouble for their parents. Even Suleiman, with five daughters and no sons, said that there was no difference between boys and girls in terms of love and affection. But a girl is welcome only if her parents have enough sons, and few or no other daughters. Only three men, each of whom already had a son, argued that boys and girls can be considered the same. A recurring theme throughout our discussions was the contrast between sons and daughters, and how much people hope that God will grant them sons.

Two boys and a girl are best

> Three children are enough. I've got one boy already so I want one more boy and a girl. If I get two more girls that would be a problem, because I

187

only want three children. I've only got a little land, and if I have more than three I won't be able to feed, clothe and educate them. My sons will be poor enough if there are two of them, never mind any more. *(Shankar)*

I was happy to be pregnant, as we had only one son and I was hoping for another. *(Maya)*

Almost everyone in Dharmnagri and Jhakri sets the value of children against their cost. For poor and middle peasants, long-term security is inseparable from the amount of land each son will probably inherit. Among the landless and poor peasants, the direct costs of feeding extra mouths and providing more clothes and medical expenses are at the front of their minds. Central to such calculations are the different destinies of sons and daughters.

In discussing ideal family size and composition, the largest category of men (19) made clear an underlying logic that one or two sons are necessary.[33] Eleven said that two boys and one girl were ideal, while eight said that two children would suffice, provided at least one was a boy. Several considered it preferable to settle the matter by having one or two sons first; thereafter, a girl might be welcome. While not wanting what they considered a large family, five said that four children would be acceptable. From nine men we could obtain no clear answer, but another eight suggested that more than four children would be acceptable. But attaining the desired number of sons and daughters is by no means straightforward and several considerations affect couples' preparedness to contemplate family limitation.

People grow old with grief when their children die

My brother's wife has just had her ninth child. All the other eight have died. Does such a woman not know the grief of a child's death? Every woman knows what it feels like when a child dies.

Matters of life and death seem uncontrollable and unpredictable. The death of young children, in particular, appears to have no design known to human beings. Some practices are indicative of the frequency of child deaths: among Hindus, a new baby's ear may be pierced and a ring inserted before the cord is cut and the placenta buried inside the house, if its elder sibling has died; in Jhakri, several women used the term "marad biyāyī" to describe a child born after its older sibling had died and such babies are said to be alert and easily startled. Even the survival of children over five-years-old cannot be assumed: every year or so an older child dies, in an accident or from a seemingly inexplicable illness so rapid in its onset that the child dies almost before people realise it is ill. Few parents feel confident that their children will reach adulthood.[34] Between about 1965 and 1980, rich and middle peasants experienced levels of child mortality at least as high as poor peasants and the landless. Since 1980, in Dharmnagri, all the children of the married women aged under 25 in the rich and middle peasant chūlhās were still alive, but such a shift has not occurred in Jhakri.

Child mortality and uncertainties about child survival have made some couples willing, almost desperate, to have more children to ensure that enough survive. This applied particularly in Jhakri, where child mortality is higher than in Dharmnagri. Six of the eight men who wanted more than four children were from Jhakri, three of whom had had at least one son die. Maqsudi had given birth five times by September 1985, but only one girl and one boy were still living; Mansur was appalled by the prospect of old age without a son. In 1983, Wasila and Wajid, had three sons, one a small baby; another boy had died by falling into boiling gur. Wasila said then that she and Wajid agreed they wanted no more children. But their oldest son died suddenly from a chest complaint in 1984 and, while Wasila still wanted no more children, Wajid had changed his mind because of their son's death.[35] Similarly, Nisar's first child (a boy) died after 17 days, his third (a girl) died aged four-and-a-half and twin girls born in 1984 died at three months. Three children remained, but he said he wanted more.

Other couples' experiences of child mortality made them hesitate to use contraception, even though they wanted no more than three or four children. In September 1985, Vir and Vimla had a girl aged three-and-a-half, and a boy of 18 months. Their first-born boy had died at 15 months, and Vir said he wanted four children in all. Similarly, Nirmala's first-born son had died (of neonatal tetanus). She had a five-year-old boy and a three-year-old girl. Another girl born in November 1984 had died in June 1985. Naresh (and also his parents) would not countenance contraception yet, saying that the son was not robust and it was unwise to do anything until another boy was born. Nirmala had another daughter in 1986. In Jhakri, nine of the 19 key informant couples had had at least one son die, and a sense of the fragility of life lay behind many men's answers to questions about ideal family size. Irfan's response typifies this view. In 1985, against considerable opposition from his elder brother Haroon, he asserted the economic rationality of a small family, although he had had six children. But three (two girls and one boy) had died:

> This just shows it has nothing to do with me. It is up to God how many children I have. God gives and He takes away: I have to take what God decides. *(Irfan)*

For some couples in both villages, then, the experience of child mortality, and the prospect of more, explicitly affects their approach to family limitation. Contraception is not yet on their personal agendas because children — particularly sons — have died.

Taking what God gives

Nevertheless, the fear of child deaths in Jhakri does not account for all the differences in responses between the two villages. Initially, some Dharmnagri men were slightly embarrassed to discuss family planning, but eventually they all did and said they accepted the principle of contraception, provided that their need for sons had been satisfied. But many Jhakri men refused to discuss the issues in any detail. They were aware of the view (widely promulgated in

189

mosques in north India) that Muslims using modern forms of contraception are committing sins which hinder their admission to Paradise in the afterlife. They were unwilling to admit publicly to any use of contraceptives (even if they acknowledged that children were expensive) and gave stock responses: God alone knows how many children they would have, and they would accept whatever God gave them.[36] Ten of the 19 male key informants in Jhakri rejected outright modern contraception for themselves or their wives. In 1985 (when Hashmi was pregnant for the eighth time), Haroon put it this way:

> I don't want more children. The three I have remaining are more than enough. But what can I do? Only God knows how many more children He will send and it is written in the Qu'rān Sharif that God will provide for the children who are born. *(Haroon)*

Suleiman said he would consider contraception only when he had a grandchild, to avoid the sharm of Sabra becoming pregnant when a grandmother. Four others gave equivocal answers, or no answer at all. Only four admitted having made some "arrangements" or considering doing so.

You could die waiting for God to give you a son

> A boy and a girl are not really the same. But if you can afford only two children and they are both girls you have to understand in your mind that a boy and a girl are on a par. You can always bring in a ghar-jamāi. If you have a son you don't have to do this, but it is better to understand your daughter the equal of a son than have five girls while trying for a son. *(Rohtash)*

Others unwilling to practise contraception were those without "enough" sons, especially those with none. In trying to attain the desired balance of boys and girls and accommodate the vagaries of child mortality, couples sometimes continue having children — or fear they will have to — even when they exceed the number they regard as ideal. Several were anxious about how long this quest might be, and feared producing a large family of daughters while waiting for a son.[37] Durgi, Lakshmi, Promilla and Viramvati in Dharmnagri, and Asghari, Ruxana, Sabra, and Tahira in Jhakri have no living sons and say they must continue to bear children until they have. Sabra had five girls in 1983; another girl born in 1984 died at 15 months and yet another was born in 1986. Not surprisingly, Suleiman said they had enough girls but wanted "a little bit of a boy" and preferably two.[38]

Men with little or no land soon feel squeezed by financial pressures.[39] When Andrew raised the issue in 1985, Viramvati was pregnant.

Andrew: What if this is a girl?
Vikram's sister: He'll certainly have a boy, we've all been praying for a boy. Surely he'll have a boy after two girls.
Andrew: Is your government right to say that two children are enough?
Vikram: Yes. Two would be enough for me. But we are having a third

to see if it will be a boy. Three or four children are plenty. Two would have been fine but we don't have a son yet.

Andrew: But what if it is a girl?

Vikram: It will be difficult to decide. I think we'll have one more.

The third child was another girl. Similarly, in Jhakri, Riasat was concerned to have a son:

Riasat: I only want one more child. A son. If it is a girl we'll have to see what else God has in store. There are two of us and two children would be enough, but one must be a boy.

Andrew: How many girls would you have in trying for a son?

Riasat: It's up to God. I don't want many children. I've only a little land. But I could look after a few children properly, give them good food and clothes and medicines if they are sick. If I have more, where will I find the money to give them anything?

More substantial farmers have greater leeway, and are more likely to hope for two sons. Ashok's only son is his second child; another boy had drowned in their well. When their fourth daughter was about seven, Adesh gave birth again, to another girl. Neighbours disapprovingly commented that this baby had been born after such a long time because Ashok was still searching for a son, but it was a sharm-kī-bāt since their oldest daughter was already married. Adesh herself commented:

Now I do not want any more children. It would all have been happily settled if this girl had been a boy. But there aren't two sons in my destiny. In the very search for a boy, yet another girl has arrived.

Mahipal, a middle peasant, admitted he was "mad for a son". His first four children were girls, the fifth a son, the sixth another girl. Five children had been more than enough, he said, but he needed two sons, one to inherit his land in Dharmnagri, one to inherit the land in Maya's pīhar. In 1985, to their great relief, Maya had a second son.

Girls come without being invited

Only if the first or second child is a boy, can the parents begin to relax a little. Otherwise, they may continue having children in the hope of "better fortune" next time. Alternatively, they may intervene to try to obtain a son. According to local belief, a baby's sex is not fixed until the end of the third month of pregnancy, and there are country medicines intended to ensure the birth of a boy. People say that no one would want treatments to obtain a girl: after all, no one seriously objects to having an extra boy. Anyway, girls are said to "come without being invited".[40]

Women who have had a succession of girls can resort to treatments called seh palat medicines for overturning the pattern (seh) of their deliveries. Tablets are generally obtained direct from local vaids or hakīms or a few renowned expert dāis and taken at the end of the second or third month of pregnancy. Some village dāis collect tablets on behalf of women requesting treatment, but do not know the ingredients. Most dāis denied giving any treatments or refused to divulge details. One dāi, however, did disclose a recipe received from her husband's grandmother, like herself illiterate, who had been given it by a hakīm. It included nutmeg, cloves and mace (all garm), saffron (thandā) and the leaves of a medicinal plant called sparrow's tongue. Cloves and gur were mentioned by another dāi, and turmeric and coconut by another. Great care must be observed by the woman taking the tablets. She should do so in secrecy, without any girl nearby. She should swallow them down with water or with milk from a cow with a male calf, using a spouted water pot. She should probably avoid bitter foods, thandā items (such as carrots), and also vegetables or dumplings in a yoghourt and chick-pea flour sauce, which are considered thandā and bādī. Urad-kī-dāl (a type of pulse) is avoided because it is bādī. Most women were uncertain how such medical and dietary regimes might work. One interpretation, however, was that women who persistently bear girls are not garm enough for the baby's sex to be fixed as male. Thus, they require a controlled intake of garm items sufficient to produce a boy but not such that a miscarriage would ensue. Bādī items would distend the woman's tubes and increase the risk of the baby falling.

Most women bear a son at some stage without intervention, and such medicines are hardly prominent features of local medical care, but their very existence is significant. Three key informants in Dharmnagri with two or more girls were intending to try seh palat medicines during their next pregnancies. Maya had obtained tablets from a healer in her pīhar before her first son was born, but Mahipal prevented her from taking them, as he does not believe they work; she wanted to obtain more during her sixth pregnancy. Durgi, with two daughters and no living sons, was also planning to get tablets from an expert dāi living near the pīhar of one of her sisters-in-law (HBW). Likewise, Promilla said that her aunt (FyBW) had promised to obtain seh palat medicines next time she was pregnant. (Both Durgi and Promilla had daughters, but Maya had a son.) That all three were looking for help outside their susrāl may just reflect where these healers (often men) happen to be. But, as with treatments for infertility, a woman's own female kin may be keen to help secure her position in her susrāl. Women are in early pregnancy when they take these medicines, and can use female networks in their natal village to obtain treatment without the knowledge of their male natal kin.

But even these women spoke of seh palat medicines in somewhat sceptical terms, and several other key informants said they had no faith in such medicines:

What, can a boy be made by taking medicines? No! It's a matter of destiny. *(Nirmala)*

I don't believe in them at all. There is no medicine that can overturn the seh. A boy comes from one's destiny. *(Viramvati)*

Muslim women were particularly adamant that God's will predominates in such matters. Despite Sabra's extraordinarily long line of girls, she said taking seh palat medicines would signify lack of faith in God. Only a minority of the dāis admitted administering them and a quarter were scathing about their efficacy, saying that they were mere deceit, that nothing can be done with medicines and that a child's sex is a matter of fate and fortune and in God's hands. Echoing several others, one dāi commented:

> There are no seh palat medicines. It is all a matter of what God gives. If it's going to be a boy or a girl, there's nothing human beings can do. Those so-called seh palat medicines are useless. Look, if boys really resulted from them, nobody would have girls, everyone would be having only boys!

Putting girls in the hands of God

Generally, women do bear the son they need, albeit sometimes only after three or four girls have arrived first. But there is another option for parents with many girls. The mortality rates for boys are appalling enough, but the significantly higher rates for girls suggest that, at some level, parents neglect some of their daughters, and at worst promote their decline. In most of the world, girls have higher survival rates than boys, but the reverse occurs in Dharmnagri and Jhakri, suggesting that mortality is not simply the outcome of natural mishaps.[41]

In the first week of life, new-born boys in Dharmnagri and Jhakri are less likely to survive than are new-born girls, as elsewhere. Thereafter, boys are sufficiently more likely to survive to skew the rates substantially in their favour. Overall, 79% of live-born boys reached their fifth birthday, but only 72% of girls. Before 1960, the differential in survival was even greater: 70% for boys and only 57% for girls.[42] In the 1960s and 1970s, girls' chances of survival rose to equal those of boys, but girls born in the 1980s have again been much more likely to die. Only 91 (about 78%) of the 117 girls born alive after January 1980 survived until September 1985, but 107 (93%) of the 115 boys did so. For the key informants, 15 of the 42 girls born to them after January 1980 were dead by September 1985; three of the 36 boys had died.

These sex differentials in child mortality are greatest among Muslims and show no signs of decreasing. Indeed, nearly half the girls born in Jhakri since January 1980 had already died by September 1985. The same patterns show up among the key informants: 76% of the boys, but only 58% of the girls born live to the Muslim key informants were still alive in 1985. In Dharmnagri, 89% of the boys and 85% of the girls born to the key informants had survived. Sex differentials in mortality are also larger among the relatively wealthy. Among rich and middle peasants, 83% of boys but only 73% of girls survived to the age of five, whereas among the poor peasants and landless, 75% of boys and 71% of girls survived.

Such patterns might suggest that those who regard daughters as most costly would have greater sex differentials in child mortality. Overall, excess female mortality is highest among the rich and middle peasants, who are most affected by dowry demands and whose women are least likely to do work seen as economically valuable.[43] But excess female mortality is greatest among Muslims, whose dowry costs and marriage expenses are lower than for comparable Hindus. Moreover, girls with one or more older sisters are not especially vulnerable: indeed, in some households, several girls in succession have died before one eventually lived.[44]

Cultural understandings mean that the processes behind these mortality differences and possible differential care are not always overtly deliberate but often deeply embedded. Consequently, they are not easily exposed by direct questioning. Boys are thought to have greater entitlements and needs (for food and medicine, for instance) and to be altogether more vulnerable than girls, especially to the evil eye or evil influences.[45] Consonant with this is the view commonly expressed, especially by those seeking husbands for marriageable daughters, that there is a deficit of boys. By contrast, women more often gave a stock response — "she just got a fever" — when asked the cause of a daughter's death. Moreover, girls should learn self-denial in preparation for life in their susrāl. Certainly, we have only fragmentary evidence of girls' being intentionally neglected. In Dharmnagri, for example, Tarabati's second daughter died at 21 months after being left at home while Tarabati helped with the wheat harvest. The children looking after her did not give her enough water to drink, and she possibly died of heat-stroke. In Jhakri, one woman's daughter died during our research, having been emaciated and suffering from diarrhoea for months beforehand. The mother said the toddler had died for want of medicines, but her husband had beaten her whenever she suggested medical care. In another case, Nisar's uncle (FB) explained only after we asked outright what happened:

> She got dryness [sukhā] but we didn't get medicine for her. We put her in the hands of God. If she was to live she would live, and if not she would die. What person can do anything if someone is going to die?

Women with several girls would sometimes comment (if one fell sick): "She does not even die." When Latifan's baby daughter was sick, a neighbour remarked (in joking tones) that the child would certainly recover and extract a dowry from her parents. The sās of Hashmi and Imrana was one of the most explicit. Holding Imrana's new-born daughter — who died about a year later — she commented on the children born to her three sons:

> Allah has sent us bad fate. My oldest son's five daughters are all fine, but one boy died of smallpox, and three others were stillborn. And the one remaining boy is useless now that he is paralysed after having fever. And, look, now Imrana has had yet another girl.

Nevertheless, it would be impossible to sustain an argument that parents systematically and callously seek the demise of their daughters. Indeed, when girls die, especially if they are no longer babies, their mothers voice their grief.[46] Shankar's aunt (FyBW) said she had even broken post-partum dietary restrictions in the hope that she would die, for she was so upset by the death of her five-year-old daughter a few days before she gave birth. She ascribed her husband's death three months later to grief. Similarly, Jamila did little but cook for Jabruddin for several weeks after their daughter died in 1983. The child had only recently begun walking (though she was nearly three) and Jamila said she was struck down by the evil eye after a neighbour remarked upon it. "She saw so little of life", she sobbed. And when Farooq's twelve-year-old sister died, her parents were devastated and relatives came from nearby villages to attend her funeral. People said she was a remarkable child, the only girl in Jhakri who had read the entire Qu'rān Sharif.

Purposeful neglect of daughters, then, is hard to establish. Nor are girls' inferior chances of survival locally perceived. Yet they are manifest almost from birth in the maternity histories. For couples in Dharmnagri and Jhakri, however, it is primarily the unpredictability of sons' deaths that enters their calculations about family size.

The domestic politics of contraceptive decision-making

> With so many children already, how could I have been happy to be pregnant? What, are all these children 'few'? But when it has happened, what could I do? It's God's will. I don't want more children, but where is men's consideration about these things? And what can we women do? *(Latifan)*

> I would like just one more child, but not quickly. Can you tell me about some medicine to make the gap long? Last month my period did not come and I was worried that I was pregnant. Then it came by itself and I was very happy. In this matter my husband prevaricates. He thinks we should have two or three more children. But my sās says nothing to us about this. *(Vimla)*

The sex and number of children born and dying, the value and costs of children, and the morality of attempting to control family size can be perceived differently by different members of the chūlhā. Thus, discerning patterns of contraceptive use also entails considering domestic decision-making.

The husband is the master

> I shall get some medicine for my wife — those pills you told me about. My wife is agreed. But if she were not, she would either do as I say or I'd show her a thick stick. *(Riasat)*

> Whatever my husband's opinion is, I have to make that my opinion too. *(Nirmala)*

Men maintained that they decide everything connected with family planning and that their wives agree with their judgements; if not, the husband's will prevails. "The husband is the master" was a refrain almost every man repeated. Almost all the women said their husband's view was decisive and that action would be taken only if he sanctioned it. Women do not go about readily nor have they much cash to spend as they wish. They cannot easily (and certainly should not) take unilateral action on family limitation; that responsibility rests with their husbands. Married women are subject to their husband's rule, whatever their class and ethnicity. Different outcomes arise because of men's differing approaches to family-building, not because they view being master of the house in different ways.

That said, about three-quarters of the key informant couples agreed about whether or not they wanted more children. For the remainder (mostly Muslims), the wives' wishes to have no more children were confounded by the husbands' different views about ideal family size and appropriate action. Such women were confronted particularly forcefully with their husband's rule. Most women agree that a son is essential, but may be satisfied with just one. Men were more likely to consider at least two sons necessary. Indeed, while Suleiman (with no sons) insisted on the need for at least one son, Sabra said she would accept what God gave but would rather have no more children at all: "Even bringing up these is hard. My health is bad and we do not have enough to eat, because we do not have the land from which to obtain grain. These are too many."

Nineteen of the 21 women with two or more living sons wanted no more children; Jumni wanted a girl, and one woman refused to talk about the subject. Ten women had only one son living in 1982. Of these, five wanted no more children, but only Rohtash and Ashok agreed with their wives. Similarly, men were more likely to cite child mortality as an explicit reason for having more children, and Maqsudi, Wakila, Vimla and Nirmala all complied with their husband's judgement on this, despite dissenting when talking to us. But, while women and men relate to childbearing in somewhat different ways, their conclusions about ideal family size (if verbal accounts can be accepted) were usually broadly in agreement. So, too, were their views that contraceptive action would be needed once they achieved their desired family. Deciding to use contraception may be the husband's decision, or presented as such, but the wife usually agrees. Indeed, she may well have wished for it earlier.

Going behind the husband

When a couple's views do not coincide, the woman generally has little option but to comply with her husband's wishes. She fears being discovered if she takes unsanctioned action, and being punished by her husband if something goes wrong. Women in their susrāl may have been inhibited in admitting that they have contravened the requirements of a dutiful wife. None the less, some women do undertake family planning "behind the husband" or said they would consider doing so. Lakshmi, for instance, who had taken fertility treatment without telling Lalit, hinted that she might seek contraception without informing him, for all that "he is the master and I should do nothing behind him". Hashmi, Dilruba and Zubeida, all with two or more living sons, said they were prepared to limit their families without their husband's agreement. While Haroon said he would accept the children God sent him, Hashmi said she was keen enough to have no more that she would go behind him if necessary: "Enough. I endure the trouble, my husband doesn't." Nevertheless, she gave birth again in 1984 and 1985. In 1983 Dilruba said she had enough children and wanted to do something about it. But Dilshad wanted as many children as God would give — and another son was born in 1985.

These examples suggest that if a bahū wants to act against her husband's wishes, she has little room for manoeuvre while she is in her susrāl. When spouses disagree about family planning, however, a woman's visits to her natal village may provide some space for action independent of her husband. Her mother is more likely to be concerned about her well-being, and to arrange for an abortion or contraception to protect her health. Several women married out of Dharmnagri, for instance, had abortions performed or IUDs inserted while staying in their parents' house, though we cannot gauge how often such secret defiance occurs.

Of the key informants, Zubeida had taken a carrot seed decoction obtained when she was in her maikā in the hope that she would not conceive again. She had two sons and a daughter at the time, and had not informed Zakir:

> He wants more children. He says, 'It's your job to rear them', so he has nothing to worry about. But I don't want any more. These three don't have enough to eat and wear even now. When I'm pregnant or a jachā I get no special food, so the children and I all become weak. *(Zubeida)*

Zakir seemed rigidly opposed to any form of contraception:

> I might have more children and I might not. It's not what I want, it's what God decides. We Muslims don't think about things like family planning. No matter how many children I have, God will look after them. Even if I thought I had too many children, where would I put them once God has given them to me?

Zubeida's daughter born in 1985 died the next year. By late 1986 Zubeida was suffering from a "gas" illness which she believed would prevent her conceiving again, so she has not used any form of modern contraceptive.

But Zubeida is unusual: most women said mothers should not participate in their daughters' contraceptive decision-making.[47] Seven of the female key informants' mothers were dead and only three of the remainder said they had even discussed family planning with their mother. The rest all said that it was not their mother's business or that mothers and daughters should not discuss such shameful matters. The mother, then, is rarely involved — and young married women have few other means of obtaining contraception without their husband's knowledge.

What can my sās say, now we are alag?

> Who listens to a sās? My husband also wants no more children. I haven't
> sought anyone else's advice — what have they to do with it? Will they
> feed our children? *(Urmila)*

A bahū's parents-in-law are much more likely to be involved in her family
planning decisions than is her mother. Moreover, whenever they are
involved, it is never to enforce contraception against the will of their son and
his wife. On the contrary, it is often to insist that more children — future
workers to provide support in old age — are necessary, despite the younger
couple's wish to use contraception. But men were unwilling to concede that
their parents played a role in family planning decisions, although their wives
generally provide a more nuanced account.

The sās who is sājhe might expect (and be expected) to influence the
bahū's fertility, yet this is not always granted. Of the seven female key
informants in this position, two said their husband would not defy their sās;
two said their parents-in-law were involved in all decisions in the chūlhā. But
three said that their sās' views were irrelevant: although Ghazala's sās agreed
that Ghazala and Ghulam should not have many children, they excluded her
from their contraceptive decision-making; Najma considered her sās so naive
that she would never discuss contraception with her; and Wasila said that
even if her sās were angry, this would not affect what she did.

Even less do the key informants consider family planning the business of
the sās who is alag. Sixteen of the 21 women key informants who were alag
saw no role for their sās: two were on such bad terms that they rarely
discussed anything; the rest intended to exclude their sās from any decision or
thought her opinion would carry no weight even if (as some suspected) she
opposed their wishes. But some women like to retain a hold over their bahūs.
The sās of Jumni and Kamla wanted to decide about contraception and only
when Jumni refused to concede the point did she tell both bahūs that she
would not interfere. The sās of Omvati, Promilla, Pushpa, Rajballa and
Santosh was particularly keen to intervene in their family planning decisions,
but succeeded only with Omvati (who is still sājhe) and Santosh (because
Sunil is afraid to defy his mother). For women who are akelī, the key figure is
generally the husband, although Adesh and Bhagirthi both reported that
their father-in-law had intervened to stop them using contraception, by
wielding authority over Ashok and Bhagwana through his continuing control
over the land.

In general, women and men key informants portrayed themselves as
decisive in family planning matters, though the husband's parents do not
always accept their relegation. But the younger generation resent their
interventions, often asserting that their elders have no right to interfere as
they will not be responsible for rearing the babies.[48] The key informants'
views are well captured by comments such as, "miyān-bīwī rāzī, kiyā karegā
Qāzī?" (if husband and wife agree, what can the lawyer do?) and "apnī apnī
daplī, apne apne rāg" (to each their own tambourine, to each their own tune).

Sticking out your leg to trip up God

The bahū herself is the most likely person to favour some kind of action to limit the number of children she bears. If she has two living sons, or sometimes only one if he is healthy and past the most vulnerable age, her husband may agree. If not, she may get some support from her mother, but her parents-in-law are still likely to be hostile to contraception, at least for the moment. But even if the couple agrees, and can ignore the views of the husband's parents, the question of which contraceptive techniques to use remains. Central considerations in this choice are perceptions of the side-effects and the moral connotations of each method.

Country ways of controlling fertility

The Ayurvedic and Unani medical systems have paid little attention to gynaecological matters. Abortifacients or medicines to delay conception are absent from the major texts. Undoubtedly some vaids and hakīms developed reputations for such treatments. But knowledge and practice of fertility control was probably basically restricted to female practitioners such as dāis, or to domestic remedies known only to women, and thus likely to escape historical enquiry. Older women in Dharmnagri and Jhakri, however, generally denied that there had ever been country medicines for limiting fertility, saying that women used to become pregnant less often and had no need to make any arrangements. People simply accepted what was given — and maybe taken away again. Trying to control the number of children born would have been considered immoral:

> In the old days, no one used medicines to stop having children. They would say it was bad to stick out your leg to trip up God in his work. However many children were in a person's fate, that many would certainly be born.

> Before, no one stopped children being born. Everyone thought that whatever fruit was in your fate would have to be taken, whatever your condition. Children were born according to your own pattern and they stopped coming in their own good time.

The older women's accounts lend considerable credence to this view, since their marital careers appear as relatively unbroken sequences of pregnancies from cohabitation to menopause or the arrival of a son's wife. Nevertheless, we cannot be certain about the prevalence of country contraceptive methods in the past, or about who might have provided them or who had access to them. And a few women did indeed describe ways of delaying pregnancies or bringing on a late period.

Treatments "to extend the gap" (seh barhānā) between pregnancies are available from some expert dāis and male healers. A dāi in Urmila's pīhar charges Rs 100 for medicine to prevent conception altogether. Carrot seeds are also believed to make a woman so exceedingly thandī that she cannot become pregnant. One old woman in Dharmnagri said the jachā who lies on her side after delivery puts her uterus askew and will only conceive again once it is straightened. One dāi said that tugging on the jachā's bed would prevent conception for three years, another that the jachā should hold her head back when she washes her hair during her chhatī bath. Generally, though, women were vague about such treatments and about the herbal and other ingredients in medicines to prevent conception, or they simply denied their existence.

More commonly, it seems, women attempted to cause "cleansing" (safāi, that is an induced abortion) particularly by effecting a late period.[49] Women whose period is late may consume very garm items "to avert a baby" (bache-ko roknā) by stimulating uterine contractions. Black tea, hot water with gur (preferably over a year old), vinegar or cotton-husk soup, fenugreek, black pepper, or a decoction of babhar grass, sesame and gur, were all mentioned. Western medicines such as anti-malaria pills are also considered very garm and may produce the same effect. According to our informants, these cause cleansing, if at all, in the first three months. Instrumental methods, such as a stick inserted into the cervix, are not favoured: they would be employed after the spirit has entered the baby and therefore entail "causing a baby to fall" (bachā girānā), a sin akin to murder. Moreover, women say, such techniques are dangerous, for the woman may haemorrhage seriously or become poisoned inside. Village dāis were not famed for performing stick abortions; all three who admitted trying to achieve cleansing said they refuse to do so if more than three months have elapsed since the woman's last menstruation. About half the dāis interviewed adamantly denied using sticks or herbal remedies as they consider any cleansing a sin. Anyway, they said, women rarely come to them.

Such information is hard to assess. Dāis cannot legally perform abortions and may have feared being reported to the authorities.[50] Similarly, village women may have under-reported abortions rather than admit to sinning. On the other hand, elderly women often said that in their lifetime dāis had known nothing about contraception and abortion. A few even suggested dāis have no interest in performing abortions as their main income is dependent upon delivering babies. Others said that country methods had fallen into disfavour with the advent of modern contraceptive and abortion methods. Several dāis said they send women seeking abortions to the government hospital in Bijnor, others that women these days rarely want abortions because they opt for sterilisation instead. None of the women who admitted having an abortion had used country methods. As with medicines to produce a son, many women were sceptical about the efficacy of country methods and regarded Western medical techniques as more reliable. While we cannot be sure about fertility control in the past, contemporary practice indicates a pre-eminence of Western medicine.

Closing the tubes

The government family planning programme was initiated in the mid-1950s and the provision of various family planning techniques throughout the rural areas has been a key feature in the spread of government health services since the mid-1960s.[51] Private practitioners in towns and villages and private clinics in the urban areas also provide contraceptives. Throughout, the mainstay of the government programme has been sterilisation or nasbandī (tube-closing). From the government's perspective, nasbandī is the most cost-effective method of preventing births: it does not require a well-established organisation to maintain a monitoring service or supply contraceptives regularly, nor does it depend on people's skill and motivation to use condoms or other methods. At first, most nasbandī was vasectomy because initially most family planning workers were male. In addition, tubectomy (the barā or big operation) required greater medical infrastructure, particularly provision for general anaesthesia. Latterly, female sterilisation has predominated since the introduction of laparoscopic sterilisation, known locally as the spyglass (dūrbīn-wālā) or one-stitch (ek-tānkā-wālā) operation, which is performed under local anaesthetic on an out-patient basis, like vasectomy.

The government's frustration with the slow rate of economic growth and its diagnosis that rapid population increase was to blame, permitted an increasingly authoritarian drift in the provision of contraception.[52] In 1975, when Indira Gandhi called a state of Emergency, suspended formal democratic processes, and jailed a number of her opponents, this tendency dramatically accelerated. Government policy became increasingly centralised in the hands of Indira Gandhi and her inner cabinet, especially her son Sanjay, one of whose favourite goals was a rapid decrease in the birth rate. In the States, Chief Ministers wanting to impress him (and through him, his mother) made vigorous efforts to set and meet high sterilisation targets. In Uttar Pradesh, State employees — even those not in the health sector — were given personal targets and threatened with dismissal or cuts in pay if they failed to meet them. By 1976, coercive methods were used to maintain the momentum of the family planning programme.

It seems that Dharmnagri's landlord, who is generally in favour of family planning, decided that a campaign under his control was preferable to the random coercion that might otherwise be applied. A sterilisation "camp" (temporary operating facilities) was held in the Dharmnagri dispensary. He persuaded 13 men from Dharmnagri, two from Jhakri, and others from surrounding villages to be sterilised. Most were independent farmers (Jats, Sahnis and Dhimars) whom the landlord promised to help if problems arose. A few were the landlord's employees, and may have feared their jobs were at stake unless they co-operated. All but one of the men from Dharmnagri and Jhakri who were sterilised already had two or more sons, with an average family size over five. People said some compulsion (or energetic persuasion) was used by local medical staff. One woman was sterilised at the Bijnor women's hospital, apparently against her will. But we were given many more lurid accounts of what had happened elsewhere in the District. As in other parts of north India, carloads of men, many widowed, divorced, unmarried, or with post-menopausal wives, were apparently taken into Bijnor and forcibly sterilised. Fearing such a general round-up, many of the remaining

Dharmnagri and Jhakri men hid in the fields for the duration of the local camp. When the landlord's elder brother was informed, we were told, he was very angry and forbad any further camps in the locality.

Nasbandī was a key factor in Indira Gandhi's defeat in the 1977 general election.[53] Indeed, population control is almost the only state programme which has been implemented over the active opposition of the mass of the target population. No one knows when or how it might be tried again and suspicion of health workers has been slow to dissipate. Family planning workers lay very low for a while after 1976 but sterilisation targets again had a high priority after Mrs Gandhi's return to power in 1979. Currently, health staff have individual targets of sterilisation "cases" to motivate, and face transfer to less desirable postings, demotion or even dismissal if they consistently fail to reach these targets. They receive motivation fees, in 1985 amounting to Rs 10 for each tubectomy and Rs 15 for each vasectomy. In addition, the "case" receives cash, officially as compensation for lost earnings and any medical expenses. In 1985 this amounted to Rs 145 for a tubectomy and Rs 125 for a vasectomy, with a bonus of Rs 20 for a tubectomy and Rs 10 for a vasectomy with three children or fewer. During special nasbandī drives, local organisations (such as the Rotary Club) donate blankets or clothing to those who agree to be sterilised. No other government programme has had such a clear priority for its workers or such a high profile in the rural areas.

ANMs are now under particular pressure to find female cases, because of men's hostility to the family planning programme. An ANM entering a village is assumed to have a family planning case to visit. The Dharmnagri ANM does not routinely visit pregnant or lactating women otherwise, nor does she normally attend deliveries. In 1983, the ANM's assistant said that when they visit villages they are always asked, "Who have you come for today?" And women in Dharmnagri complained that the ANM's solicitous behaviour evaporates once the individual has been sterilised. Village women thus view government health staff with an eye to their ulterior motives, and a lurking and perhaps not ill-founded fear of a return to direct coercion. Maternal and child health services are approached cautiously, because women want to avoid putting themselves in debt to the health staff. The meaning of these services for health staff was well captured in numerous incidents we observed. For instance, the Dharmnagri ANM complained to us in 1982 about a third village, saying, "I've done so much for them but they haven't given me any cases." Moreover, both she and her assistant repeatedly denied the existence of alternative methods of contraception and tried to persuade women to be sterilised. And in 1985, the new Dharmnagri ANM refused to give Santosh ante-natal tetanus injections unless she promised to be sterilised after her second child was born. Santosh resorted to the dispensary compounder, who charged her Rs 10 to administer injections that should have been free.

Coercion, however, is but part of the story. For several reasons, many people in Dharmnagri and Jhakri do not regard nasbandī as the ideal contraceptive.[54] Many people fear operations and contact with medical professionals in general:

Dilruba: I myself won't have the operation, even thinking about it makes me afraid.
Patricia: Is that because of religion or because of fear?
Dilruba: It's partly a matter of religion, but basically I fear the operation — they cut your whole belly open!

The cash incentives are considered insufficient to allow for post-operative recovery, especially as operating conditions are not always conducive to clean healing of the wound. Men often regarded vasectomy as an undesirable option for them because even a few days off work would have serious implications, and all the more so if the wound becomes infected. Of couples recently contemplating nasbandī, only Ishwar Das said he should be sterilised: Imarti was already weak but his step-son was now doing most of his heavy work. One landless woman in Dharmnagri said her husband could not risk having nasbandī: "How would we feed the children? After the operation, he would be weak and could not ride his rickshaw." It is also rumoured that, in the long-term, vasectomy is weakening, affecting men's ability to work and their sexual potency. Udayan's father died in 1982, and Udayan's mother considered this a result of his nasbandī six years previously:

After having nasbandī he couldn't lift heavy weights. I wouldn't let him do heavy work. He had stomach pains all the time. Another man had nasbandī at the same time and he died after three or four months.

Although some sterilised men reported no adverse symptoms, men and women are generally apprehensive. Nowadays, however, female sterilisation is more common. As Shankar's father commented: "Men have no reason to be afraid of the operation, it won't be done on them but on their wife!" Men commonly said, "I shall have my wife sterilised" and women accepted that it would be their nasbandī rather than their husband's. But women, too, sometimes wonder what will happen to them afterwards:

People like me cannot have nasbandī. I have five children and I don't want any more. But I can't afford nasbandī. I spend all day in the fields doing heavy work, otherwise we could not eat. How can I have an operation?

Patricia's bantering suggestion that women should call their nand to help was greeted with amusement: a good idea, possibly, but not realistic, since women are not entitled to help after nasbandī, although a sās might provide a few days' respite. Nasbandī is not a matter of celebration, so how could they expect their nand to come? Sometimes, too, female nasbandī is not straightforward. One woman in Dharmnagri was sterilised in 1982, but the incision did not heal properly and left her in pain for several weeks. Others blamed chronic problems on nasbandī: "I have been sick since my nasbandī and can't even do my house-work. I still take sleeping pills every day."

Such examples influence the general view of nasbandī. At the very least, couples considering nasbandī are cautious about the timing of the operation. People believe that the damp monsoon heat makes infection likely, so they often delay until the winter, when wounds heal quickly and ready cash is more easily available for medicines if necessary.

The moral connotations of nasbandī, however, are often a much more powerful barrier. Nasbandī is the archetypal means of "tripping up God": some older Hindus and Harijans and almost all the adults in Jhakri consider nasbandī to be a greater sin than any other form of contraception. Many Muslims insist that Allah provides for all the children in a person's allocation, that nasbandī amounts to blood murder, and that Muslims who have been sterilised forfeit a place in Paradise.[55] Some Muslim family planning workers we encountered during our survey even said they made laparoscopic sterilisation acceptable to potential Muslim cases by claiming that it is a contraceptive injection effective for ten years.[56]

In all, 22 men in Dharmnagri and Jhakri (19 from Dharmnagri) had nasbandī, all before 1977. Of the 26 women sterilised up to the end of 1986, just two were from Jhakri. The sterilised Muslims felt they had had no choice. One man, for instance, was the landlord's ploughman and he told us (and the ANM confirmed this) that his operation had been done under compulsion. His brother had nasbandī because his first wife had died in childbirth and the second narrowly missed doing so. Of the two women, Dilruba's nand was sterilised in hospital after an obstructed labour and Caesarian section which nearly killed her. In Dharmnagri, some people reported being pressurised by circumstances or by the health staff, but most had undergone nasbandī freely, having attained their desired family size and composition.

If one consequence of the Emergency is that knowledge of nasbandī is widespread, understanding what it involves is somewhat limited.[57] Vasectomy is believed to close the tubes through which a man's seeds pass, but people were uncertain about why men might become thandā (cold, impotent) after nasbandī rather than garm (because his seeds accumulate within the body). According to local views, a woman's contribution to the growing foetus is nourishing the man's seed with her menstrual blood. Since sterilised women continue to menstruate, women in Dharmnagri and Jhakri had difficulty explaining how nasbandī prevents conception. One dāi suggested that nasbandī closes the tube that takes blood to the uterus and the man's seeds fail to develop for want of nourishment. Another thought the tube where a baby would lodge and grow was cut and knotted. But most women simply refused to speculate.

None the less, people are very clear that nasbandī does not "extend the gap" nor "avert a baby": nasbandī "puts a stop to children" (bachon-ko band karnā). This finality is the major key to resistance to it in an environment of high child mortality. There are no local facilities for micro-surgery and going further afield for such an operation was unknown and would anyway be prohibitively expensive. Nasbandī is thus a high risk strategy and there was much talk about (rumoured) cases where several children died after one parent had been sterilised. In Jhakri, indeed, soon after the ploughman's nasbandī his younger son died and they were left with only one son, who was often sick. In 1985, Nirmala said she would have wanted nasbandī if one of her daughters had not died earlier that year and her son were not weak, but she was under pressure to have more children. Even Muslims who resist nasbandī on religious grounds provide more nuanced accounts after further questioning, in which fear of child deaths is at the forefront:

I am praying for no more children. What else can I do? Two of my children have died. Since we have no idea when our children might die, how can we think of nasbandī? *(Wasila)*

Wajid explained his views like this:

Wajid: I can't say how many children I want. That is God's decision. Last winter I had four sons and I thought that was more than enough, though God has not given me a daughter. Then one son died. Another is now ill with a cough — who knows if he will survive?
Andrew: Is your government right to say that two children are enough, then?
Wajid: In one way they are right. If you have two, you can feed and clothe them properly. But God decides how many children you have, not the government. With nasbandī, the government can take away the ability to have children, but it can't give you back the children who die.

Mansur took a similar line, as did many others:

Two children are not enough. If you have only two and they die after you have nasbandī you will be in great trouble, with neither a daughter to give away nor a son to look after your farm. The government is wrong to say two are enough. They don't give children nor can they take them away. Only God can do that.

Rajballa's sās was one of the older Hindu women most opposed to nasbandī. She had been unable to prevent her daughter's husband (with three boys and two girls) and her eldest son (with four daughters and three sons) having nasbandī in Dharmnagri dispensary in 1976. She was also unable to control Rohtash. Before Rajballa's Caesarian operation, Rohtash was asked if he would consent to nasbandī. He readily agreed, astounding all observers, local and expatriot alike. Even the ANM asked if he felt under compulsion, but he said that he and Rajballa had already decided on nasbandī even if the second unborn baby were another girl. When his mother learnt of this she let forth a diatribe of abuse about his imprudence. Looking back two years later, Rohtash and Rajballa were happy to endorse the decision:

Rohtash: 'Two is enough' is right for me. With two children I get some ease and we can stay happy. It cost me enough trouble when the second child was born and we had to mortgage some land to pay off the debts. We couldn't do that again. If we had any more children, we'd have to work morning and night to prevent them going naked.

Rajballa: Yes! People with many children are worried the whole time wondering how they will feed their children.

Rohtash: With four or five children, one or other would always be sick or hungry and take food from the others' mouths. The smaller your family the better when you're poor.

But few would have been prepared to take such a decision before knowing the outcome of the delivery. Even having nasbandī with one son, or when sons are still small, requires considerable optimism and courage. In 1985 for instance, Mahipal was delighted by his second son's birth and planned for Maya's nasbandī — but this had still not taken place over a year later. Nasbandī may also be delayed by couples still seeking a son, as was the case with Vikram after his third daughter was born. Records from the Primary Health Centre for the area indicated that no couples without one or more sons came forward for nasbandī, although 10% of couples had no daughter.[58] As Liaqat commented, "Who ever heard of people having nasbandī after three daughters?"

Causing a cleansing

Medical termination of pregnancy (MTP) by a qualified doctor and virtually on demand has been legal in India since 1972. Locally, surgical abortion, injections and oral abortifacients are covered by the general term "cleansing" (safāi), as also is dilatation and curettage (D and C).

Surgical abortions are not performed in the Dharmnagri dispensary, but the government women's hospital and the two private women's clinics in Bijnor offer surgical abortion facilities and over one-third of the dāis claimed to refer women wanting abortions there. But surgical abortion can be expensive. The notionally free treatment at the government hospital is rarely so and conditions there make it an unpopular choice anyway: women complained about dirtiness and we heard of abortions conducted without any anaesthesia. Private clinics charge Rs 300 or more. Moreover, a few women's requests for surgical abortions were refused because the doctor said they were too weak for an operation — though apparently strong enough to undergo pregnancy and childbirth. For women seeking abortions, then, the health services are an unsatisfactory option.

Further, surgical abortions are likely to be recommended only after the spirit has entered the baby and involve "causing a baby to fall". They also entail being exposed and are considered more hazardous and violating than medical methods: opening the woman's cervix leaves her vulnerable to dangerous influences, just as after delivery. Indeed, some women reported refusing a surgical abortion and some men used these arguments to prevent their wives having an abortion. Hiran, for instance, felt that her third pregnancy was too soon after her second. She went to Bijnor with Harwan but when they were told that she would need a surgical abortion he refused to proceed. She carried the baby to term but subsequently had nasbandī.

Adesh, too, had not wished to continue with her seventh pregnancy, but Ashok would not countenance a surgical abortion saying, "The child is no one else's — let it live."

Oral abortifacients (such as ergot) and injections are available both within and outside the formally licenced structure of abortion facilities. The compounder at the Dharmnagri dispensary sometimes writes prescriptions for abortifacient medicines which women buy for a few rupees from chemists in Bijnor, although the medicines can easily be purchased without prescription. If they are used before the child has taken root, they are regarded as medicines for "averting a baby". Since the spirit has not yet entered the child, this does not carry quite the sinful taint of surgical abortions. Even so, Omvati was prevented from aborting her fifth pregnancy by oral means because of the moral objections of Om Prakash and his mother; she continued with the pregnancy and had a daughter (who died at about 18 months). And after Ghazala's aborted second pregnancy became known to her sās, Fatima and other women in their courtyard, she was the butt of jibes if she ever mentioned feeling unwell: "There are pills for headaches too, you know." Oral abortifacients and injections may also be employed after the spirit has entered the child, when they are considered most likely to be effective if the foetus is male, just as a male foetus is believed to be more vulnerable to falling if the woman is too garm. The female foetus has a reputation for greater tenacity. Sabra bitterly regretted taking abortifacient medicines after having vaginal bleeding during the fifth month of her second pregnancy; the baby was male. She interpreted her subsequent lack of sons as divine punishment.[59]

While many Muslims express vehement religious objections to abortion, more bahūs in Jhakri than in Dharmnagri reported wanting or attempting to procure one, though not always successfully. Among them, in 1982, Imrana wanted to abort her fourth pregnancy, but not without Irfan's consent. She considered abortion a threat to her life and a sin, yet wanted no more children. So she persisted in asking Irfan to buy abortifacient medicines until, "in anger", he gave way. But they failed, and she had a daughter (who died aged one year). In early 1984, Imrana again unsuccessfully tried to abort her next pregnancy, and gave birth to twins. Pregnant once more in 1985, she again took abortifacient pills (without informing Irfan) but to no avail. Around the same time, Qudsia was trying to abort her fifth pregnancy; she had four children, the eldest aged six. With Qadir's knowledge, she had twice obtained abortifacient pills from the dispensary compounder, but they had no effect. So Imrana and Qudsia (with the consent of Irfan and Qadir) went to one of the private women's clinics in Bijnor and had injections and more pills. Still nothing happened. Qudsia returned to the doctor, by now rather annoyed with the turn of events; she was given another mixture and aborted ten days later. Imrana's pregnancy was more advanced and the doctor refused to perform a surgical abortion, saying Imrana was not strong enough. She later had another son.

Women seeking abortions portrayed their quest as a desperate last resort about which they were uneasy, rather than a positive or desirable option. The greater frequency of recent abortion attempts among the Muslims does not indicate that abortion is regarded favourably in Jhakri. Rather, the greater resistance to nasbandī in Jhakri means more women there are contending with unwanted (generally high parity) pregnancies.

Modern methods of extending the gap

Those who are unready to take the irreversible step of nasbandī or the morally dubious and dangerous route of abortion do have other options. Government policy since the 1950s has been to make condoms widely available. They are supplied free on request by the male family planning worker at the Dharmnagri dispensary, but few couples in Dharmnagri and Jhakri reported ever using them.[60] Intra-uterine devices (IUDs) have long been second to nasbandī in the government family planning programme. More recently, hormone-based contraceptives have become available, currently only in oral pills not as injectables or implants.[61] Locally, IUDs and contraceptive pills are regarded as means of extending the gap between pregnancies. Women tendered no explanations of how the pill and IUD work: just one dāi surmised that an IUD dries up the woman's tubes and the man's water cannot remain inside (just as with some women who are unable to conceive).

Like nasbandī and abortion, neither IUDs nor oral contraceptives are considered wholly satisfactory by women in Dharmnagri and Jhakri.[62] Until recently, IUDs (known locally as "loop" and "Copper T") have had equivocal reputations. Only seven women (all in Dharmnagri) had a Lippes loop inserted in the five years before 1982. Three reported menstrual problems and pelvic pains; Bhagirthi even removed her loop herself. Menstrual irregularity or spotting (which repeatedly defile the woman), heavy menstrual bleeding (which is considered weakening) and painful menstruation were common fears. Some women also believed that the loop can cause cancer. The Copper T has caused fewer problems. By 1983, one Dharmnagri woman had switched to it from the loop and reported less menstrual discomfort. Another Dharmnagri woman had a Copper T inserted in 1979, and reported no pain and normal periods in 1983. By 1985 her periods had become very heavy so she had it removed and opted for nasbandī. Several women, however, feared that a Copper T could damage their tubes and even disappear inside them. Crucially, there is no formalised monitoring of women with IUDs and the ANM usually only sees women who come to her with problems. Some women said the ANM refused to change IUDs and will remove them only if the woman agrees to nasbandī instead. This probably inhibits women from consulting the ANM; several women, indeed, had an IUD for some years without any check-up.

The dispensary had no stocks of oral contraceptives when we arrived in 1982. The ANM denied that any such medicines were available in India, even though they were easily purchasable without prescription from pharmacists in Bijnor. Women in Dharmnagri or Jhakri had not heard of oral contraceptives until they asked Patricia to list family planning methods. Several Muslim men refused to believe that there could be pills to stop women having children because the government — usually so keen to prevent children being born — had not mentioned such a technique. Since 1983, however, free oral contraceptives have been stocked at Dharmnagri dispensary. Family planning workers receive a small incentive fee for each cycle they administer (without medical tests or follow-up) and several women in Dharmnagri and Jhakri obtain oral contraceptives from the ANM. Others prefer to buy them privately rather than accept the ANM's favours and come under pressure to have nasbandī. But this makes them dependent on their husbands, and they cannot rely on regular supplies because the men do not always remember to replenish the stocks. Otherwise, women appear to have no problems taking oral contraceptives regularly, but are anxious about side-effects and whether they should take the pills with hot or cold milk or water. Some took the pill for only a few cycles because they were affected by garmī caused by a light menstrual flow, and evidenced in giddiness and other symptoms of garmī in the head. Others were perturbed by the frequent defilement caused by spotting.[63]

God gives sunlight but people use parasols

> Once a woman has three-four children, I myself suggest that she has nasbandī. Even though I am a Muslim, I am not against nasbandī. After all, God gives sunlight but people use parasols. *(dāi)*

In retrospect, we sense that we first arrived in Dharmnagri and Jhakri at a crucial point in the demographic history of the two villages. Fertility was still high, but mortality had been declining for at least 20 years. People still perceived an overriding need to have enough children (particularly sons) to ensure that some would survive a highly risky childhood. This requirement was in tune with the local system of marriage arrangements and residence patterns, a subordinate role for the bahū and a labour-intensive economy. These features have hardly changed, but new parameters now require very different responses. The changes of the Green Revolution probably contributed to the decline in mortality by raising living standards. But people increasingly believe that they are living on borrowed time; with a sense of foreboding, most realise that their sons will inherit parcels of land too small to generate sufficient income and that their daughters' marriages may push them too heavily into debt to maintain even what little they have. Again, women react somewhat differently from men, as they try to cope with their work responsibilities alongside what seem to be more frequent pregnancies and the increasing demands of childcare as child mortality declines. This was grudgingly admitted by many couples in the early 1980s, but had become a major concern by 1986. More and more people feel a pinch developing and they try to reach their desired number of sons with a small completed family.

People are not all affected equally. Each woman has a particular experience of fertility — how rapidly children arrive, and the balance of boys and girls — and of child mortality, which combine to set a different context for each chūlhā. But some similarities can be discerned for couples within class groupings, and the ethnic dimension distinguishes Dharmnagri and Jhakri. Overall, however, few couples are insulated from the pressures. Almost all are being impelled to consider contraception by the changing logic of their own positions. Government propaganda plays a small part in this.[64] Three features bring home the fluidity of the situation very forcefully: comparing the rhetoric of Muslim men with contraceptive behaviour in Jhakri; the different responses to us and our questions between our arrival in early 1982 and our departure in 1983 and on our subsequent visits; and the contrast between contraceptive use in early 1982 and that by the end of 1986.

When Andrew questioned men in Dharmnagri about contraception in 1985, their answers were mostly straightforward, confirmed by their wives, and bore a close relation to behaviour. Only Udayan (whose interview was in front of several other men) gave equivocal and joking answers. He insisted that he would use some local medicines, but he could not say what they were nor where he would obtain them. In 1986 Urmila had nasbandī, as she had said she would. In Jhakri, however, only four male key informants said they ever had or ever would consider contraception of any kind. But some others who had voiced adamant religious objections to contraception had been involved in their wives' abortions and other efforts at contraception. These men's rhetorics seem to have co-existed with ambivalence, delay and disputes between husbands and wives, not the outright rejection which they claimed. Consider, for example, Qadir, who told Andrew in 1985 that his four children were enough:

Qadir: If the post office is shut now, that's fine by me.
Andrew: But will you try to shut it yourself?
Qadir: No. I do not want any more children but we will have to see what God has in store for us. I've never used family planning and I never will. My wife agrees, and even if she didn't she would do what I say. I'm the master and she does what I tell her.

But at that very time Qudsia was taking oral contraceptives, she had had an abortion (with Qadir's knowledge, according to her account) and she was still taking pills over a year later. In 1985, Jabruddin and Nisar also said they would never use contraception:

Jabruddin: I will take as many children as God gives.
Andrew: God is the master, but what do you think in your own heart?
Jabruddin: Three children are enough, but only God knows the future. We have never used any contraception and we never will. The government is wrong to say that two is enough. Although I think three is enough, I will still do nothing about it.
Nisar: Don't bother asking anyone else in Jhakri, you'll be wasting your time! All the men will give you the same answer. My wife's a Muslim, she'll say the same.

But Najma and Jamila gave rather different stories:

Najma: Ha! I was very happy to be pregnant again! What happens as a result of being happy? It was a calamity. If it were within my control I wouldn't have had a single child, but what should I have done? Children are not within my control. Whatever God gives will have to be accepted. My husband is not the sort of man who would bring pills. He is very straight and doesn't know anything about such matters.
Swaleha: Do you want any more children at all, then?
Najma: Another 50 girls and 50 boys! ...... No, really, I do not need either a girl or a boy.

Jamila's first two boys had died (one aged just over two, the other at 17 days), then she had a boy who is still living, followed by a girl (who died in 1983) and another boy born in 1982. By 1983 she wanted a break from childbearing, but could do nothing without Jabruddin's consent. In 1985, she reported that she had persuaded Jabruddin to obtain abortifacient pills when she was pregnant the previous year. She did not take them as she was four months pregnant by the time he brought them, so she had another son. But Jabruddin then obtained two cycles of oral contraceptives. And in 1986, Jamila and Najma, along with Latifan, had Copper Ts inserted.

Farooq was also adamant that he would never consider contraception: "Really, I think I've got enough now. I shall pray for no more, but that's all. We will have to see what God has in store for us." Farida also claimed that prayer was their only resort, though she added an ironic twist: "The more we don't want children, the more God sends them. So now I'm going to give God this prayer, 'Please send me lots more children'!" But in 1986, she too had a Copper T fitted at the Dharmnagri dispensary.

Contrasts between 1982 and 1986 can be seen most dramatically by comparing our first days in the villages and our last. In February 1982 we explained our interest in childbearing in the villages. Even in Dharmnagri, but especially in Jhakri, many women were suspicious that we were employed by the family planning programme. Furthermore, when Patricia and Roger were quizzed about how they had been married so long but only had one daughter, questions about family planning followed. Several women in Jhakri ran away when Patricia replied to their questions about how they could stop having children, and she was abused when she tried to ask them about their families.

But before long, women's fears gave way to constant requests for contraceptives. Khurshida sought our involvement twice over. With Khalil's consent, she first asked us for pills in 1982 on her own behalf and (extraordinarily) for her mother too. We insisted that they had medical check-ups from a woman doctor in Bijnor, though these were so perfunctory that no contra-indications could possibly have been determined. Khurshida continued taking oral contraceptives for just two cycles and reported suffering from garmī. She soon became pregnant and had a son in 1984. Then in 1985, she considered an abortion, with Khalil's agreement: he said that she

211

was weak and had to work alone, and additional children would only make matters worse. They obtained abortifacient pills that failed to work. Then Khurshida asked Patricia to accompany her to a clinic and oversee a surgical abortion, but a couple of days later she had decided she was too afraid to proceed. In the end, she had a six-month miscarriage. Some women in Dharmnagri saw us as a route preferable to the ANM, because the pressure on them to have nasbandī increased if they used the government services. In general, however, women in Dharmnagri were less opposed to nasbandī, had lower child mortality rates, and could generally handle the (Hindu) ANM more successfully than could the Muslim women. Thus, Jhakri women were the main source of requests for help. By the time we left in April 1983, the same women who had fled in terror a year earlier asked Patricia why she was not leaving them some "souvenir" by which (after Patricia had misunderstood) they explained they meant contraceptive pills.

This grass-roots demand had evolved into widespread contraceptive use by December 1986. In 1982 fewer than ten of the 160 married women then under the age of 45 were "protected" by IUD, tubectomy or their husband's vasectomy. By 1986, 41 women had Copper Ts and eight more women had been sterilised. Eight others (seven from Jhakri) were regularly obtaining oral contraceptive pills from the ANM and others were obtaining them privately. In total, about one-third of the women then below the age of 45 were protected from conceiving. Only Hindus are willing to seek nasbandī. In both villages, however, women are using methods which do not have the same finality, though Jhakri women are generally coming to modern contraception at higher parities than Hindu women.

Aside from the prospects of a financial squeeze, some of this change was possibly due to our presence, some to the more general change in government policy to make contraceptive methods other than nasbandī more prominent, and some to the arrival of a new ANM who resides at the dispensary and seems inclined to provide more comprehensive maternal and child health care. But the shift is dramatic, and one about which we are far from happy. Certainly, women wanting to limit their fertility are increasingly obtaining the means to do so. But this must not obscure the profound problems surrounding contraception, particularly with respect to the side-effects of the currently available techniques and the politics of their provision. Modern methods of contraception are all unsatisfactory, even possibly dangerous. Nasbandī operations are carried out without after-care facilities. The other methods should be carefully monitored through regular check-ups, but they are not. Women experience the costs of childbearing most directly and are the main source of demand for contraception, but the potential dangers mostly affect women, the focus of almost all local family planning efforts. As currently constituted, the medical infrastructure does not have the resources to provide follow-up for women adopting modern contraception. Perhaps more seriously, the government's stress on nasbandī and the excesses of the Emergency have highlighted its preoccupation with population control, rather than family planning in tune with the wishes of childbearing women and their husbands. Health workers' cash incentives for motivating contraceptive cases provide them with no reason to give after-care any priority. Furthermore, the government's irritation at the slow decline in the birth rate could result in a return to overt coercion. The limitations of government services for women's reproductive health and child survival could easily turn women away, not only from the available contraceptive methods but also from government health services generally. The situation is extremely volatile.

Father cuts sugar-cane while his children play

9.   Village Homes and Government Offices

The government doesn't think about the poor when they sterilise them.
If you go and get medicine for your sick children after nasbandī they
just look the other way. They aren't interested. *(Usman)*

We began this book with Muni giving birth in the apparent privacy of her
small village home. But the childbearing careers we described in the chapters
that followed are tied into much wider social relationships, most obviously
connected with domestic structures, class position and ethnicity. Broadly
speaking, women like Muni face considerable risks of a delivery culminating
in a maternal or infant death and suffer the physical costs of frequent
childbearing, and the longer-term prospects for their children are poor. In
terms of maternal and child well-being, then, there is considerable scope for
improvement at each stage: in pregnancy, during delivery, in the immediate
post-partum period or in the next few years.

Childbearing in north India is not the concern solely of childbearing
women and their close female susrāl kin, nor even of the wider kin groups to
which they belong and which the new babies (if they survive) will join. The
Government of India claims to be concerned about the health of mothers and
their babies and to have the right to intervene to limit the number of children
born, in the wider interests of society. The government, then, might seem the
most obvious source of action to improve the prospects for childbearing
women in north India. Our experience and analysis, however, suggest that
government policy will have little direct or positive effect on childbearing
women in the foreseeable future. Central features of Dharmnagri and
Jhakri's social structure are common to thousands of villages across the
Ganges plain. There may be local exceptions — an outstanding hospital,
effective health workers, active women's groups or grass-roots political
organisations — but, in general, neither the wider spread of conventional
medical services nor attempts to support and improve traditional maternity

215

care arrangements have much chance of success.

Conventional medical services

On the face of it, the government might tackle the conditions of childbearing most effectively through better maternal and child health services. Conventionally, this has entailed top-down, bureaucratically organised clinics, staffed by full-time professionals or para-professionals. In central government policy statements, key targets for "Health for All by the Year 2000" include reducing the maternal mortality rate from its current level of around five per 1,000 live-births to around two and the infant mortality rate from the national figure of over 10% of all live-births to less than 6%. The main method proposed to achieve such ends is increasing the number of health centres and sub-centres to between two and three times as many in the year 2000 as in 1980, so that each cluster of villages with a population of 5,000 is served by at least one ANM.[1]

In some parts of India, this policy may provide accessible skilled medical care and a monitoring and referral service which safeguards women and children at risk. Some progress may also be possible in preventing neonatal tetanus and reducing maternal anaemia. But we remain sceptical about how far or how fast such programmes will succeed in north India.[2] Women's medical services have a lower priority within the structure of health service provision than those for children or men, and their quality is poorer; furthermore, they are subordinated to the population control programmes.[3] Government staff receive an incentive for each nasbandī case they motivate. Surgeons receive a special fee for each nasbandī operation they perform. Consequently, during the main months for family planning campaigns (usually December to March) virtually all the energies of maternal and child health staff may be directed towards those ends.[4] Financial inducements corrupt the medical services and bias them towards nasbandī. No similar incentives or special fees encourage work aimed at improving women's reproductive health or reducing child mortality, unless such action can rapidly guarantee higher levels of family planning achievement.

Even in maternal health work itself, staff do not operate according to the national policy goal of taking health services to the rural population. Doctors regard obstetrics as an urban, hospital-based speciality. No serious attempt is made to run ante-natal clinics in sub-centres or to create effective liaison between hospital doctors and ANMs. In urban maternity units, rural referrals are not welcomed and receive no priority. There is, then, no real chain of referral from lower to higher levels of care.

These structures are based on models of health services derived from the experiences of Britain and the United States.[5] In relation to childbearing, the ultimate goal is full ante-natal screening by doctors and nurses, with most (if not all) babies delivered under medical supervision in medical institutions. Leaving aside the criticisms of these models in the West, to spread such medical services to the rural Indian population would be a very slow and expensive business. The considerable demands already made on the mainly curative health services from the urban population and from landlord and some rich peasant families are far from being met at current levels of resources. Doctors and nurses are fully occupied, in private practice or in government service. Even to meet the urban demand, not enough women doctors are being trained, and not enough blood banks or anaesthetists are available. Furthermore, spreading medical facilities to the villages would necessitate extra outlays to provide a rural social infrastructure — speedy and cheap transport, schooling and housing, reliable electricity supplies — with which to tempt doctors away from the towns. Additionally, rural services for women are hampered because problems of personal security for female staff inhibit the recruitment of educated young women.

Even were such government services feasible, however, most rural women would find many aspects of them unpalatable. Although access to hospital itself is free or very cheap, entering hospital to give birth in complicated cases can practically ruin a poor or middle peasant family. Landless people should obtain free services, but few believe that this entitlement really operates. Sometimes, drugs and other medical supplies are simply unavailable; in other cases, they are prescribed only to those whose personal ties to the doctor or pharmacist give their demands a higher priority. Some drugs are cynically presumed to have been stolen and sold by the health staff, and the remainder diluted. Only bribes or "unsolicited gifts" are believed to entice government servants to provide what they are supposed to. Doctors and other staff are said to be increasingly interested only in "heating" their own pockets:

> In the past, doctors didn't ask for so much money. They would take whatever people could afford. But these days, the first thing they say is that this much money will be needed. If it is available then the patient will be treated. But if not, they do nothing. *(Jumni's sās)*

In addition, medical treatment may be provided in a very demeaning and threatening manner. Urban-educated health workers' theories of anatomy and physiology, disease and treatment, often diverge from those of their rural clients, a cultural gap which can be a barrier to health care. It is manifested in disparagement of patients by staff under stress: patients are accused of being dirty, incapable of understanding instructions or following hospital procedures and of exaggerating their poverty to avoid paying for treatment. The poor fear being sent to the end of queues or denied entry if they arrive late, perhaps after long and tortuous journeys.[6] Often, treatment appears conditional on agreeing to contraception. Indeed, only nasbandī cases seem really welcomed; their costs are reduced and they receive various gifts, but after the operation, even they receive no favours:

> The government persuades you to have nasbandī and they take away the possibility of your having children. But when your children are sick they never look at you. If you go to the hospital and pay your 50 paise you get useless broken pills, powdered and old. If a man has nasbandī and then his children fall sick, you can expect the government to do

nothing and the children will die. *(Khalil)*

Muslims are more alienated from government services than Hindus: they repeatedly told us that the British Raj had been replaced by a Hindu Raj. All the health staff at the Dharmnagri dispensary were Hindu, and the Bijnor government hospitals had Hindu or Christian doctors and nurses. Muslims fear they will receive second-class treatment at best and hesitate to use government facilities: this probably contributes to the higher child mortality rates in Jhakri. But Hindus and Muslims alike agree that patients are not treated on the basis of need. Money and status are persuasive in hospital, just as elsewhere. Not surprisingly, private doctors, with their more predictable fees and more courteous manner, may be preferred.

Strengthening traditional medical services

The conventional top-down clinic-based approach to providing medical services in the Third World has been widely criticised in Geneva, New Delhi and elsewhere for its cost, limited effectiveness, and the problems generated by the cultural and social gulf between health workers and their clients.[7] The critics are correctly sceptical of the value of medicalised maternity provision for the vast majority of deliveries; they deploy the work of medical anthropologists and others as evidence of the benefits of home deliveries and argue for grass-roots provisions, particularly the use of traditional birth attendants, as an alternative means of providing widespread and accessible medical services.[8] In many countries, these criticisms have been ignored, perhaps because they are still offering top-down strategies rather than responding to the grass-roots situation.

Indian health planners, however, have accepted the critics' premises and presume that dāis are socially and culturally acceptable sources of health care. In some parts of India, voluntary health projects have indeed demonstrated that dāis with training are capable of delivering safe, cheap and cost-effective maternity services.[9] In 1977, with WHO and UNICEF support, critiques of conventional medical services led to government programmes throughout India to train dāis to use antiseptic techniques and maternity kits and to detect high-risk pregnancies and refer them speedily to health staff. Under this scheme, the training programme has entailed three-week courses held at sub-centres or Primary Health Centres. Local health workers do the training, using rudimentary visual aids. It is not clear what most dāis learn during these courses, nor what effects the training has on their future practice.[10] In rural Bijnor, dāis who had been trained appreciated the stipend they received during the course but gave little indication of having changed their obstetric practice. Furthermore, many other dāis had refused training for fear of being too closely associated with the nasbandī programme. Other women with a marginal interest in becoming dāis have sometimes taken the opportunity to be paid to attend the training in their place. ANMs should maintain contact with dāis, who are offered replacements for their maternity kits and an incentive of Rs 2 for referring pregnant women to the ANM for ante-natal care. But most dāis have no contact with pregnant women until the delivery, and the dāis' incentive payments have such a low priority in the government health budget that few have ever received their due. Furthermore, since dāis tend to be middle-aged when they start the work, such benefits of training as there are may be short-lived. The training programme has nearly run its course and there are no plans for a continuation. Yet most deliveries are still being handled by elderly untrained dāis, and more somewhat younger untrained women are continually taking on the work as others become too old or die.

In any case, even trained dāis are not necessarily the best route through which to enhance the quality of care for childbearing women. The Harijan dāi is welcome only while the new mother is herself unclean; the Caste Hindu dāi is tainted by her work. Only for a Muslim among Muslims or a Harijan among Harijans, and then not always, are the barriers between a dāi and her client at a minimum. Government health staff, as urban superiors, are socially distant in one direction, while the dāi, as a polluted menial, is socially distant in the other. During the delivery the dāi does defiling-work, some of which could undoubtedly benefit from being performed more hygienically. But training by itself does not enable the dāi to insist on sterilised instruments to cut cords or hot water to wash herself and labouring women, to play a more prominent role in managing labour or to be summoned before deliveries start if complications are suspected. Indeed, perhaps only broader-based campaigns of appropriate health education for all school girls and every sās could have much impact on the conditions of childbirth. But in north India today, such proposals are impracticable and unrealistic.

A historical perspective strengthens our scepticism, because the idea of training dāis is by no means as novel as its contemporary advocates would have us believe.[11] Indeed, the problem of providing cheap and accessible maternity care has exercised Indian policy-makers for well over a century. Dāi training programmes started in the 1860s and they have been reinvented every 20 years or so. But the failures of earlier programmes have not informed later ones. Basically, the north Indian dāi training programmes have failed to comprehend dāis and birthing practices in a wider framework of childbearing, particularly in relation to the structural constraints on bahūs in their susrāl and local understandings of childbearing which entail shame and pollution.

Nowadays, too, attempting to use dāis to improve the conditions of childbearing ignores how their position is being undermined by the impact of medical care provided beyond the government health services. For instance, male practitioners using powerful modern drugs are already encroaching on childbirth, in particular by using oxytocin to stimulate contractions. Such interventions, whether in childbirth or in other spheres, are not part of formal government policy, but government inertia in the face of them, is, in a sense, official policy. The nature of the Indian state is shown not only in government pronouncements, but also in what the state's agents do and fail to do in the countryside. Senior government staff are widely believed to take bribes to ignore illegal medical practice, behaviour which is thought to be condoned all the way up to New Delhi:

> It's so shameful that such officers ask for such small amounts of money. All they do is sit under a fan and count their bribes all day. But it's not fair that the ones at the bottom get such a bad name. People forget that they themselves have to sweeten their superiors to get their own work done. Bribes go right from the bottom to the very top. *(Mahipal)*

In practice, then, the state is demonstrating no firm commitment to maternal medical services, either of the conventional clinical kind or the so-called grass-roots version put forward as an alternative. Commercial and other interests prevail, thereby reducing official policy to empty rhetoric.[12]

Health planning

In any case, necessary though medical services are, they are insufficient in themselves to solve women's reproductive health problems. Medical services — providing mainly curative care in clinics and hospitals — tend to perceive only the isolated individual client who has medical symptoms needing treatment using medical technologies. By contrast, the advocates of public health set general health problems firmly in a wider context, and argue that they are best dealt with outside the walls of hospitals and clinics, for instance through changes in diet or housing.[13] One strategy is to change health-threatening aspects of the environment without requiring people to alter their habits very much. Examples include cleaning and protecting water supplies, draining ponds, spraying insecticides to prevent mosquitoes breeding, or introducing nutritional supplements to everyday foodstuffs like salt. All these have been tried, and have had some limited success.

More radical attempts to deal specifically with maternal and child health problems focus on some of the deeper causes of poor maternity outcomes, through nutritional programmes and health education. Following the experimental Integrated Child Development Scheme, feeding centres are being established throughout India for pre-school children and pregnant and nursing mothers.[14] They are based on women's groups co-ordinated by Social Education Officers, and they employ local women. ANMs can refer undernourished pregnant or lactating women and their children to the feeding centres, and can go there themselves to teach women about better nutrition.

But western Uttar Pradesh has no tradition of women's groups to form the organisational core of this programme. We suspect that any attempts to create such groups would be bedevilled by class and ethnic hostilities which could exclude the women in most need. Evidence from elsewhere also suggests that women and children who attend feeding centres then receive even less food at home.[15] These programmes, then, will only slightly reduce the proportion of mothers who are too small and light to have a reasonable chance of safely delivering children big enough to survive. Furthermore, health education in India emphasises women's roles as mothers. Better mothers (of fewer children) are expected to serve more nourishing food in a hygienic way and to use government health facilities in cases of illness. No account is taken of financial and time constraints already affecting women attempting to combine mothering with their other work. Such health education messages rarely reach the women of Dharmnagri and Jhakri, but even if they did, they would surely be ignored for their irrelevance.[16]

The context of motherhood

Basically, we believe that attempts to use medical and public health services to deal with the problems of childbearing are likely to fail because they address only part of the social, political and economic context within which childbearing women live. Poor maternal and child health reflects, in microcosm, the problems facing the bahū. In north India, women are controlled and valued for their childbearing capacity, but their needs associated with that role are given little weight. One reason for the inadequacies of medical services for women and children is that medical workers deal only with those who demand their services, and bahūs can rarely do so at their own whim.[17] Decisions about the seriousness of their own or their child's illnesses, about ante-natal care, tetanus toxoid injections, strengthening food or rest, are rarely made by the woman alone. Nor do her views carry most weight with those in her susrāl who might act on her behalf. Health planners, however, in practice ignore this and regard childbearing women as individualised patients; but real people are tied into social relationships which offer differing opportunities for action. Young bahūs are subject to controls (whether overt or not) which have crucial implications for their own and their children's health.

In any case, looking to the government for solutions usually involves ignoring the extent to which the government itself contributes to the problems. The government may be capable of little more than moderating some broader social changes which are detrimental to women; it may be actively encouraging others which counteract the health programmes. Rajiv Gandhi's government employs a rhetoric of commitment to women's issues and he created a Department of Women's Welfare in New Delhi in 1985, but within the Indian government, the interests of powerful men still predominate and define the issues. State activities provide goods and services for which there is a demand (antibiotics or credit, fertilisers or clinics) but what is given with one hand is partly taken back with the other, directly in bribes by local state officials (in health services as in other spheres) or because the growth of expert services undermines traditional forms of caring and draws people more deeply into commercialised relationships. The state's clients see the potential benefits of modern science and technology, of credit and organisational power; but there is widespread local cynicism about the state's advance, because these resources are provided in an alienating or disempowering way. Much government action seems less designed to provide the rural populace with services than to widen employment opportunities for educated urbanites, who can then extract more from villagers in new ways. Indeed, such processes may be central rather than peripheral features of state actions, since class and other interests tend to dominate policy implementation, if not policy proposals themselves.[18] The balance of powers, then, are such that the state is unlikely to implement policies that might generate decisive changes for the majority of rural women. Transforming marriage arrangements and domestic relationships and people's access to personal property and inheritance rights is notoriously difficult; but the government's toleration of changes contrary to women's interests leaves daughters undesired and the young bahū relatively powerless.

Health planners find it difficult to conceptualise maternal health programmes to take account of the effect of these structural forces on women.[19] In most WHO documents, sociological explanations of women's position are reduced to socio-economic indicators such as age, parity, social class, housing quality and location. The problem is seen as merely one of attitudes and motivation, not something constantly established and reinforced through systems of kinship, marriage and property and class relationships, which are all shot through with gender differentiation. Effective maternal health programmes would require changes in the ranking of priorities within domestic units to raise the interests of the bahū in comparison with her husband and his parents. Equally, within hospitals and clinics, women would have to be granted the treatment and sympathetic respect currently reserved for the powerful or wealthy. The chances of this happening revolve around three aspects of young married women — as wealth-bringers, workers and bearers of children — and the dynamics of change in each of them, whether originated by government action or not.

A woman's role as a wealth-bringer is most obvious in the dowry and other gift exchanges that begin when a marriage is arranged. She is a conduit for wealth most of which she herself does not own; the non-productive property in gift-exchanges is often specifically for redistribution to her susrāl kin, and she can take little of it with her in the event of separation or divorce. Far from such patterns being challenged, the law abolishing dowry is largely unenforced. Indeed, some people even said that parents call their daughters for visits less often nowadays because they cannot afford the giving expected of them, and that men try to loot their in-laws by sending their wives to their natal villages to fetch cash or other items. With agriculture becoming more commercialised, the demands of dowry and len-den are locally believed to be increasing, generating new problems for young women and their parents and reinforcing the undesirability of daughters. This is linked to the exclusion of women from the ownership of property (especially land), which also applies, though to a lesser extent, amongst the landless. Again, legislation granting property rights to women is ignored. Women's exclusion from inheritance of land is facilitated by their migration away from that land when they marry. Marriage migration also cuts women off from important sources of social support, particularly the young women they have known from birth who are despatched in different directions themselves.

These material consequences of the kinship system help to explain why women in western Uttar Pradesh have neither organised to demand better services, nor provided facilities for themselves. The few examples of successful rural women's self-help organisations in India are in States like Gujarat, Kerala or Bengal, where women's issues have been taken up by women's groups or by wider political movements within established communist or socialist parties.[20] There is little such tradition in the male-dominated politics of Uttar Pradesh, and women themselves are barely organised beyond the level of the chūlhā or closely related chūlhās. The prospects for grass-roots women's organisations, then, are not good. At the village level, female marriage migration and the derision of the ghar-jamāi remain unquestioned, and women do not claim their rights in productive property. Thus, the divisions among women are left intact, son preferences are undisturbed, and no other changes are clearly mitigating their effects.

Women's roles as workers, the evaluation of their work and the access of women to the fruits of their efforts are also almost entirely ignored by government programmes. Women's contribution to agricultural production is hidden, but women's workloads have changed as a result of these programmes. Mechanisation, declining sources of firewood and reduced fodder crop production, for instance, all have a direct impact on women's work. Some women's work has been intensified, that of others reduced. But changes in the social organisation of women's work seem minor by comparison. Rising life expectancies and changes in economic opportunities probably mean that chūlhās divide earlier, and that more women spend most of their marital careers in separate chūlhās than was so previously. This change, apparently offering women more scope for self-expression and autonomy in work and decision-making, has its drawbacks. While their work is so labour-intensive, women gain their limited measure of independence only at the expense of losing help with their work. They may have little time or energy to build upon their freedom from the direct control of their sās. Overall, no section of women has benefited in an unqualified way. In any case, detailing the changes that have taken place in the tasks women do and the social relationships within which they work should not obscure crucial continuities. Women's work is still devalued, even trivialised; their entitlements to food, consideration or care remain very limited; they still have little control over what they produce, because they neither market it nor have access to the income it generates; and they remain subject to their husband's rule.

Some changes seem to be affecting women in their childbearing roles, but they too must not be exaggerated or seen as wholly positive. Adolescent girls are still very constrained by the need to maintain an indisputable sexual purity which is not expected of young men. Women have little or no say in deciding when and to whom they are married and they are still subject to restraints on their behaviour and mobility within their susrāl. And a woman still needs to bear children, if in moderation.

Few direct changes have enhanced the conditions of childbearing; indeed, most changes pertain only to preventing it or reducing its frequency. Deliberate fertility regulation is increasing, despite the way contraceptive services are offered in the government programme. This shift could have several effects. If women have fewer children, can space them, and stop bearing them at an earlier age, maternal and infant mortality should decline, even if no other improvements are made to the conditions of childbearing.[21] Also, if women's subordination is compounded by the energy and time lost through childbearing and childrearing, having fewer children might facilitate their taking more active roles within their chūlhās. Conversely, women might simply be under greater 'pressure to be high-quality mothers, investing as much time and energy in their fewer children as is currently spread over several. They may also spend more time improving the family's prestige, by becoming more involved in educating children, engaging in more extravagant len-den or in improving the domestic environment.[22] If that happens, women will still be largely restricted to the domestic sphere and their work will probably remain undervalued. Crucially, too, because patterns of inheritance and post-marital residence remain unchanged and unquestioned, it is now much more important that the first or second child is a son. This consideration lies behind the expansion of private clinics (so far restricted to the major cities and some larger towns) offering amniocentesis tests that detect the sex of the foetus, and an abortion if it is female.[23] Quite apart from our reservations about the safety and monitoring of the available contraceptive techniques and the means used to encourage their adoption, we are very doubtful of any straightforwardly liberating effects of contraceptive use for women.

Government activities are achieving few positive effects for women as wealth-bringers, workers and mothers. Nor are wider social changes clearly moving in women's favour either. Additionally, there are few signs of grass-roots challenges to women's own views of themselves. We saw and heard no opposition to either women's exclusion from property-ownership or the consequent preferences for sons. Women's work is portrayed by men as light and unimportant, and women tend to be unwilling to reject this view publicly. Women are still ashamed of their sexuality, and regard themselves as polluting to others when they menstruate or give birth. Common shame is a poor basis for common action.[24]

The ambiguities of social change

Social change always has contradictory and double-edged effects, and no easy summary is possible. We have stressed the negative side, but government programmes are not an unmitigated disaster for childbearing women. Many services provided by the state remain desired even after adding on the costs of bribes, loss of dignity, or dangers of excessive surveillance, for otherwise even basic provisions would be unavailable to the poor. Rajballa's case epitomises the dilemmas involved. The poor quality of ante-natal monitoring and the cost and form of her treatment in the hospital highlight the inadequacy of government provision; but without it, she and her son would not have survived. Leaving such services to the working of the market imposes other costs, and is hardly likely to be a better solution. Similarly, the Green Revolution has had some negative effects on many women's lives, yet as it spreads and deepens, it clearly facilitates rising output, improved living standards and nutritional levels, and lower child mortality for almost all social classes. Although the expanding population creates fears of land fragmentation, and commercialisation provides new uncertainties, more cash is in the pockets of men and some women from almost all social classes. New urban or industrial jobs are also providing a living for some landless and poor peasant men. But the relatively powerless (in this case, young bahūs in their susrāl) seem least able to take advantage of such new opportunities as these changes offer.

Standing where the concerns of feminism, demography and political economy intersect can alert us to some issues which are crucial for women and men alike. But it cannot provide solid ground for predicting the future. In order for the position of bahūs such as Muni to have changed much for the better by the year 2000, dramatic changes would be required in patterns of landholding and employment, in women's work and access to property, in evaluations of their worth, and in the systems of kinship, residence and marriage which constrain them. Such changes would strike at the very basis of rural society in western Uttar Pradesh. The signs are not encouraging. But the future is always open: bahūs might use their limited opportunities and the small spaces which are opening up to organise with others to demand changes in their conditions, or to take advantage of what is supposedly already available to them. We can discern little on the local horizon that harbingers a better future but we still hope to be proven wrong in our pessimistic predictions.

Appendix 1: Research Strategy

In the Preface we outlined some of the issues raised by studying childbearing as a socially organised phenomenon. Alongside our general interest in biological reproduction and women's subordination in an agrarian setting, the three of us brought different backgrounds and concerns to the research. Following her research among Muslim women in Delhi, Patricia was particularly interested in the implications of marriage arrangements for women's support networks: a comparison between Hindus (who generally marry their daughters at some distance) and Muslims (who often marry their daughters nearby) seemed a promising way to explore aspects of women's experiences of childbearing. Roger wanted to pursue issues which had arisen from his research on health policy in India, particularly the provision of health services for rural women and children and the role of dāis (traditional birth attendants), who seemed to provide an interesting case of women's expertise crying out for exploration. And Andrew brought an interest in fertility and population processes to his work for his doctoral thesis.

These considerations, then, set the context for our research. We decided to work in the Indian State of Uttar Pradesh because Patricia and Roger already spoke Hindi. We chose Bijnor District because, like Uttar Pradesh as a whole, it is characterised by high levels of fertility as well as of young child mortality, has a very adverse sex ratio (about 863 females per 1,000 males), and had been known for female infanticide in the 19th century. Furthermore, Bijnor District has a high proportion of rural Muslims (about 30%). (See Appendix 3, Table 1.)

In early 1982, we established a base for the three of us and Laura Jeffery (aged 2) in a disused operating theatre in a government dispensary, to conduct research in two adjacent villages, Dharmnagri and Jhakri; these are not pseudonyms as they are so easily identifiable. Dharmnagri's population is Hindu, that is Caste Hindu and Harijan (Scheduled Caste), while that of Jhakri is Muslim. We wanted to concentrate not on women as a whole but on a particular segment of the female population. Thus, our prime concern was neither with older women who may have attained a degree of domestic power, nor with the most economically disadvantaged, those in female-headed households. Rather, we focussed on young married women in the childbearing years, whose livelihood depended on their own and their husband's efforts and for whom childbearing and fertility control were issues of the moment: in other words, those who have not yet attained seniority in their affinal village. Allowing the boundaries of the base villages to dictate the field of research makes us vulnerable to accusations of being androcentric. The "village study" is the classic form of sociological research in south Asia and can be criticised for failing to take seriously the relationships that straddle village boundaries, for instance, those which link in-married women with their natal kin elsewhere and out-married women with the base village. This point has rather less force than it might, however, since childbearing women in Bijnor have more restricted access to their natal kin than at other times. Conducting research on childbearing in areas where women return to their parents' home to give birth would have presented great practical difficulties.

For ourselves, the experience of working together was immensely valuable. The ideas incorporated into the research are the outcome of planning the work together and of discussing with one another and our local women research assistants the ideas generated by the material as it was being collected. Since returning from India, our discussions have continued — albeit at a rather less intense level — and it would scarcely be possible now to attribute the origins of many themes that we have pursued. Moreover, working as a team of women and men enabled us to explore issues that one person alone could not have done. This is only partly an issue of quantity. More importantly, working in a society where there are marked separations between the activities and knowledge of females and males, we were able to straddle the gender divide.

Patricia, Roger and Andrew recorded information collected separately, initially largely based on memory and (once local suspicions subsided) derived from notes taken during conversations and observations. We generally typed in English, though particularly resonant turns of phrase were recorded in Hindi using Roman script. Initially, the research assistants accompanied Patricia and noted conversations which they later recorded in detail. Patricia checked these records, amplified them and clarified queries, translated them into English, and noted what needed to be followed up either generally or with particular informants. Later, when we used more semi-structured interview schedules, the assistants sometimes conducted these on their own. Our three assistants, two of whom (Swaleha Begum and Radha Rani Sharma) worked for us for most of 1982-83 and again in 1985, made an incalculable contribution to our understanding of Bijnor life. They helped us come to terms with the Bijnor dialect and they also acted as cultural interpreters, elaborating information which we found particularly puzzling as well as explaining us to our informants.

We embarked on the research with a general framework within which we wanted to operate, but we also wished to ensure that our work would not be entrapped by our preconceptions. We therefore spent the first few months in work which was open-ended and exploratory, aiming to obtain a broadly based view of the agricultural cycle, labour use, birthing procedures and so forth. This entailed mixing widely in the two villages, talking to anyone about the issues which concerned them and us, watching people at work and checking out our impressions with our assistants. Indeed, some aspects of the material we collected surprised and disappointed us. We had, for instance, expected Muslim women to be better placed in their affinal villages than are Hindus, because of the proximity of their parents. We had also hoped to correct the negative view of dāis so often presented in the literature, only to be confronted with their extremely problematic position in the local social structure.

This initial research provided the basis for the main strands of our work, a survey of recently delivered women in other villages in Bijnor District and systematic data collection from selected key informants in Dharmnagri and Jhakri. Essentially, the survey was to check that the rich material we were obtaining in the base villages was not seriously unrepresentative of women's childbearing experiences in the locality. In Dharmnagri and Jhakri there are few Jats (the dominant landowners in the District), water for irrigation is more accessible than in villages on higher land (which affects cropping and therefore work patterns) and the two villages are close to medical and other services in Bijnor town. We randomly selected eleven villages in the District and aimed to interview every woman in them who had given birth in the previous twelve months. This resulted in the completion of 300 pre-coded interviews, detailing household composition, work, contacts with natal kin, maternity histories and most recent pregnancy and delivery. Radha Rani Sharma also interviewed the dāis whom those women listed. The *dāi schedule* covered their family background, work history, accounts of the biology of normal and abnormal pregnancy and delivery, birthing practices, and views of their work. Roger gathered basic village data and interviewed the male medical practitioners who served those villages. The picture obtained from the survey is broadly in line with that derived from the base villages.

Meanwhile, on the basis of our census data from Dharmnagri and Jhakri, we selected 41 key informant couples, 22 from Dharmnagri and 19 from Jhakri and carried out a series of directed yet discursive discussions over the following months, Patricia and the assistants concentrating on the women and Andrew on the men. We used several criteria for selecting the key informants. Primarily we sought women who had recently given birth or were pregnant. We included couples of different caste and ethnic group membership, covering a range of economic positions, household structures and parities. In some instances, we selected men who were brothers or paternal first cousins, which enabled us to control somewhat for land-ownership, caste and ethnicity while obtaining a window on such matters as differential fertility and diverse accounts of household separation. (See Appendix 2 for a listing and fuller details.)

With the women, we completed *maternity histories* (covering their pregnancies, lactation and child spacing, child deaths and family planning).

We talked about their *last pregnancy* (discussing their work, diet, and health care during pregnancy, delivery, and the post-partum period, and family planning). The *chūlhā* (household) schedule explored domestic and sexual politics, women's support networks in their affinal village, changes in women's chūlhā composition since their marriage, patterns of work and co-operation with other women, contacts with their own natal kin and with their husband's married sisters. The *maikā/pīhar* (natal village) and *nand* (husband's sister) schedules further explored the links which married women retain with their natal kin, the conditions under which they may visit them, the gift exchanges which occur especially after they or their brothers' wives or husband's sisters give birth. We also attempted systematic collection of *time-use* data: this is a time-consuming and difficult procedure but we wanted to dovetail a study of women's work at different seasons with different stages of pregnancy. This did not proceed as far as we wished, for our informants were very resistant to a task which they found boring and (they claimed) a mere repetition of the earlier round of questions, but it gave broad indications of variations in women's work.

The male key informants were asked about *crops* in a schedule which Andrew administered four times in the agricultural cycle (choice of seed, fertiliser, use of irrigation, yields and consumption, and use of family and other labour), about *land and loans* (amount and type of land, timing and reasons for sales and purchases, other assets, and loan taking and giving), and about *animal husbandry* (number and type of livestock, their feeding throughout the year, milk yields, veterinary care, responsibility for animal husbandry).

The work in 1985 entailed up-dating our census of Dharmnagri and Jhakri and completing maternity histories from the 236 ever-married women in the two villages. In addition, the female key informants' *1985 schedule* covered family planning intentions and decision-making, in relation to domestic politics in their affinal village and their contacts with their natal kin; we also up-dated their maternity histories. The male key informants were asked about *family-building* (family planning, the value of children and ideal family size) and *kinship networks* (marriage arrangements, their own and their wife's contacts with the wife's natal village, visits to their sisters' affinal villages and associated gift exchanges). *Oral history schedules* with selected elderly men and women covered information on agricultural practices and landholding and how changes have affected people's work, marriage arrangements, dowry and sexual politics.

Throughout, we also had extensive contacts with the dāis who work in Dharmnagri and Jhakri as well as with the staff at the dispensary, and recorded other conversations and observations about village life in general. We consulted archival material, including land records from the local land revenue offices, records of loans, purchases of sugar-cane and sales of fertiliser by the Co-operative Cane Society, family planning records held by the District health staff, and historical material on Bijnor (especially on the eradication of female infanticide in the District). We had neither the funds nor the time for anthropometric work or for detailing dietary intakes, energy expenditures or nutritional status, which would (in any case) have been even more intrusive than the methods we adopted. Our priority was to focus on the social meanings and practices associated with childbearing.

Combining qualitative and quantitative methods has allowed us to explore the topic in ways which would have been impossible had we restricted ourselves to fewer methods — as we often fervently wished we had done whenever we became overwhelmed with data. Perforce, we are deploying some material here more than others, particularly the key informant schedules. They are also the main source of the quotations in the text; these are not verbatim but, in translation, we have tried to retain the flavour of our informants' speech. We have indicated where these quotations reflect the generality of comments and where they represent illuminating individual experiences. Unattributed quotations are from people not closely related to our key informants. Clearly, the richness of our shared experiences cannot be adequately captured in a single monograph. Other aspects of our work have been explored in publications listed in the bibliography.

This account of our data collection is, however, something of a travesty. It falsely suggests that our only experience of research was to make plans which remained fully under our control, and that our informants were passive victims of our research design, while we were simply inquisitorial observers. But interviews were often diverted by events or hijacked by bystanders' comments; discussions often wandered far from the track we had intended and had to be completed at a later date.

Furthermore, the residents of Dharmnagri and Jhakri found it very difficult to comprehend us. Some people thought we were spying on the villages prior to their being uprooted to make way for a nuclear power station nearby on the banks of the Ganges, a rumour that evaporated when officials countered our questions with instructions to mind our own business. Others thought we were an advance guard for a returning British Raj, although they were easily convinced that the British would not try to rule India again, since they were having such trouble retaining the Falkland Islands. A more lingering fear (and one that proved harder to dispel) was that we were employed in the Government of India's family planning programme. Why else were we preoccupied with such shameful and dirty matters as childbirth, why did we enquire about their children? The credibility of this opinion was undoubtedly enhanced because the operating theatre where we lived was last used for sterilisation operations and because our jeep was similar to those used by family planning workers. Initially, then, we were very circumspect. Using our jeep to take men on wedding parties, or just giving lifts to and from Bijnor certainly helped to allay anxieties, but taking Rajballa to hospital one night proved the dramatic watershed in our acceptability. A few days later, the maulwī in Jhakri even summoned one of our informants for us over the mosque tannoy system. Eventually, our intentions were more clearly understood; long before we left, the same people who had run away rather than answer our questions would complain if we failed to record their comments verbatim.

We have ceased to be dangerous, but continue to be perplexing. Our behaviour remains a constant source of questions, in general conversation or during "interviews", queries that themselves often generate ideas and new types of data. Was it not a failure of maternal love that Patricia left her daughter to sleep on a bed by herself? Did she really prefer her husband to her daughter? Was the child not afraid — and what would happen if she needed to go to the latrine in the night? Our solution of providing a torch and potty was scorned as yet further evidence of dereliction of duty. What was more, how had Patricia and Roger contrived to have only one child? And had they not taken total leave of their senses when they adopted a baby girl? God had fated them with one daughter — was it not an act of utter perversity to acquire another one by choice? Did they intend to educate her? And provide her with a dowry? And why did Patricia not understand that feeding the baby mashed banana in mid-winter might cause her to die of cold? Thus, having a small child and acquiring a baby during our research generated a mine of comments on family planning, son preferences and infant care. Certainly, if Patricia had not been a mother herself, the research would have been impossible. As is always the case, who we are and what we did affected what we were told, what we were allowed to see, who wanted to spend time with us and who withdrew from our company as soon as was decently possible. All told, we had a lot of explaining to do and our weird and sometimes shocking behaviour was generally tolerated with an undeserved geniality.

On our side, too, there was much we found hard to accept. Fortunately, we could provide one another with practical and psychological support, for it is unpleasant to be seen as dangerous and often tiresome to have no privacy. Our research was a full-time existence: women give birth, people fall sick, stolen buffaloes need to be retrieved or visitors rap on the door at any time of day or night. Moreover, trying to maintain our acceptability with a wide range of people meant treading a tight-rope of decisions. Living in the dispensary helped us avoid too close an identification with either Dharmnagri or Jhakri — but the initial cost was being linked too closely to the medical establishment. Our vegetarian and teetotal kitchen saved us from causing offence: but how were we to deal with wedding feasts, when Muslims might ply us with beef or Hindus might serve pork and local liquor? And what effect did our brazen insistence on accepting food from Harijans and Muslims have on our relationships with Caste Hindus?

Ethnic and inter-caste distaste and mistrust aside, we found much else unpalatable. Initially, at least, Patricia complied fairly stringently with norms of female modesty by keeping her head covered in the presence of men, and demurely retreating inside when men came to chat on our veranda at dusk. Throughout, Roger and Andrew found it hard to be fully at ease with men who openly admitted to wife-beating and exerting sexual power over their wives. We were all depressed by hearing women and men alike devaluing women's work, or commenting that women cannot live together without fighting. And how much joy could we really experience listening to the bawdy songs sung only after a boy's birth? We often had little space for manoeuvre between dissembling and wrecking our rapport by indicating our disapproval.

Intensive research like this is always challenging, often harrowing, and sometimes fun. Many of our "informants" became good friends, who warmly welcome us when we return, and ask when we will live among them again. Overall, it was certainly an experience that none of us would have missed.

Appendix 2: Key Informants

Notes

For the key informants we have used pseudonyms, Hindu names for key informants from Dharmnagri and Muslim ones for those from Jhakri. Spouses' names share the same initial letter, and this also indicates their class position, for we ranked them in order of wealth (basically, landholding per adult male). In Dharmnagri, the following are real brothers: Ashok and Bhagwana; Jagram and Krishnu; Om Prakash, Pratap, Punni, Rohtash and Sunil; and Shankar and Tulsi. Mahipal and Devinder are half-brothers. In addition, Gopal and Harwan, Vikram and Vir are paternal cousins. In Jhakri, Bashir is Suleiman's father; Farooq and Ghulam, Haroon and Irfan, and Wajid and Zakir are real brothers; Jabruddin and Khalil are paternal first cousins; Liaqat is their paternal uncle.

Tables 1 and 2 detail the couples and their class, caste, chūlhā and production unit in April 1982 when we conducted the first census and selected the key informants. Production units are classified from the husband's perspective, as joint (with his father, adult brothers etc.), separate or alone; and chūlhās are classified from the wife's perspective (in relation to her sās). Class categories are as follows: II = rich peasants; III = middle peasants; IV = poor peasants; V = landless.

Tables 3 and 4 detail the woman's marriage and childbearing. Estimated ages of marriage are at cohabitation (each time, if the woman has been married more than once). Marriage distances are rounded and allow for normal travelling routes. Data concerning children give the situation in September 1985 so that they are comparable with data in Appendix 3.

Table 1: Dharmnagri: Caste, Class, Production Unit and Chūlhā

Woman's Name	Husband's Name	Caste	Class	Production Unit	Chūlhā (Household)
Adesh	Ashok	Rajput	II	Joint F & B	Alone
Bhagirthi	Bhagwana	Rajput	II	Joint F & B	Alone
Chandresh	Chet Ram	Jatab	II	Joint F	Alone
Durgi	Devinder	Sahni	III	Joint F & B	Separate
Gita	Gopal	Dhimar	III	Joint F & B	Joint
Hiran	Harwan	Dhimar	III	Joint F & B	Joint
Imarti	Ishwar Das	Sahni	III	Alone	Alone
Jumni	Jagram	Dhimar	III	Joint F & B	Separate
Kamla	Krishnu	Dhimar	III	Joint F & B	Joint
Lakshmi	Lalit	Sahni	III	Joint B	Alone
Maya	Mahipal	Sahni	III	Separate	Separate
Nirmala	Naresh	Jatab	III	Joint F & B	Separate
Omvati	Om Prakash	Dhimar	III	Joint 2B	Joint
Promilla	Pratap	Dhimar	III	Joint 2B	Separate
Pushpa	Punni	Dhimar	III	Joint 2B	Joint
Rajballa	Rohtash	Dhimar	IV	Alone	Separate
Santosh	Sunil	Dhimar	IV	Alone	Separate
Shakuntala	Shankar	Chamar	IV	Joint F & 2B	Separate
Tarabati	Tulsi	Chamar	IV	Joint F & 2B	Separate
Urmila	Udayan	Sahni	IV	Joint F	Separate
Viramvati	Vikram	Jatab	V	Alone	Separate
Vimla	Vir	Jatab	V	Alone	Separate

Table 2: Jhakri: Caste, Class, Production Unit and Chūlhā

Woman's Name	Husband's Name	Caste	Class	Production Unit	Chūlhā (Household)
Asghari	Ahmad	Sheikh	II	Joint F	Joint
Bilquis	Bashir	Sheikh	II	Alone	Alone
Dilruba	Dilshad	Sheikh	II	Joint F	Joint
Fatima	Farooq	Sheikh	III	Joint F & 2B	Separate
Ghazala	Ghulam	Sheikh	III	Joint F & 2B	Joint
Hashmi	Haroon	Sheikh	III	Joint 2B	Separate
Imrana	Irfan	Sheikh	III	Joint 2B	Separate
Jamila	Jabruddin	Sheikh	III	Joint 3FB	Alone
Khurshida	Khalil	Sheikh	III	Joint F, 2FB & FBS	Alone
Latifan	Liaqat	Sheikh	III	Joint 2B & BS	Alone
Maqsudi	Mansur	Sheikh	III	Joint F & B	Separate
Najma	Nisar	Sheikh	III	Joint F & 3FB	Joint
Qudsia	Qadir	Sheikh	III	Joint F	Separate
Ruxana	Riasat	Teli	III	Alone	Alone
Sabra	Suleiman	Sheikh	IV	Separate	Separate
Tahira	Taslim	Sheikh	V	Joint B	Alone
Umrao*	Usman*	Teli	V	Alone	Alone
Wasila	Wajid	Teli	V	Joint F	Joint
Zubeida	Zakir	Teli	V	Separate	Separate

* Jhakir is Umrao's natal village. Her parents are dead. Umrao has no contact with her step-mother-in-law and is classified as alone. Similarly, Usman has no contact with his father and is also classified as alone.

Table 3: Dharmnagri: Marriage and Childbearing

Woman's Name	Age at Marriage	Marriage Type	Marriage Distance (Kms)	Age at 1982	Sex and Parity of Sampled Birth	Full-term Deliveries			
						Boys		Girls	
						Ever-born	Alive in 1985	Ever-born	Alive in 1985
Adesh	14	Normal	60	40	Girl-7	2	1	5	5
Bhagirthi	15	Normal	60	35	Boy-6	3	3	4	3
Chandresh	15	Normal	30	20	Boy-1	1	0	0	0
Durgi	16	Normal	30	27	Girl-4	1	1	3	2
Gita	15	Normal	25	20	Girl-2	3	1	3	2
Hiran	18	Normal	30	23	Boy-3	3	3	0	0
Imarti	16 & 23	Levirate	40	33	Boy-8	3	3	5	3
Jumni	16	Normal	25	33	Boy-4	4	4	1	0
Kamla	15	Normal	11	25	Boy-3	2	2	2	2
Lakshmi	13, 15 & 30	Husband's 7th, bought	50	31	Girl-1	0	0	2	2
Maya	18	Normal	45	32	Girl-6	2	2	5	4
Nirmala	21	Normal	40	27	Girl-3	2	1	2	1
Omvati	15	Normal	40	26	Girl-5	3	3	3	2
Promilla	17	Normal	25	23	Girl-2	0	0	3	3
Pushpa	16	Normal	15	17	Boy-1	1	1	1	1
Rajballa	25	Bought	60	30	Boy-2	1	1	1	1
Santosh	15	Normal	25	18	Girl-1	1	1	1	1
Shakuntala	16	Normal	25	18	Boy-1	1	1	0	0
Tarabati	16	Normal	30	22	Girl-3	2	2	2	2
Urmila	16	Normal	45	24	Girl-3	2	2	2	2
Viramvati	14	Normal	15	22	Girl-2	0	0	3	3
Vimla	20	Normal	30	23	Girl-2	2	1	1	1

Note: Chandresh died in 1984; Maya's husband, Mahipal, was a ghar-jamāi for several years.

236

Table 4: Jhakri: Marriage and Childbearing

Woman's Name	Age at Marriage	Marriage Type	Marriage Distance (Kms)	Age at 1982	Sex and Parity of Sampled Birth	Full-term Deliveries			
						Boys		Girls	
						Ever-born	Alive in 1985	Ever-born	Alive in 1985
Asghari	15	Normal	1	23	Girl-1	0	0	1	1
Bilquis	15 & 18	Husband's 2nd	5	36	Girl-12	7	4	5	2
Dilruba	15	Normal	6	26	Boy-5	4	4	2	1
Fatima	14	Normal	3	24	Boy-5	4	3	2	1
Ghazala	17	Normal	1	19	Boy-1	1	1	0	0
Hashmi	12	Normal	4	27	Girl-6	2	2	4	1
Imrana	15	Normal	3	24	Girl-4	3	2	3	1
Jamila	15	Normal	2	25	Boy-5	5	3	1	0
Khurshida	14	Normal	2	21	Girl-3	2	2	2	2
Latifan	16	Within-village	0	34	Girl-8	7	6	2	2
Maqsudi	17	Normal	3	25	Girl-4	3	2	3	1
Najma	17	Normal	3	26	Girl-4	3	2	4	2
Qudsia	17	Normal	2	22	Boy-3	2	2	2	2
Ruxana	14	Normal	5	20	Girl-1	0	0	2	1
Sabra	17	Normal	4	30	Girl-4	0	0	6	5
Tahira	15 & 20	Husband's 2nd, bought	300	22	Boy-2	1	0	2	1
Umrao	16	Ghar-jamāi	25	38	Boy-9	5	2	4	2
Wasila	17	Normal	30	29	Boy-4	5	3	0	0
Zubeida	15	Husband's 2nd	30	23	Boy-3	3	3	1	1

Appendix 3: Statistical Tables

Table 1: Population of Bijnor District, 1981 Census

Residence/Sex	Muslim	Caste Hindu ('000)	Harijan	Total
Rural:				
Male	239	340	194	786
Female	208	286	167	672
(Sex ratio	870	841	861	855)
Urban:				
Male	167	70	17	255
Female	151	57	16	226
(Sex ratio	904	814	941	886)
All:				
Male	406	409	211	1041
Female	359	344	183	899
(Sex ratio	884	841	867	864)

Note: The total column includes other religious minority groups (Christians and Sikhs). Totals do not tally because of rounding. The sex ratio is the number of females per 1,000 males. The all-India sex ratio in 1981 was 935.

Table 2: Combined Populations of Jhakri and Dharmnagri by Class and Caste, 1985

Religion/Caste		I Land-lord	II Rich	III Middle	IV Poor	V Land-less	Total
			Peasants:				
Muslim	H/holds		5	28	6	6	45
Sheikh	Popn.		33	177	34	30	274
Others:	H/holds		0	4	0	14	18
	Popn.		0	22	0	71	93
Total:	*H/holds*		*5*	*32*	*6*	*20*	*63*
	Popn.		*33*	*199*	*34*	*101*	*367*
Caste Hindu:	H/holds		4	3	0	1	8
Jat etc	Popn.		25	24	0	6	55
Sahni:	H/holds		3	14	10	12	39
	Popn.		37	80	55	58	230
Dhimar:	H/holds		0	7	2	2	11
	Popn.		0	53	7	12	72
Others:	H/holds	1	0	3	5	4	13
	Popn.	5	0	15	23	9	52
Harijan:	H/holds		0	15	10	6	31
Chamar:	Popn.		0	93	62	27	182
Jatab:	H/holds		1	1	3	6	11
	Popn.		3	10	14	30	57
Other:	H/holds		0	0	3	1	4
	Popn.		0	0	19	9	28
Total Hindu:	*H/holds*	*1*	*8*	*43*	*33*	*32*	*117*
	Popn.	*5*	*65*	*275*	*180*	*151*	*676*
TOTAL	*H/holds*	*1*	*13*	*75*	*39*	*52*	*180*
	Popn.	*5*	*98*	*474*	*214*	*252*	*1043*
Percentages:	H/holds	0	7	42	22	29	100
	Popn.	0	9	46	21	24	100
KEY INFORMANTS			6	23	6	6	41
Percentages			15	56	15	15	101

Table 3: Ever-married Women in Jhakri and Dharmnagri by Age and Household Position, 1985

Household Position *Women aged 15-44*	*Muslim*	*Caste* *Hindu*	*Harijan*	*All*
Living with sās (Sājhe)	19	22	9	50
Living separately (Alag)	22	26	11	59
Alone (Akelī)	18	15	11	44
Other	2	1	2	5
All	*61*	*64*	*33*	*158*
Women aged over 45				
Living with married son (Sājhe)[1]	14	17	6	37
Living separately (Alag)[2]	7	5	6	18
Alone but supported (Akelī)[3]	5	8	5	18
Alone, not supported (Akelī)[4]	1	4	0	5
All	*27*	*34*	*17*	*78*

[1] Living with at least one bahū; includes women who are separate from one or more other bahūs as well as those with no other bahūs.
[2] Living with unmarried children, at least one bahū alag but none joint.
[3] Living with husband and/or unmarried children, no bahūs and no sās.
[4] Living alone with no husband, either with no children alive or none resident in the same village.

Table 4: Average Number of Live-born and Stillborn Children to Ever-married Women in Jhakri and Dharmnagri by Ethnicity, 1985

Age of Woman	Muslim	Caste Hindu	Harijan	All
15-24	1.1	1.3	1.7	1.3
(N)	(24)	(17)	(9)	(50)
25-34	4.6	3.5	3.8	3.9
(N)	(21)	(28)	(16)	(65)
35-44	6.8	6.2	5.7	6.4
(N)	(18)	(19)	(8)	(45)
45+	8.5	7.1	8.4	7.8
(N)	(25)	(34)	(17)	(76)
All	*5.2*	*4.9*	*5.3*	*5.1*
(N)	*(88)*	*(98)*	*(50)*	*(236)*
Average age of women	36	39	38	38

Note: N is the number of women in each category.

Table 5: Average Number of Live-born and Stillborn Children to Ever-married Women in Jhakri and Dharmnagri, by Class, 1985

Age of Woman	Class				
	I & II	III	IV	V	All
15-24	1.2	1.4	1.2	1.3	1.3
(N)	(6)	(18)	(11)	(15)	(50)
25-34	4.3	4.3	3.8	3.3	3.9
(N)	(4)	(29)	(17)	(15)	(65)
35-44	7.2	6.5	5.7	5.6	6.4
(N)	(9)	(22)	(6)	(8)	(45)
45+	7.5	8.4	7.9	7.2	7.8
(N)	(6)	(27)	(21)	(22)	(76)
All	*5.4*	*5.4*	*5.0*	*4.5*	*5.1*
(N)	*(25)*	*(96)*	*(55)*	*(60)*	*(236)*
Average age of women	38	37	39	37	38

Note: N is the number of women in each category.

241

Table 6: Number of Stillbirths, Live-births and Infant Deaths to Ever-married Women in Jhakri and Dharmnagri, 1985

				Infant Deaths:	
	Still-births	Live-births	Less than one week	Between 1 & 4 weeks	Between 1 month & 1 year
Class:					
Rich and middle peasants	19	644	23	26	31
Poor peasants and landless	17	530	16	9	22
Sex:					
Male	21	626	22	19	18
Female	15	548	17	16	35
Year of birth:					
Up to 1965	18	429	18	16	28
1966-1985	18	745	21	19	25
Total	*36*	*1174*	*39*	*35*	*53*

Table 7: Perinatal and Infant Mortality Rates of Children Born to Ever-married Women in Jhakri and Dharmnagri, 1985

	Perinatal	Neonatal	Post-neonatal	Infant
Class:				
Rich and middle peasants	65	76	48	124
Poor peasants and landless	60	47	42	89
Sex:				
Male	66	65	29	94
Female	57	60	64	124
Year of birth:				
Up to 1965	81	82	65	147
1966-1985	51	52	33	86
All	*62*	*63*	*45*	*108*

Note:

Perinatal mortality rate = stillbirths plus deaths in the first week per 1,000 live-births and stillbirths combined.

Neonatal mortality rate = deaths in the first month per 1,000 live-births.

Post-neonatal mortality rate = deaths between the end of the first month and the end of the first year per 1,000 live-births.

Infant mortality rate = deaths in the first year per 1,000 live-births (i.e. neonatal + post-neonatal mortality)

Table 8: Percent of Children Born Alive to Ever-married Women in Jhakri and Dharmnagri Surviving to Age 5

| | Caste | | | | | | | |
| | Muslim | | Hindu | | Harijan | | All | |
Class	Boy	Girl	Boy	Girl	Boy	Girl	Boy	Girl
	Born up to 1965							
Rich and Middle								
Peasants	74	55	86	67	63	58	78	61
(N)	(39)	(38)	(57)	(43)	(19)	(19)	(115)	(100)
Poor Peasants and								
Landless	56	47	57	65	67	52	59	56
(N)	(34)	(36)	(46)	(43)	(30)	(25)	(110)	(104)
	Born 1966-80							
Rich and Middle								
Peasants	77	75	89	88	79	81	82	81
(N)	(83)	(67)	(66)	(52)	(34)	(21)	(183)	(140)
Poor Peasants and								
Landless	67	58	90	93	90	93	82	81
(N)	(42)	(36)	(48)	(43)	(30)	(29)	(120)	(108)
	All born up to 1980							
Rich and Middle								
Peasants	76	68	88	79	74	70	81	73
(N)	(122)	(105)	(123)	(95)	(53)	(40)	(298)	(240)
Poor Peasants and								
Landless	62	53	73	79	78	74	71	69
(N)	(76)	(72)	(94)	(86)	(60)	(54)	(230)	(212)

Note:

N is the number of live-births in each category. Children born after 1980 are excluded from this table as they had not reached the age of 5 when the maternity histories were collected in September 1985.

These rates are expressed as survivorship rates, or the proportions of children born in a particular period who reached their fifth birthdays, because we are following a different method of calculation from child mortality rates, which are deaths in a particular year of children aged under 5 per 1,000 children of that age.

Appendix 4:
Food Classification

	Garm	Neither Garm nor Thandā	Thandā
Halka	meats, eggs, fish		
	mūng-kī-dāl		
	masūr-kī-dāl		
	barley, wheat-flour		
	aubergine		squash, cucumber
	garlic, onion		carrot, spinach
	tea, warm water		cold water
	heated milk		cow's, goat's milk
			yoghourt, buttermilk
	(old) gur		cane-juice, sugar
			honey
	most spices (cloves,		cinnamon
	nutmeg, turmeric,		
	mace, dried ginger,		
	chilli), ajwain		
	most nuts		coconut
	mosty dried fruits	raisins	most fresh fruits
Bādī	channa-kī-dāl		boiled rice
	urad-kī-dāl		
	kidney beans	maize	
	flat bean pods		
	peas, potatoes	cauliflower	
	sweet potato	ladyfinger	
	almonds		
	ghī		buffalo milk

Note: These are just a few examples of foods readily available in villages in Bijnor. It is very difficult to produce a listing which everyone would accept because different people sometimes allocate items to different categories.

Notes

Chapter 1

1. Muni is an affectionate nickname meaning "little one" that may be used for a woman of any religious, caste or class group.

2. Many of the issues raised in passing in this chapter are dealt with in more detail in Chapter 5. Appendix 1 contains a description of how we carried out the research.

3. Burhiya is an affectionate nickname meaning "old one" that may be used for a woman of any religious, caste or class group.

Chapter 2

1. W. Crooke, 1897, p.230.

2. H. Papanek, 1984, pp.127-148.

3. We use career in the sense developed in H. Becker, 1963, pp.24-39; and by E. Goffman, 1961, Chapter 3.

4. For some general accounts of village life in plains north India see W.H. Wiser and C.V. Wiser, 1971; and O. Lewis, 1958. Accounts which stress inequality and social change include D.B. Miller, 1975; M. Sharma, 1978; U. Sharma, 1980; U. Patnaik, 1987.

5. For example, F. Edholm et al., 1977, pp.101-30; C. von Werlhof, 1980, pp.33-42; L. Vogel, 1983; J. Sayers et al. (eds), 1987.

6. V. Beechey, 1979, pp.66-82; I. Young, 1980, pp.169-88; G. Omvedt, 1986, pp.30-50. For statements of similar arguments based, however, on an interpretation of "reproduction" which is restricted to the narrower concerns of demography, see D. Levine, 1987; and for a Marxist version, W. Seccombe, 1983, pp.22-47. C. Meillassoux, 1981, provides a theoretical account of the control over biological reproduction, but it is uninformed by feminist perspectives. M. Sharma, 1985, pp.57-88, in an otherwise interesting account of eastern Uttar Pradesh, locates production in the public sphere and reproduction in the private sphere, a dualism which we do not find useful.

7. L. Beneria, in L. Beneria (ed.), 1982, pp.119-147.

8. L. Beneria and G. Sen, 1981, pp.279-298; B. Agarwal, 1986a, pp.165-220.

9. O. Harris, in K. Young et al. (eds), 1981, pp.49-68; F. Edholm, in E. Whitelegg et al. (eds), 1982, pp.166-177; N. Folbre, 1986, pp.245-255.

10. M. Cain et al., 1979, pp.405-38; see also U. Sharma, 1980; I. Palmer, 1977, pp.97-107.

11. Classic discussions of north Indian kinship can be found in I. Karve, 1968,

pp.127-37; D. G. Mandelbaum, 1970, pp.58-94; L. Dumont, 1961, pp.75-95. These all tend to take a man's perspective, as pointed out by U. Sharma, 1981, pp.34-38. Of the few accounts that give equal weight to women's perspectives see S.S. Wadley, in N. Falk and R. Gross (eds), 1980, pp.94-109; and L. Bennett, 1983. An accessible discussion of recent writing is T. Dyson and M. Moore, 1983, pp.35-60.

12.　For a vivid description of men's perspectives on this shift in residence, see M. Marriott, in M.N. Srinivas (ed.), 1955, p.101: "Behind this organisation of marriage is the feeling that one's daughter and sister at marriage becomes the helpless possession of an alien kin group." A woman's perspective is given as, "Early marriage to a stranger and the separation from the mother's house", I. Karve, 1968, p.127. See also M.S. Luschinsky, 1962, and L. Dube, 1988, pp.WS-11 to WS-19.

13.　L. Beneria, in L. Beneria (ed.), 1982, tends to fall into this error, as also does B. Rogers, 1980. A. Phillips, 1987, pp.99, 102-3, provides a critique of this tendency.

14.　See, for instance, J. Brenner and M. Ramas, 1984, pp.33-71; M. Barrett, 1984, pp.123-128.

15.　Although we are dealing with biological reproduction and women's roles, we distance ourselves from those feminists who see women's position rooted solely in their childbearing and consider that women share a common experience (as a sex-class) because of childbearing, for example, S. Firestone, 1971. We endorse the perspective advanced in L. Segal, 1987.

16.　R. Gupta, 1982, gives a 1981 rural population of 91 million, or 93 million in 1982; Registrar-General of India, 1985, gives a crude birth rate of 40 per 1,000 population in 1982 and a perinatal mortality rate (stillbirths and deaths of children under one week per 1,000 live-births and stillbirths) of 80 for 1982 in rural Uttar Pradesh; these generate figures of 10,200 births per day, 820 of whom die by the end of their first week. WHO, 1986, gives estimates of maternal mortality in rural India ranging from 500 to 1,200 per 100,000 live-births; for the calculation in the text, the lower figure has been used, though a higher rate almost certainly applies to Uttar Pradesh. For comparison, in England and Wales in 1984, the perinatal mortality rate was 10. The maternal mortality rate was 8; but in 1936 it too was about 500.

17.　C.M. Cassidy, in N. Scheper-Hughes (ed.), 1987, pp.293-324; W. Mosley and L. Chen (eds), 1984; R. Cash et al. (eds), 1987. A reassertion of the importance of women's reproductive health, in its own right and also as a contributor to child survival, can be seen from the papers for the Safe Motherhood International Conference, Nairobi, 1987. For example, D. Maine et al., 1987.

18.　D. Maine et al., 1987, Table B, argue that complete ante-natal surveillance would be a very expensive way of preventing deaths in developing countries today, but the alternative policy options — improving obstetric facilities as close to labouring women as possible and minimising delays in referral — require the selection of high risk maternities before labour starts if they are to be fully successful. See also note 43, Chapter 4.

19.　For a more detailed description see O.H.K Spate and A.T.A. Learmonth, 1972.

20.　*Statistical Diary, Bijnor*, 1981, shows 2,102 inhabited villages in the District, and a rural population of 1,458,451 (average village size 694), approximately half of whom lived in villages of between 250 and 1,000 people.

21.　We detail exceptions to this pattern later in this chapter.

22.　More details on our research can be found in Appendix 1. This chapter draws heavily on material from the men on *land and loans* and *kinship networks*. The accounts of women's experiences of being a daughter-in-law and their contacts with their natal kin are based on the responses to the *chūlhā, maikā/pīhar*, and *nand* schedules. Views of social change draw heavily on the *oral history* schedules.

23.　Bijnor town is essentially an administrative and market centre; Nagina and Najibabad, the other two large towns, have some small-scale manufacture. According to the CMIE index of economic development, with the 1980 all-India figure set at 100, Bijnor scored 83, Saharanpur 105, Muzaffarnagar 108, and Uttar Pradesh as a whole, 73; CMIE, 1985.

24.　In the text we use "Hindu" to include Caste Hindus and Harijans (e.g. the population of Dharmnagri) and differentiate between them only when necessary. Mahatma Gandhi attempted to popularise the term "Harijan" (literally, children of God) for those regarded as "Untouchable". Caste Hindus usually avoid physical and social contacts and (in particular) food from their hands. Since 1950, these castes have also been known as "Scheduled Castes" because they are listed in a Schedule of the Constitution of India.

25.　Some of these castes have traditionally been associated with particular occupations: Sahnis are known as vegetable-growers; Dhimars as water-carriers and cooks; Rajputs as warriors; Chamars as leather-workers; Telis as oil-pressers and Julahas as weavers. Jatabs claim to be distinct from Chamars, but others contest this: we have chosen to group people according to their own statements of caste membership. More information on local castes can be found in W. Crooke, 1896. Full details of the distribution of the population by caste is given in Appendix 3, Table 2.

26.　Muslims and Hindus do not always live in separate villages: several local villages were mixed.

27.　Details of the key informants are provided in Appendix 2. Appendix 1 describes how they were selected, and how the research was carried out.

28.　This "transformation" is at best a mixed blessing. Two accessible sources on the Green Revolution in India are B.H. Farmer (ed.), 1983; and T.J. Byres and B. Crow, 1985.

29.　Scrubland is not, of course, unproductive, but is a source of common grazing, firewood, grasses and reeds for rope-making and thatching, for example. For a recent discussion focussing on women's role in managing and restoring these resources, see I. Dankelman and J. Davidson, 1988.

30.　The best account of the abolition of zamīndārī in Uttar Pradesh is provided in W.C. Neale, 1962.

31.　In addition, by 1983 almost all the land previously owned in many small plots had been consolidated into fewer, more sizeable fields for each owner.

32.　In doing so we are aware that apparently similar arguments of J. Goldthorpe, 1983, pp.465-488, have generated considerable recent criticism, e.g. M. Stanworth, 1984, pp.159-170. But however strong the argument of principle that women should be treated separately and should not have their class position derived from that of their husbands, it loses much of its force when women do not engage in paid employment outside the family enterprise (see A.F. Heath and N. Britten, in *Sociology*, vol.18, 1984, pp. 475-490) or, as in north India, do not own property (see B. Agarwal, 1986b). The other extreme position, for example as advanced by C. Delphy, 1977, that all women share the same class position because of the unpaid labour they have to perform for their husbands, obliterates the very real differences in life-chances of women whose husbands are located differently in the class structure. Somewhat diffidently, then, we have elected to use the conventional approach as the most useful for our purposes.

33.　For similar discussions of class categories in rural India see L.I. Rudolph and S.H. Rudolph, in M. Desai et al. (eds), 1984, especially pp.310-322; U. Patnaik, 1976, pp.A-82 to A-108; and U. Patnaik, 1987. The distribution of households by class category appears in Appendix 3, Table 2.

34. Those who owned no land but rented or sharecropped it were classified as poor peasants, but this affects very few farmers in the two villages.

35. We have given the key informants pseudonyms according to rules set out in Appendix 2.

36. The details on each example given here and on the following pages date from 1982; because animal-ownership is fluid, the situation in 1985 was often slightly different.

37. Members of Scheduled Castes have preferential rights to jobs, loans and other economic benefits, and to elected positions — privileges not granted (for example) to Muslims or Caste Hindus in comparable economic positions.

38. Fish are caught in the Ganges and brought to the villages by itinerant salesmen, often from the Bengali settlement near Dharmnagri. Muslims are prohibited from eating pork but may eat beef; the reverse is true for Hindus. Despite the low levels of meat consumption, inter-ethnic hostility can be generated through contrasts of this kind.

39. For discussions of similar changes elsewhere in north India see references cited in notes 28 and 33 above.

40. Appendix 1 describes the conventions we are following in presenting "quotations" like this one.

41. For a description of similar processes in south India, see e.g. J. Caldwell et al., 1982, pp.689-727.

42. For more detailed discussion of this point see U. Sharma, 1980.

43. Contrasts in the implications of widowhood are described in M. Cain, 1981, pp.435-474; M. Cain et al., 1979, pp.405-38; and S.S. Wadley, 1987.

44. Pīhar is associated with pitr (father), and means the father's house or his ancestral village; maikā is associated with mā (mother) and means one's mother's house — which is usually not the mother's own father's house but that of her sasūr (father-in-law), her susrāl.

45. This is discussed further in many places: see, for example, D.B. McGilvray, in C.P. MacCormack (ed.), 1982, pp.25-73.

46. Garm-thandā are not the only paired opposites in local thinking; dry-wet is another common one. In addition, some foods have a bādī influence, usually translated as windy or flatulence-creating; others are halkā, light or easily digestible. See Appendix 4 for a classification of common local foods using these principles. F. Zimmerman, 1988, discusses the links between this system of classification and theories of climate and environment.

47. See for example, M. Carstairs, 1957, and D.B. McGilvray, in C.P. MacCormack (ed.), 1982, p.33.

48. A man with nocturnal emissions is regarded as a garmī-kā-marīz — suffering from garmī which would decline if he had sexual intercourse.

49. Women in a polluted state — such as menstruating women — should not perform religious duties or visit temples or mosques. Hindu women should also not cook while they are menstruating, but in chūlhās with only one adult woman, the full prohibition can rarely be observed. Muslim women attached to the shrine of Hazrat Nizamuddin Auliya, New Delhi, continue to cook for others within the chūlhā when they are menstruating, but do not prepare food which is to be blessed in the shrine for distribution to pilgrims; P.M. Jeffery, 1979, pp.110-115. For more general discussions of menstrual taboos and their implications see also N. Yalman, 1963, pp.25-58; F. Young and A. Bacdayan, 1965, pp.225-40; P. Hershman, 1974, pp.274-298; and C.S. Thompson, 1985, pp.701-11.

50.   Only a small minority of married couples in the two villages were not married in this fashion; we discuss deviations from this pattern, and their consequences, below.

51.   Hindus talk of kanyā dān, the gift of a virgin. Muslims do not use this phrase, but there are many parallels in the meanings and structural implications of marriage for the two religious groups.

52.   Many castes are divided into smaller groups, known in English as sub-castes, within which most marriages take place.

53.   Data on Hindu marriage practices in north India are well summarised in D. Mandelbaum, 1970, or in I. Karve, 1968, and outlined in T. Dyson and M. Moore, 1983, pp.35-60. Descriptions of Muslim patterns are much more uncommon; see V. Das, 1973, pp.30-45; P.M. Jeffery, 1979, and I. Ahmad (ed.), 1976. Note, however, that the contrasts between marriage systems are not as clear-cut as the simple models suggest. For example, within-village marriage is common among Hindus in Garhwal, in the foothills of the Himalayas not far from Bijnor; G.D. Berreman, 1972. As in Jhakri, close-kin and within-village marriages probably account for a minority of north Indian Muslim marriages.

54.   In north Indian kinship systems, people distinguish between relatives who are not differentiated in English. For example, "uncle", "aunt" and "cousin" have very different meanings if they refer to people related through the father rather than the mother. We have used the English words in the text, but in brackets have made the relationships involved clear through the shorthand explained in the Glossary.

55.   The extent of within-village marriage or close-kin marriage among Muslim populations has rarely been studied closely, nor the implications of these patterns considered. Thus M. Cain et al., 1979, p.406, describe marriage patterns in Bangladesh and note that 29% of women in one village were in-married, but nothing is said about the distribution or effects of this kind of marriage for women, which are discussed in P.M. Jeffery, 1979. The marriage distances of our key informants are listed in Appendix 2. The contrast between Muslim and Hindu marriage patterns was one consideration in our choice of research site, as indicated in Appendix 1.

56.   Most expenses on each side are met by the parents of the bride and groom respectively, but the mother's brothers of the couple usually make a substantial contribution, at least at the wedding of their sister's eldest child. See further below.

57.   Among Muslims the only cash sum involved is usually the mahr, which may be listed in the marriage contract as a settlement on the wife by the husband. In practice this is generally merely notional and no actual payment is ever made, but it may become significant if disputes are taken to court after divorce.

58.   For Muslim patterns of gift-giving see, for example, Z. Eglar, 1960; Naveed-i-Rahat, in T.S. Epstein and R.A. Watts (eds), 1981; and P.M. Jeffery, 1979. For Hindu patterns, as well as those to be found in the general ethnographies listed above, see S. Vatuk, 1975, pp.155-196; and G.G. Raheja, 1988.

59.   An elder sister may give, if she is married to a ghar-jamāi (in-married son-in-law) who controls his father-in-law's ancestral property.

60.   Holi is a spring festival; see M. Marriott, in M. Singer (ed.), 1966, pp.200-212. Tijo, at the beginning of the monsoon, is known as the festival of swings; see also S.S. Wadley, in N. Falk and R. Gross (eds), 1980, pp.94-109. The major Muslim festivals are the two Eids marking the end of Ramzan and the tenth day of Zulhaj. See the Glossary for further details.

61.   The argument that dowry is pre-mortem inheritance is made by J. Goody and S.J. Tambiah, 1974, and is criticised by (among others) U. Sharma, 1980, and by M.N. Srinivas, 1986.

62.   Rand (widow) is often used as a term of abuse, as in chudāi-rand (prostitute-

widow) and marī-rand-saukan (dead widow co-wife).

63.   See Chapter 6 below for more detail on gift-giving after a birth.

64.   Here we agree with M.N. Srinivas, 1986, and R. Ahmad, 1987, pp.WS-2 to WS-26, that the crucial difference from the past is that demands are now being made by the groom's family. B. Miller, 1980, pp.95-129, argues by contrast that dowry is rising because of the increase in women's dependence and their exclusion from the labour force. See also B. Miller, 1981. In some areas of rural north India, dowry payments may not be rising in real terms, in the sense that the rise in cash payments may be not far out of line with general inflation, and dowry payments may bear roughly the same relationship to cash incomes: see M. Macdornan, 1986.

65.   See S. Vatuk, in H. Papanek and G. Minault (eds), 1982; U. Sharma, in P. Caplan and J. Bujra (eds), 1978; U. Sharma, 1980; P.M. Jeffery, 1979; and D.G. Mandelbaum, 1986, pp.1999-2004.

66.   This is generally true for Muslims as well, since within-village and close-kin marriages are minority forms.

67.   We detail the effects of shifts from the initial sharing of a chūlhā, to becoming separate or alone, in Chapter 3. Some key informants did not follow this pattern: Zubeida never shared with her sās because Zakir and his first wife (Zubeida's sister) had separated from his parents; and in other cases the sās was already dead before the woman was married.

68.   Some scepticism must be attached to these estimates: most women were very vague about their current age, and their ages at marriage and at cohabitation.

69.   C.S. Thompson, 1981, pp.39-53 contrasts "good sharm" which is respectful behaviour, and "bad sharm" which is the feeling of embarrassment which comes when a person breaches moral rules of propriety.

70.   Women were reticent about discussing this kind of matter, and we have little evidence about how common this was nor what women thought about it. The sās' control of sexual access could protect the bahū from excessive sexual demands from her husband or could represent the sās' attempt to maintain her dominance over her son and bahū by restraining the development of their relationship.

71.   Even on trips into Bijnor, Jhakri women did not wear a burqā, a veiled garment that completely covers a woman's body. The few, relatively wealthy women who owned one rarely wore it for trips to neighbouring villages. For everyday wear, cotton was the commonest fabric. More desirable (and expensive) was "tery-cot" (cotton and artificial fibres) which may be worn or given on special occasions.

72.   In general, Muslim and Hindu women observed purdah in approximately the same situations and in similar ways. More extended discussions of parallels and contrasts can be found in S. Vatuk, in H. Papanek and G. Minault (eds), 1982; and D.G. Mandelbaum, 1986, pp.1999-2004.

73.   See note 54 above. A woman's husband's older brother (her jeth) and his wife (jethānī) relate to her differently from her husband's younger brother (devar) and his wife (devrānī). We call these relatives her brothers- and sisters-in-law, and mark the difference (where appropriate) by using the shorthand HeB, HyB etc. (see the Glossary). Her husband's sister is called "nand", and her brother's wife, "bhābī". Because the nand plays an important role in childbirth arrangements, she will always be referred to by the Hindi word.

74.   The role of women as managers of other women on behalf of senior men is discussed by, for India, U. Sharma, in P. Caplan and J. Bujra (eds), 1978; and more generally, by M.Z. Rosaldo, 1980, pp.389-417.

75.   In Karimpur, further south in Uttar Pradesh, it is said that, "Women never have friends in their susrāl" (S.S. Wadley, personal communication).

76.　Access to natal kin is used by T. Dyson and M. Moore, 1983, pp.35-60, as one indicator of women's autonomy in India. D.G. Mandelbaum, 1986, p.2000, notes how refusal to permit a visit to her natal village may be "a considerable penalty on a young wife" while refusing to bring her back is "perhaps worse".

77.　Only the landlord's house has a telephone, and few people in Dharmnagri and Jhakri can read or write; villagers rarely asked someone to write a letter for them, or to read a letter back to them. Most contact and transfer of news is therefore face-to-face.

78.　These contrasts between a woman's behaviour in her natal village and in her susrāl give the lie to those who stereotype Indian women as "passive" by nature; passivity is maintained by powerful social forces, and when they are relaxed, women are assertive and active. The dangers of stereotyping Indian women as passive are discussed in P. Parmar, in Centre for Contemporary Cultural Studies, 1982; and by P. Trivedi, 1984, pp.37-50.

79.　Young married Hindu women usually return to their natal village for a few days rest and relaxation at Holi and Tijo; Muslim women are less likely to get permission to visit their parents at Eid — a contrast brought home to us when Eid and Tijo fell on the same day in 1982.

80.　To call a man "sālā" is to claim to be having a sexual relationship with his sister, which threatens his prestige at its core.

81.　We were surprised at the lack of support among Muslim men and women for close-kin and within-village marriages, since these are positively valued in Nizamuddin, studied previously by P.M. Jeffery, 1979, and in northern Pakistan, H. Donnan (personal communication).

82.　"Bahin-chūt" (literally sister's vulva) implies that the man has sexual relations with his own sister.

83.　"Ganjā" (bald) also means effaced or destroyed; "kāliyā" (black one) also implies low-status or devalued.

84.　Note that the brothers of these men who had bought a bride were in orthodox dowry marriages: we are not dealing here with a shift in marriage practice from bridewealth to dowry, as discussed in I. Rajaraman, 1983, pp.275-79; and S. Randeria and L. Visaria, 1984, pp.648-52; see also G.G. Raheja, 1988, p.236.

Chapter 3

1.　The 1981 Census gives a participation rate of 10.6% of the total rural female population in Uttar Pradesh; R. Nayyar, 1987, pp.2207-2216, uses National Sample Survey sources for 1983 to produce a figure of 30.0%, including women who said their secondary occupation involved "work". Problems in using these sources are further discussed by S. Bhattacharya, in D. Jain and N. Banerjee (eds), 1985.

2.　This point is stressed, for example, by E. Boserup, 1970, and by K. Young et al. (eds), 1981. On how socialist societies have tended to regard women's position, see, for example, M. Molyneux, 1981, pp.1-35; and E. Croll, 1981, pp.361-374.

3.　B. Rogers, 1980, makes much of this argument.

4.　An early statement of women's time-use in a village north of Delhi can be found in T.P.S. Chawdhari and B.M. Sharma, 1961, pp.643-650; see also M. Cain et al., 1979, pp.405-438; M. Buvinic et al. (eds), 1983; D. Jain, in D. Jain and N. Banerjee (eds), 1985; G. Sen and C. Sen, 1985, pp.WS-49 to WS-56; and K. Bardhan, 1985, pp.2207-2217. A call for more information is made in L. Beneria (ed.), 1982. B. White, in C.P. White and K. Young (eds), 1984, pp.18-32, notes that a labour-use survey can be a very valuable way of getting an initial overview of who does what, but it is a time-consuming exercise and needs to be justified very carefully in the context of other priorities.

5. We collected *time-use* information from key informant women but they said repeat questioning would be pointless and we did not complete the full seasonal range we had intended. This material is complemented by women's answers to the *chūlhā*, *maikā/pīhar* and *nand* schedules, by information from the men concerning *crops* and *animal husbandry*, and observational data to check under-reporting of women's activities. More details are given in Appendix 1.

6. House-work is not the same as domestic labour in the West, since it entails a much greater range of tasks involving more basic processing of foodstuffs and very different maintenance tasks. We use house-work (with a hyphen) to signal that the term has a different meaning from that in the West. The other forms of work we distinguish in this way are defiling-, animal-, field-, outside- and dung-work.

7. See, for a similar point, M. Chen, 1986, pp.217-222; and L. Beneria and G. Sen, 1981, pp.279-299.

8. For discussions of the theoretical location of such activities, see H. Papanek, 1979, pp.775-781; P. Caplan, 1985; and U. Sharma, 1986.

9. M. Cain et al., 1979, pp.405-438, demonstrate a similar pattern in Bangladesh.

10. The Gandhi Ashram is a voluntary organisation established in the Gandhian tradition which, among other things, encourages home industries such as spinning.

11. The increased use of dung for fuel, and a probable reduction in the number of cattle because of encroachments on common grazing land, mean an even greater reliance on the chemical fertilisers introduced with the new seeds.

12. This mixed picture of the effect of the Green Revolution on women's work is described for other parts of north India in B. Agarwal, 1986a, pp.165-220. See also G. Sen, in L. Beneria (ed.), 1982.

13. The patterns of development of residential arrangements in India are described as domestic cycles in I. Karve, 1968, D. Mandelbaum, 1970, and A. M. Shah, 1974. However, these accounts do not elaborate on the effects of different residential arrangements on men and on women, and on their work. Nor do they discuss how residential and property relationships interact and affect women's work, which we discuss below; a brief account can also be found in U. Sharma, 1978, pp.218-33.

14. Being sājhe not only allows a bahū to obtain leave more easily but also affects the help she receives with her work during her pregnancies and after her deliveries, as we discuss in Chapters 4 and 7 below.

15. D. Mandelbaum, 1986, pp.1999-2004, describes the interplay of male and female interests in residing jointly or separately, and notes that the blame for a break-up is "usually put on the wives"; see also P. Kolenda and L. Haddon, in P. Kolenda, 1987.

16. During pregnancy and in the post-partum period, a woman's access to her natal kin may be an indicator of her ability to get leave from her work more generally, making a material difference to her general experience of childbearing.

17. Appendix 3, Table 8 shows that for all ever-married women in the two villages, 69% of their sons born before 1965 survived to the age of 5; of those born between 1966 and 1980, 82% survived. We can put no figures on the increasing life expectancy of adults in the two villages.

18. Because more sons are surviving now, more joint households are possible now than in the past, as P. Kolenda, 1987, points out. However, because married brothers rarely live in joint chūlhās, most chūlhās are still separate.

19. Estimated age of cohabitation for ever-married women in Jhakri and Dharmnagri born in the 1940s is 16; in the 1950s, 16.2; and in the 1960s, 16.4. Given

women's uncertainties over their ages, these differences are too small to be significant.

20. For estimates of women's energy expenditures see S. Batliwala, in D. Jain and N. Banerjee, (eds), 1985; for a survey of material on feeding patterns see B. Harriss, mimeographed, 1986. See also A. Appadorai, 1981, pp.494-511; and S. Vatuk, mimeographed, 1983.

21. Landless widows are the only exceptions to this generalisation; if they have no son prepared to support them they have to find what work they can. Some of them become dāis (see below in this chapter).

22. The general picture is well captured in T. Dyson and M. Moore, 1983, pp.35-60. In the "normal" pattern, the excess of male births is counteracted by an excess of male deaths, both in infancy and at later ages. See also J. Kynch and A. Sen, 1983, pp.363-80.

23. The population of these States in 1981 was 175 million; if growth at 2% per annum continues, the 1991 figure will be about 215 million.

24. See Appendix 3, Table 1 for more details of the Bijnor rates; other tables in Appendix 3 give village-level data on mortality of children by sex. Estimates of age-specific mortality rates for males and females in rural Uttar Pradesh are provided in the annual series *Sample Registration System*, produced by the Vital Statistics Division, Office of the Registrar-General, India, Ministry of Home Affairs, New Delhi.

25. See, for example, Government of India, 1974; B.R. Nanda (ed.), 1976; J. Liddle and R. Joshi, 1986; N. Desai and V. Patel, 1985.

26. Family law in India is different for the main religious groups; civil marriage is relatively rare. We do not have space here to discuss the law on divorce, maintenance or custody of children, which also differs for each religious group. The recent Shah Banno case demonstrates the continuing political significance of such laws, but they affect Bijnor village women even less than the laws on the age of marriage, dowry and inheritance.

27. D. Engels, 1983, pp.107-134; G. Forbes, 1979, pp.407-419. The whole topic was made an international issue by the publication of K. Mayo, 1927; this is discussed in D. Engels, unpublished paper given to the European Modern South Asian Studies Conference, Heidelberg, July 1986.

28. Government of India, 1974; B.R. Nanda (ed.), 1976; J.M. Everett, 1981. Anon. 1984, pp.1609-1610, discusses the attempts to reform the 1961 legislation.

29. There are recurrent newspaper reports of the deaths of young brides which are either encouraged suicides or outright murder. Reports suggest that "dowry deaths" are particularly a feature of lower middle-class urban north India; but given the unwillingness of the women's parents to report these deaths, and of the police to investigate them, the frequency and social location of these deaths is not well established; see M. Kishwar and R. Vanita (eds), 1984, pp.203-241.

30. Government of India, 1974; B.R. Nanda (ed.), 1976; A. De Souza (ed.), 1980.

31. The effects of education on women's position in the home, fertility and mortality is considered by J.C. Caldwell et al., 1985, pp.29-51.

32. The female literacy rate in rural Uttar Pradesh in 1981 was 15%.

33. For details, see U. Sharma, 1980; B. Rogers, 1980; N. Nelson, 1979.

34. More details are provided in R. Jeffery, 1988; D. Banerji, 1985; M. Chatterjee, 1988.

35. See Appendix 3, Tables 6-8. Few mortality studies in India report rates by social class; the best indicators available are mother's education and housing type. See, for example, Registrar-General, India, 1983; and A.K. Jain and P. Visaria (eds), 1988.

36. H.R. Nevill, 2nd. edit., 1928.

37. The under-use of primary health facilities, coupled with extreme overcrowding in district and medical college hospitals, has often been reported in India; see D. Banerji, 1985; R. Jeffery, 1988.

38. The problems faced by female staff posted alone to a rural sub-centre include the fear of rape or other sexual harassment; young women living without the protection of a husband or father are widely assumed to be of "loose" character.

39. Nīm-hakīm is translated as a half-trained doctor or quack in J.T. Platts, Reprint Edit., 1977, p.1169; our research assistants, however, described a nīm-hakīm as a travelling healer, likely to be found sitting under a nīm tree.

40. Discussions of the range of available healers, and strategies of consultations, can be found in C. Leslie (ed.), 1976; see also G.R. Gupta (ed.), 1981; and R. Jeffery, 1988.

41. A more extended discussion of medical services for women in India can be found in P.M. Jeffery, R. Jeffery and A. Lyon, 1985.

42. Other discussions of dāis in north India can be found in W.H. Wiser and C.V. Wiser, 1971, pp.44-45; D.N. Kakar, 1980; M.S. Luschinsky, 1962; H. Gideon, 1962, pp.1220-1234.

43. The information we discuss here comes from interviews with the dāis who practised in Dharmnagri and Jhakri and in the villages where we conducted a survey of recently delivered women. For more details, see Appendix 1.

44. The main exception is a literate married Punjabi woman in her early 30s whose husband was an untrained medical practitioner and who conducts deliveries in order to complement her husband's work. However, she leaves the more "defiling" tasks to a Harijan woman who usually accompanies her.

45. The dāi who works in Dharmnagri is a widowed Muslim; but the husbands of the two Muslim women who conduct most deliveries in Jhakri are still alive. More detail on these women is given in Chapter 5.

46. Chapter 5 gives more detail on appropriate attendants at deliveries.

47. Chapter 9 includes a more detailed discussion of dāi training schemes.

48. See for example the sources used by K. Mayo, 1927; also J. Roberton, 1846, pp.308-319; files in the National Archives of India: Home, Medical, August 1887, No.32-A; Home, Public, 1872, Nos.266-267-A; and J.E. Mistry, in V. Anstey, 1936.

49. The data on pauperisation and its effects on women presented by B. Agarwal, 1986a, pp.165-220, do not, however, show a clear trend for rural Uttar Pradesh as a whole since the early 1960s; the long-term data held by S.S. Wadley and B. Derr for Karimpur, further south in Uttar Pradesh, also provide little evidence for an increase in, for example, the number of widows being left to live alone; S.S. Wadley, 1987.

Chapter 4

1. Unless otherwise specified, the material used in this and the following chapters is mainly drawn from the *last pregnancy*, *1985 schedules*, and the maternity histories, and usually refers to the key informants' pregnancies and deliveries which took place in 1982-3. These are the ones we used to select the women for our sample; for more details of the sex and parity of the births, see Appendix 2.

2. South Indian practice is different: see for example G.E. Ferro-Luzzi, 1974b, pp.113-161. The contrasts are discussed by S. S. Wadley, in S.S. Wadley (ed.), 1980, pp.153-170. O. Lewis, 1958, p.47, discusses a garbha sanskāra (pregnancy ritual) in a village near Delhi; C. S. Thompson, unpublished Ph.D. thesis, London University, 1984, discusses pregnancy rites in a central Indian village.

3. If a woman is in a polluted state she should not visit a temple or mosque or read

the scriptures, but women in Dharmnagri and Jhakri rarely do these at any time. Childbirth pollution is discussed in more detail in Chapters 6 and 7 below. G.E. Ferro-Luzzi, 1973a, pp.165-172, says that although pregnant Tamil women are not usually regarded as polluting, they are forbidden to visit temples, especially once their pregnancy is advanced.

4. If, as we have argued in Chapter 3, a young married woman's natal kin offer her most emotional and practical support, her inability to visit them from late pregnancy until a month or more after the baby has been delivered (see Chapters 6 and 7 for more details) poignantly encapsulates her lack of autonomy.

5. S. Vatuk, in H. Papanek and G. Minault (eds), 1982, p.74, also notes that "it is because of sharm that a woman does not visit the natal home when in an advanced state of pregnancy or in order to give birth" in western Uttar Pradesh. This latter point is discussed in more detail in Chapter 5 below; see also references in note 4 to that chapter.

6. The case of Pushpa is discussed in more detail below.

7. The same can, of course, be said of Western medical science.

8. This lack of knowledge is not unique to north India. It is widespread in the West, too, where these matters are also regarded as the preserve of "experts".

9. Two dāis told us that women have two uteri, one on the left for girls and one on the right for boys.

10. Most of these terms suggest that the man takes the initiative, as in chūt lenā (to take the vulva), but mauz lenā and mauz khānā (to eat or consume the banana, that is, penis) portray the woman in an active way.

11. A few dāis — mostly those with Government training — also said that women produce seeds and mentioned a fertile period. The farming analogy is discussed by L. Dube, in L. Dube et al. (eds), 1986, pp.22-53. C.E. Taylor et al., 1983, p.73, report that in Punjab the analogy of the field is common, but that fertility is thought to decline midway between menstrual periods because the field slowly closes.

12. Hindus and Muslims follow twelve-month lunar calendars to set the dates of religious festivals, but Hindu months begin with the full moon whereas Muslim months begin at new moon. Lunar months last 29 or 30 days and lunar years are therefore about 10 days shorter than the solar year. The Hindu calendar inserts an extra month every three years to bring the two calendars back into line, but the Muslim calendar does not. Both groups also use the Western solar calendar used by the Government for public events such as schooling etc.

13. The foetus is also called a māns-kā-golā or a golā-kā-pindā.

14. Note that if the causative form of the verb is used (girānā) it means "to cause an abortion"; abortion is discussed further in Chapter 8 below.

15. More generally, thailī means a sack; while a burqā is the veiled garment used by some Muslim women to achieve seclusion.

16. As we shall show in Chapter 7, toddlers are not always weaned before a younger sibling is born.

17. We did not attempt to collect systematic data on dietary intakes, energy expenditures or nutritional status (see Appendix 1). Data from elsewhere in rural India suggest that most pregnant women receive a diet which is lacking in several respects and which probably has adverse effects on maternal and child health, and we judge that women in Dharmnagri and Jhakri are similarly disadvantaged. See C. Gopalan, 1985, pp.159-166.

18. The costs to women and children are discussed further in Chapter 7.

19. Appendix 4 is a tabulation of common foods according to their characteristics as garm/thandā and bādī/halkā.

20. The apparent absence of food avoidances in pregnancy is also reported for south India in G.E. Ferro-Luzzi, 1973b, pp.259-266, and elsewhere in Uttar Pradesh in M.S. Luschinsky, 1962, p.62. C. Laderman, 1983, p.92, notes for coastal Malaysian villages that women usually fail to observe food avoidances in pregnancy. Only if something unpleasant happens might these failures be scrutinised to account for what went wrong.

21. The fear of large babies amongst women in Karnataka is discussed in M. Nichter and M. Nichter, 1983, pp.235-246. This fear does not necessarily lead women to restrict their food intake: some women think a large stomach reduces the space available for the baby to grow (p.239). This article also describes a folk theory of the relationship between garmī and pregnancy similar to that described above.

22. Two Jhakri key informants — Latifan and Umrao — were resident in their natal village but neither had any natal kin who could help.

23. This was not Tahira's first pregnancy because she had one child (already dead) in her first marriage.

24. We discuss below some exceptions when women become very ill.

25. Seasonal factors might influence not only a woman's work during pregnancy but also whether the baby and mother survive; see R. Chambers et al. (eds), 1981. But our numbers are small and mothers' memories of the season of birth or death of children are very unreliable. We are thus unable to comment on the impact of such factors as climatic variation or seasonal poverty on women's childbearing experiences.

26. This section is largely derived from the responses to the *chūlhā* schedule (see Appendix 1).

27. Omvati, Promilla, Pushpa and Santosh were the wives of four of six brothers.

28. Chapter 7 deals with work in the post-partum period when a woman is both polluted and polluting.

29. Contacts between the dāi and her clients are discussed further in Chapter 5, and the effects of these relationships for maternal and child health programmes are discussed in Chapter 9.

30. Post-natal tetanus toxoid injections are discussed in Chapter 6.

31. This is elaborated in Chapter 8 below.

32. Inampur is about 8 kms to the north-north-east; Nizampur is 40 km. away to the east; Najibabad is 45 kms away (see Map 1); Sahanpur is 48 kms away, just beyond Najibabad; Nehtaur is 35 kms east-south-east of Jhakri.

33. No women living in either village had in fact been returned to their parents and remained unmarried. Some women who never gave birth, and others who had seen all their children die, continue to live with their husband. Despite these local examples, childlessness remains a powerful threat to the continuation of a woman's marriage.

34. Though we asked specifically about delayed periods and miscarriages when collecting maternity histories, we doubt that women reported every event. The numbers involved are very small: 12 "late periods" and 24 "babies falling". These rates — 10 and 20 per 1,000 reported pregnancies — are lower than we would expect, given the poor nutritional status of these women.

35. We discuss in Chapter 8 how women also say attempted abortions are more likely to be successful if the woman is carrying a male baby.

36. In Chapter 5 we describe how this build-up of garmī relates to uterine contractions at the time of delivery.

37. We are using the medically correct term "dilatation", not the commoner "dilation".

38. Direct translations of these symptoms into Western disease categories are

problematic because there are not always exact equivalents.

39. This combination of symptoms probably indicates pre-eclampsia.

40. Her symptoms would probably lead a Western doctor to a diagnosis of pulmonary tuberculosis.

41. This was probably eclampsia.

42. In Western medical terms, this indicates high blood pressure and possibly pre-eclampsia.

43. A. Oakley, 1984, has argued that ante-natal care in the West is a recent development, and not a wholly welcome one. There is little evidence of its value in reducing morbidity, and it represents excessive surveillance over women which is unnecessary in most cases. However, having little access to medical services is arguably a worse situation. The key issue is the quality of care and the politics of its provision, which we discuss further in Chapter 9.

Chapter 5.

1. This description is based on the births attended by Patricia, others to which she was not called but heard about (usually the following day), those described by key informants when asked about their "last pregnancy", or discussed in general conversations. There are relatively few descriptions of birthing practices in north India. Men are almost totally excluded, but even female ethnographers seem to have found difficulty in attending or reporting births. In the mid-1950s, in a major social research project in eastern Uttar Pradesh, "project staff members were never allowed to attend deliveries", M.S. Luschinsky, 1962, p.78. C.S. Thompson, 1984, p.312, also reports not being allowed to attend a delivery because she was young, unmarried and childless. More extended descriptions are provided by D. Jacobson, in N.A. Falk and R.M. Grass (eds), 1980; H. Gideon, vol.64, 1962, pp.1220-1234; and T. Blanchet, 1984.

2. "Natural" childbirth, of a kind sometimes invoked by Western writers, is a myth, because birthing practices are always socially constructed. S. MacIntyre, 1977, pp.13-22 points out that writers who appeal to a romanticised past or anthropological present tend to homogenise "primitive" societies in order to use them as contrast comparisons to highlight aspects of modern childbirth that they wish to criticise.

3. Crises during deliveries are discussed below.

4. Only about 3% of deliveries reported by women in the survey and by women in Dharmnagri and Jhakri took place in hospital or clinic, or elsewhere; all the rest took place in the woman's husband's house. This degree of restriction is unusually severe; in Punjab, women usually return to their natal village for their first delivery, sometimes for their second, and may do so for a few more births; but negotiating this may cause friction; H. Gideon, 1962, pp.1220-1234; P. Brown et al., in Cambridge Women's Study Group, 1981. Further east in Uttar Pradesh, the ideal is for women to stay in their susrāl, but "childbirth in the woman's parents' house is not uncommon", M.S. Luschinsky, 1962, p.94. In Bangladesh, a cultural ideal for the more wealthy is that at least the first birth should take place in the woman's natal village: T. Blanchet, 1984. In the north of Madhya Pradesh (south of Uttar Pradesh) women are prohibited from going to their natal village for the first delivery, but may do so later; but 100 miles further south, and in south India generally, the first delivery is most likely to be in the natal village, with a declining frequency thereafter; D. Jacobson, in N.A. Falk and R.M. Grass (eds), 1980, p.80; C.S. Thompson, 1984. See also I. Karve, 3rd. ed., 1968, p.403. It is not clear why such variations exist nor what their consequences are, but most of the above sources are agreed that women who give birth in their natal village

are more relaxed and better treated, and have a more supportive environment in which to deliver.

5.   The sources mentioned in note 4 above also suggest that when women return to their natal village to give birth it may be in the hope of breaking a sequence of miscarriages, stillbirths, neonatal deaths or births of girls; or if, for other reasons, a woman is not thought to be getting adequate care in her susrāl.

6.   If there is a choice of rooms, the innermost may be used. It is regarded as the most garm, most appropriate for intercourse and childbirth; see G.G. Raheja, 1988, p.85.

7.   Sharm is felt in relation to a woman's own mother and sister (particularly an older one) but not so much by a woman in front of her own daughter or daughter-in-law, because they are susrāl relatives.

8.   Chamars and Dhanuks — traditionally mat-makers — are reported as the castes which provide dāis in W. Crooke, 1896. See also the references cited in note 42, Chapter 3.

9.   See Map 2 for the location of Itawa, Chandpuri and Qaziwala.

10.   Their husbands follow the traditional caste occupation of butchery.

11.   This is just a specific instance of women's reliance on men's mobility and control over most means of transport.

12.   We are not endorsing these practices, but mention them merely to show that the dāi's internal examinations are the only interventions different from those of the other women present.

13.   The left hand is used for all tasks considered "dirty", such as washing the genital area after defaecating, or touching the genitals in sexual intercourse; the right hand is thereby kept "clean" and is reserved for eating etc.; see R. Hertz, 1960, pp.89-113; and V. Das, 1982, Chapter 4.

14.   G.G. Raheja, 1988, pp.72, 82-3, notes how one-and-a-quarter is a quantity frequently used as a means of removing inauspiciousness. Circling a small dish of grain and/or money round the head is also done during other rituals, and is known as wa-pher.

15.   Evil spirits are thought to fear iron, and the use of an iron instrument or charm in this way is also reported by C.S. Thompson, 1984.

16.   An extended discussion can be found in P. Hershman, 1974, pp.274-298.

17.   Raising the head of the bed to speed delivery is the reverse of the practice of raising the foot of the bed to avoid a miscarriage, mentioned in Chapter 4 above.

18.   We did not expect women would deliver lying on their backs. The predominant image of non-Western birthing practices is that, "Traditionally, women in developing countries go through labour and give birth in upright or semi-upright positions, such as sitting, squatting, half-reclining, kneeling or standing, and often adopt several of them in sequence." B. Jordan, 1987, p.314; see also N. Newton and M. Newton, in J.G. Howells (ed.), 1972; C.S. Ford, 1945, p.58; and C.P. MacCormack, in C.P. MacCormack (ed.), 1982, p.14. Similarly, in Bangladesh, T. Blanchet, 1984, p.87, reports a universal upright position, either kneeling or squatting. But in Punjab, the Khanna study found that "care was taken that the patient was flat on her back, knees drawn up, and the belief prevailed that shifting of position led to trouble"; J.E. Gordon et al., 1965, p.737. We have no reason to believe that either the pattern described in Punjab nor what we describe here has resulted from the introduction of recent Western medical theories about appropriate birthing positions.

19.   Ajwain is trachyspermum ammi, a kind of caraway, used to counteract the effects of worms and flatulence. Similar ways of trying to accelerate labour through garm food or drink are described in J.E. Gordon et al., 1965, p.737; and by C.S.

Thompson, 1984, p.274.

20. Reports of childbirth in India or Sri Lanka stress the importance of silence and the exclusion of outsiders (particularly men) from knowledge of the woman's distress; see H. Gideon, 1962, p.1224; M.S. Luschinsky, 1962; C.S. Thompson, 1984, p.273; D.B. McGilvray, in C.P. MacCormack (ed.), 1982. The sharm that exaggerates the secrecy of childbirth, and the pollution that inheres in the delivering woman, seem to prevent women from using this sphere of women's business as a basis for independent social organisation that might give them the kind of resources for status and action outside men's control described, for example, by C.P. MacCormack, in C.P. MacCormack (ed.), 1982. See also C.S. Thompson, 1984, p.308, who argues that "the rituals surrounding birth make female physical sexuality seem low status and degrading. Birth isolates women from one another, from their own caste mates and from men and it is not seen as a source of prestige or power".

21. Other reports suggest that death pollution is the most severe, but women are not normally affected as much by death as by birth pollution; G.E. Ferro-Luzzi, 1973a, pp.165-166. Discussions of the place of childbirth pollution in the overall patterns of Hindu pollution practices and beliefs can be found in E.B. Harper, in E.B. Harper (ed.), 1964; and H. Orenstein, in M. Singer and B. Cohn (eds), 1968. Childbirth pollution as it affects the mother and how the baby is cleaned is described in more detail in Chapter 6.

22. These practices leave the baby vulnerable to neonatal tetanus. The sole exception was Chandresh, whose baby was delivered by the ANM's assistant, who used scissors to cut the cord.

23. As a bought bride she also has no contact with her natal kin; nor does she with her nand, because of a feud. Lalit's yBW had an affair with Lalit's ZH, whose son discovered this and murdered Lalit's yBW.

24. These Faqirs had no special religious position, nor were they travelling beggars, as the term often signifies; but they were landless, and depended on various casual jobs. At the other extreme, Ahmad's mother is in a rich peasant chūlhā, but her cutting of cords creates no social barriers for her or her family. Contrasts between Muslim and Hindu behaviour with respect to childbirth pollution in Bangladesh are discussed in T. Blanchet, 1984; although Muslims describe childbirth as polluting, many poor women have no dāi and cut the cord themselves.

25. We return to the significance of these ethnic differences in Chapter 7 below.

26. Reports from elsewhere in north India suggest that Hindus normally bury the placenta in the room where the birth took place; see D. Jacobson, in N.A. Falk and R.M. Gross (eds), 1980, p.82; H. Gideon, 1962 p.1226; M.S. Luschinsky, 1962, pp.72-73; C.S. Thompson, 1984, p.275. T. Blanchet, 1984, pp.89-91, reports that all placentas are buried, but regional variations exist in whether they are buried in the house or at the edge of a field. Care must be taken to ensure that they are inaccessible, either by digging a very deep hole or by burying it within the house. In none of these accounts are differences between the treatment of a boy's and a girl's placenta discussed, nor differences by caste.

27. The labouring woman is not in control, which parallels the situation in the West, but in the West, she is also subjected to an alien medical repertoire.

28. Most discussions of midwifery in the Third World see only two potential kinds of relationships, and ignore the possibility of the inequality being loaded against the birth attendant, as here. This point is discussed further in R. Jeffery, P.M. Jeffery and A. Lyon, 1988.

29. These dāis are unusual in their assertiveness and willingness to "drum up custom" in this way, perhaps because they have been trained, are from relatively

higher social backgrounds, and are married.

30. Women who cut cords but do not accept payment (especially the Sheikh women described above) avoid some of the taint attached to carrying out the task; see also T. Blanchet, 1984, pp.145-149.

31. W.H. Wiser, 1936, is the classic source on such relationships; like most commentators, he gives much less attention to relationships involving female services. In general, we know very little about whether dāis used to have exclusive rights to serve and be paid in kind by particular families from dominant caste groups. However, E.A.H. Blunt, 1931, pp.242-243, noted that in some castes — Dhanuks and Chamars — dāis had their own clients, and a caste council might impose a fine on a dāi who delivered the baby of another dāi's client.

32. Sīdhā normally means upright, and ultā upside down; but in this usage, sīdhā means with the head down.

33. The potential of oxytocin to accelerate labour was recognised in 1909. Initially it was administered intramuscularly, but after 1949 intravenous infusion became more popular. Intramuscular usage was condemned by authoritative obstetric sources as early as 1959, because its effects are immediate and uncontrollable; see P.W. Howie, in T. Chard and M. Richards (eds), 1977, p.84. Its use in rural Bijnor dates from about 1975, roughly the same time as tetanus toxoid injections became common.

34. In 1982, only about 2% of rural and 16% of urban births — 4% combined — in Uttar Pradesh took place in hospital, maternity or nursing home or health centre; Registrar General, India, 1985, p.111.

35. These celebrations and gift exchanges are described in Chapter 6 below.

36. In the West, hospitals also offer the possibility of having pollution removed, and this apparently attracts some members of ethnic minorities and travelling women in Britain to hospital deliveries; see J. Okely, in S. Ardener (ed.), 1975. Women in Bijnor see no comparable benefits, and additionally, they fear being sterilised without being informed; see Chapters 8 and 9 below.

37. The barrage across the Ganges and the new roads connecting it with Bijnor and Meerut were not then open: the journey now takes under 2 hours by jeep.

38. This practice is described in Chapter 6 below.

39. This is a narrower definition of maternal mortality than that used in most comparative statistics, which include maternity- or abortion-related deaths occurring much later after the delivery. The small absolute numbers of maternal deaths in Dharmnagri and Jhakri make any attempt to estimate a rate very unreliable; but the experiences of these villages are not out of line with the rates listed for north India in WHO, 1986.

40. Women who die in childbirth are not normally returned to their natal villages for burial; this case reflects the very poor relationship between the woman in question and her susrāl kin.

41. See Appendix 3, Tables 6 and 7 for more details of infant and child mortality in Dharmnagri and Jhakri. The perinatal mortality rate reported for rural Uttar Pradesh in 1982 was 80 per 1,000 deliveries: Registrar-General, India, 1985. In our sample of about 1,200 live-births, stillbirths and late miscarriages (7th month or later), 86 failed to survive to the end of the first week of life, a perinatal mortality rate of 71 per 1,000.

Chapter 6

1. Balmikis, more commonly known as Bhangis, are Harijans whose hereditary occupation is sweeping and cleaning latrines.

2.   See also M.S. Luschinsky, 1962, pp.81-84; C.S. Thompson, 1984, Appendix 1; and D. Jacobson, 1975, pp.45-59, for descriptions of women singing after a birth.

3.   The details in this chapter are largely drawn from the *last pregnancy* and *nand* schedules, and observations.

4.   The classic discussion of the need to mark transitions in the life-cycle — birth, marriage and death in particular — was provided by A. van Gennep, 1st edit., 1906. He argues that rituals mark a separation from the old state, a period of danger or liminality while the person is between states, and a period when the person is aggregated to a new condition or returned (reaggregated) to the old. Birth is a classic case, since the new baby breaks the boundaries of the woman's body and introduces a new body whose arrival must be marked socially so that it can be placed and recognised. "The child is not a 'complete' member by physical birth alone; on the contrary, a child must be incorporated into its group by certain ceremonies"; H. Callaway, in S. Ardener (ed.), 1978, p.165. M. Douglas, 1966, argues that whenever boundaries are unclear or are broken, concepts of dirt and pollution are involved and social mechanisms are invoked to reorder and reassert these boundaries. For specifically south Asian material see note 21 in Chapter 5 above; and H. Orenstein, in M. Singer and B. Cohn (eds), 1968. L. Bennett, 1976, p.28 states that in Nepal, the baby's father and his close kin are also put into a state of ritual impurity by the birth. However, D. Jacobson, in N.A. Falk and R.M. Gross (eds), 1980, p.84, notes that in central Madhya Pradesh and Punjab, as in Bijnor, birth pollution only spreads by contact, not by virtue of the relationship of an individual to the woman who has given birth. See also C.S. Thompson, 1984, p.289; P. Hershman, 1974, p.285; and G. Buhler, (trans.), 1886, V57-V61.

5.   The idea that a new mother is "cold" can also be found in Spanish America as well as Sri Lanka and south India; see S. Cosminsky, and D.B. McGilvray, in C.P. MacCormack (ed.), 1982.

6.   These general patterns of gift exchanges are discussed in Chapter 2; see the references in note 49 to that chapter.

7.   B. Miller, 1981, summarises and discusses ethnographic accounts of the ways new-born boys and girls are greeted in India. In south India, few ethnographic accounts comment on any differences, whereas in north India differences are apparently universal.

8.   This conversation highlights the complexities of relationships among Muslims who can be married in their natal village and/or to cousins. Najma married her cousin (FZS); her sister was also married in Jhakri to Nisar's cousin (FBS). Here this sister's adolescent daughter is talking about her aunt (MBW) and Najma's brother's wife in Qaziwala. Mansur's sister is in a within-village marriage in Jhakri.

9.   These are probably symptoms of tetanus or of septicaemia. More extended discussions of "evil eye" beliefs can be found in C. Maloney (ed.), 1976; S.G. Singh, 1883, pp.205-210. M.S. Luschinsky, 1962, pp.84-96 and C.S. Thompson, 1984, pp.276-7 both also discuss the confinement of women after delivery in terms of the pollution attaching to mother and baby and the vulnerability of mother and baby to evil influences.

10.   A person with an amulet (tawīz) also cannot enter a house where a death has taken place for one-and-a-quarter months after the amulet is tied.

11.   The centrality of food transactions to the ideology and day-to-day practice of inter-caste relationships is classically discussed by M. Marriott, in M. Singer and B.S. Cohn (eds.), 1968, and by L. Dumont, 1972, Chapter 6.

12.   Our informants were so offended by questioning about sexual relationships that we have no reliable picture of post-partum taboos.

13. Among Muslims, a family elder whispers the call to prayer (azān) into the baby's ears before it is placed beside the mother; alternatively, the maulwī may be called from the mosque to do this task; see also M.H. Raza, 1894, pp.186-193. About Rs 15 are then paid to mosque funds, and sweets are distributed.

14. Some Hindus said that bathing on a Monday was not advisable.

15. W.S. Blunt, 1896, p.289, suggests that it is because one of the chief tasks of the dhobī (washerwoman) is to "wash the clothing of women after childbirth" that the caste is stamped as specially impure. C.S. Thompson, 1984, p.276, observes that in one part of Madhya Pradesh, the dāī refuses to wash these clothes but for most castes an older woman of the household will wash them; whereas D. Jacobson, in N.A. Falk and R.M. Gross (eds.), 1980, p.84, states that further north in the same State the washerwoman washes the dirty bedding and clothes or else they are thrown away. Blood spilt at childbirth is like highly concentrated and stagnant menstrual blood. See also L. Bennett, 1976, p.28. Women in Dharmnagri and Jhakri normally wash their own menstrual cloths and re-use them.

16. Asār, also known as Sār, is a Hindu lunar month roughly corresponding to June. M.S. Luschinsky, 1962, pp.86-108, D. Jacobson in N.A. Falk and R.M. Gross (eds), 1980, p.85, and C.S. Thompson, 1984, Chapter 6, all describe the role of women from the barber caste in a number of ceremonies after the delivery; they do not come into close contact with the jachā until the greatest pollution is over and the jachā has bathed, and the caste is not regarded as polluted by the tasks it carries out.

17. Diwālī is a Hindu festival of lights, taking place in Kartik (October).

18. In Chapter 7 we describe jachās' reports of ill-health, and in particular deal with gole-kā-dard, griping after-pains, which some said results from an excess of bādī food.

19. For other reports of post-partum feeding practices, see G.E. Ferro-Luzzi, 1974a, pp.7-15; H. Gideon, 1962, p.1230; D. Jacobson, in N.A. Falk and R.M. Gross (eds), 1980, p.83; C.S. Thompson, 1984, p.278; M.S. Luschinsky, 1962, pp.84-85; L. Bennett, 1976, pp.34, 51; D.B. McGilvray, in C.P. McCormack (ed.), 1982, p.59; T. Blanchet, 1984, pp.113-116; B.G. Prasad et al., 1969, p.52.

20. By contrast, D. Jacobson, in N.A. Falk and R.M. Gross (eds), 1980, p.83, suggests that in northern Madhya Pradesh the special post-partum foods may be expensive "but that miserly in-laws can hardly balk at providing" them.

21. Throughout south Asia women prefer not to breast-feed the new baby until the third day, and a garm drink is provided instead. See, for example, L. Visaria, 1985, p.1404; L. Bennett, 1976, p.31; C.S. Thompson, 1984, p.276; T. Blanchet, 1984, pp.112-113; K. Mahadevan et al., in K. Mahadevan (ed.), 1986, H. Gideon, 1962, p.1223. M.S. Luschinsky, 1962, p.87, notes that the Chamar dāī might suckle the baby during the first two days, in a situation where the dāī generally stayed with the jachā until the chhatī; we had no hint of this happening. O. Lewis, 1958, p.48, surprisingly states that breast-feeding begins on the same day but not immediately: birth syrup is given first, and a dūdh-dhulāi performed before the baby is given the breast. In Europe until the eighteenth century the colostrum was commonly drawn off and thrown away, and the new-born was fed honey and purgatives to help expel the meconium; see V. Fildes, 1987.

22. Cooking bovine khīs in gur helps to reduce its adverse effects, but people still take only small quantities. For a more extended discussion of the nature of breast milk in general, and the parallels with khīs in particular, in north India and south Nepal, see N. Reissland and R. Burghart, no date, unpublished paper.

23. Home-made or patent birth syrup from the market may also be fed to growing infants to treat stomach upsets, given in warm water if the child is constipated and in

cold water to treat diarrhoea.

24. These are the flat bean dolichos lablab.

25. In Punjab, this may be done by a pre-pubertal girl; see H. Gideon, 1962, pp.1228-1229; but according to S.G. Singh, 1883, this is the job of the nand. G.G. Raheja, 1988, p.95, also says that in Saharanpur District (to the west of Bijnor, across the Ganges) this ceremony is done by the nand, but there it is known as chhūchhī dhulāi. M.S. Luschinsky, 1962, p.89 reports no dūdh-dhulāi but a common practice of the mother cleaning her breasts with mustard paste or water; L. Bennett, 1976, p.31, also describes washing the breasts to make the milk come, but does not suggest that this has any other special significance.

26. For other descriptions of these ceremonies, see M.S. Luschinsky, 1962, pp.99-105; D. Jacobson, in N.A. Falk and R.M. Gross (eds), 1980, pp.85-89 (where the chhatī is called a chauk); and G.G. Raheja, 1988, pp.95-101. A different ceremony called a sūraj pūjā (sun pūjā) is described by C.S. Thompson, 1984, pp.280-286; this seems to combine the bahārī and the chhatī, and is similar to the patterns described in eastern Uttar Pradesh and Rajasthan in S.L. Srivastava, 1971, pp.181-196. Jasthawn is the commoner local pronunciation, but according to J.T. Platts, 1st. edit. 1885, p.517, it is the dasūthan, from das (ten) and ūthnā (getting up), and is the jachā's bath on the 10th day after delivery.

27. If P. Hershman, 1974, is correct, this may mark the time after which the woman can resume sexual relations with her husband without polluting him, but we have no indication of this.

28. When a woman gives birth in her natal village, these rituals take different forms, since the nand is not present, and news of a birth (particularly of a first-born or a son) must be sent immediately to her susrāl; see M.S. Luschinsky, 1962, pp.94-99. The basic principles of gift-giving remain those created by continuing obligations to married daughters and sisters and their susrāl kin.

29. These rituals may also be held rapidly if the jachā is sick or has no helper; see Chapter 7 below.

30. M.S. Luschinsky, 1962, pp.95-99 also describes sending news to the wife's parents and how they respond by preparing gifts for the jachā, her baby and her affinal kin. See also D. Jacobson, in N.A. Falk and R.M. Gross (eds), 1980, p.90. G.G. Raheja, 1988, pp.99-100, gives chhūchhak as the term in use among Hindus, and says the word is derived from a word for breast, chhūchhī.

31. The pressure to increase the expense of gifts at childbirth parallels the increased pressure to give generously in the dowry.

32. The size of a bīghā is not standard throughout India. See Glossary.

33. However, Pushpa's parents had paid for her medical treatment during her pregnancy, which also generated a lot of hostility among her susrāl kin.

34. G.G. Raheja, 1988, discusses in detail the distinctions between neg and other giving (especially dān), and suggests that neg does not transfer inauspiciousness to others (unlike some of the payments made to the dāi after a delivery). For the purpose of neg the married nand is still regarded as a member of the jachā's husband's kin group. In other settings and for different gift-giving, she may be regarded as a member of her husband's kin group, and therefore "other" and an appropriate channel for removing inauspiciousness from her natal family.

35. This may be related to the concerns described in note 34 above; we did not discuss the distinctions between the different kinds of gifts noted by Raheja, but a feeling that the nand should take away inauspiciousness may have motivated nands to prefer jewellery from the jachā's natal village. Alternatively, nands might be expressing their competition with their brother's wife, and a desire to reduce the

burden on their own parents.

36.   Contacts between Lakshmi and her nand were non-existent because of a feud; see note 23, Chapter 5.

37.   Son preferences are discussed further in Chapter 8 below.

38.   These abusive terms stress the lowest positions to which women can fall. A widow has outlived her husband, and a co-wife is a woman's arch-rival; both positions suggest that she has failed in her wifely duties. Widows are also suspected of being forced (or choosing) to become prostitutes, which is made explicit in the quote below.

39.   D. Jacobson, 1975, pp.55-56 and C.S. Thompson, 1984, pp.392-393 also cite birth songs in which the jachā weeps over the way her susrāl kin continually demand money for the various services they render after a birth. Sanwāliyā is a term often used of Lord Krishna, so a woman using this word is referring to her husband as a God. Like many birth songs, this is difficult to translate because the words often have several meanings. For example, "luchchī" has connotations of wanton licentiousness but also of tight-fistedness. "Bhārū" is a term of abuse which strictly means pimp or cuckold, but it is used in much the same way as "bastard" is in English.

40.   These are not Hindu shrines to immolated widows, but to devoted wives. These sites are associated with good-luck signs (sathiyā), and are also visited by new brides in Dharmnagri.

41.   Women who are normally very prudish and will only hint at sexual activities may dance and display such explicit sexuality in a number of women-only settings, for example after the men from a groom's family have left to collect a bride. See D. Jacobson, 1975, pp.56-57; and P.M. Jeffery, 1979, p.95.

42.   In Dharmnagri, after a boy's birth, a well ritual (kūa pūjā) may be carried out. This domestic ritual is very varied in content and timing, and does not involve gift-giving. The jachā should not draw water for family use until it has been performed. See also C.S. Thompson, 1984, pp.301-305 for a discussion of the parallels between this ritual and one during the marriage celebrations. Water symbolically links the fertility of the soil and the fertility of a woman, as well as being a medium which cleanses and cools.

43.   Only Muslims practise male circumcision; no ethnic group practises female circumcision.

44.   L. Dube, 1988, pp.WS-11 to WS-19, refers to this and to the effects on girls' socialisation of songs and lullabies that stress the unluckiness of being a girl.

45.   More detail on these deaths can be found in Appendix 3, Tables 6 and 7. Registrar-General, India, 1985, p.110, reports higher rates for rural Uttar Pradesh in 1982, with stillbirths and neonatal mortality accounting for about one in nine (114 per 1,000) births, compared with the Dharmnagri and Jhakri figures derived from maternity histories (and therefore going back much further in time) of one in twelve (81 per 1000). The differences might reflect problems of recall among our informants, but they could result from the greater wealth of Bijnor, compared with central and eastern Uttar Pradesh. In an analysis of nearly 20,000 births in Bangladesh in 1966-1970, A.K.M.A. Chowdhury, 1981, also reports little variation in neonatal mortality by sex and class.

46.   For other examples, see P. Chowdhury, 1987, pp.2060-2066. "Ūt" means sonless and also has connotations of being a blockhead or useless.

47.   On the basis of a study in eastern Uttar Pradesh, G.B. Simmons et al., 1982, pp.371-389; and C.M. Smucker et al., 1980, pp.321-335, report much higher levels of tetanus mortality than we found. One crucial difference seems to be the choice of dressings for the cut end of the umbilical cord: a mixture of ash and cow-dung was more commonly reported there than in Bijnor.

Chapter 7

1. Most other ethnographic accounts merely state the ideal position, and give no hint of how far this is met in practice, nor who actually takes over the jachā's responsibilities. For example, for material on Muslims in West Bengal, see L. Fruzetti, in I. Ahmad (ed.), 1981, p.102; on Muslims in Bangladesh, T. Blanchet, 1984, p.99. For Punjab, H. Gideon, 1962, pp.1231-2, refers only to a woman who has delivered in her natal village, and thus does not have to fulfil her susrāl obligations. D. Jacobson, in N.A. Falk and R.M. Gross (eds), 1980, p.89, notes a graded reintroduction to work responsibilities, with women permitted many routine tasks after a week to ten days, but not cooking until the end of 40 days; she does not, however, discuss variations from these norms. In our preliminary research, people's first responses also referred to standard observances of sawā mahīnā, or five weeks, but more detailed questioning of the key informants revealed a more complex picture. The material for this chapter is largely drawn from the *nand, chūlhā* and *last pregnancy* schedules; for details see Appendix 1.

2. Here we are largely concerned with women's views about their entitlements and how far these are met in practice, rather than to compare them with what Western medicine currently holds to be best. In any case, what might be relevant for well nourished European or north American women cannot be applied unthinkingly to women whose workloads and nutritional status are so very different.

3. We refer to the occasional exceptions later in this chapter.

4. Muslims call these gifts "chīllā badalnā", the 40th-day exchange.

5. Because these visits prevent sexual intercourse, they might have some effect on the timing of the jachā's next conception; O. Lewis, 1958, p.48, even suggests that such visits are arranged "to avoid conceiving too soon", but they were never explained to us in those terms, and the jachā is normally back in her susrāl before the separation could have much effect.

6. See note 49 to Chapter 2 for further discussion of menstrual pollution and its effects.

7. See Chapters 2 and 3 above for discussions of the structural tensions between a woman and her brother's wife, and the differences between the expectations of a woman with respect to her observances of purdah and to her work in her natal village and in her susrāl.

8. G.G. Raheja, 1988, p.216, reports a saying that when neg is involved, everyone fights for their own rights and may ask for specific items.

9. Although the sex of the baby was a major factor for Hindus in deciding whether or not to call the nand, someone else would usually help out if the nand did not come. Among Muslims, however, the sex of the baby had a greater impact on how much help the jachā received from any helper.

10. Rohtash's sister's husband was sterilised in 1976, so Rohtash's sister has not been pregnant herself recently, which might otherwise have helped to explain her lack of assistance.

11. Ishwar Das himself would not eat food cooked by his virgin daughter and he made his own food. The daughter cooked for Imarti and the other children.

12. To be pregnant after one's daughter or, especially, one's son is married, or to be a "pregnant grandmother" is a sharm-kī-bāt; the effects of this, and cases of women who were exceptions to this rule, are discussed further in Chapter 8.

13. Maqsudi's pregnancy was discussed in more detail in Chapter 4 above.

14. Since most marriages are of couples from roughly the same economic

background, the jachā and her nand are likely to have similar work obligations. Thus the jachā in most need of help is likely to have a nand who can be spared from her own susrāl only with great difficulty.

15.   A common response was "ten-fifteen days", or a formulaic "fifteen days" and for less recent births we had to be satisfied with estimates like this.

16.   Similar differences were indicated by the survey.

17.   In Chapter 2 above we noted how some Muslim women are easily called back by their susrāl kin, and tend to make only short visits as a result.

18.   As pregnancy is not a polluting state, the compulsion to protect others from the effects of pollution are absent, and women cannot achieve the rest they feel they deserve in late pregnancy, as we discussed in Chapter 4 above.

19.   T. Blanchet, 1984, pp.105-112, is one of the few authors to have compared Muslim and Hindu birth practices in the same area; however, she concentrates on the ritual observances and celebrations, and says little about women's work obligations.

20.   We tried several ways to collect information on "post-natal depression", both as a short-term period of misery and as a longer-term psychiatric illness. We asked individual women when we took their maternity histories, and we asked more generally, looking for a folk category to explain unusual behaviour of women after giving birth. None of these methods generated substantial results; but we cannot be sure that such disorders were absent.

21.   The aetiology and nature of post-natal depression are contested issues. Of those who stress the role played by women's isolation and loss of social support in pregnancy and in the post-natal period, A. Oakley, 1979 provides an eloquent example. G.W. Brown and T.O. Harris, 1978, in a more restrained analysis based on a larger sample and a sophisticated battery of tests and scores, suggest that (among other factors) heavy domestic responsibilities, indicated by having young children to look after, and lack of social support, from husband, mother, or in the form of employment outside the home, contribute strongly to the chances of depressive disorder for married women in London. Other writers, mainly medical scientists, stress the role of hormones associated with post-partum changes, or genetic factors in the creation of depression.

22.   For more detail, see Registrar-General, India, 1985. The differential in mortality rates by sex is greatest among young adults, but in absolute numbers of deaths, excess female mortality is largely accounted for by infant and child deaths. Female mortality rates are above those of men until the age-band 45-49 in Uttar Pradesh. In those Indian States where women have fewer children and stop having them at an earlier age than Uttar Pradesh, the cross-over point to excess male mortality comes much earlier, for instance at the 25-29 age-band in Kerala and Tamil Nadu. Women in these States also tend to be better educated and to be less subject to harrassment over dowry; "accidental" deaths and "suicides" contribute heavily to urban death rates of young married women in north India; see M. Karkal, 1985a, p.1424.

23.   See Appendix 1 for more detail on the limitations of our data on women's time-use. In general, childcare can be combined with these women's work obligations (though at a cost to the mother and child that we deal with in the next section), in part because so few women have any paid employment. Further, their field-work and other outside-work is usually done close to home.

24.   We came across no infants being fed with milk reconstituted from milk powder or baby formula. Such milk is prohibitively expensive; in local terms, it is also regarded as inferior to breast-milk or to a feed based on cow or buffalo milk. For a more extended discussion of the nature of breast-milk in north India and southern

Nepal, see N. Reissland and R. Burghart, no date, mimeographed.

25. Breast-milk alone is an inadequate diet for a baby over the age of nine months, though it provides a hygienic and nourishing source of fluid where the water supply is easily contaminated. But young children also need additional water in hot weather, and rarely receive it. "Weanling diarrhoea" is a major cause of death of young children aged between one and three years old; see M. Karkal, 1985b, pp.1835-37; and G. Donoso, 1979, pp.103-113. See also our discussion in Chapter 4 above.

26. We collected the maternity histories of all ever-married women in the two villages in 1985; see Appendix 1 for more detail on this material, summarised in Appendix 3, Tables 4-8. One of the weakest parts of our data on maternity careers is the gaps between deliveries: many women gave standard answers, saying that all their children came two years, or three years, etc., after the previous one. We attempted to use season of birth as a check, but women frequently could not tell us this. We therefore often had to estimate gaps between deliveries, using other information, such as the age of the youngest child, or the age at which older children were married.

27. A longer discussion of child mortality is provided in Chapter 8 below; see also the tables in Appendix 3.

28. Ethnic differences in relationships with Government health services are discussed further in Chapters 8 and 9 below.

Chapter 8

1. Many discussions of decision-making on matters of fertility in rural India exist: early classics are T. Poffenberger, 1969; and J.F. Marshall, 1972. See also J. Caldwell et al., 1982, pp.689-727.

2. Literature surveys which stress the significance of cultural factors in fertility, and the role of small-scale research projects in uncovering the processes behind large-scale demographic analyses, include T.H. Hull, and R.A. Levine and S.C.M. Scrimshaw, in R.A. Bulatao and R.D. Lee (eds), 1983; R. Anker et al. (eds), 1981; D.P. Warwick, 1988, pp. 1-18.

3. Accounts of the Indian family planning programme's development can be found in D. Banerji, 1971; N. Demerath, 1976; R. Cassen, 1978; A. Mitra, 1978; R. Ledbetter, 1984, pp.736-758; and K. Srinivasan, 1983, pp.7-25.

4. Data used in this chapter come largely from the general *maternity histories* for all the ever-married women in the two villages; *last pregnancy* schedules; *1985 schedules*; and the men's *family-building* schedules.

5. North Indian demographic patterns are well summarised by T. Dyson and M. Moore, 1983, pp.35-60.

6. More general discussions of trends in mortality and fertility in India can be found in P.N. Mari Bhat et al., 1984; and J.R. Rele, 1987, pp.513-30. In Bijnor, mortality rates which are higher for females than for males contribute to the sex ratios referred to in Chapter 3 and discussed further below; see also Appendix 3, Tables 6-8.

7. Since our numbers are small, these and other demographic rates quoted in this chapter are subject to quite wide statistical margins of error, and should all be interpreted cautiously. The Crude Birth Rate is the number of live-births occuring in a twelve-month period, divided by the total population, and expressed as a rate per 1,000 population. More detailed fertility information is provided in Appendix 3, Tables 4 and 5.

8. Evidence to support the argument that some female births are missing from our maternity histories comes from comparing the reported sex ratio at birth (115 males per 100 females) to the predicted maximum rate (108 to 110 males per 100 females).

The disparity may be accounted for by female births which are not reported if the girl then died at or soon after birth; see B. Miller, 1981. Using data from Karimpur, in Mainpuri District (south-west Uttar Pradesh), S. Wadley and B. Derr, 1986, report a sex ratio at birth of 112 and locate sex ratios more adverse to females among certain castes and for the "struggling poor", especially for women in their 40s and 50s. These patterns are not reflected in our Bijnor data.

9.   We have not attempted a full analysis of the proximate determinants of fertility, since we do not have reliable information on all the relevant variables. Here we select only those where our material suggests some differences in social behaviour which might affect overall fertility. See J. Bongaarts, 1978, pp.105-132.

10.   The wish to avoid being a "pregnant grandmother" is described in D.G. Mandelbaum, 1974, pp.29-33.

11.   Average reported ages at marriage in the two villages as a whole have risen from 15.0 for women born in the 1940s to 16.2 for those born in the 1960s. Age at cohabitation has remained almost stationary at 16 years or so. Mean gaps from cohabitation to first conception for these same cohorts have declined from 2.6 years to 1.8 years respectively.

12.   The 1971 census reported 252 people living in Jhakri, compared to 393 in 1985, a 56% rise over the 14 year period, just under 3% per year. Unfortunately, the census division for Dharmnagri includes the Bengali colony with the same name, so we cannot calculate population growth rates there for the same period. Migration, the third factor in population changes, is more difficult to assess, but between our village censuses of April 1982 and September 1985, 34 people emigrated and 24 immigrated, including those women moving in or out on marriage, reducing overall population growth in the two villages by about 1%.

13.   The main reported causes of death for children under the age of 5 were fever (43), evil spirits (20), tetanus (18), diarrhoea (17), typhoid (motī jārā) (14), smallpox (13) and pneumonia (11). In addition, 15 were said to have died suddenly, for no apparent reason.

14.   More detail on young child mortality can be found in Appendix 3, Table 8.

15.   Most of these deaths were of girls; the sex differential in mortality is discussed further below. Since some of these children could still have died before reaching their fifth birthday, these deaths are not final totals.

16.   For further details, see Appendix 3, Table 8.

17.   As noted below, however, since 1980 a gap has apparently opened in Dharmnagri between women from classes II and III and those from classes IV and V; but this picture could be changed by mortality since 1985. A relative lack of class differentials in child mortality rates since 1971 is also reported by S. Wadley and B. Derr, July 1986. They note, however, that mother's education is closely correlated with lower mortality rates, a finding also shown for the whole of rural Uttar Pradesh in Registrar-General, India, 1983. Although more high class women are likely to be educated, very few have as many as five years of schooling, and this factor thus has little impact on class variations, in Uttar Pradesh generally as well as in Dharmnagri and Jhakri.

18.   Classic examples of the argument that young children have an economic value that helps to explain high levels of fertility are B. White, in M. Nag (ed.), 1975; M. Nag et al., 1978, pp.293-301; M. Vlassoff, 1982, pp.45-60; and M. Cain, 1977, pp.201-227. M. Mamdani, 1972, argues that villagers are economically rational to want many children, and stresses the longer-term benefits derived from adult children. The restatement of demographic transition theory in J. Caldwell, 1982, also hinges on a shift from a situation in which children provide net benefits for their parents to one

where they become net costs.

19. This argument is sometimes described as the "old-age security hypothesis". See a recent debate on its significance in India, M. Vlassoff and C. Vlassoff, 1980, pp.487-499; J.B. Nugent, 1985, pp.75-97.

20. M. Mamdani, 1972, in his classic discussion of the economic benefits from high fertility, tends to fall into the trap of using the demand for several sons to explain large families. What this might mean for the excess daughters born is discussed by M. Das Gupta, 1987, pp.77-100.

21. One of our research assistants is unmarried. This was a cause of great comment in Dharmnagri and Jhakri, for people said that parents of an unmarried village girl would be severely criticised for "eating her earnings", using terms which connote living like a pimp off a prostitute. See the discussion in D.G. Mandelbaum, 1974, p.18. The kinship patterns described in Chapter 2 above help to explain people's desire to be in a position to continue to give to one's daughter and not be forced to take from her.

22. The problems that Mamdani's respondents had in obtaining economic benefits from their sons emerged from a repeat survey, reported by M. Nag and N. Kak, 1984, pp.661-678.

23. D.G. Mandelbaum, 1974, pp.21-23, interprets the religious comfort provided to a man who has a son to carry out memorial rites on his behalf as "a sure means of prolonging something of one's self beyond the mortal span." He does not discuss how women achieve the same goal.

24. As this discussion suggests, labour-saving technology is not considered an alternative strategy: these peasants are not rich enough to invest in a level of technology which would markedly reduce their labour needs. The rich peasants in our sample all had only young sons: some older men in roughly similar economic positions were using their sons to diversify, e.g. establishing a shawl weaving factory, working cane-crushers, or leasing and harvesting guava or mango orchards.

25. Of the three other rich peasant informants, Chet Ram was not asked with the others in 1985 because Chandresh had died in 1984; Ahmad's answer stressed the problems of having children at all, because Asghari was sick with T.B. and he had only one child; and Bashir was one of our most unforthcoming respondents and refused to answer questions of this kind, though since Bilquis had had 12 children (two stillborn) by 1985 we can guess his likely answer.

26. An alternative possible route to security is through education and urban employment, but few in Dharmnagri and Jhakri have any reason to believe that they or their children will succeed in this. Even the most educated young men (with B.A. and B.Comm. degrees) cannot find permanent urban employment and are still living in the village, working on the land. Where urban opportunities are greater and educational levels higher, people may express their desire for fewer children in different terms: compare J.C. Caldwell et al. 1982, pp.36-60; and S.S. Wadley and B. Derr, 1986.

27. Latifan subsequently had a stillbirth.

28. For some men, "children" equal "sons"; see the quote from Ashok above. Men often list their sons first, in descending order of age, and then their daughters afterwards. Since men are also often hazy about the ages of their children, it is sometimes difficult to get a coherent picture of birth orders from them.

29. Calculations of the economic value of an unmarried girl's work are thus beside the point: a girl is there, so it is better if she can do something useful, but noone would consider economic benefit a reason for having a daughter. Similar arguments apply for sons, though with less force. R. Cassen, 1976, pp.33-70, also argues that one must distinguish ex ante from ex post rationality when it comes to fertility decision-making.

30.   Rakshā bandan is a Hindu festival when sisters tie protective threads around their brothers' wrists to wish them long life, to express a sacred and mutually protective relationship; see also S.S. Wadley in N. Falk and R. Gross (eds), 1980, pp.94-109.

31.   The exception is if there are no brothers and the sister is in a ghar-jamāi marriage; but only an elder sister may give.

32.   D.G. Mandelbaum, 1974, p.22, notes that giving a daughter in marriage is less important than raising a son, but still "of high religious merit". As he points out, however, surrogates are possible, and rarely do people let the chance of such merit make a significant difference to their fertility behaviour. G.G. Raheja, 1988, emphasises the out-married daughter's role as a channel for the removal of inauspiciousness from her natal kin: no one in Dharmnagri spoke in these terms as a reason for having a daughter.

33.   This is in line with other surveys of ideal family size in India; see, for example, J.C. Bhatia, 1978, pp.3-16. There are many problems with asking questions of this kind: people may give the answer they think the questioner expects or wants to hear, rather than think hard about hypothetical situations; see, for example, D.G. Mandelbaum, 1974, p.14; L. Stone and J.G. Campbell, 1984, pp.27-37. We did not ask such questions at all on our first visit, but waited until 1985 when we think we were not identified in any way with the Government family planning programme. However, some answers may have been coloured by our respondents' knowledge of Patricia's maternity history.

34.   The argument that increasing chances of child survival will reduce levels of fertility has been discussed in many places, and underlies the original understanding of "the demographic transition": see S.H. Preston (ed.), 1978. The reverse argument — that contraception will help reduce mortality rates — is challenged by J. Bongaarts, 1987, pp.323-334.

35.   Possibly from asthma or pneumonia.

36.   D.G. Mandelbaum, 1974, p.22, discusses some of the problems of interpreting answers such as "It is in God's hands", or "It is God's will" to questions about fertility limitation. Such answers may mean that respondents feel they have no knowledge or power to act, or are afraid to do so.

37.   " 'No sons beget many children' is an apt popular saying." D.G. Mandelbaum, 1974, p.18.

38.   Sabra's aborted second pregnancy was a boy: see further below.

39.   M. Nag and N. Kak, 1984, pp.661-678, note that similar points were made by Punjabi respondents who had not foreseen the effects of their large number of sons on their landholdings.

40.   These remedies are well-known in north India, with local variations, and have been discussed on the woman's pages of local newspapers. For other discussions of theories of how the sex of the foetus is determined, see S.B. Mani, in G.R. Gupta (ed.), 1981, and D.B. McGilvray, in C.P. MacCormack (ed.), 1981. Tightening the strings on a bed at dusk was the only technique we encountered for obtaining a girl.

41.   For the argument that high levels of infant mortality among infants of either sex may result from high levels of fertility, through conscious or subconscious mechanisms at the family level, see S. Scrimshaw, 1978, pp.383-404. An account of the logical extreme — female infanticide — and its history in north India is in B. Miller, 1981. See also T. Dyson and M. Moore, 1983, pp.35-60; S.S.Wadley and B. Derr, 1986; and M. Das Gupta, 1987, pp.77-100.

42.   The differential is probably greater than it appears because some female babies who died rapidly are likely to have been omitted by women.

43.   This is what B. Miller, 1981, predicts, but she excludes Muslims from her

discussion.

44. M. Das Gupta, 1987, pp.77-100, shows that, in her sample, girls with elder sisters are more vulnerable than those without.

45. For a well-documented report on these differentials, see L.C. Chen et al., 1981, pp.55-70; see also A. Sen and S. Sengupta, 1983, pp.855-62.

46. M.S. Luschinsky, 1962, p.82, reports a similar ambivalence to baby girls: "One day this Thakur woman held her baby granddaughter up in the air and said 'Now she should die. I tell her she should die.' Often when she thought of the consequences of another female member of the family she spoke in this way, but always in her personal relations with the baby she was loving and affectionate."

47. In a village near Delhi, none of the 65 male and 39 female respondents said that their mother was an ideal or actual person to be consulted concerning family planning decisions: S.B. Mani, 1973, pp.10-19.

48. S.B. Mani, 1973, pp.10-19, notes that the mother-in-law was consulted by one-sixth of the Gujar women, but by no one else.

49. As in most developing countries, illegal abortions are presumed to be very common: one estimate for India is of 6 million per year, and between 6,000 and 60,000 associated deaths, giving an idea of both the scale of the problem and the level of ignorance about it: *Population Reports*, 1980, Series F, no. 7, pp.110, 135. For discussions on attitudes towards abortion and the role of dāis in this, see J.C. Bhatia, 1973, pp.275-285; and S. Islam, 1981.

50. Abortion has been legalised in India as Medical Termination of Pregnancy since 1972, but only registered medical practitioners are legally permitted to do abortions, and then only in specified circumstances; see further below.

51. See the recent surveys of the Indian family planning programme listed in note 3 above.

52. The latent authoritarianism in the Indian family planning programme is discussed in M. Vicziany, 1983, pp.373-401 and pp.557-592.

53. The impact of family planning coercion on the 1977 election is discussed in D. Gwatkin, 1979, pp.29-59.

54. Discussions of perceptions of nasbandī by men and women include J. Pettigrew, 1984, pp.995-1002.

55. Muslim unwillingness to be sterilised was cited by some of our Hindu informants as grounds for Hindus not using contraception, though we have no evidence that such considerations affected any individual's behaviour. For a discussion of the role of family planning in communal hostility, see T.P. Wright, in W.C. McCready (ed.), 1983, pp.405-427.

56. We are not condoning this deception, though we would point out that workers are under great pressure to meet their targets. Most Muslim women sterilised in this way are 35 or older.

57. There is widespread ignorance about the mechanisms of sterilisation, as well as of other contraceptive methods, in the West also.

58. We collected detailed information on family sizes reported by men and women being sterilised in two local Primary Health Centres: see R. Jeffery and P.M. Jeffery, 1984, pp.1207-1212.

59. For these reasons, we almost certainly under-counted abortions among the women in Dharmnagri and Jhakri.

60. The male family planning worker was a Bengali, and most of his clients came from the neighbouring Bengali colonies.

61. Women might be attracted to implants or injectables because they can be administered without a husband's knowledge; but these methods would probably be

unacceptable as they interfere with normal menstruation. However, there are many criticisms of the long-term health effects of these contraceptive methods and of the ways they have been introduced in India, let alone elsewhere. See, for example, V. Balasubrahmanyan, 1984, p.371; P. Prakash, 1986, pp.733-34; and B. Sadasivam, 1986, pp.1886-87.

62.   The high level of dissatisfaction with IUDs was a major cause of slow progress in the family planning programme in the early 1970s.

63.   The dangers of the contraceptive pill have been much discussed in the West; they are likely to be much greater where medical check-ups are rare, when women start using the pill at a young age, and when many women are anaemic and undernourished.

64.   Government propaganda is resisted, and its rationale is often irrelevant to the perceived needs of the villagers; but the information it provides about available methods and the possibility of family limitation has had much greater impact.

Chapter 9

1.   Indian Government health policy statements are most easily accessible in the Plan documents: see, for example, Government of India, 1985. Discussions of the assumptions behind these Plans, and how far they have been implemented, can be found in R. Jeffery, 1988; A. Bose, 1988; and M. Chatterjee, 1988.

2.   The health service infrastructure is much better developed and health staff are better trained and motivated in Kerala and Tamil Nadu, in south India, and in West Bengal, than in what A. Bose, 1988, calls BIMARU, the "sick" region of north India comprising Bihar, Madhya Pradesh, Rajasthan and Uttar Pradesh.

3.   This pattern of inadequate development of women's health services is documented in K.G. Rao and S. Kumar, no date, and discussed in R. Jeffery, 1988, and M. Chatterjee, 1988.

4.   Another indicator of the priority given to achieving family planning targets is that family planning has been part of the "Twenty-Point Programme" of the Government of India first under Mrs Gandhi and latterly under Rajiv Gandhi. Figures of sterilisations carried out and IUDs inserted have to be collected very rapidly and sent to New Delhi to appear on the Prime Minister's desk every month.

5.   Rural health services in general have been based on the concept of the health centre, but the medical training offered to obstetricians has been almost entirely carried out in large hospitals. "Community obstetrics" is almost unknown; most obstetricians see their contribution to rural provision as getting high risk labouring women into hospitals to deliver.

6.   S. Zurbrigg, 1984, describes how patients are forced to suffer rude, threatening treatment from hospital staff if they want treatment in Tamil Nadu.

7.   The classic criticisms can be found in K. Newell (ed.), 1975, and in V. Djukanovich and E.P. Mach (eds), 1975; see also J. B. Srivastav, 1975, and V. Ramalingaswami, 1980. Anthropological critiques stressing the social and cultural distance between health staff and patients include chapters in G.R. Gupta (ed.), 1981, by M. Nichter and by K. van der Veen.

8.   Traditional birth attendants have been used for many years in Third World countries for the delivery of family planning services: a full survey appeared in Population Reports, Series J, no.22, 1980.

9.   For surveys of the achievements of voluntary sector community health projects in India, see M. Hardiman, in T. Dyson and N. Crook (eds), 1984; D.R. Gwatkin et al., 1980; and R. Faruqee and E. Johnson, 1982.

10.   Several studies of dāi training programmes in north Indian States report

conditions very similar to those we found in Bijnor; see, for example, B.C. Ghosal et al., no date; A. Kumar et al., 1982; and G. Narayana and J. Acharya, 1981; H.S. Gandhi and R. Sapru, 1980.

11.   This history is discussed in P.M. Jeffery, R. Jeffery and A. Lyon, in H. Afshar (ed.), 1987.

12.   In a sense, the Government has admitted its own failures in its 1983 Statement of National Health Policy (available as a pamphlet from the Foundation for Research in Community Health, Bombay).

13.   One discussion with specific relevance to tropical maternal and child health services is G.J. Ebrahim, 1985.

14.   Aspects of these nutrition programmes as they affect children are discussed in C. Gopalan and M. Chatterjee, 1985; for effects on maternal nutrition, see C. Gopalan, 1985, pp.159-166.

15.   Government nutrition programmes, and their limitations, are discussed in R. Cassen, 1978.

16.   B. Rogers, 1980; C.P. White and K. Young (eds), 1984.

17.   M. Chatterjee, no date, suggests that the use women make of health services depends in part on the availability of services, but as crucially on the way in which their health "needs" are limited by the fact that they must obtain permission to use services and be able to do so.

18.   Health policy and its implementation in India is discussed in R. Jeffery, 1988.

19.   The weakness of sociological analysis in WHO documents is discussed in J. Justice, 1986.

20.   Women's self-help groups in India are discussed in D. Jain (ed.), 1980.

21.   This is because the chances of infant mortality are raised if the mother is under 19 or over 40, if the birth is of parity five or over, and if a birth follows rapidly after another.

22.   The shift to "higher quality mothering" is sometimes held to explain why the time spent on childcare has not declined much in China, despite the one-child policy and the emphasis there on releasing women to take up more productive roles; see, for example, J. Robinson, 1985. For similar material from urban south Asia, see U. Sharma, 1986, and H. Papanek, in H. Papanek and G. Minault (eds), 1982. Rural women may also be withdrawn from field-work as much because of the increasing demands of animal husbandry, hospitality etc., as because of considerations of family honour.

23.   For discussions of the use of amniocentesis in India to select female foetuses for abortion, and the likely impact on women's positions, see A. Ramanamma and U. Bhambawala, 1980, pp.107-110; D. Kumar, 1983, pp.61-64; and L. Dube, 1983, pp.279-80.

24.   A similar argument is made by C.S. Thompson, 1985, pp.701-711.

Bibliography

Afshar, H. (ed.), 1987, *Women, State and Ideology*, Macmillan, London.

Agarwal, B., 1986a, 'Women, Poverty and Agricultural Growth in India', *Journal of Peasant Studies*, vol.13, pp.165-220.

Agarwal, B., 1986b, 'Women, Land Rights and the Household in India', unpublished paper given to the European Modern South Asian Studies Conference, Heidelberg, 1986.

Ahmad, I. (ed.), 1976, *Family, Kinship and Marriage among Muslims in India*, Manohar, Delhi.

Ahmad, I. (ed.), 1981, *Ritual and Religion Among Muslims in India*, Manohar, Delhi.

Ahmad, R., 1987, 'Changing Marriage Transactions and Rise of Demand System in Bangladesh', *Economic and Politicial Weekly*, vol.XXII, pp.WS-2 to WS-26.

Anker, R., M. Buvinic & N.H. Youssef (eds),1982, *Women's Roles and Population Trends in the Third World*, Croom Helm, London.

Anon, 1984, 'Dowry Amendment Bill: Another toothless legislation', *Economic and Political Weekly*, vol.XIX, pp.1609-1610.

Anstey, V., 1936, *The Economic Development of India*, Longmans Green, London.

Appadorai, A., 1981, 'Gastropolitics in Hindu South Asia', *American Ethnologist*, vol.8, pp.494-511.

Ardener, S. (ed.), 1975, *Perceiving Women*, Malaby Press, London.

Ardener, S. (ed.), 1978, *Defining Females*, Croom Helm, London.

Balasubrahmanyan, V., 'Mass Use of Injectable Contraceptive', *Economic and Political Weekly*, vol.XIX, no.9, 1984, p.371.

Banerji, D., 1971, *Family Planning in India*, People's Publishing House, New Delhi.

Banerji, D., 1985, *Health and Family Planning Services in India*, Lok Paksh, New Delhi.

Bardhan, K. , 1985, 'Women's Work, Welfare and Status: Forces of Tradition and Change in India', *Economic and Political Weekly*, vol.XX, pp.2207-2217.

Barrett, M., 1984, 'Rethinking Women's Oppression: a reply to Brenner and Ramas', *New Left Review*, no.146, pp.123- 128.

Becker, H., 1963, *Outsiders*, Free Press, New York.

Beechey, V., 1979, 'On Patriarchy', *Feminist Review*, vol.3, pp.66-82.

Beneria, L. (ed.), 1982, *Women and Development: The Sexual Division of Labor in Rural Societies*, Praeger, New York.

Beneria, L. & G. Sen, 1981, 'Accumulation, Reproduction and Women's Role in Economic Development: Boserup Revisited', *Signs*, vol.7, no.2, pp.279-298.

Bennett, L., 1976, 'Sex and Motherhood Among the Brahmins and Chhetris of East-central Nepal', *Contributions to Nepalese Studies*, vol.3, pp.1-51.

Bennett, L., 1983, *Dangerous Wives and Sacred Sisters: Social and Symbolic Roles of High-caste Women in Nepal*, Columbia University Press, New York.

Berreman, G.D., 1972, *Hindus of the Himalayas*, California University Press, Berkeley.

Bhatia, J.C., 1973, 'Abortionists and Abortion-seekers', *Indian Journal of Social Work*, vol.34, pp.275-285.

Bhatia, J.C., 1978, 'Ideal Number and Sex Preference of Children in India', *Journal of Family Welfare*, vol.24, pp.3-16.

Blanchet, T., 1984, *Women, Pollution and Marginality: Meanings and Rituals of Birth in Rural Bangladesh*, University Press, Dhaka.

Blunt, E.A.H., 1931, *The Caste System of Northern India*, 1969 reprint edit., S.Chand, New Delhi,

Bongaarts, J., 1978, 'A Framework for Analyzing the Proximate Determinants of Fertility', *Population and Development Review*, vol.4, pp.105-132.

Bongaarts, J., 1987, 'Does Family Planning Reduce Infant Mortality Rates?', *Population and Development Review*, vol.13, pp.323-334.

Bose, A., 1988, *From Population to People*, B.R. Publications, Delhi.

Brenner, J. & M. Ramas, 1984, 'Rethinking Women's Oppression', *New Left Review*, no.144, pp.33-71.

Brown, G.W. & T.O. Harris, 1978, *Social Origins of Depression: A Study of Psychiatric Disorder in Women*, Macmillan, London.

Boserup, E., 1970, *Woman's Role in Economic Development*, St. Martin's Press, New York.

Buhler, G. (translator), 1886, *The Laws of Manu*, Oxford University Press, Oxford.

Bulatao, R.A. & R.D. Lee (eds), 1983, *Determinants of Fertility in Developing Countries*, 2 vols., Academic Press, New York and London.

Buvinic, M., M.A. Lycette, & W.P. McGreevey (eds), 1983, *Women and Poverty in the Third World*, The Johns Hopkins University Press, Baltimore and London.

Byres, T.J. & B. Crow, 1985, *The Green Revolution in India*, Open University Press, Milton Keynes.

Cain, M, 1977, 'The Economic Activities of Children in a Village in Bangladesh', *Population and Development Review*, vol.3, pp.201-227.

Cain, M., 1981, 'Risk and Insurance: Perspectives on Fertility and Agrarian Change in India and Bangladesh', *Population and Development Review*, vol.7, no.3, pp.435-474.

Cain, M. et al., 1979, 'Class, Patriarchy and Women's Work in Bangladesh', *Population and Development Review*, vol.5, no.3, pp.405-38.

Caldwell, J., 1982, *Theory of Fertility Decline*, Academic Press, London.

Caldwell, J.C., P.H. Reddy & P. Caldwell, 1982, 'The Causes of Demographic Change in South India', *Population and Development Review*, vol.8, pp.689-727.

Caldwell, J.C. et al., 1985, 'Educational Transition in South India', *Population and Development Review*, vol.11, pp.29-51.

Cambridge Women's Study Group, 1981, *Women in Society*, Virago Press, London.

Caplan, P., 1985, *Class and Gender in India: Women and Their Organisations in a South Indian City*, Routledge and Kegan Paul, London.

Caplan, P. & J. Bujra (eds), 1978, *Women United, Women Divided*, Tavistock, London.

Carstairs, M., 1957, *The Twice-Born*, Hogarth Press, London.

Cash R. et al. (eds), 1987, *Child Health and Survival: the UNICEF GOBI-FF Program*, Croom Helm, London.

Cassen, R., 1976, 'Welfare and Population: Notes on Rural India since 1960', *Population and Development Review*, vol.1, pp.33-70.

Cassen, R., 1978, *India: Population, Economy, Society*, Macmillan, London.

Centre for Contemporary Cultural Studies, 1982, *The Empire Strikes Back*, Hutchison, London.

Chambers, R. et al. (eds), 1981, *Seasonal Dimensions to Rural Poverty*, F. Pinter, London.

Chard, T. & M. Richards, (eds), 1977, *Benefits and Hazards of the New Obstetrics*, Heinemann, London.

Chatterjee, M., (1988), *Implementing Health Policy*, Manohar, New Delhi.

Chatterjee, M., no date, 'Women's Access to Health Care: a Critical Issue for Child Health', mimeographed.

Chawdhari, T.P.S. & B.M. Sharma, 1961, 'Female Labour of the Family Farm in Agriculture', *Agricultural Situation in India*, vol.16, pp.643-650.

Chen, L.C. et al., 1981, 'Sex Bias in the Family Allocation of Food and Health Care in Rural Bangladesh', *Population and Development Review*, vol.7, pp.55-70.

Chen, M., 1986, 'Poverty, gender and work in Bangladesh', *Economic and Political Weekly*, vol.XXI, pp.217-222.

Chowdhury, A.K.M.A., 1981, *Infant Deaths, Determinants and Dilemmas*, International Centre for Diarrhoeal Disease Research, Dhaka.

Chowdhury, P., 1987, 'Socio-economic Dimensions of Certain Customs and Attitudes: Women of Haryana in the Colonial Period', *Economic and Political Weekly*, vol.XXII, pp.2060-2066.

CMIE, 1985, *Profiles of Districts: Part 1 A-K*, Centre for Monitoring the Indian Economy, Bombay.

Croll, E., 1981, 'Women in Rural Production and Reproduction in the Soviet Union, China, Cuba and Tanzania', *Signs*, vol.7, no.2, pp.361-374.

Crooke, W., 1896, *The Tribes and Castes of the North Western Provinces and Oudh*, Superintendent of Government Publications, Calcutta.

Crooke, W., 1897, *The North-Western Provinces*, Methuen, London.

Dankelman, I. & J. Davidson, 1988, *Women and Environment in the Third World*, Earthscan, London.

Das, V., 1973, 'The Structure of Marriage Preferences: an Account from Pakistani Fiction', *Man*, vol.8, pp.30-45.

Das, V., 1982, *Structure and Cognition*, 2nd. edit., Oxford University Press, Delhi.

Das Gupta, M., 1987, 'Selective Discrimination against Female Children in Rural Punjab, India', *Population and Development Review*, vol.13, pp.77-100.

Delphy, C., 1977, *The Main Enemy*, WRRC, London.

Demerath, N., 1976, *Birth Control and Foreign Policy*, Harper Row, New York.

Desai, M. et al. (eds), 1984, *Agrarian Power and Agricultural Productivity in South Asia*, Oxford University Press, Delhi.

Desai, N. & V. Patel, 1985, *Indian Women: Change and Challenge in the International Decade 1975-85*, Popular Prakashan, Bombay.

De Souza, A. (ed.), 1980, *Women in Contemporary India and South Asia*, Manohar, New Delhi.

Djukanovich V. and E.P. Mach (eds), 1975, *Alternative Approaches to Meeting Basic Health Needs in Developing Countries*, World Health Organisation, Geneva.

Donoso, G. 1979, 'Weanling Diarrhoea: Overview of its Nutrition and Public Health Significance', *Indian Journal of Nutrition and Dietetics*, vol.16, no.4, pp.103-13.

Douglas, M., 1966, *Purity and Danger*, Routledge and Kegan Paul, London.

Dube, L., 1983, 'Misadventures in Amniocentesis', *Economic and Political Weekly*, vol.XVIII, pp.279-80.

Dube, L., 1988, 'On the Construction of Gender: Hindu Girls in Patrilineal India', *Economic and Political Weekly*, vol.XXIII, pp.WS-11 to WS-19.

Dube, L., E. Leacock & S. Ardener (eds), 1986, *Visibility and Power: Essays on Women in Society and Development*, Oxford University Press, New Delhi.

Dumont, L., 1961, 'Marriage in India: the Present State of the Question', *Contributions to Indian Sociology*, vol.5, pp.75-95.

Dumont, L., 1972, *Homo Hierarchicus*, Paladin, London.

Dyson, T. & M. Moore, 1983, 'On Kinship Structure, Female Autonomy and Demographic Behaviour in India', *Population and Development Review*, vol.9, no.1, pp.35-60.

Dyson, T. & N. Crook (eds), 1984, *India's Demography*, South Asian Publishers, New Delhi.

Ebrahim, G.J., 1985, *Social and Community Paediatrics in Developing Countries*, Macmillan, London.

Edholm, F., O. Harris & K. Young, 1977, 'Conceptualising Women', *Critique of Anthropology*, vol.3, no.9-10,

Engels, D., 1983, 'The Age of Consent Act of 1891: Colonial Ideology in Bengal', *South Asia Research*, vol.3, pp.107-134.

Engels, D., 1986, 'Sex, marriage and social reform: Bengal in the 1920s', unpublished paper given to the European Modern South Asian Studies Conference, Heidelberg.

Eglar, Z., 1960, *A Punjabi Village in Pakistan*, Columbia University Press, New York.

Epstein, T.S. & R.A. Watts (eds), 1981, *The Endless Day*, Pergamon Press, Oxford.

Everett, J.M., 1981, *Women and Social Change in India*, Heritage, New Delhi.

Falk, N. & R. Gross (eds), 1980, *Unspoken Worlds: Women's Religious Lives in Non-Western Cultures*, Harper and Row, New York.

Farmer, B.H. (ed.), 1983, *Green Revolution?*, Cambridge University Press, Cambridge.

Farooq, G.M. & G.B. Simmons (eds), 1985, *Fertility in Developing Countries: an Economic Perspective on Research and Policy Issues*, Macmillan, London.

Faruqee, R. & E. Johnson, 1982, *Health, Nutrition and Family Planning in India*, World Bank Staff Working Paper 507, Washington D.C.

Ferro-Luzzi, G.E., 1973a, 'Food avoidances at puberty and menstruation in Tamilnad,' *Ecology of Food and Nutrition*, vol.2, pp.165-172.

Ferro-Luzzi, G.E., 1973b, 'Food avoidances of pregnant women in Tamilnad', *Ecology of Food and Nutrition*, vol.2, pp.259- 266.

Ferro-Luzzi, G.E., 1974a, 'Food avoidances during the puerperium and lactation in Tamilnad', *Ecology of Food and Nutrition*, vol.3, pp.7-15.

Ferro-Luzzi, G.E., 1974b, 'Women's pollution periods in Tamilnad (India)', *Anthropos*, vol.69, pp.113-161.

Fildes, V., 1987, *Breasts, Bottles and Babies*, Edinburgh University Press, Edinburgh.

Firestone, S., 1971, *The Dialectic of Sex*, Bantam, New York.

Folbre, N., 1986, 'Hearts and Spades: Paradigms of Household Economics', *World Development*, vol.14, pp.245-255.

Forbes, G., 1979, 'Women and Modernity: the Issue of Child Marriage in India', *Women's Studies International Quarterly*, vol.2, pp.407-419.

Ford, C.S., 1945, *A Comparative Study of Human Reproduction*, Yale University Press, New Haven.

Gandhi, · H.S. & R. Sapru, 1980, 'Dais as Partners in Maternal Health', mimeographed, National Institute for Health and Family Welfare, New Delhi.

Gennep, A. van, 1906, *Les Rites de Passage*, E. Guilmote, Paris, translated and published in English as *Rites of Passage*, Chicago University Press, Chicago, 1960.

Ghosal, B.C. et al., no date, *Dais Training Scheme in Haryana – an Evaluation*, Central Health Education Bureau, New Delhi.

Gideon, H., 1962, A Baby is Born in Punjab, *American Anthropologist*, vol.64, pp.1220-34.

Goffman, E., 1961, Asylums, Penguin Books, Harmondsworth.

Goldthorpe, J., 1983, 'Women and Class Analysis: In Defence of the Conventional View', *Sociology*, vol.17, pp.465-488.

Goody, J. & S.J. Tambiah, 1974, *Bridewealth and Dowry*, Cambridge University Press, London and New York.

Gopalan, C., 1985, 'The Mother and Child in India,' *Economic and Political Weekly*, vol.XX, no.2, pp.159-166.

Gopalan, C. & M. Chatterjee, 1985, *Use of Growth Charts For Promoting Child Nutrition*, Nutrition Foundation of India, New Delhi.

Gordon, J.E., H. Gideon & J. Wyon, 1965, 'Midwifery Practices in Rural Punjab, India', *American Journal of Obstetrics and Gynaecology*, vol.93, pp.728-737.

Government of India, 1974, *Towards Equality: Report of the Committee on the Status of Women in India*, Department of Social Welfare, New Delhi.

Government of India, 1985, *Seventh Five Year Plan*, Planning Commission, New Delhi.

Gupta, G.R. (ed.), 1981, *The Social and Cultural Context of Medicine in India*, Vikas, Delhi.

Gupta, R. *Census of India 1981, Series 22 Uttar Pradesh, Paper-1 of 1982: Final Population Totals*, Director of Census Operations, Uttar Pradesh, Lucknow, 1982.

Gwatkin, D.R., 1979, 'Political Will and Family Planning', *Population and Development Review*, vol.5, pp.29-59.

Gwatkin, D.R., J.R. Wilcox & J.D. Wray, 1980, *Can Health and Nutrition Interventions Make a Difference?*, Overseas Development Council, Washington D.C.

Harper, E.B. (ed.), 1964, *Religion in South Asia*, University of Washington Press, Seattle.

Harris, B., 1986, 'The Intrafamily Distribution of Hunger in South Asia', mimeographed.

Heath, A.F. & N. Britten, 1984, 'Women's Jobs do Make a Difference', *Sociology*, vol.18, pp.475-490.

Hershman, P., 1974, 'Hair, Sex and Dirt', *Man*, vol.9, pp.274-298.

Hertz, R., 1960, *Death and the Right Hand*, translated by R. and C. Needham, Cohen and West, London.

Hirschon, R. (ed.), 1984, *Women and Property, Women as Property*, Tavistock, London.

Howells, J.G. (ed.), 1972, *Modern Perspectives in Psycho-obstetrics*, Oliver and Boyd, Edinburgh.

Islam, S., 1981, *Indigenous Abortion Practitioners in Rural Bangladesh*, Women for Women, Dhaka.

Jacobson, D., 1975, 'Songs of Social Distance', *Journal of South Asian Literature*, vol.11, pp.45-59.

Jain, A.K. & P. Visaria (eds), 1988, *Infant Mortality: Differentials and Determinants*, Sage, New Delhi.

Jain, D. (ed.), 1980, *Women's Quest for Power: Five Indian Case Studies*, Vikas, Ghaziabad.

Jain, D. & N. Banerjee (eds), 1985, *Tyranny of the Household: Investigative Essays on Women's Work*, Shakti, New Delhi.

Jeffery, P.M., 1979, *Frogs in a Well: Indian Women in Purdah*, Zed Press, London.

Jeffery, P.M., R. Jeffery & A. Lyon, 1985, *Contaminating States and Women's Status*, Indian Social Institute, New Delhi.

Jeffery, R. & P.M. Jeffery, 1984, 'Female Infanticide and Amniocentesis: a Research Note', *Social Science and Medicine*, vol.19, no.11, pp.1207-1212.

Jeffery, R., P.M. Jeffery & A. Lyon, 1988, 'Traditional Birth Attendants in Rural North India', unpublished paper given to the Wenner-Gren Conference on Analysis in Medical Anthropology, Portugal.

Jeffery, R., 1988, *The Politics of Health in India*, California University Press, Berkeley and London.

Jordan, B., 1987, 'High Technology: The Case of Obstetrics', *World Health Forum*, vol.8, p.314.

Justice, J., 1986, *Policies, Plans and People: Culture and Health Development in Nepal*, California University Press, Berkeley and London.

Kakar, D.N., 1980, *Dais: The Traditional Birth Attendant in Village India*, New Age, Delhi.

Karkal, M., 1985a, 'How the Other Half Dies in Bombay', *Economic and Political Weekly*, vol.XX, p.1424.

Karkal, M., 1985b, 'Maternal and Infant Mortality', *Economic and Political Weekly*, vol.XX, pp.1835-37.

Karve, I., 1968, *Kinship Organisation in India*, 3rd edit., Asia Publishing House, Bombay.

Kishwar, M. & R. Vanita, (eds), 1984, *In Search of Answers: Indian Women's Voices from Manushi*, Zed Books, London.

Kolenda, P., 1987, *Regional Differences in Family Structure in India,* Rawat Publications, Jaipur.

Kumar, A. et al., 1982, *Report of Evaluation of Traditional Birth Attendants (Dais) in the State of Uttar Pradesh*, Population Centre, Lucknow.

Kumar, D., 1983, 'Male Utopias or Nightmares?', *Economic and Political Weekly*, vol.XVIII, pp.61-64.

Kynch, J. & A. Sen, 1983, 'Indian Women: Well-being and Survival', *Cambridge Journal of Economics*, vol.7, pp.363-80.

Laderman, C., 1983, *Wives and Midwives: Childbirth and Nutrition in Rural Malaysia*, California University Press, Berkeley and London.

Ledbetter, R., 1984, 'Thirty Years of Family Planning in India', *Asian Survey*, vol.XXIV, pp.736-758.

Leslie, C. (ed.), 1976, *Asian Medical Systems*, California University Press, Berkeley.

Levine, D., 1987, *Reproducing Families: The Political Economy of English Population History*, Cambridge University Press, Cambridge.

Lewis, O., 1958, *Village Life in Northern India*, Random House, New York.

Liddle, J. & R. Joshi, 1986, *Daughters of Independence: Gender, Caste and Class in India*, Zed Books, London.

Luschinsky, M.S., 1962, 'The Life of Women in a Village of North India: A Study of Role and Status', unpublished Ph.D. thesis, Cornell University.

MacCormack, C.P. (ed.), 1982, *Ethnography of Fertility and Birth*, Academic Press, London.

Macdornan, M. 'Contemporary Marriage Practices in North India: Evidence from three Uttar Pradesh Villages', unpublished Ph.D. thesis, Australian National University, 1986.

MacIntyre, S., 1977, 'Childbirth: the Myth of the Golden Age', *World Medicine*, 15 June, pp.17-22.

Mahadevan, K. (ed.), 1986, *Fertility and Mortality: Theory, Methodology and Empirical Issues*, Sage, New Delhi.

Maine, D. et al., 1987, 'Prevention of Maternal Mortality in Developing Countries: Program Options and Practical Considerations', mimeographed.

Maloney, C. (ed.), 1976, *The Evil Eye*, Columbia University Press, New York.

Mamdani, M., 1972, *The Myth of Population Control*, Monthly Review Press, New York.

Mandelbaum, D.G., 1970, *Society in India*, University of California Press, Berkeley and Los Angeles.

Mandelbaum, D.G., 1974, *Human Fertility in India*, Oxford University Press, Delhi.

Mandelbaum, D.G., 1986, 'Sex Roles and Gender Relations in North India', *Economic and Political Weekly*, vol.XX1, no.46, pp.1999-2004.

Mani, S.B., 1973, 'Ideal Versus Actual: Patterns of Inter-personal Communication in Family Planning in an Indian Village', *Journal of Family Welfare*, vol.19, pp.10-19.

Mari Bhat, P.N. et al., 1984, *Vital Rates in India, 1961-1981*, National Academy Press, for the Panel on India, Committee on Population and Demography, Washington D.C.

Marshall, J.F., 1972, 'Culture and Contraception: Response Determinants to a Family Planning Programme in a North Indian Village', unpublished Ph. D thesis, University of Hawaii.

Mayo, K., 1927, *Mother India*, Harcourt Brace, New York.

McCready, W.C. (ed.), 1983, *Culture, Ethnicity and Identity*, Academic Press, New York.

Meillassoux, C., 1981, *Maidens, Meal and Money: Capitalism and the Domestic Economy*, Cambridge University Press, Cambridge.

Miller, B., 1980, 'Female Neglect and the Costs of Marriage in Rural India', *Contributions to Indian Sociology*, vol.14, pp.95-129.

Miller, B., 1981, *The Endangered Sex*, Cornell University Press, Ithaca, N.Y.

Miller, D.B., 1975, *From Hierarchy to Stratification*, Oxford University Press, Delhi.

Mitra, A., 1978, *India's Population: Aspects of Quality and Control*, 2 vols., Abhinav Publications, New Delhi.

Molyneux, M., 1981, 'Socialist Societies Old and New: Progress towards Women's Emancipation', *Feminist Review*, no.8, pp.1-35.

Mosley, W. & L. Chen (eds), 1984, *Child Survival: Strategies for Research*, Cambridge University Press, London and New York.

Nag, M. (ed.), 1975, *Population and Social Organization*, Mouton, The Hague.

Nag, M. et al., 1978, 'An Anthropological Approach to the Study of the Economic Value of Children', *Current Anthropology*, vol.19, pp.293-301.

Nag, M. & N. Kak, 1984, 'Demographic Transition in a Punjab Village', *Population and Development Review*, vol.10, pp.661-678.

Nanda, B.R. (ed.), 1976, *Indian Women: From Purdah to Modernity*, Vikas, Delhi.

Narayana, G. & J. Acharya, 1981, *Problems of Field Workers: Study of Eight Primary Health Centres in Four States*, Administrative Staff College of India, Hyderabad.

Nayyar, R., 1987, 'Female Participation Rates in Rural India', *Economic and Political Weekly*, vol.XXII, pp.2207-2216.

Neale, W.C., 1962, *Economic Change in Rural India*, Yale University Press, New Haven.

Nelson, N., 1979, *Why Has Development Neglected Rural Women?*, Pergamon, Oxford.

Nevill, H.R., 1928, *Bijnor: A Gazetteer, Being Volume XIV of the District Gazetteers of the United Provinces of Agra and Oudh*, 2nd. edit., Government Press, Allahabad.

Newell, K. (ed.), 1975, *Health By The People*, World Health Organisation, Geneva.

Nichter, M. & M. Nichter, 1983, 'The Ethnophysiology and Folk Dietetics of Pregnancy', *Human Organisation*, vol.42, no.3, pp.235-246.

Nugent, J.B., 1985, 'The Old Age Security Motive for Fertility', *Population and Development Review*, vol.11, pp.75- 97.

Oakley, A., 1979, *Becoming a Mother*, Martin Robertson, London.

Oakley, A., 1984, *The Captured Womb: a History of Medical Care for Pregnant Women*, Basil Blackwell, Oxford.

Omvedt, G., 1986, '"Patriarchy:" the Analysis of Women's Oppression', *Insurgent Sociologist*, vol.13, pp.30-50.

Palmer, I., 1977, 'Rural Women and the Basic Needs Approach', *International Labour Review*, vol.115, no.1, pp.97-107.

Papanek, H., 1979, 'Family Status Production: the "Work" and "Non-work" of women', *Signs*, vol.4, pp.775-781.

Papanek, H., 1984, 'False Specialisation and the Purdah of Scholarship — A Review Article', *Journal of Asian Studies*, vol.44, no.1, pp.127-148.

Papanek, H. & G. Minault (eds), 1982, *Separate Worlds: Studies of Purdah in South Asia*, Chanakya, Delhi.

Patnaik, U., 1976, 'Class Differentiation Within the Peasantry' *Economic and Political Weekly*, vol.XI, no.39, pp.A-82 to A-108.

Patnaik, U.,1987, *Peasant Class Differentiation*, Oxford University Press, Delhi.

Pettigrew, J., 1984, 'Problems Concerning Tubectomy Operations in Rural Areas of Punjab', *Economic and Political Weekly*, vol.XIX, pp.995-1002.

Phillips, A., 1987, *Divided Loyalties: Dilemmas of Sex and Class*, Virago Press, London.

Platts, J.T., 1885, *A Dictionary of Urdū, Classical Hindī and English*, 1977 reprint edit., Oriental Books, New Delhi.

Poffenberger, T., 1969, *Husband-wife Communication and Motivational Aspects of Population Control in an Indian Village*, Central Family Planning Institute, New Delhi.

Population Reports, Series J, no.22, 1980, *Traditional Midwives and Family Planning*, Johns Hopkins University, Baltimore.

Population Reports, Series F, no.7, 1980, *Complications of Abortion in Developing Countries*, Johns Hopkins University, Baltimore.

Prakash, P., 1986, 'Hormonal Methods of Contraception: Government Indifferent to Dangers', *Economic and Political Weekly*, vol.XXI, no.17, pp.733-34.

Prasad, B.G. et al., 1969, 'A Study on Beliefs and Customs in a Lucknow Village in Relation to Certain Diseases, Menstruation, Child Birth and Family Planning', *Indian Journal of Social Work*, vol.XXX, pp.45-54.

Preston, S.H., (ed.), 1978, *The Effects of Infant and Child Mortality on Fertility*, Academic Press, London.

Raheja, G.G., 1985, 'Kinship, Caste and Auspiciousness in Pahansu', unpublished Ph.D. thesis, University of Chicago.

Raheja, G.G., 1988, *The Poison in the Gift*, University of Chicago Press, Chicago.

Rajaraman, I., 1983, 'Economics of Bride-Price and Dowry', *Economic and Political Weekly*, vol.XVIII, no.8, pp.275-79.

Ramalingaswami, V., 1980, 'Health for All: an Alternative Strategy', mimeographed, Report of·the Indian Council of Social Science Research and Indian Council of Medical Research Joint Study, New Delhi.

Ramanamma, A. & U. Bhambawala, 1980, 'The Mania for Sons', *Social Science and Medicine*, vol.14B, pp.107-110.

Randeria, S. & L. Visaria, 1984, 'Sociology of Bride-Price and Dowry', *Economic and Political Weekly*, vol.XIX, no.15, pp.648-52.

Rao, K.G. & S. Kumar, no date, 'Impact of Health Services on Health Status of Women in Post-Independence India', National Institute of Health and Family Welfare, New Delhi.

Raza, M.H., 1894, 'Customs at and before Birth, at Circumcision and at Betrothal — Mahomedans, Upper Ganges-Jamnah Doab', *North Indian Notes and Queries*, vol.3, pp.186-193.

Registrar-General, India, 1983, *Survey on Infant and Child Mortality 1979*, Office of the Registrar-General, India, New Delhi.

Registrar-General, India, 1985, *Sample Registration System 1982*, Ministry of Home Affairs, Office of the Registrar-General, India, New Delhi.

Registrar-General of India, 1986, *Sample Registration Bulletin*, vol.20, no.1.

Reissland, N. & R. Burghart, no date, 'The Transmission of Illness Through Mother's Milk: Beliefs and Practices of Maithil Women', mimeographed.

Rele, J.R., 1987, 'Fertility Levels and Trends in India 1951-81', *Population and Development Review*, vol.13, pp.513-30.

Roberton, J., 1846, 'On Hindu Midwifery', *Edinburgh Medical and Surgical Journal*, vol.65, pp.308-319.

Robinson, J., 1985, 'Of Women and Washing Machines: Employment, Housework, and the Reproduction of Motherhood in Socialist China', *China Quarterly*, no.101.

Rogers, B., 1980, *The Domestication of Women: Discrimination in Developing Societies*, Kogan Page, London.

Rosaldo, M.Z., 1980, 'The Use and Abuse of Anthropology: Reflections on Feminism and Cross-cultural Understanding', *Signs*, vol.5, pp.389-417.

Rosaldo, M.Z. & L. Lamphere (eds), 1974, *Women, Culture and Society*, Stanford University Press, Stanford.

Sadasivam, B., 1986, 'Injectable Contraceptives in Mass Programmes: Alarming Scope for Misuse', *Economic and Political Weekly*, vol.XXI, no.43, pp.1886-87.

Sayers, J. et al. (eds), 1987, *Engels Revisited: New Feminist Essays*, Tavistock, London.

Scheper-Hughes, N. (ed.), 1987, *Child Survival*, D. Reidel, Dordrecht.

Scrimshaw, S., 1978, 'Infant Mortality and Fertility Behaviour in the Regulation of Family Size', *Population and Development Review*, vol.4, pp.383-404.

Seccombe, W., 1983, 'Marxism and Demography', *New Left Review*, no.137, pp.22-47.

Segal, L., 1987, *Is the Future Female? Troubled Thoughts on Contemporary Feminism*, Virago, London.

Sen, A. & S. Sengupta, 1983, 'Malnutrition of Rural Children and the Sex Bias', *Economic and Political Weekly*, vol.XVIII, pp.855-62.

Sen, G. & C. Sen, 1985, 'Women's Domestic Work and Economic Activity', *Economic and Political Weekly*, vol.XX, no.17, pp.WS-49 to WS-56.

Shah, A.M., 1974, *The Household Dimension of the Family in India*, California University Press, Berkeley.

Sharma, M., 1978, *The Politics of Inequality: Competition and Control in an Indian Village*, University Press of Hawaii, Honolulu.

Sharma, M., 1985, 'Caste, Class and Gender: Production and Reproduction in North India', *Journal of Peasant Studies*, vol.12, pp.57-88.

Sharma, U., 1978, 'Women and Their Affines: The Veil as a Symbol of Separation',

Man, vol.13, pp.218-233.

Sharma, U., 1980, *Women, Work and Property in North-West India*, Tavistock, London.

Sharma, U., 1981, 'Male Bias in Anthropology', *South Asia Research*, vol.1, no.2, pp.34-38.

Sharma, U., 1986, *Women's Work, Class and the Urban Household*, Tavistock, London.

Simmons, G. et al., 1982, 'Post-neonatal Mortality in Rural India: Implications of an Economic Model', *Demography*, vol.19, pp.371-389.

Singer, M. (ed.), 1966, *Krishna: Myths, Rites and Attitudes*, East-West Center Press, Honolulu.

Singer, M. & B.S. Cohn (eds), 1968, *Structure and Change in Indian Society*, Aldine, Chicago.

Singh, S.G., 1883, 'Memorandum on the Superstitions Connected with Child Birth, and Precautions Taken and Rites Performed on the Occasion of the Birth of a Child among the Jats of Hoshiyarpur in the Punjab', *Journal of the Asiatic Society of Bengal*, vol.52, pp.205-210.

Smucker, C.M. et al., 1980, 'Neo-natal Mortality in South Asia: the Special Role of Tetanus', *Population Studies*, vol.34, pp.321-335.

Spate, O.H.K. & A.T.A. Learmonth, 1972, *India and Pakistan: a general and regional geography*, 3rd revised edit., Methuen, London.

Srinivas, M.N. (ed.), 1955, *India's Villages*, West Bengal Government Press, Calcutta.

Srinivas, M.N., 1986, *Dowry*, Oxford University Press, Delhi.

Srinivasan, K., 1983, 'India's Family Planning Programme: its Impact and Implications', *Journal of Family Welfare*, vol.30, pp.7-25.

Srivastav, J.B., 1975, 'Report of the Group on Medical Education and Support Manpower', mimeographed, Ministry of Health and Family Planning, New Delhi.

Srivastava, S.L., 1971, 'Birth-rites: a Comparative Study', *Eastern Anthropologist*, vol.24, pp.181-196.

Stanworth, M., 1984, 'Women and Class Analysis: A Reply to Goldthorpe', *Sociology*, vol.18, pp.159-170.

Statistical Diary, Bijnor, 1981, (in Hindi), no date, mimeographed.

Stone, L. & J.G. Campbell, 1984, 'The Use and Misuse of Surveys in International Development: an Experiment from Nepal', *Human Organisation*, vol.43, pp.27-37.

Taylor, C.E. et al., 1983, *Child and Maternal Health Services in Rural India: the Narangwal Experiment*, Johns Hopkins University Press, Baltimore and London.

Thompson, C.S., 1981, 'A Sense of *sharm*: its Implications for the Position of Women in Central India', *South Asia Research*, vol.1, no.2, pp 39-53.

Thompson, C.S., 1984, 'Ritual States in the Life-Cycles of Hindu Women in a Village of Central India', unpublished Ph.D. thesis, London University: School of Oriental and African Studies.

Thompson, C.S., 1985, 'The Power to Pollute and the Power to Preserve: Perceptions of Female Power in a Hindu Village', *Social Science and Medicine*, vol.21, no.6, pp.701-711.

Trivedi, P., 1984, 'To Deny our Fullness: Asian Women in the Making of History', *Feminist Review*, no.17, pp.37-50.

Vatuk, S., 1969, 'A Structural Analysis of the Hindi Kinship Terminology', *Contributions to Indian Sociology*, vol.3, pp.94-115.

Vatuk, S., 1975, 'Gifts and Affines in North India', *Contributions to Indian Sociology*, vol.9, pp.155-196.

Vatuk, S., 1983, 'Sharing, Giving and Exchanging of Food in South Asian Societies', mimeographed.

Vicziany, M. 1983, 'Coercion in a Soft State', *Pacific Affairs*, vol.55, no.3, pp.373-401 and no.4, pp.557-592.

Visaria, L., 1985, 'Infant Mortality in India: Level, Trend and Determinants', *Economic and Political Weekly*, vol.XX, pp. 1352-59, 1399-1405, and 1447-50.

Vlassoff, M., 1982, 'Economic Utility of Children and Fertility in Rural India', *Population Studies*, vol.XXXVI, pp.45-60.

Vlassoff, M. & C. Vlassoff, 1980, 'Old Age Security and the Utility of Children in Rural India', *Population Studies*, vol.34, pp.487-499.

Vogel, L., 1983, *Marxism and the Oppression of Women*, Pluto Press, London.

von Werlhof, C., 1980, 'Notes on the Relation Between Sexuality and Economy', *Review*, vol.4, pp.33-42.

Wadley, S.S. (ed.), 1980, *The Powers of Tamil Women*, Maxwell School, Syracuse, N.Y.

Wadley, S.S., 1987, 'Patriarchy and Widows in Rural North India', mimeographed.

Wadley, S.S. & B. Derr, 1986, 'Child Survival and Economic Status in a North Indian Village', unpublished paper presented at the European Modern South Asian Studies Conference, Heidelberg.

Warwick, D.P., 1988, 'Culture and the Management of Family Planning Programs', *Studies in Family Planning*, vol.19, pp.1-18.

White, C.P. & K. Young (eds), 1984, *Research on Rural Women: Feminist Methodological Questions*, Institute of Development Studies, Brighton.

Whitelegg, E. et al. (eds), 1982, *The Changing Experience of Women*, Blackwells, Oxford.

WHO, 1986, *Maternal Mortality Rates: A Tabulation of Available Information*, 2nd edit., World Health Organisation, Geneva.

Wiser, W.H., 1936, *The Hindu Jajmani System*, Lucknow Publishing House, Lucknow.

Wiser, W.H. & C.V. Wiser, 1971, *Behind Mud Walls 1930-1960, with a Sequel: the Village in 1970*, University of California Press, Berkeley.

Yalman, N., 1963, 'On the Purity of Women in the Castes of Ceylon and Malabar', *Journal of the Royal Anthropological Institute*, vol.93, pp.25-58.

Young, F. & A. Bacdayan, 1965, 'Menstrual Taboos and Social Rigidity', *Ethnology*, vol.4, pp.225-40.

Young, I., 1980, 'Socialist Feminism and the Limits of Dual Systems Theory', *Socialist Review*, vol.10, no.2/3, pp.169-88.

Young, K., C. Wolkowitz & R. McCullagh (eds), 1981, *Of Marriage and the Market*, CSE Books, London.

Zimmerman, F., 1988, *The Jungle and the Aroma of Meats*, California University Press, Berkeley and London.

Zurbrigg, S., 1984, *Rakku's Story*, George Joseph, Madras.

Index